CONTENT ESSENTIALS™ for Science

Vocabulary

Content

Literacy

Wright Group

The McGraw·Hill Companies

www.WrightGroup.com

Printed in the United States of America.

Send all inquiries to:
Wright Group/McGraw-Hill
P.O. Box 812960
Chicago, IL 60681

ISBN 978-1-4045-6747-4
MHID 1-4045-6747-X

1 2 3 4 5 6 7 8 9 QWD 14 13 12 11 10 09 08

Author

Margarita Calderón, Ph.D.
Senior Research Scientist and Professor
Johns Hopkins University

Content Consultant

James A. Shymansky, Ph.D.
E. Desmond Lee Professor of Science Education
University of Missouri, St. Louis

Reviewers

Amy Diedrichsen Bates
Curriculum Specialist
Plano Independent School District
Plano, Texas

Lillian Vega Castaneda, Ed.D.
Professor, Language, Culture, and Literacy
California State University,
Channel Islands, California

Susan Greca
Director of Second Language Programs
Freeport Public Schools
Freeport, New York

Elizabeth Jiménez
English Learner Consultant
GEMAS Consulting Co.
Pomona, California

Sandra Ann Madriaga
Supervisor of World Languages, English as a Second Language and High Ability Programs
Evansville-Vanderburgh School Corporation
Evansville, Indiana

Janie Perez Martin
Physics Instructor
Southwest Independent School District
San Antonio, Texas

Vyagale D. Maryland
Title III/ESL & Languages Other than English Specialist
Montgomery Public Schools
Curriculum and Instruction
Montgomery, Alabama

Ann L. Rifleman
Teacher
Mesa Unified School District
Mesa, Arizona

Elma Alicia Ruiz
Humanities Coordinator
Denver Public Schools, Department of Teaching and Learning
Denver, Colorado

Linda Thompson, Ed.D.
Director of Curriculum, Instruction, and Assessment
Carmel Clay Schools
Carmel, Indiana

Contents

PHYSICAL SCIENCE 194

Part Two Literacy Essentials 310

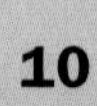

How to Use This Book

Your book has two parts. You can use the first part to learn about science topics. If you need help reading or writing about science, use the second part.

Part One Science Essentials

LIFE SCIENCE Life science is the study of living things. You will learn about many types of living things, what they are made of, and how they live.

EARTH SCIENCE Earth science is the study of many topics. It includes what makes up Earth and facts about fossils, weather, water, and space.

PHYSICAL SCIENCE Physical science is the study of matter and energy. These lessons explain matter and how energy causes change.

STUDYING SCIENCE Science is about asking and answering questions. These lessons show you how scientists solve problems.

Part Two Literacy Essentials

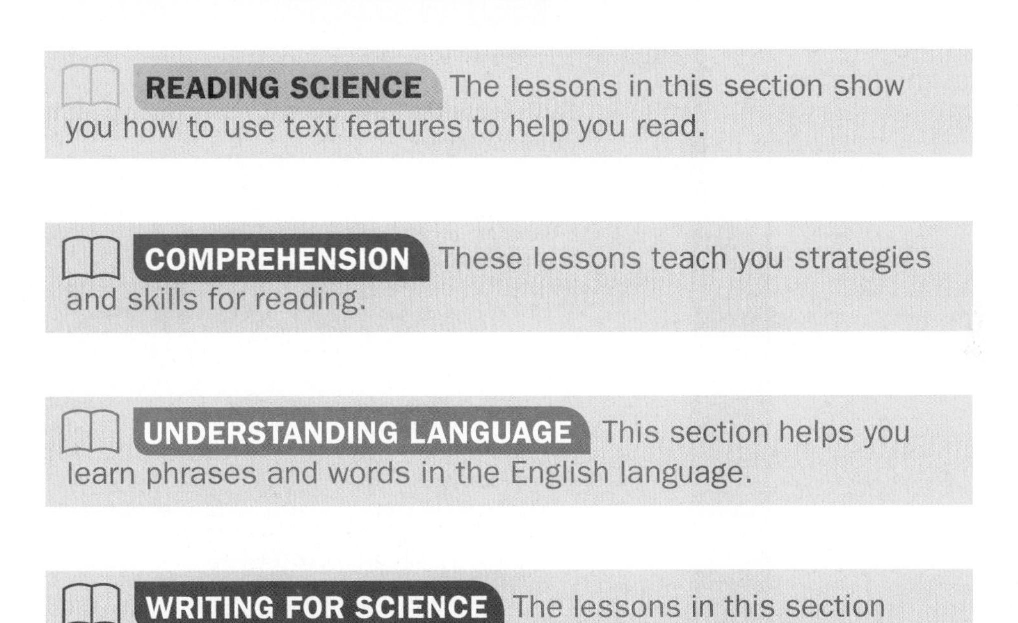

READING SCIENCE The lessons in this section show you how to use text features to help you read.

COMPREHENSION These lessons teach you strategies and skills for reading.

UNDERSTANDING LANGUAGE This section helps you learn phrases and words in the English language.

WRITING FOR SCIENCE The lessons in this section show you how to write a science report.

Previewing Lessons

Each lesson has the same text features, such as an Essential Idea, photographs, labels, and Why It Matters, to help students easily find and comprehend the topic information.

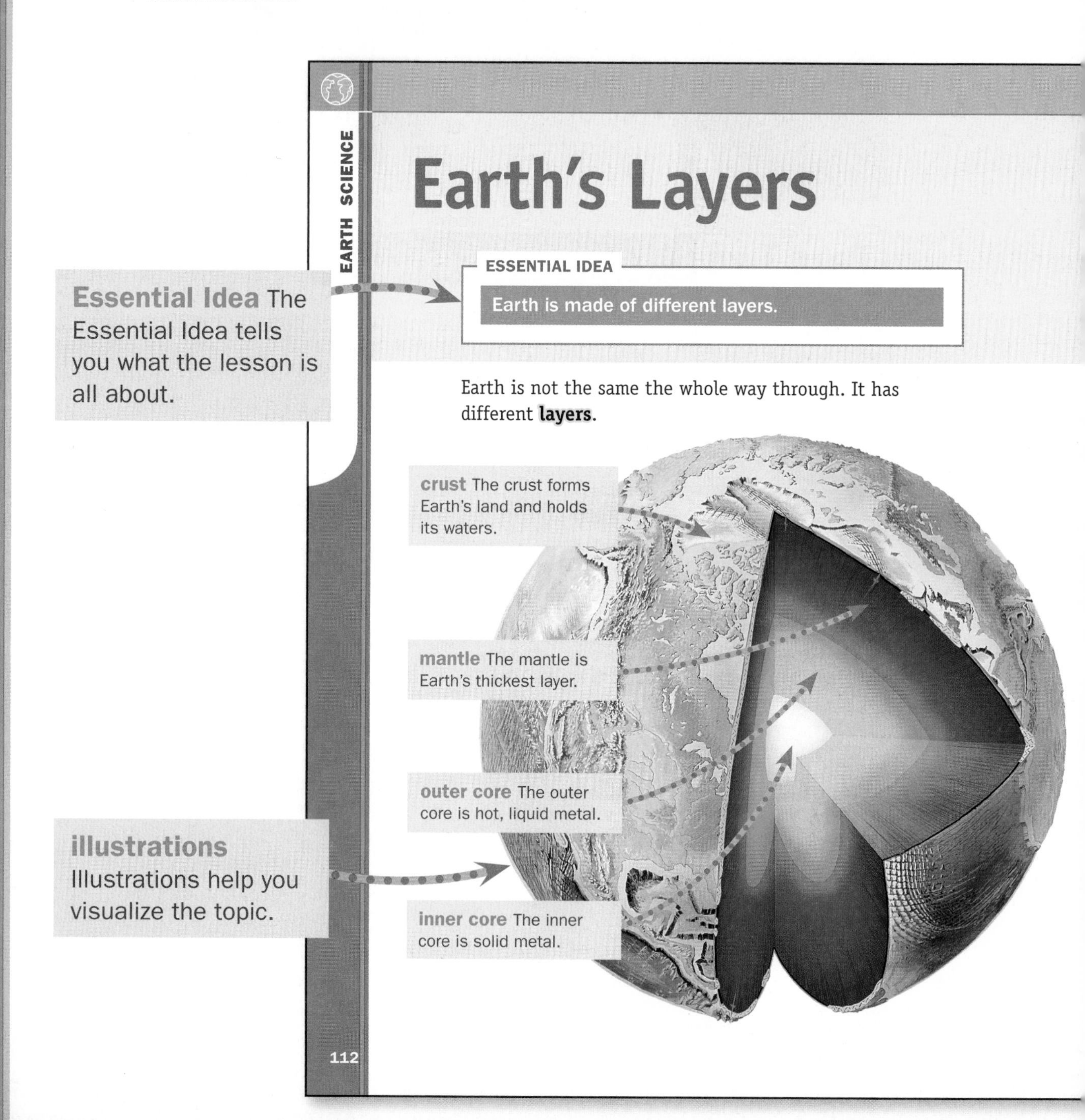

Learning Academic Vocabulary

You need to know academic vocabulary, or words used in school subjects, to learn. Each lesson highlights the words you will need to understand ideas in science.

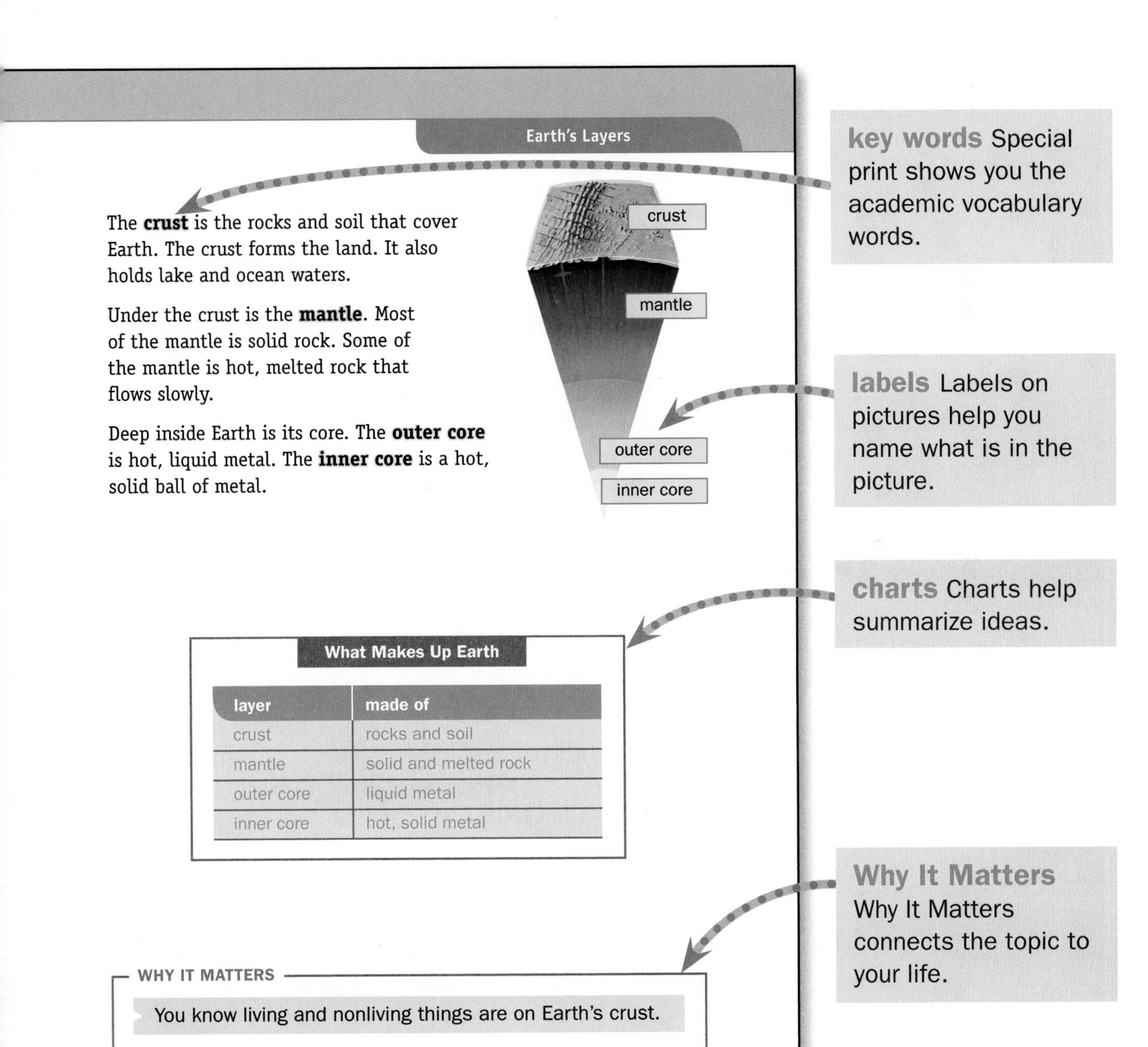

key words Special print shows you the academic vocabulary words.

labels Labels on pictures help you name what is in the picture.

charts Charts help summarize ideas.

Why It Matters Why It Matters connects the topic to your life.

Part One

Science Essentials

In this part of the book, you will learn all about the basics of science.

Life science is the study of living things. You will learn about many types of living things, what they are made of, and how they live.

Earth science is the study of many topics. It includes what makes up Earth and facts about fossils, weather, water, and space.

Physical science is the study of matter and energy. These lessons explain matter and how energy causes change.

Science is about asking and answering questions. These lessons show you how scientists solve problems.

Life Science

Living Things

ESSENTIAL IDEA

All living things do seven life processes.

Nature is filled with living and nonliving things. **Living things** include plants and animals. Rocks and water are **nonliving** things.

Living things are called **organisms**. **Life processes** are the things organisms do to stay alive.

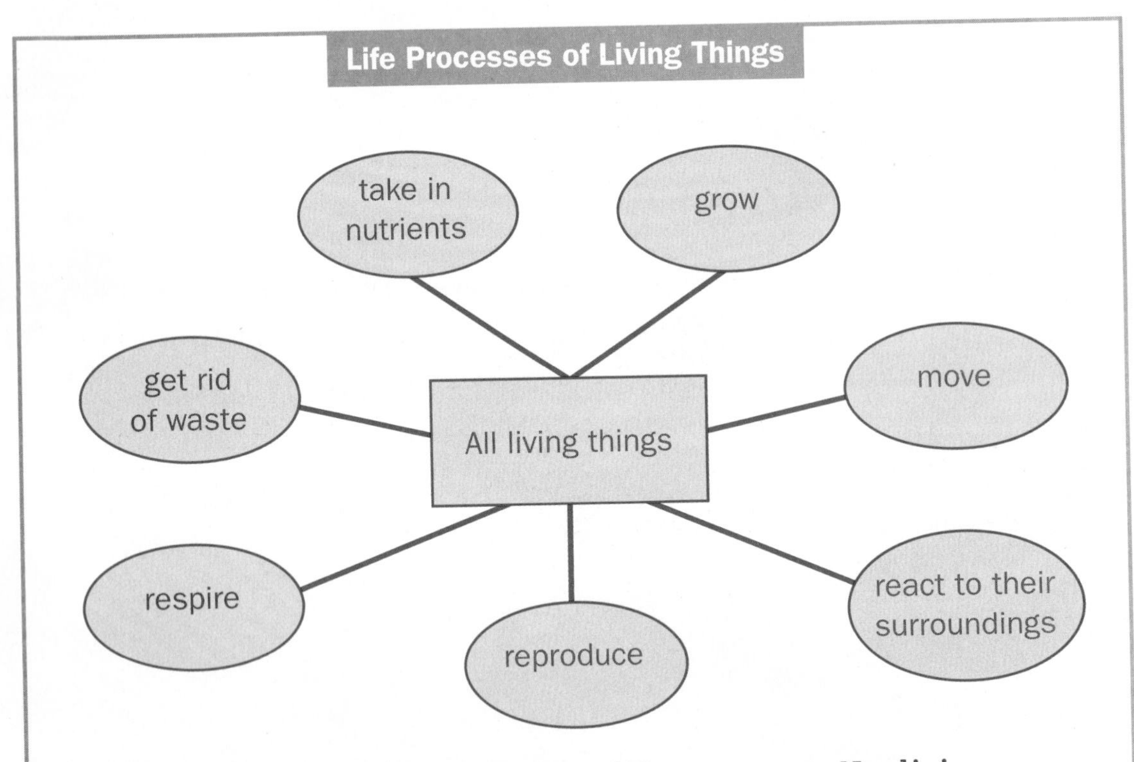

Living things must do all of these life processes. Nonliving things may do some of these functions, but not all of them. For example, water moves but does not grow.

Take in Nutrients

Organisms need **nutrients**, such as vitamins, to live. Animals get nutrients by eating food. Plants get nutrients from the soil using their roots.

A mother bird feeds its offspring to provide them with nutrients.

Grow

Nutrients help organisms grow. Organisms grow into adults.

plant

Plants grow from seeds.

Move

Living organisms move. Animals move their bodies to get to different places.

All animals move.

React to Their Surroundings

Living things **react** to what happens in their surroundings.

Plants react to light.
They bend toward the light.

Reproduce

Organisms grow into adults. Adult organisms **reproduce**, or make more organisms like themselves.

Elephants reproduce to make more of their own kind.

Respire

All living things **respire**, or breathe. Animals use oxygen in the air to give them energy to move and grow.

Get Rid of Waste

All living things get rid of **waste**, such as water and gas. For example, humans release carbon dioxide into the air.

When you breathe in, you bring in oxygen. When you breathe out, you get rid of carbon dioxide as a waste.

All living things:

- take in nutrients
- grow
- move
- react to their surroundings
- reproduce
- respire
- get rid of waste

WHY IT MATTERS

- You eat food to get nutrients so you can move and grow.
- You react to the Sun, rain, and other organisms in your environment.

LIFE SCIENCE

Cells

ESSENTIAL IDEA

Cells are the basic structures of all living things.

All living things are made up of **cells**. Living things have at least one cell. Cells have **structures**, or parts. Each structure has a different **function**, or job.

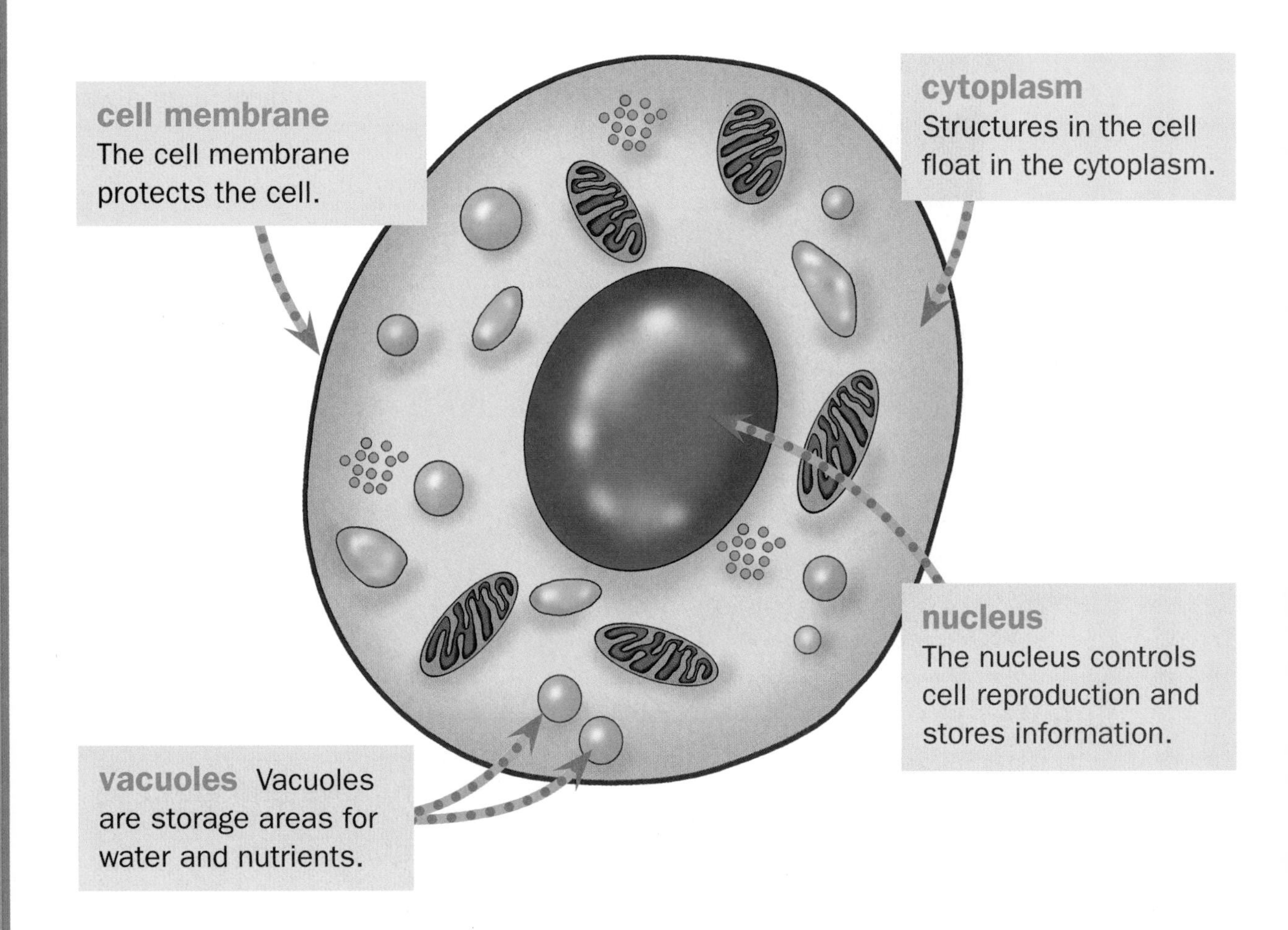

The **cell membrane** holds the cell together. It controls what moves into and out of the cell.

The **nucleus** controls how the cell reproduces. Information about the cell is stored in the nucleus.

Cytoplasm is a jellylike substance that supports all the structures in the cell.

Vacuoles in the cell store water and nutrients.

Parts of a Cell

Here are the parts of a cell and their functions.

part of a cell	function
cell membrane	holds cell together
nucleus	controls the cell and stores information
cytoplasm	supports cell structures
vacuoles	store water and nutrients

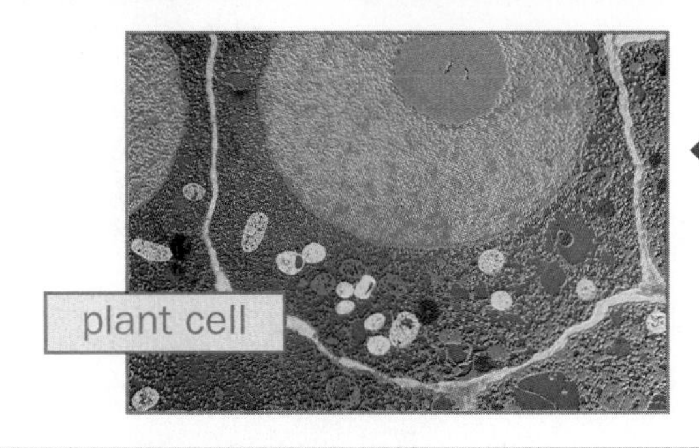

This is a plant cell. The yellow dots are vacuoles.

WHY IT MATTERS

- You are made up of millions of cells.
- Your cells carry out different functions, or jobs.

LIFE SCIENCE

What Cells Do

ESSENTIAL IDEA

Each type of cell does a certain job. Cells work together to form the parts of a living thing.

All living things are made of cells. Different types of cells have different **functions**, or jobs. A **tissue** is a group of cells that **performs** a certain function.

In animals, for example, some cells work together to form **muscle tissue**. Muscle tissue allows animals to move.

Muscle tissue in a giraffe's neck helps the animal reach for food.

Plants also have **specialized** groups of cells. Cells in leaves change the Sun's energy into food. The trunk of a tree contains several different kinds of cells. Cells in the bark protect the softer cells inside.

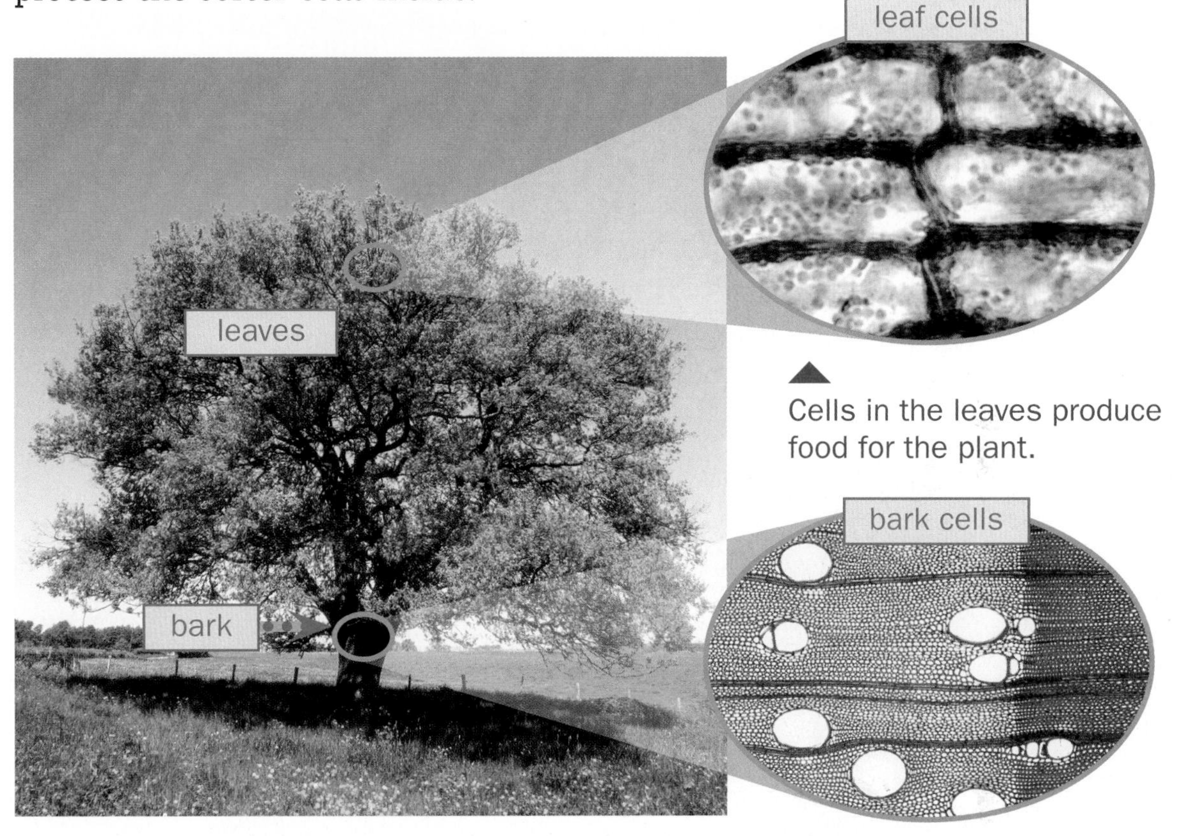

Cells in the leaves produce food for the plant.

Cells in the bark produce new cells that make the tree thicker and harder.

Both plants and animals have specialized cells that do different jobs.

WHY IT MATTERS

- Like plants and animals, you have specialized cells in your body.
- All of your cells work together to keep you alive.

LIFE SCIENCE

How Organisms Grow

ESSENTIAL IDEA

Cells make other new cells by dividing. Each new cell gets all the information it needs from the parent cell.

Your body is made of millions of cells. The nucleus of each cell contains chromosomes. **Chromosomes** contain information about **traits**, such as your hair and eye color.

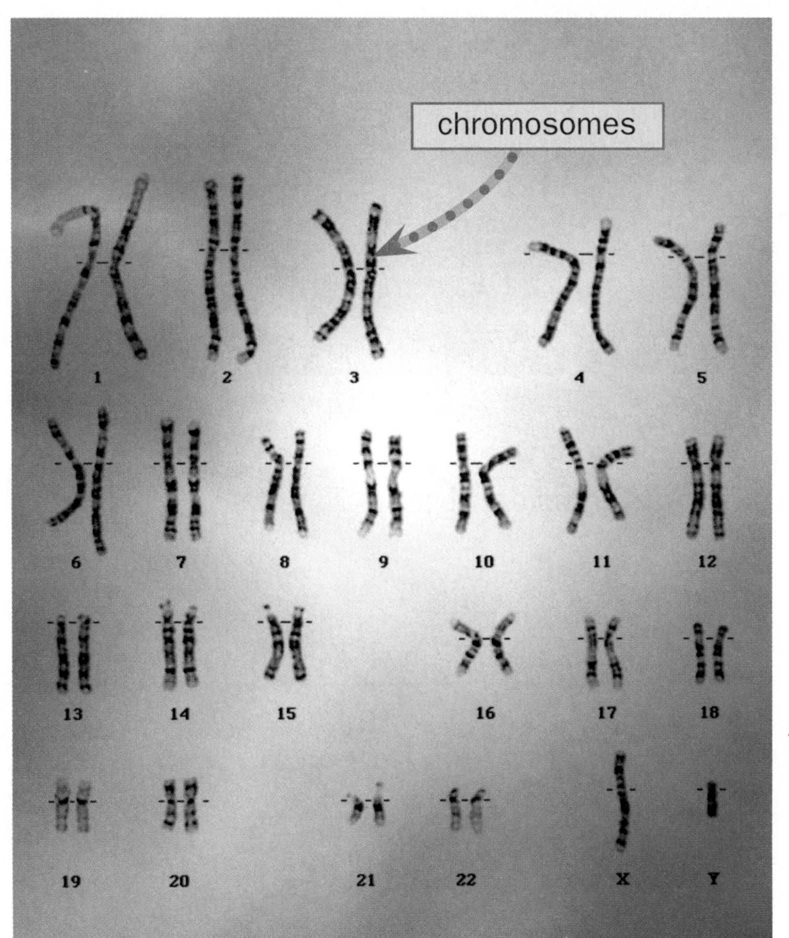

All humans have 23 pairs of chromosomes.

As your body grows, cells **divide**, or split, into two. When cells divide, they produce exact copies of themselves. This process is called **mitosis**.

How Cells Divide

1 Chromosomes in the parent cell make copies and form pairs.

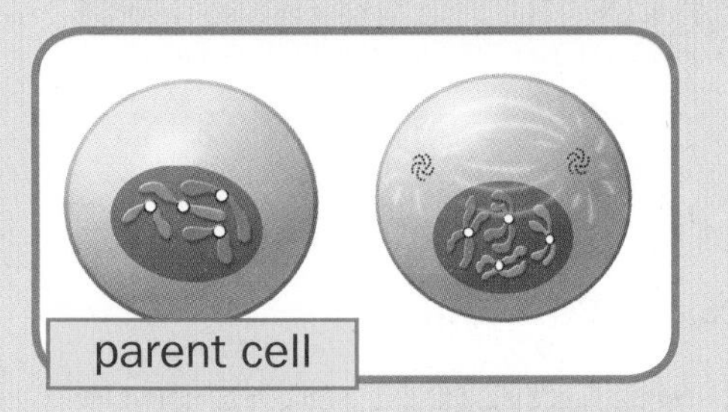

2 Chromosome pairs line up along the center of the cell.

3 Fibers form and attach to one half of the chromosome pair.

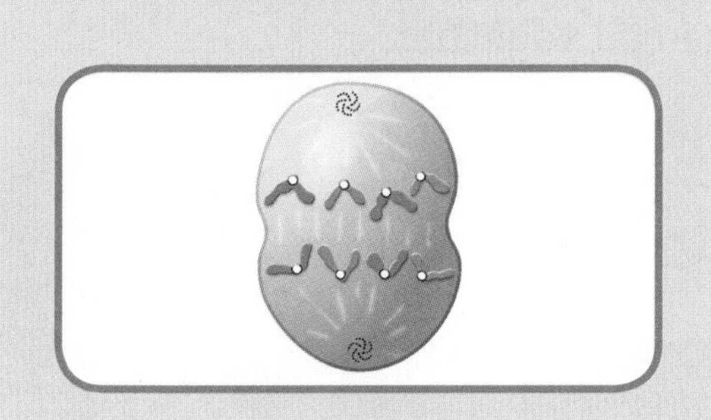

4 Fibers pull the chromosome pairs apart. After division, two new daughter cells are made.

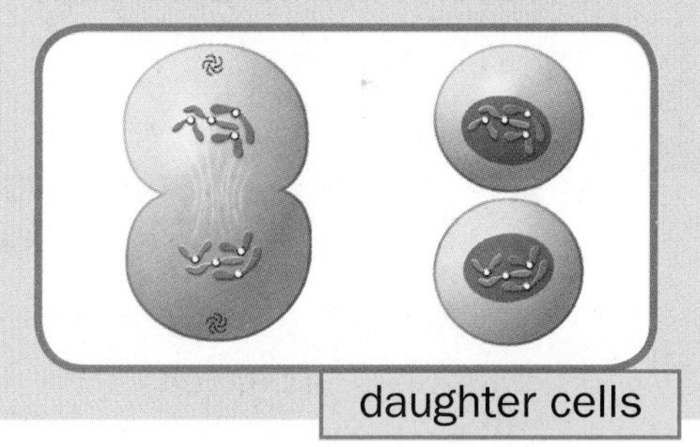

Chromosomes in the **daughter cells** have exactly the same information as the chromosomes in the **parent cell**.

WHY IT MATTERS

As your cells divide, you build more tissue and muscle.

LIFE SCIENCE

Comparing Plant and Animal Cells

ESSENTIAL IDEA

Plant and animal cells are both similar and different.

Plant and animal cells are alike in many ways. They have many **organelles**, or structures, in common.

Both cells have **mitochondria**. The mitochondria in a cell turn nutrients into energy. Both plant and animal cells have a **nucleus** and **chromosomes**. They control the cell's reproduction. Both types of cells also have **cell membranes** that hold the cell together.

Plant and Animal Cell Parts

organelle	animal cell	plant cell
mitochondria	✓	✓
nucleus	✓	✓
chromosomes	✓	✓
cell membrane	✓	✓
cell wall		✓
chloroplasts		✓

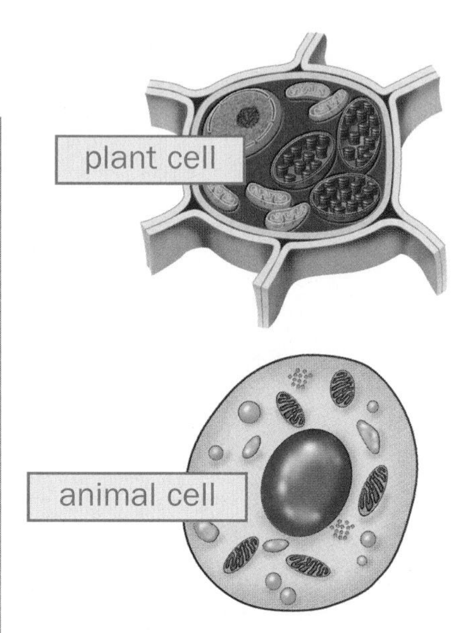

Plant Cells

Plants cells have several organelles that animal cells don't have.

Plants have a **cell wall**. The cell wall supports and protects the cell. Plant cells also contain chloroplasts. The **chloroplasts** contain chemicals that capture the Sun's energy.

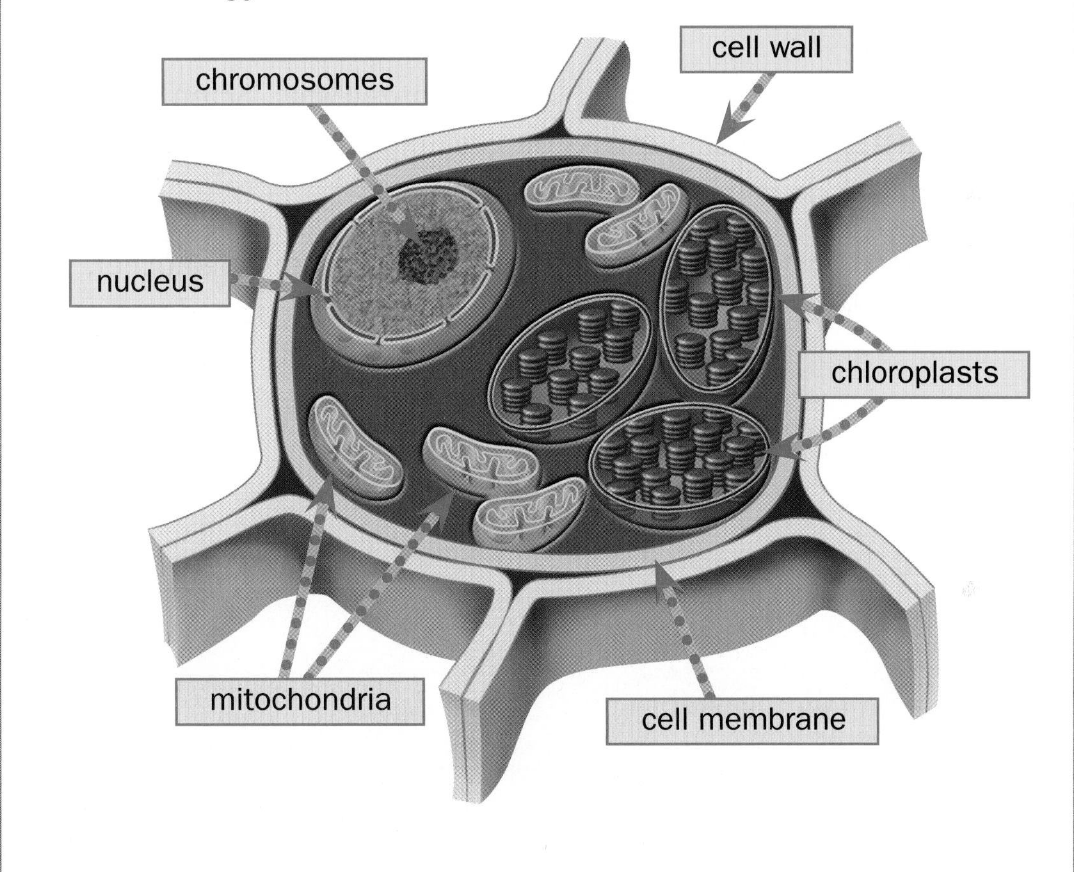

WHY IT MATTERS

Mitochondria in your cells turn the food you eat into energy for your body.

LIFE SCIENCE

How Living Things Are Classified

ESSENTIAL IDEA

Scientists classify living things into five main groups.

There are many different kinds of organisms. Scientists **classify** organisms into groups called **kingdoms**. A kingdom is the largest division in classifying living things.

Animals make up one kingdom. Plants make up another. Other organisms are divided into three more kingdoms.

Organisms in the **fungi** kingdom can't make their own food. Fungi get their nutrients only from the soil and other plants. Mushrooms are fungi.

The **moneran** kingdom includes all bacteria. Many bacteria are useful. Others can harm other organisms. Organisms in the moneran kingdom only have one cell.

Most organisms in the **protist** kingdom have only one cell. Protists are grouped together because they are unlike other kingdoms.

WHY IT MATTERS

- You are a member of the animal kingdom.
- Knowing how living things are alike and different can help you understand them better.

LIFE SCIENCE

How Plants Are Classified

ESSENTIAL IDEA

Scientists classify plants by their parts and by the way they reproduce.

Scientists classify plants into two main groups: plants without tubes and plants with tubes.

Plants without Tubes

Plants without tubes are called **nonvascular plants**. Nonvascular plants, like mosses, are simple plants that grow close to the ground. Mosses live in wet places because they do not have true roots to help them get water.

Moss cannot grow tall, but it can grow wide.

Plants with Tubes

Some plants have cells that look like long **tubes**. These cells carry water and nutrients up and down to the roots, stems, and leaves. Plants with tubes are called **vascular plants**.

Trees, grasses, and bushes are all kinds of vascular plants. These plants can grow tall because tubes support their stems.

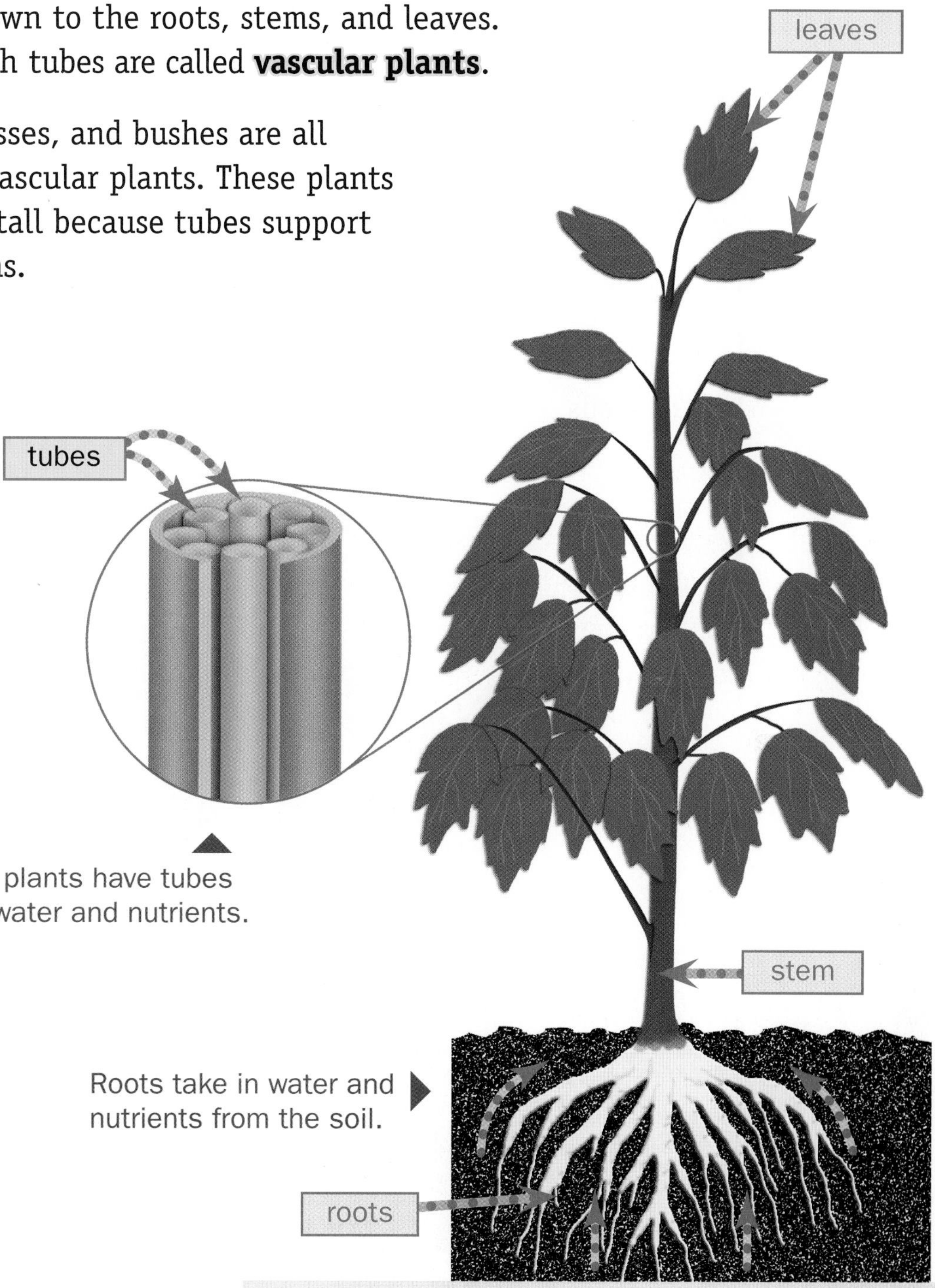

leaves

tubes

Vascular plants have tubes to carry water and nutrients.

stem

Roots take in water and nutrients from the soil.

roots

Plants are also classified by how they **reproduce**.

Seed Plants

Flowering plants make seeds in flowers. In some flowering plants, the flowers change into fruit that holds the seeds. **Conifers** are trees that have cones and needlelike leaves. The seeds of conifers come from the cones.

Kinds of Seed Plants

Seed plants reproduce from seeds. There are many kinds of seeds.

flowering plants

conifers

Nonseed Plants

Some plants do not use seeds to reproduce. Seedless plants, such as ferns, reproduce by dropping **spores** on the ground.

fern

spores

vascular plants

WHY IT MATTERS

- You use many flowering plants for food.
- You see many different kinds of plants in your daily life.

LIFE SCIENCE

How Plants Make Food

ESSENTIAL IDEA

Plants make their own food through a process called photosynthesis.

Plants are **producers**. They produce, or make, their own food through a process called **photosynthesis**. Photosynthesis takes place in the leaves of plants.

Trees produce food by photosynthesis.

Plants use **chlorophyll** in their leaves to trap light energy. Plants also take in carbon dioxide and water to make **starch**. When plants make food, they release oxygen.

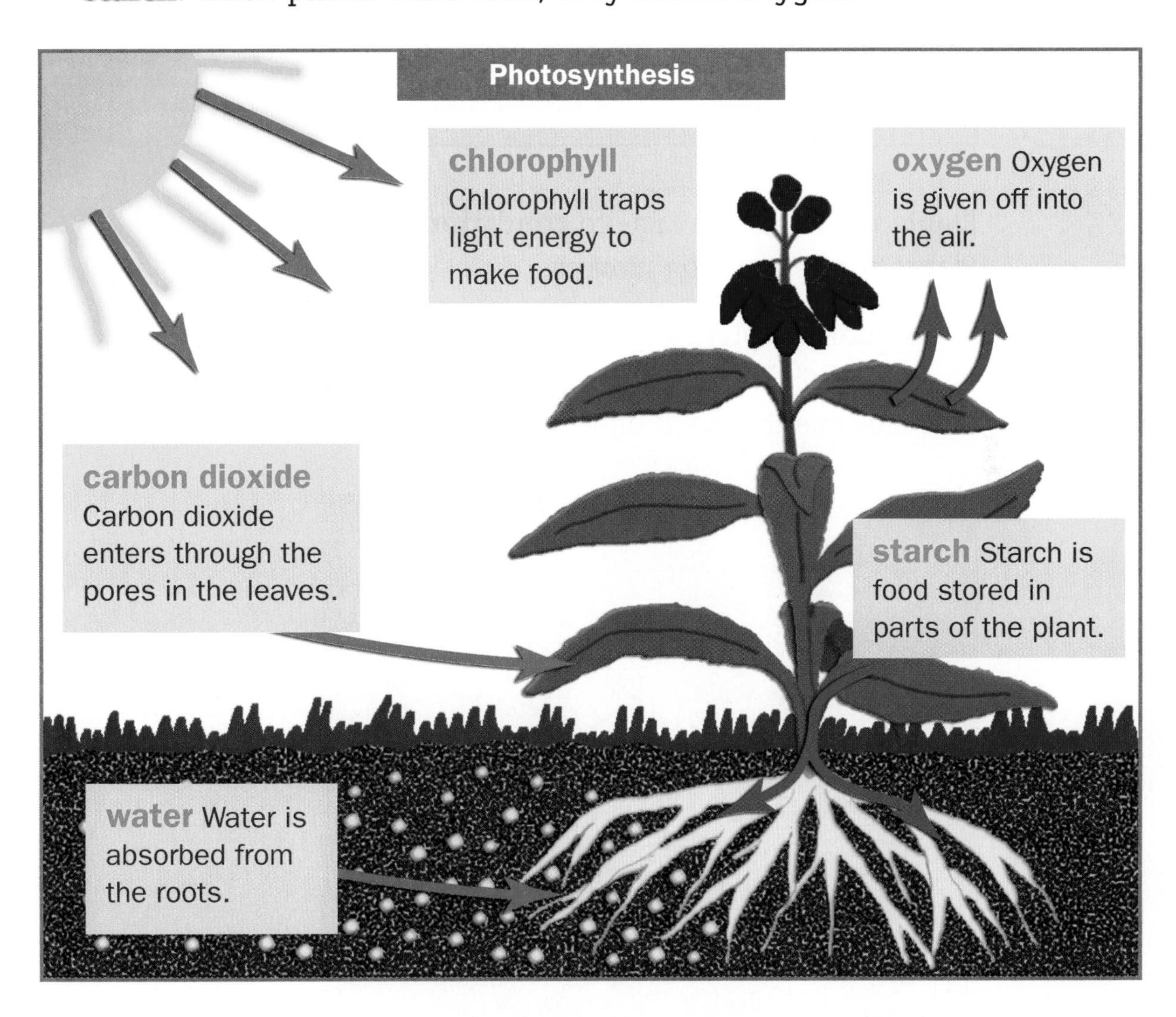

WHY IT MATTERS

- A lot of nutrients you eat come from food produced by plants.
- Plants also produce oxygen that you breathe.

LIFE SCIENCE

How Plants Respond

ESSENTIAL IDEA

Plants respond to conditions in their environment.

Plants **respond**, or react, to **conditions** around them. Plants can respond by moving.

A **tropism** is a plant's response to something in the environment. For example, a plant will grow toward light. This movement toward light is called **phototropism**.

This plant was lit from the side. It grew toward the sunlight.

The roots of plants grow down into the soil. The roots are responding to Earth's gravity. This is called **geotropism**. Plants can respond to different conditions.

WHY IT MATTERS

Like plants, you respond to your environment.

How Animals Are Classified

ESSENTIAL IDEA

Animals belong to one of two large groups: vertebrates and invertebrates.

Scientists classify animals into two main groups. Animals that have **backbones** are called **vertebrates**. Cats, fish, and birds are all examples of vertebrates. They have backbones made of small bones called **vertebrae**.

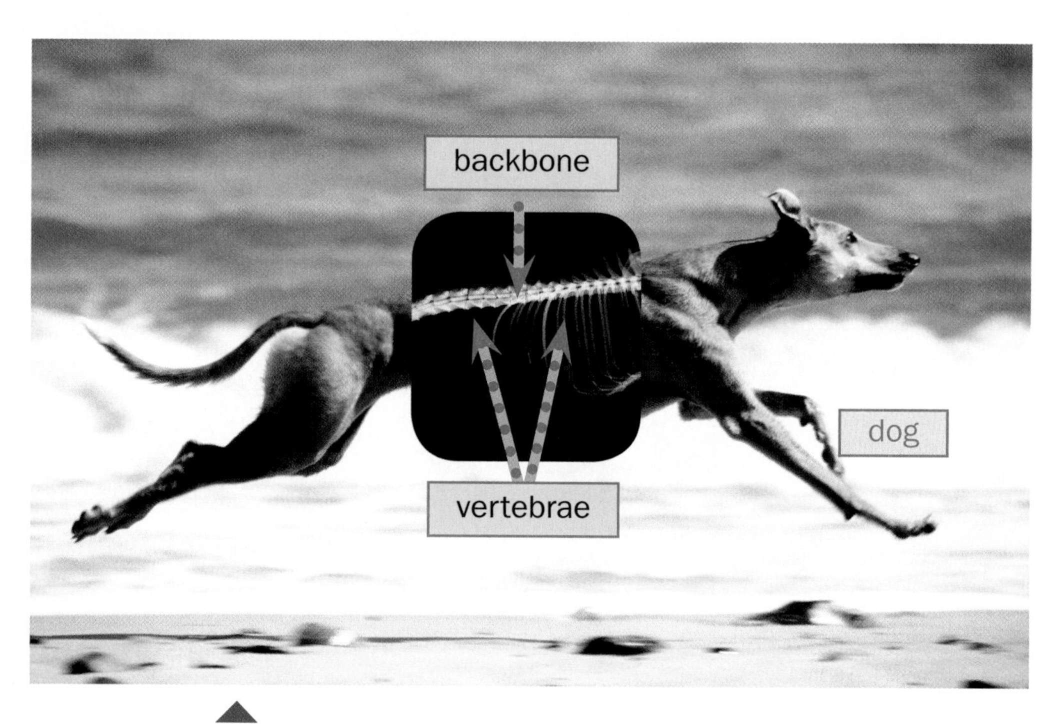

Dogs are vertebrates.

The other animal group is **invertebrates**. Invertebrates are animals that do not have a backbone. Most animals in the world are invertebrates. Some invertebrates, like snails and worms, live on land. Other invertebrates, like jellyfish, live in the ocean.

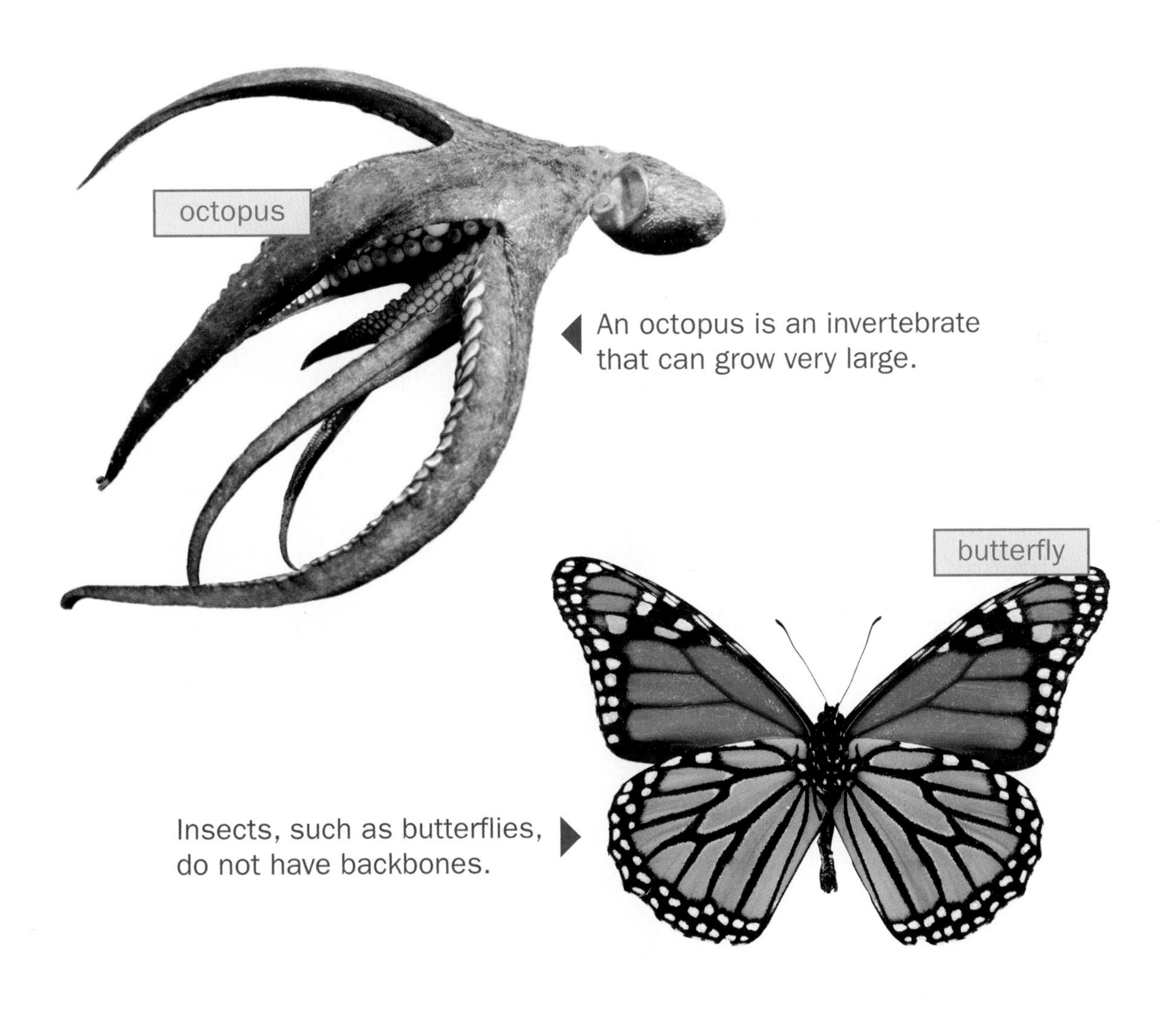

An octopus is an invertebrate that can grow very large.

Insects, such as butterflies, do not have backbones.

WHY IT MATTERS

- You have a backbone, so you are a vertebrate.
- Insects and spiders that you see are invertebrates.

Invertebrates

ESSENTIAL IDEA

Most animals on Earth are invertebrates.

More than 95 percent of the animals living on Earth are invertebrates. Many invertebrates live in water. Worms, insects, and spiders live in and on the soil.

The simplest animals are **sponges**. Sponges have no muscle or nerve cells. They absorb food through **pores**, or openings, in their bodies.

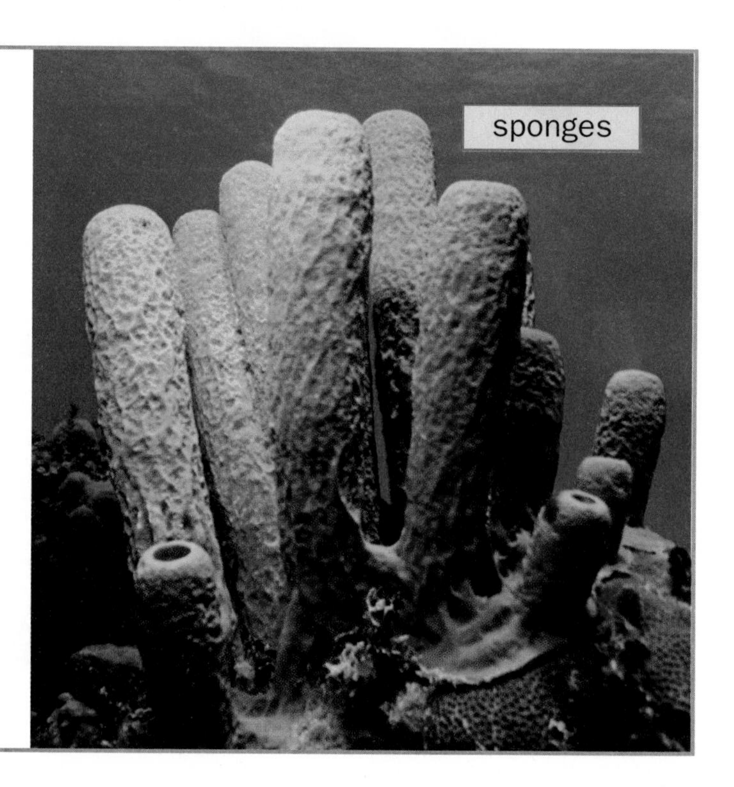

Snails and squid are invertebrates called **mollusks**. They have soft bodies. Many mollusks, such as snails, have a hard shell that grows with their body.

Shrimp, lobster, and crayfish are invertebrates called **crustaceans**. Crustaceans have **exoskeletons**, or hard shells, on the outside of their bodies.

Annelids are invertebrates with long bodies made of many parts. The parts look like rings and move separately. Worms and leeches are annelids.

annelids

leech

worms

There are more than a million different kinds of **insects** on Earth. Insects have **antennae** and six legs. Their bodies have three parts. Like crustaceans, insects have exoskeletons.

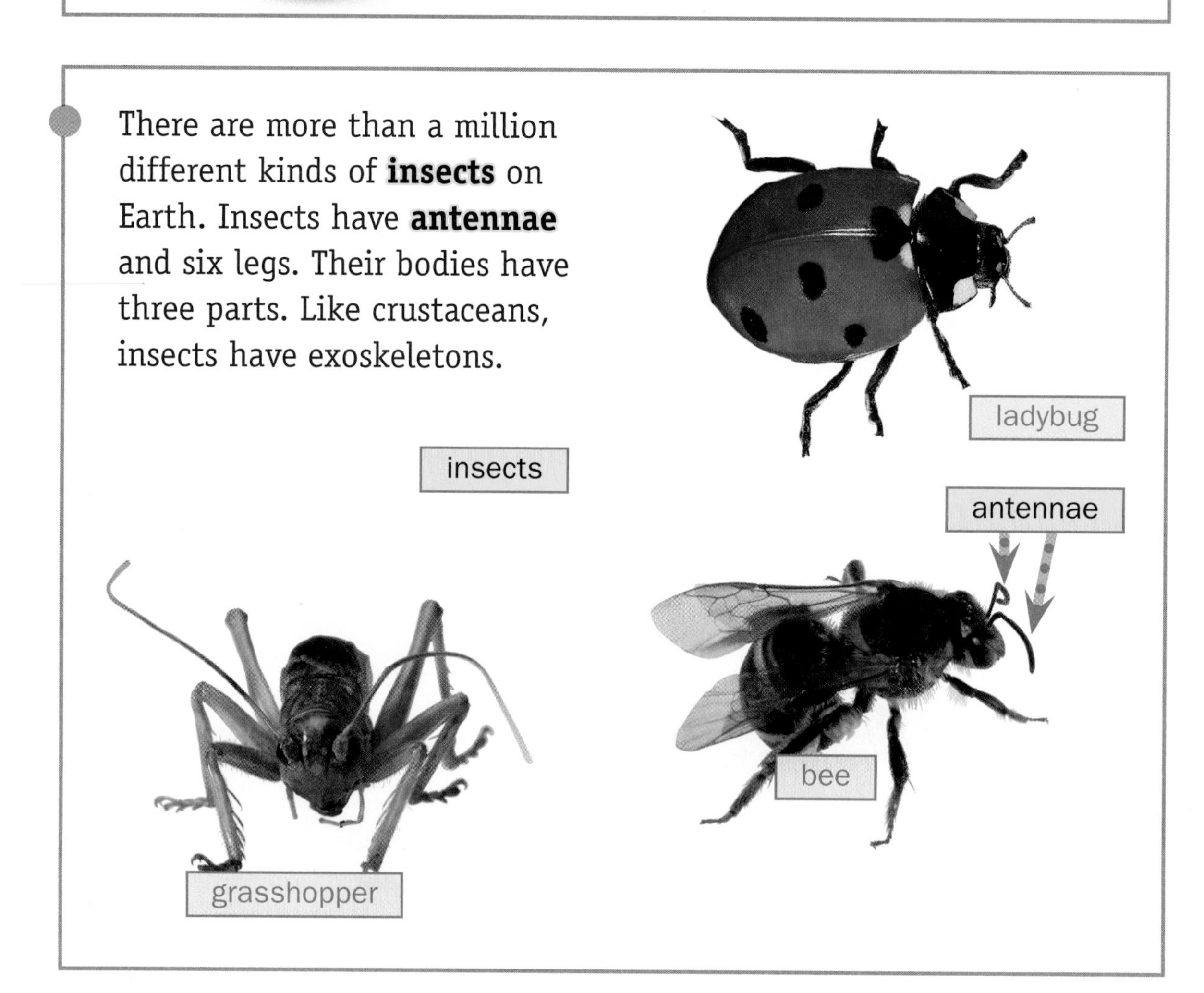

Spiders have eight legs and no antennae. They have two body parts. Many spiders spin webs to catch insects for food.

spider

Invertebrates

types of invertebrates	traits
sponges	live in water absorb food through pores
mollusks	live on soil or in water have soft bodies some have shells
crustaceans	live in water have exoskeletons
annelids	live on soil or in water have long bodies
insects	live in or on soil have exoskeletons, six legs, antennae, and three body parts
spiders	live on soil have eight legs and two body parts

WHY IT MATTERS

- There are thousands of invertebrates around you every day.
- Invertebrates often help you. For example, insects help fruit reproduce, and you eat fruit.

Vertebrates

ESSENTIAL IDEA

There are five types of vertebrates.

Many of the animals you see every day are vertebrates, or animals with backbones. Vertebrates are divided into five main classes. Each **class** has a group of traits that separate the animals from other classes.

Mammals are **warm-blooded** animals. Mammals' bodies are adapted to help them keep a constant temperature. Outside temperatures do not change the temperature of the animals.

Birds are warm-blooded animals that have feathers. Most birds use their wings to fly.

Most **fish** are **cold-blooded**. They have the same temperature as their environment.

Reptiles are cold-blooded animals that have scales. They live on land or in water. Reptiles reproduce by laying eggs. Snakes and lizards are reptiles.

Amphibians are cold-blooded. They spend part of their lives in water and part on land. Frogs reproduce in water and live on land as adults.

more about **Vertebrates**

Mammals

Mammals are warm-blooded. They can **regulate**, or control, their body temperature. Their temperature stays about the same all the time. Hair or fur on the bodies of most mammals acts as **insulation** to keep their bodies warm.

Mammal **offspring**, or babies, form inside the mother's body. The mothers **nourish**, or feed, the offspring with milk produced in their bodies.

Mammals care for their offspring until they are old enough to find food on their own.

Some mammals live in a **marine** environment. Marine mammals depend on the ocean for their food. They come to the surface to breathe oxygen from the air.

Whales, dolphins, and manatees live their whole lives in water. Their babies are born alive underwater.

Manatee offspring live under water but breathe oxygen.

Dolphins come to the surface to breathe.

Mammal traits

warm-blooded
most have hair or fur
breathe oxygen
babies fed with milk

more about **Vertebrates**

Birds

Like mammals, birds are warm-blooded. Birds have two legs. Their front **limbs** are **wings** that most birds use to fly. Their bodies are covered with **feathers**. Some birds have **claws** on their feet.

The bones of birds are hollow. Birds are light because their bones are filled with air.

An eagle can lift a fish out of the water with its claws.

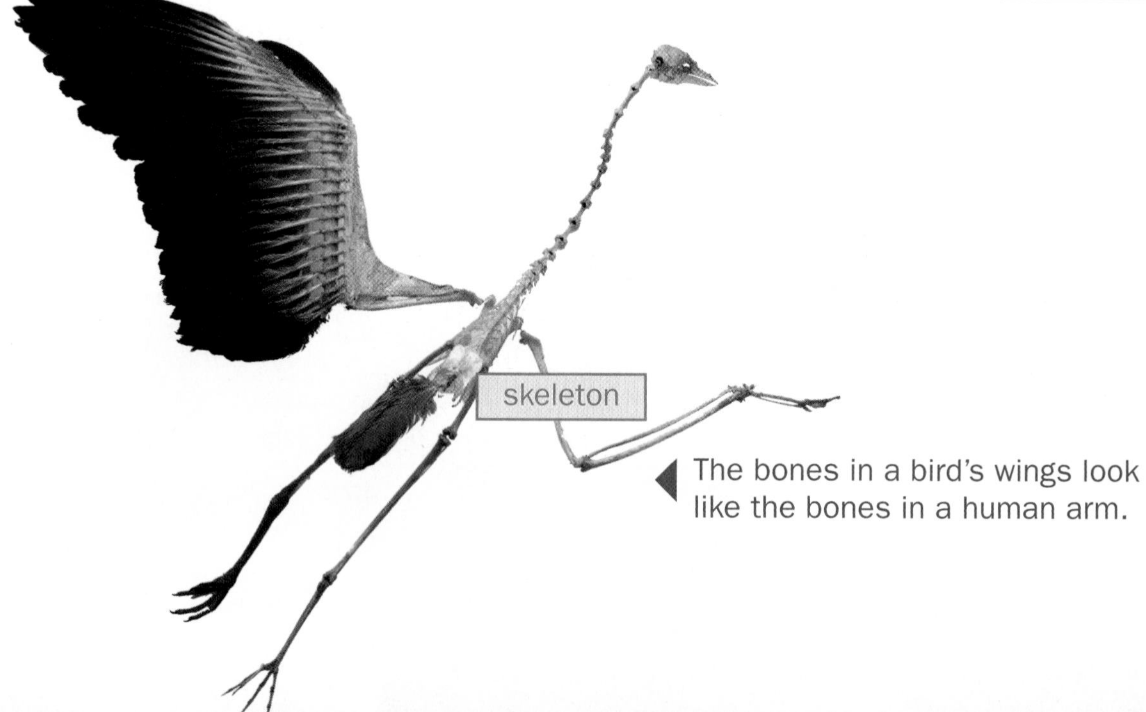

The bones in a bird's wings look like the bones in a human arm.

Birds lay eggs. The birds keep the eggs warm and safe in nests. When the offspring are large enough to survive, the babies break through the eggs. Baby birds **rely** on their parents to bring them food.

Baby birds are blind and helpless at birth.

Bird traits

warm-blooded
two legs, two wings
feathers
hollow bones
reproduce by eggs

Some birds, such as ostriches, do not fly. Their long legs help them run fast.

Fish

All fish live in either freshwater or salt water. Their bodies are **streamlined** to help them move easily through water. Fish have **gills** instead of lungs. As water flows over their gills, the gills remove oxygen from the water.

Most fish have **scales** that protect their bodies. Fish have **fins** on their sides, top, and bottom that help them swim. A tail fin helps them move forward in the water.

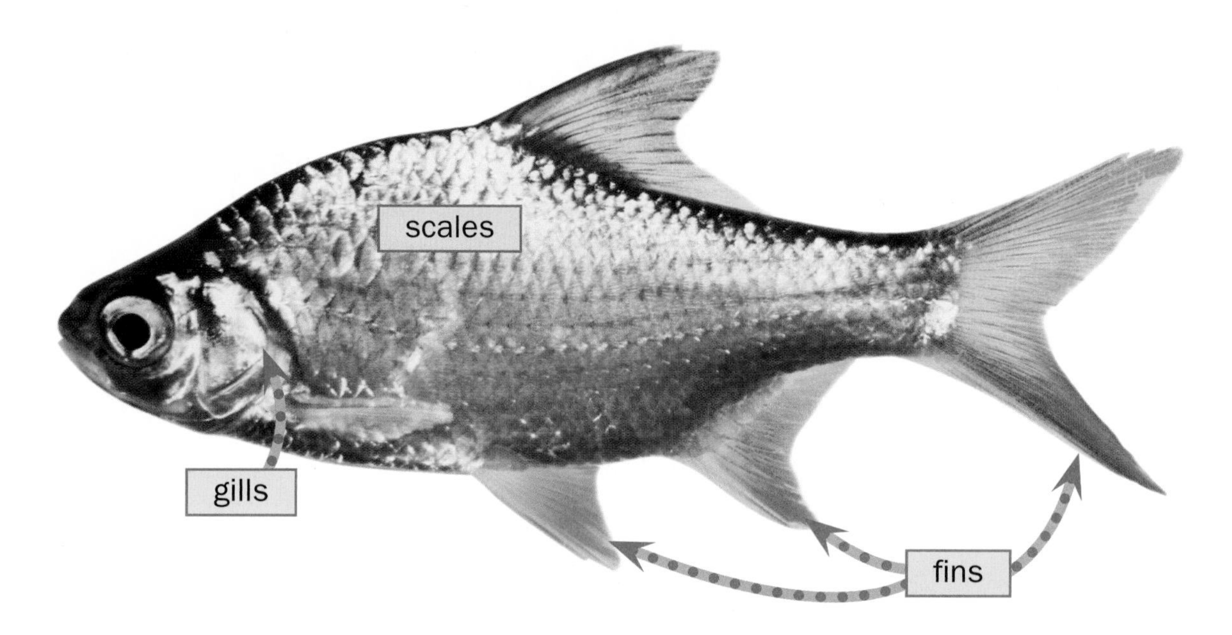

Bony Fish

Bony fish have **skeletons** that are made of bone.

Sharks and Rays

The skeletons of sharks and rays are made of cartilage rather than bone. **Cartilage** is a tough, bendable tissue, like the tip of your nose or your ears.

Most sharks live in salt water.

Fish traits

cold-blooded
gills, fins
skeletons made of bone or cartilage

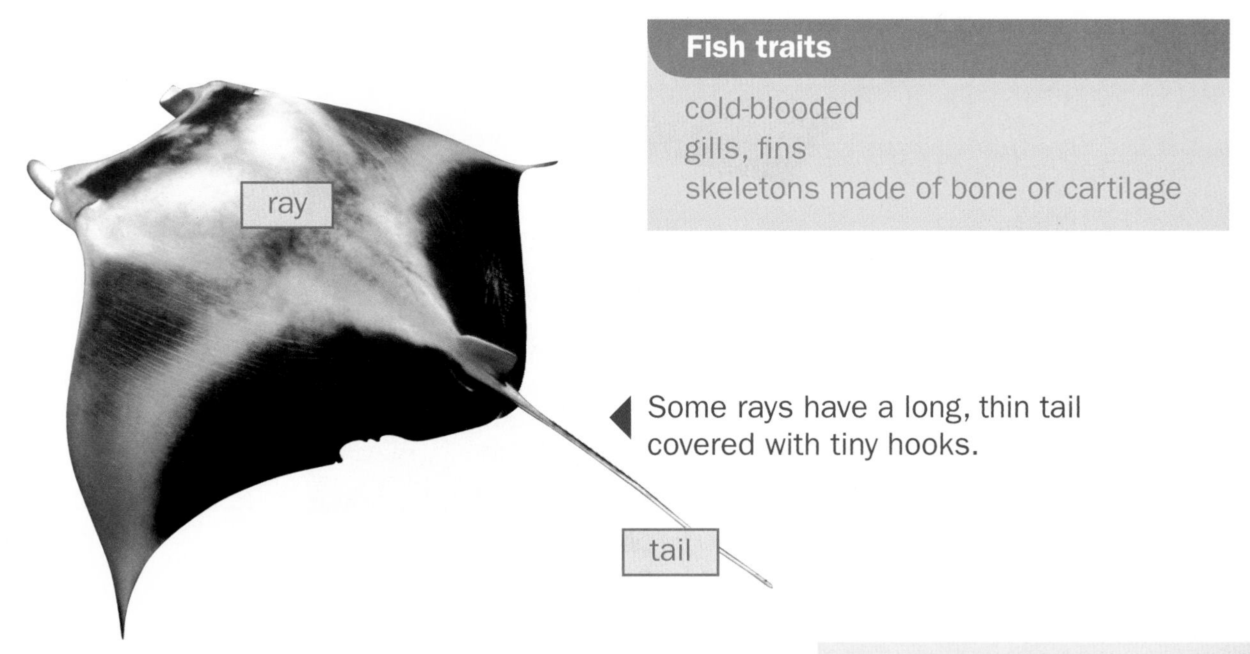

Some rays have a long, thin tail covered with tiny hooks.

Reptiles

Reptiles include turtles, snakes, lizards, and alligators. All reptiles have lungs to breathe with and skin that does not need to stay wet. They produce eggs with a leathery **shell**. It protects the offspring inside from drying out.

Snakes hatch from eggs.

Reptiles are **ectothermic**, or cold-blooded. Some reptiles use the Sun's energy to keep warm. Their bodies are covered in hard scales. The scales help keep their bodies from drying out.

Most turtles spend their lives on land and in the water. Turtles have **flippers** instead of legs to **propel**, or move, them through the water.

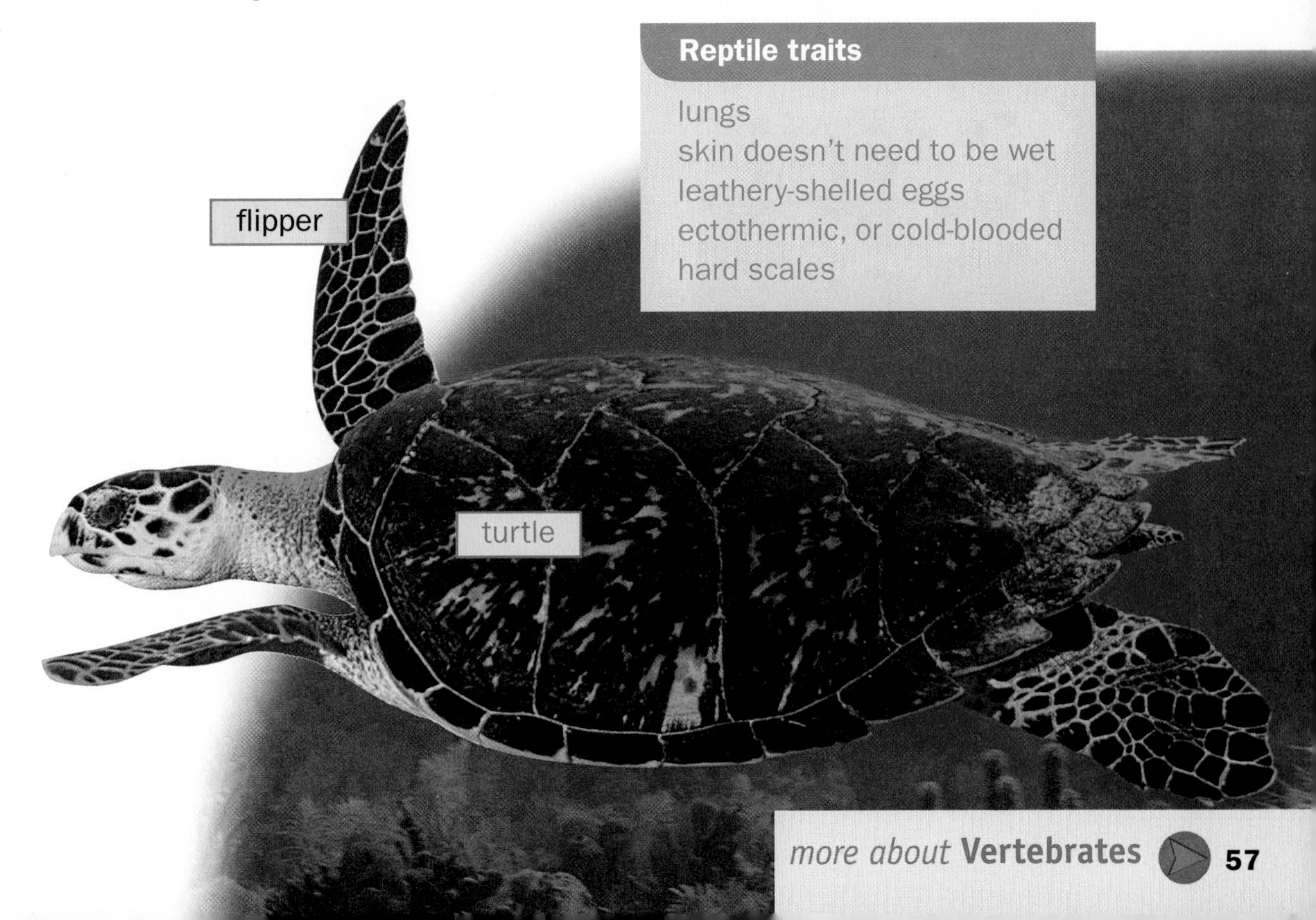

Reptile traits

lungs
skin doesn't need to be wet
leathery-shelled eggs
ectothermic, or cold-blooded
hard scales

Amphibians

Amphibians live both in water and on land. Amphibians start life with gills, like fish, and later develop lungs to breathe air.

Amphibians reproduce by laying **eggs** in water. This keeps the eggs **moist**, or wet, until the animals hatch. Amphibians are born with tails.

Baby frogs are called **tadpoles**. Frogs lose their **tails** as they grow.

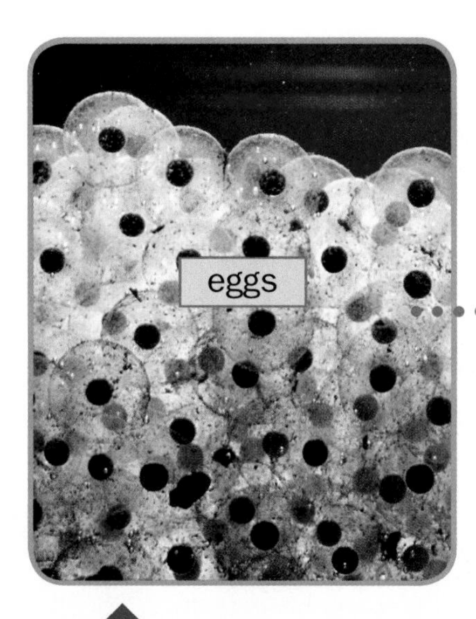

Mother frogs lay eggs in water.

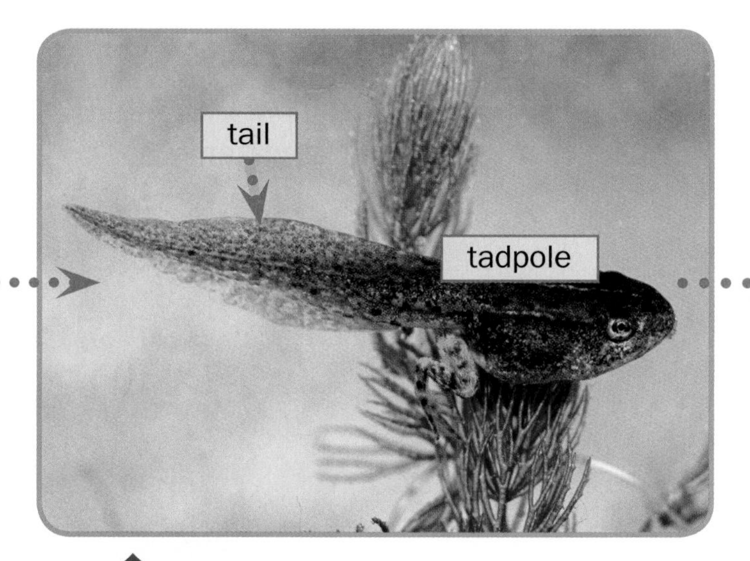

Tadpoles live in water all the time. This tadpole has started to develop its back legs.

After amphibians develop lungs, they can live on land. Amphibians can get oxygen through their lungs or skin. Their skin needs to stay moist, so they always live near water.

Amphibian traits

born from eggs in water
live on land as adults
cold-blooded
skin stays moist

Frogs are amphibians with lungs and smooth, moist skin.

WHY IT MATTERS

You are a vertebrate, so you have a backbone.

You are also a mammal, so you are warm-blooded.

Life Cycles

ESSENTIAL IDEA

Plants and animals are living things that have life cycles.

All living things go through different **stages** of a life cycle. Organisms are **born** and **grow** over time. They **develop** into **adults**. As adults, organisms **reproduce** to make more of their own kind.

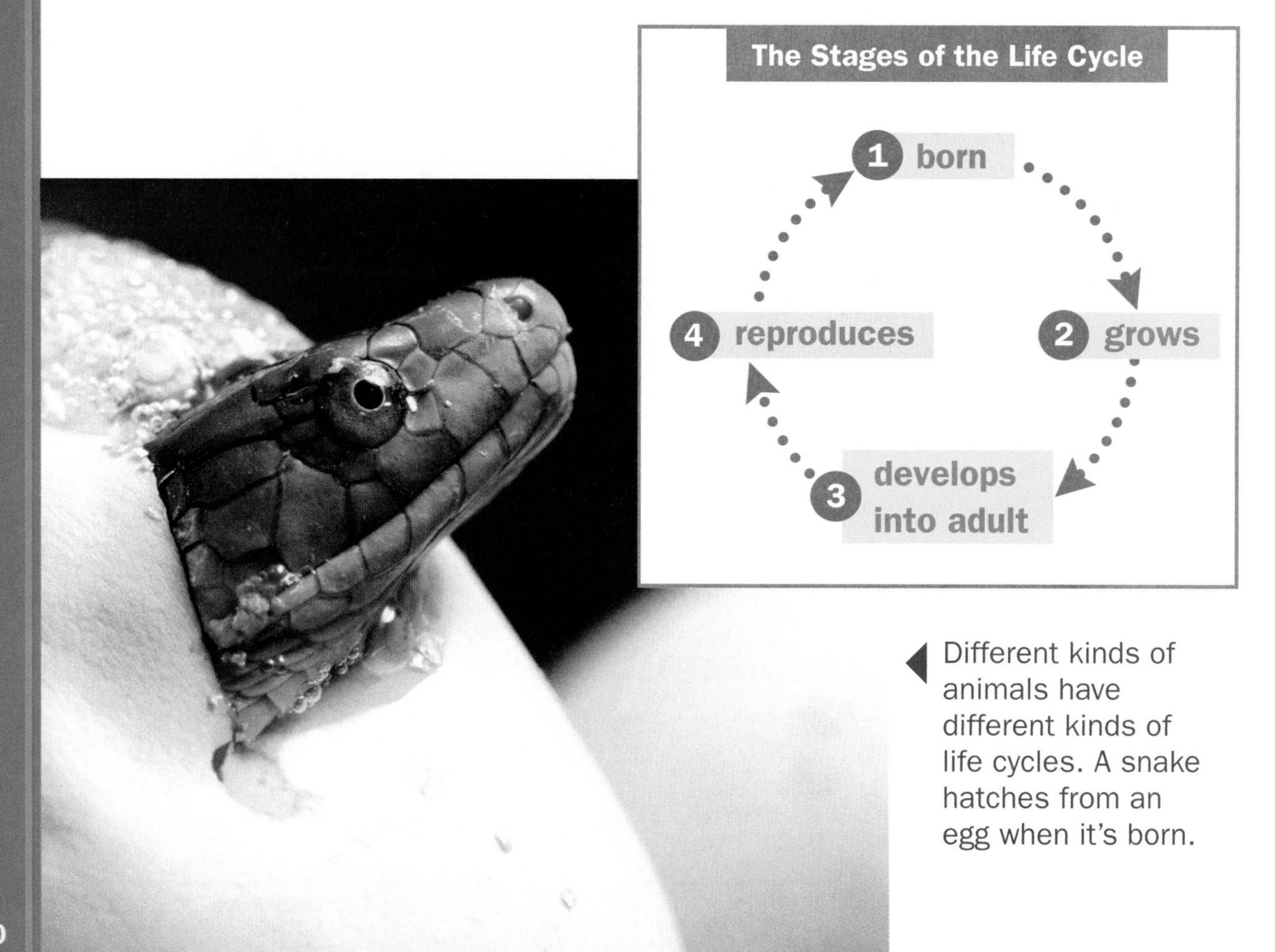

Different kinds of animals have different kinds of life cycles. A snake hatches from an egg when it's born.

Animal Life Cycles

Many animals look a lot like their parents when they are born. Other kinds of animals change forms as they develop.

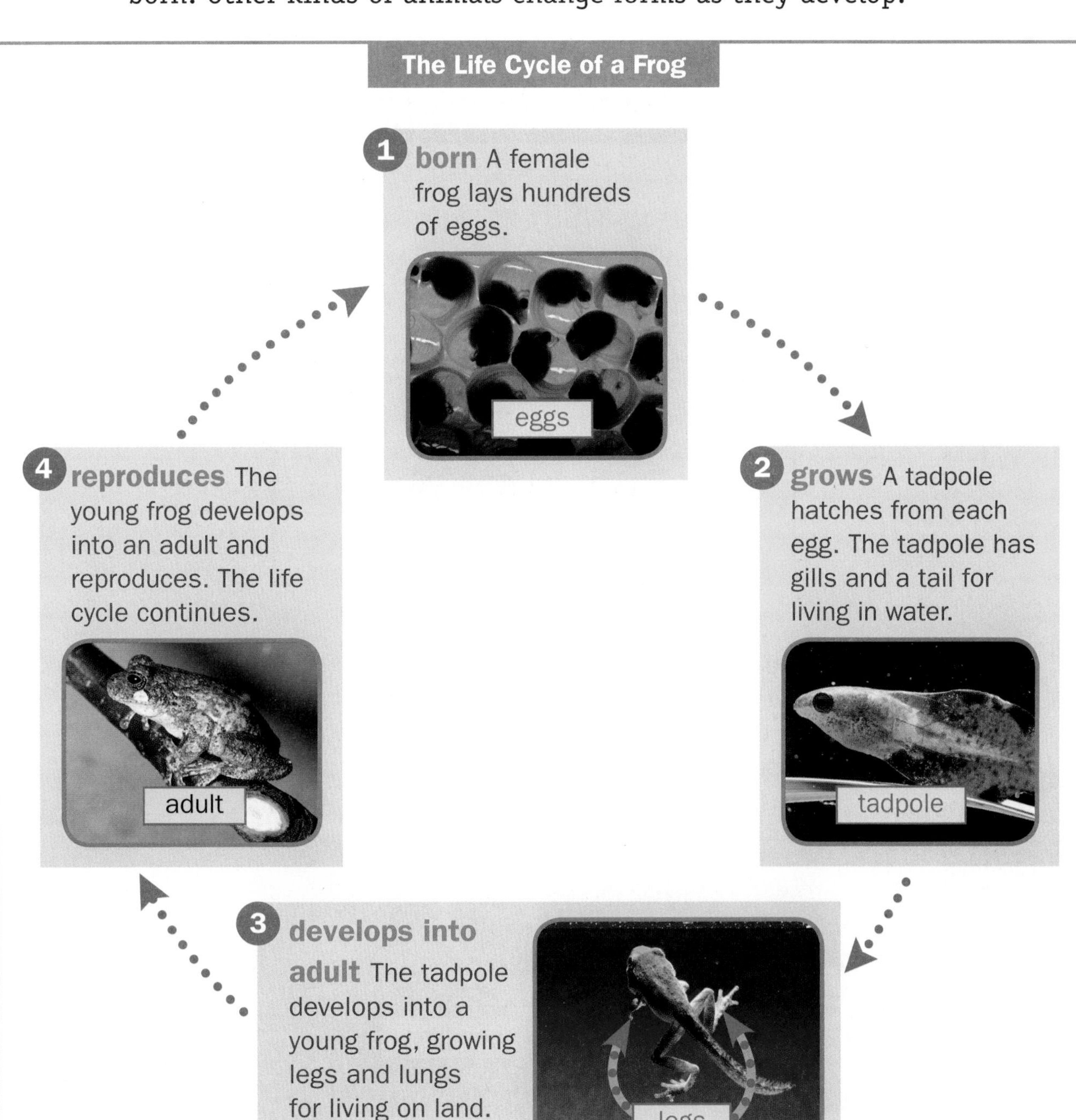

more about **Life Cycles**

Plant Life Cycles

The life cycle of many plants begins with a **seed**. Seeds grow into **seedlings** and develop roots.

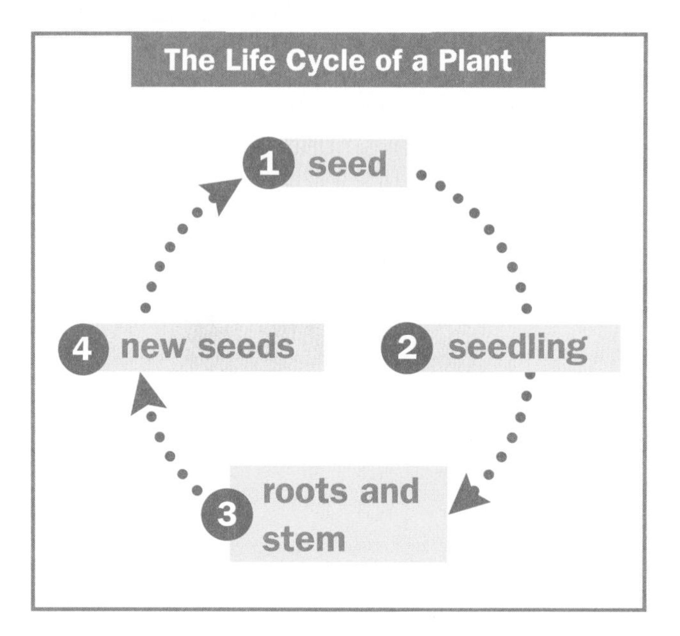

Stems grow taller and leaves develop. Adult plants can reproduce by making seeds.

WHY IT MATTERS

- You go through the stages of a life cycle.
- Your life cycle began when you were born.
- Your body changes as you grow.
- You develop into an adult.

3 roots and stem Some plants develop leaves. The plant's roots and stem grow longer.

4 new seeds As adults, plants make new seeds, and the life cycle continues.

LIFE SCIENCE

Adaptations in Plants

ESSENTIAL IDEA

Adaptations are traits that help a plant survive in its environment.

Plants have different **traits**, or qualities. Traits are features, such as what the plant looks like and how it responds to its environment. The traits are **inherited**, or passed down, as new plants form.

An **adaptation** is a trait that helps a plant survive in its environment. For example, the **spines** on a cactus keep animals from eating its fruit.

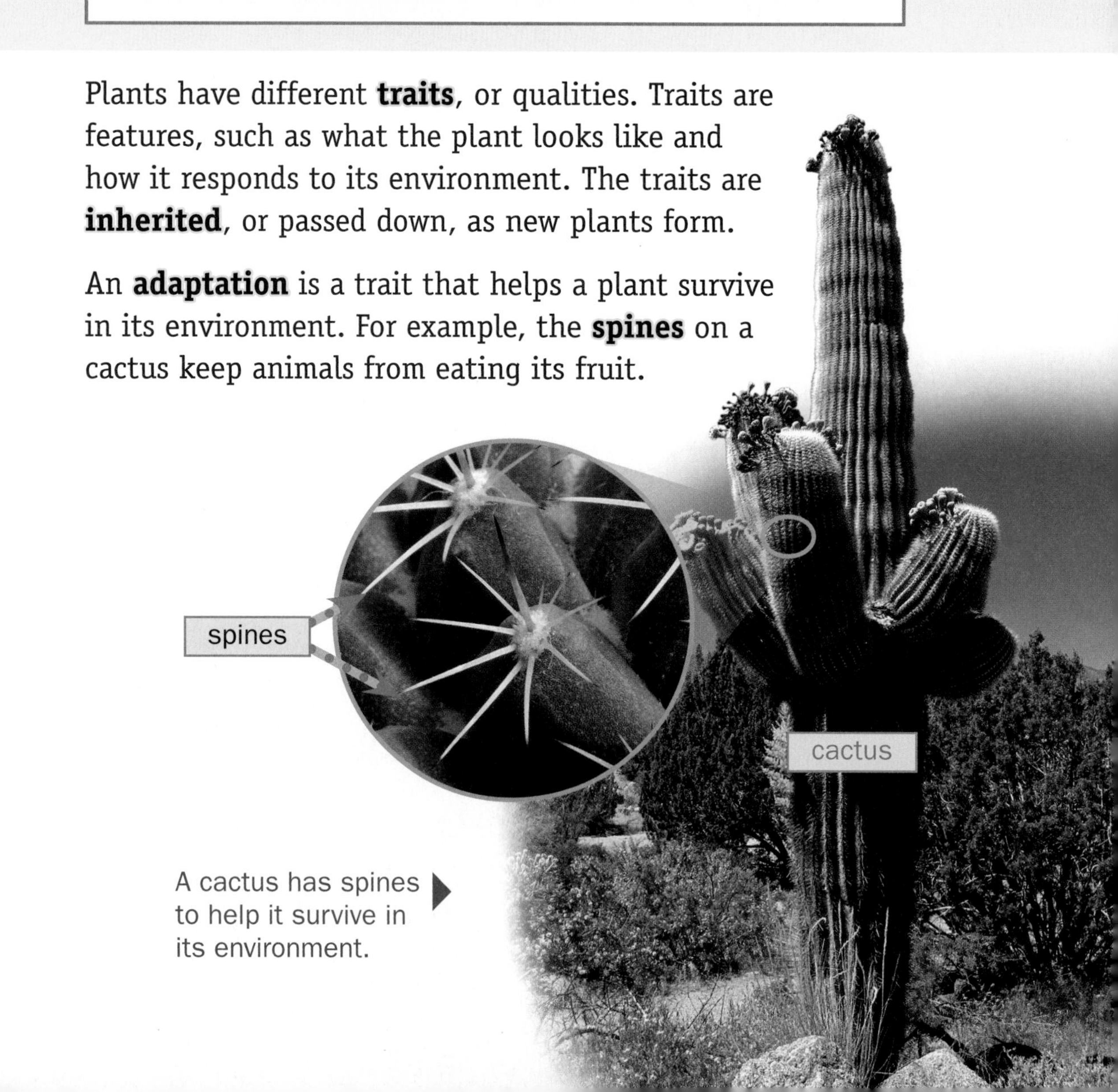

A cactus has spines to help it survive in its environment.

These wildflowers bloom in the spring. They grow before leaves on the trees develop and block the sunshine.

This water lily has leaves that float on top of the water. The leaves float so the plant gets sunlight. Water lilies have flexible stems that can move under water and not break.

WHY IT MATTERS

Some plants grow well in your environment, but others may not be adapted to live there.

LIFE SCIENCE

Adaptations in Animals

ESSENTIAL IDEA

Adaptations help animals survive in their environment.

Parents pass **characteristics**, or traits, to their offspring. **Adaptations** help organisms survive in their environments.

leopard The leopard's spots make it easier to sneak up on prey without being seen.

hippopotamus The hippo's nostrils, eyes, and ears are high on its head so it can stay low in the water. When it goes under the water, it can hide from predators.

Physical adaptations help animals get food and hide from their **prey** or their **predators**.

flamingo A flamingo's long legs and neck let it stand in water to feed. It uses its long beak to get food.

hedgehog The hedgehog's body is covered with sharp spines. It can roll into a ball if attacked by a predator.

WHY IT MATTERS

Like all animals, you are adapted to live in your environment.

LIFE SCIENCE

Natural Selection

ESSENTIAL IDEA

Over long periods of time, populations that survive and reproduce can become new species.

A **species** is a group of organisms with features that make them different from other organisms. A **population** is the members of a species that live in the same area.

Most members of a population have the same traits. But sometimes individuals are born with **mutations**, or changes. Over a long period of time, organisms with these mutations may become a new species.

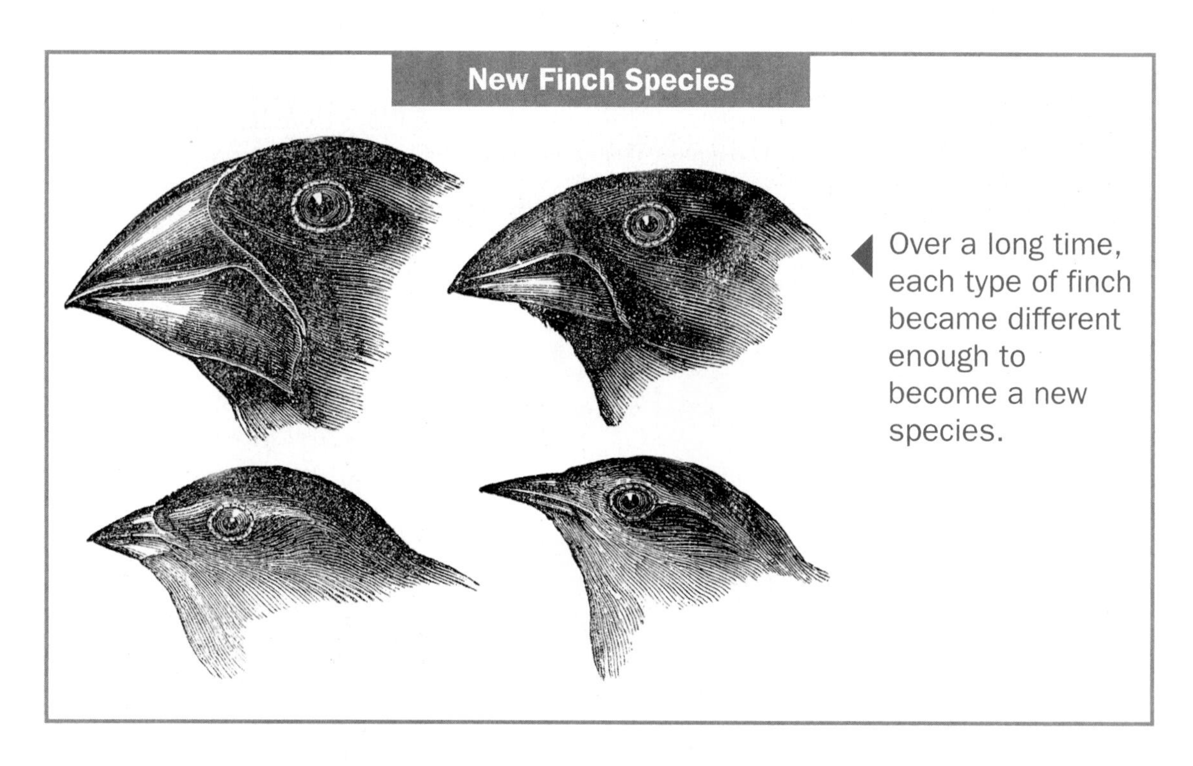

New Finch Species

Over a long time, each type of finch became different enough to become a new species.

Natural Selection of Peppered Moths

Peppered moths are either light or dark. The dark-colored moths were once uncommon. Birds would eat the dark moths because they were easy to see on light-colored trees.

Burning coal in factories caused pollution, and trees became a darker color. The light moths became easy to see on the dark trees. Over time, the dark moths became the most common. This is an example of **natural selection**.

In 1848 only 1 percent of peppered moths were dark.

Around 1948 about 90 percent of peppered moths were dark.

WHY IT MATTERS

Your area has populations of humans, cats, dogs, and different insect species.

Human Body Systems

ESSENTIAL IDEA

Each body system has a specific job. All the systems of the body work together to keep you alive.

Groups of cells with the same job are called **tissues**. Tissues that share the same task form **organs**. Organs join together to form **organ systems**.

Each organ system has a **specific** function. This means each organ system is important to your body in a different way.

Muscular and Skeletal Systems

The **muscular system** gives the body the ability to move. Muscle cells work together to form muscle tissues. Muscles are attached to bones of the skeletal system.

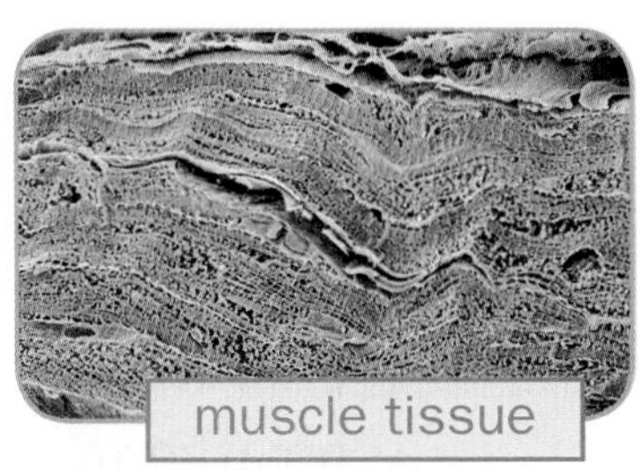

The **skeletal system** supports the body and protects organs inside the body. In the skeletal system, bone cells join to form bone tissue. Bone tissue forms bones.

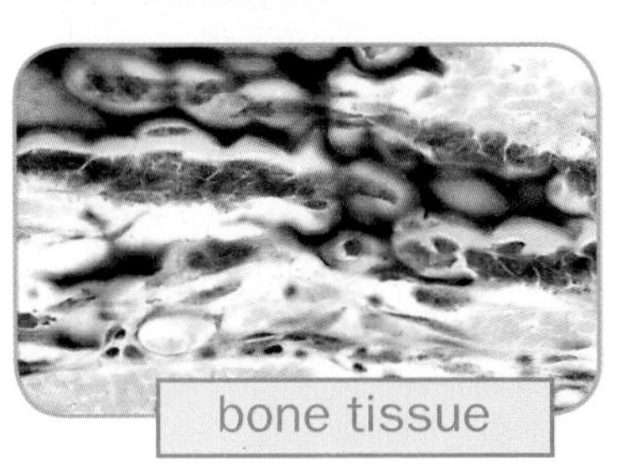

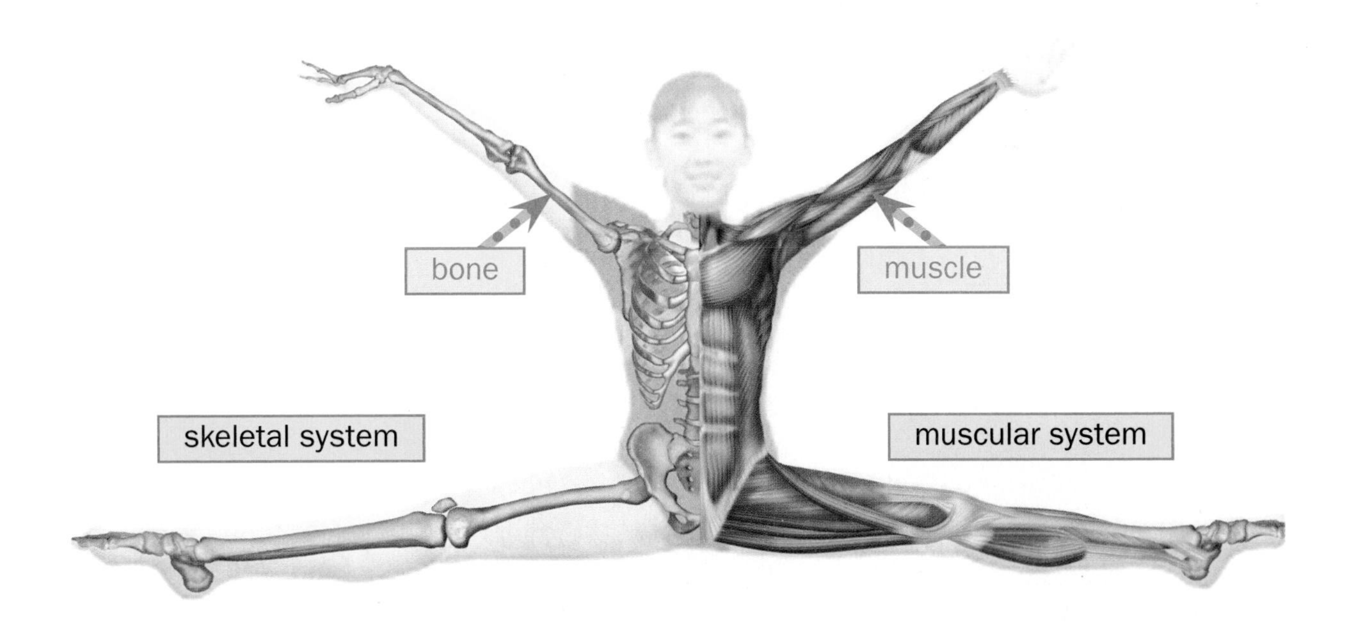

The Respiratory System

The **respiratory system** contains the organs you use to breathe.

Cells in your body need **oxygen** from the air. The cells produce **carbon dioxide** as waste. When you **inhale**, or breathe in, your lungs take in oxygen. When you **exhale**, or breathe out, your lungs push out carbon dioxide.

The organs of your respiratory system include the nose, **windpipe**, **lungs**, and **air sacs**.

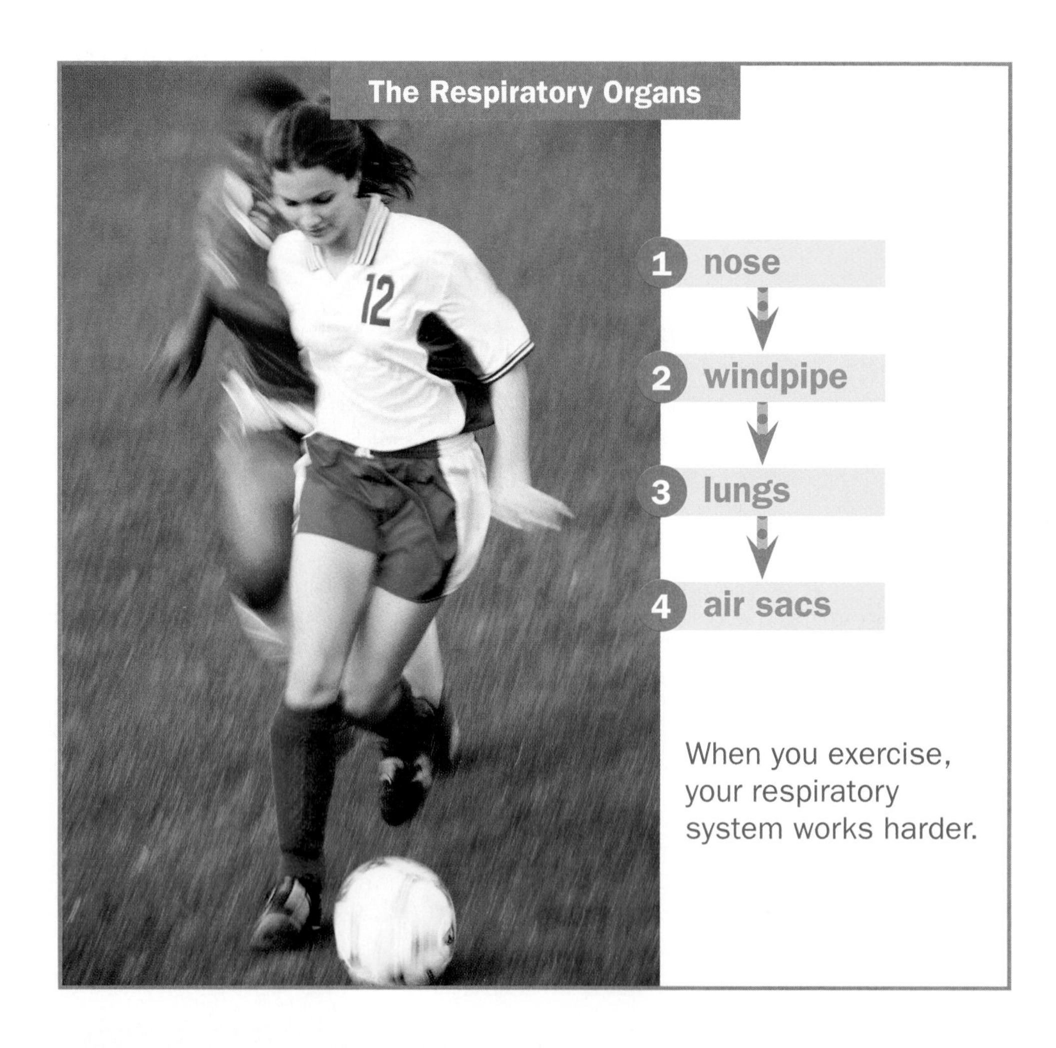

When you exercise, your respiratory system works harder.

How the Respiratory System Works

1 nose When you inhale, air enters the body through the nose.

2 windpipe The windpipe carries air to the lungs.

3 lungs In the lungs, the air fills millions of tiny air sacs.

4 air sacs Oxygen moves from the air sacs into the blood.

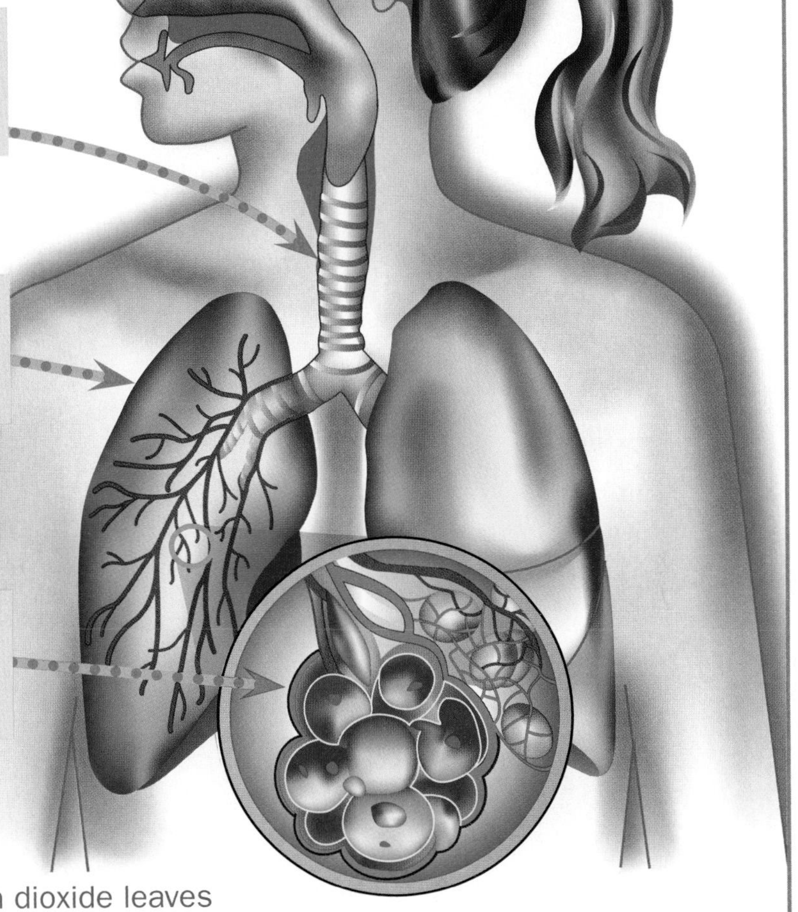

When you exhale, carbon dioxide leaves the body.

The Circulatory System

The main job of the **circulatory system** is to move nutrients, gases, and waste through the body. The major parts in the circulatory system are the **heart**, **blood vessels,** and **blood**.

How the Circulatory System Works

The heart pumps blood from the lungs to all parts of the body. Blood moves into and out of the heart with each beat.

Veins and **arteries** are blood vessels. Veins carry blood toward the heart. Arteries carry blood away from the heart. **Capillaries** are tiny blood vessels that connect arteries and veins.

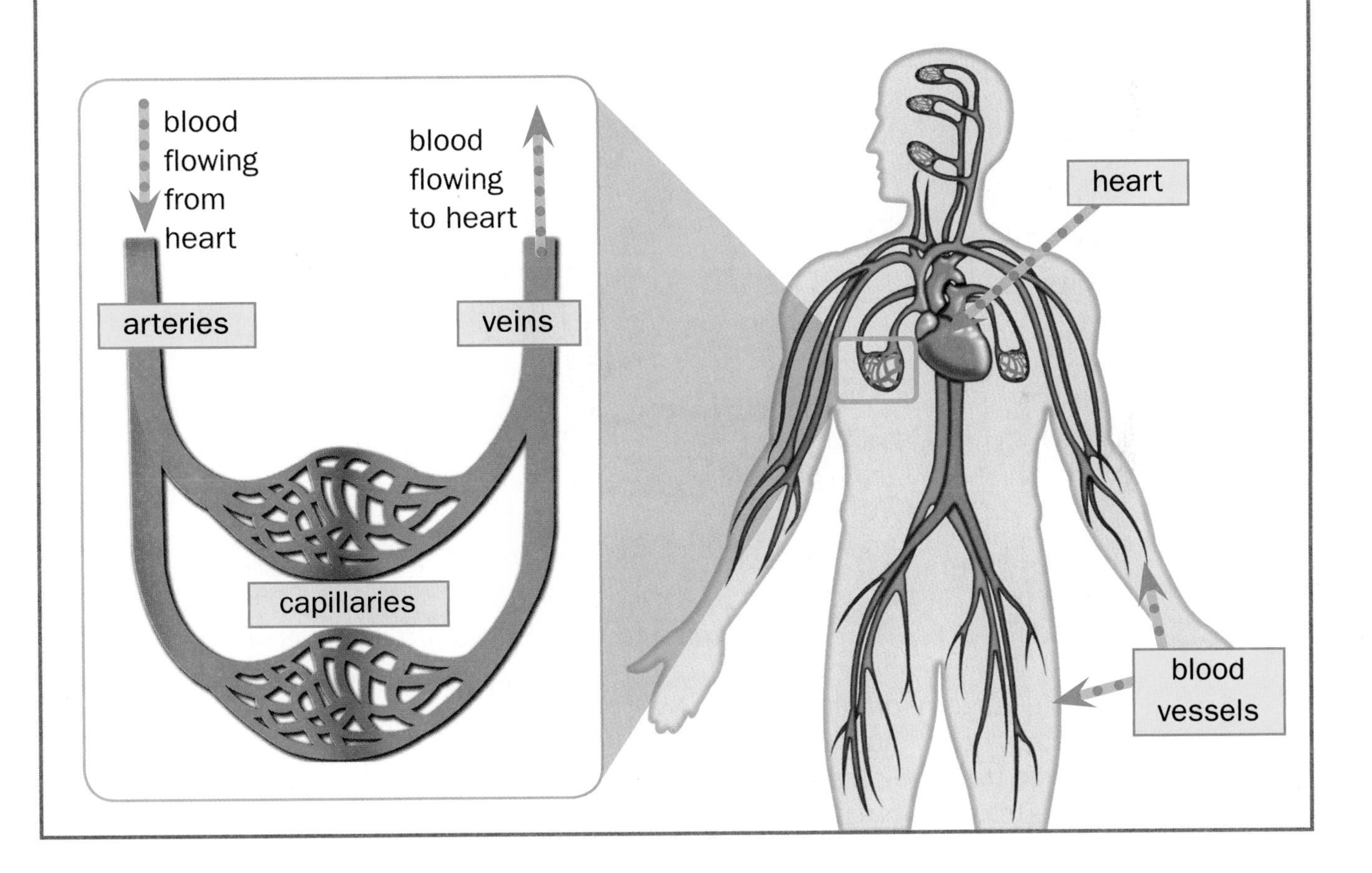

The Nervous System

The **nervous system** allows parts of the body to communicate. The major organs of the nervous system are the **brain**, **spinal cord**, and **nerves**.

Your **senses** pick up information from the environment. Nerve cells send this information to different parts of the brain. The brain reads the information and tells your body what to do.

The Sensory Regions of the Brain

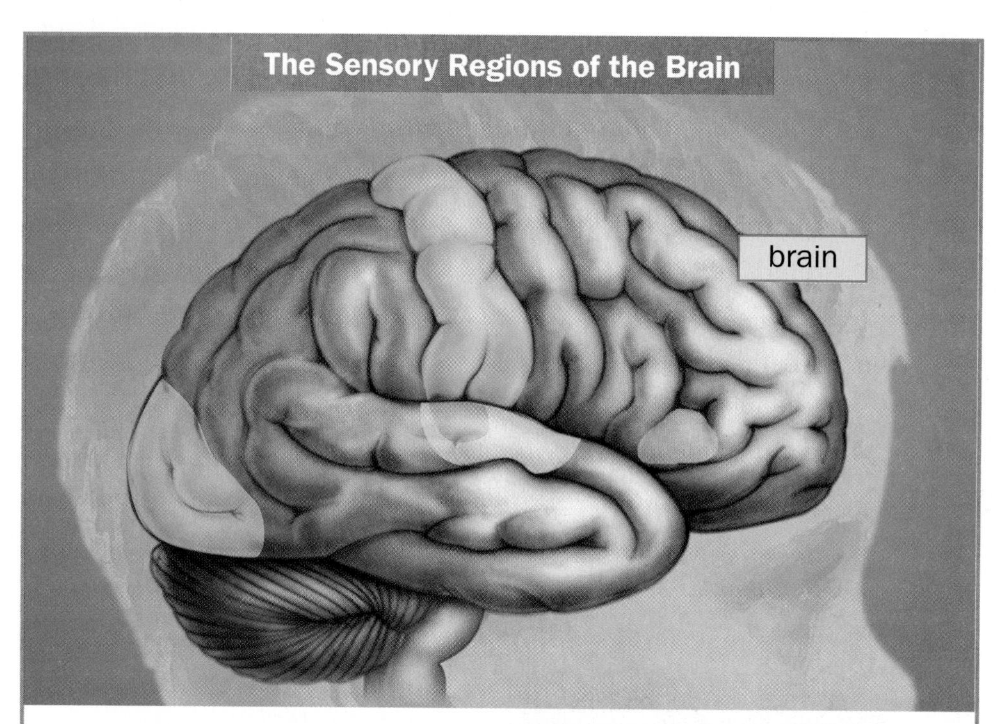

Messages from the eyes, ears, nose, mouth, and skin travel to different parts of the brain.

region	message from
■	eyes
■	skin
■	ears
■	mouth
■	nose

The spinal cord controls your **reflexes**, or automatic responses.

When you touch something hot, the signal from nerves in your finger reaches the spinal cord. Then, a return message tells the finger to move away from the heat. Even before you think, you pull your finger away. This is called a reflex.

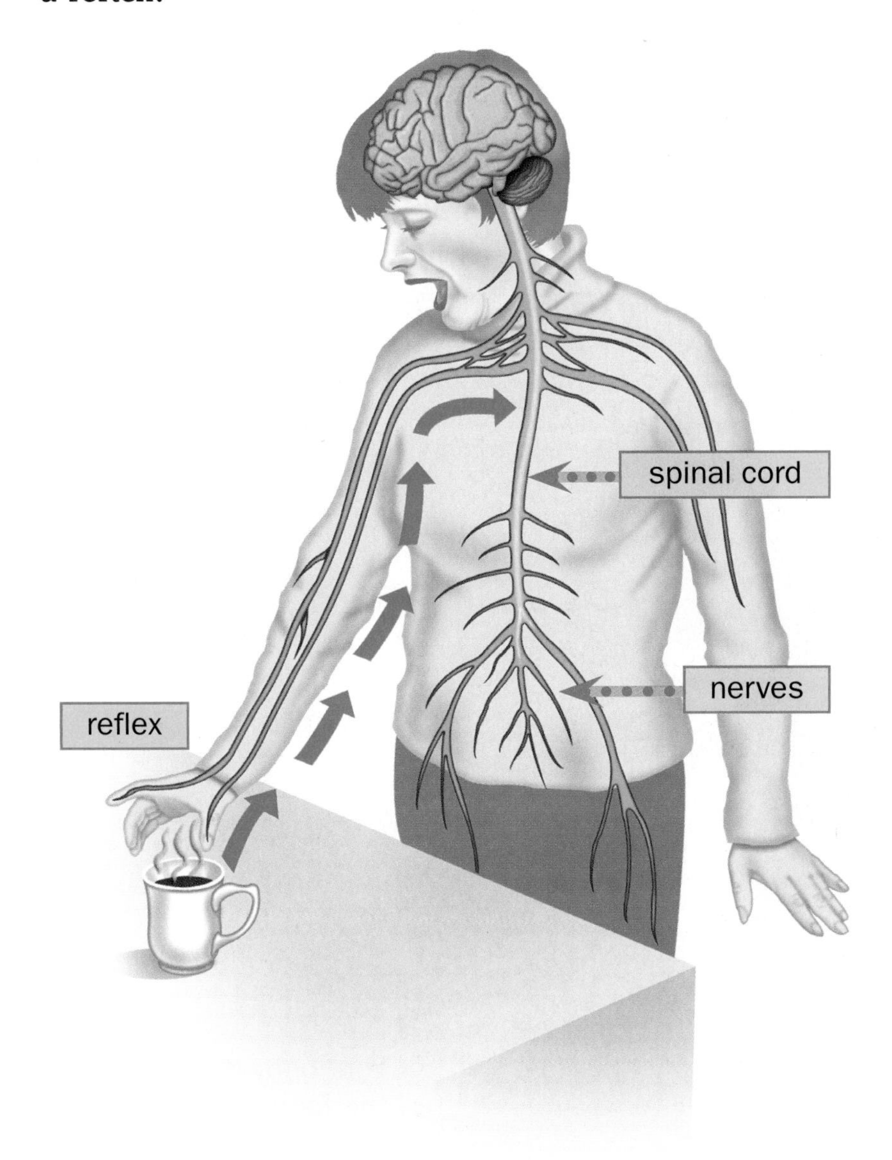

The Digestive System

Both the excretory and digestive systems help your body get rid of waste. The digestive system removes solid waste.

The digestive system **digests**, or breaks down, food. The digestive system removes nutrients from the food and **transfers**, or moves, them to the blood. Your blood then carries the nutrients to the cells of the body.

The main organs of the digestive system are the mouth, **esophagus**, **stomach**, **small intestine**, and **large intestine**.

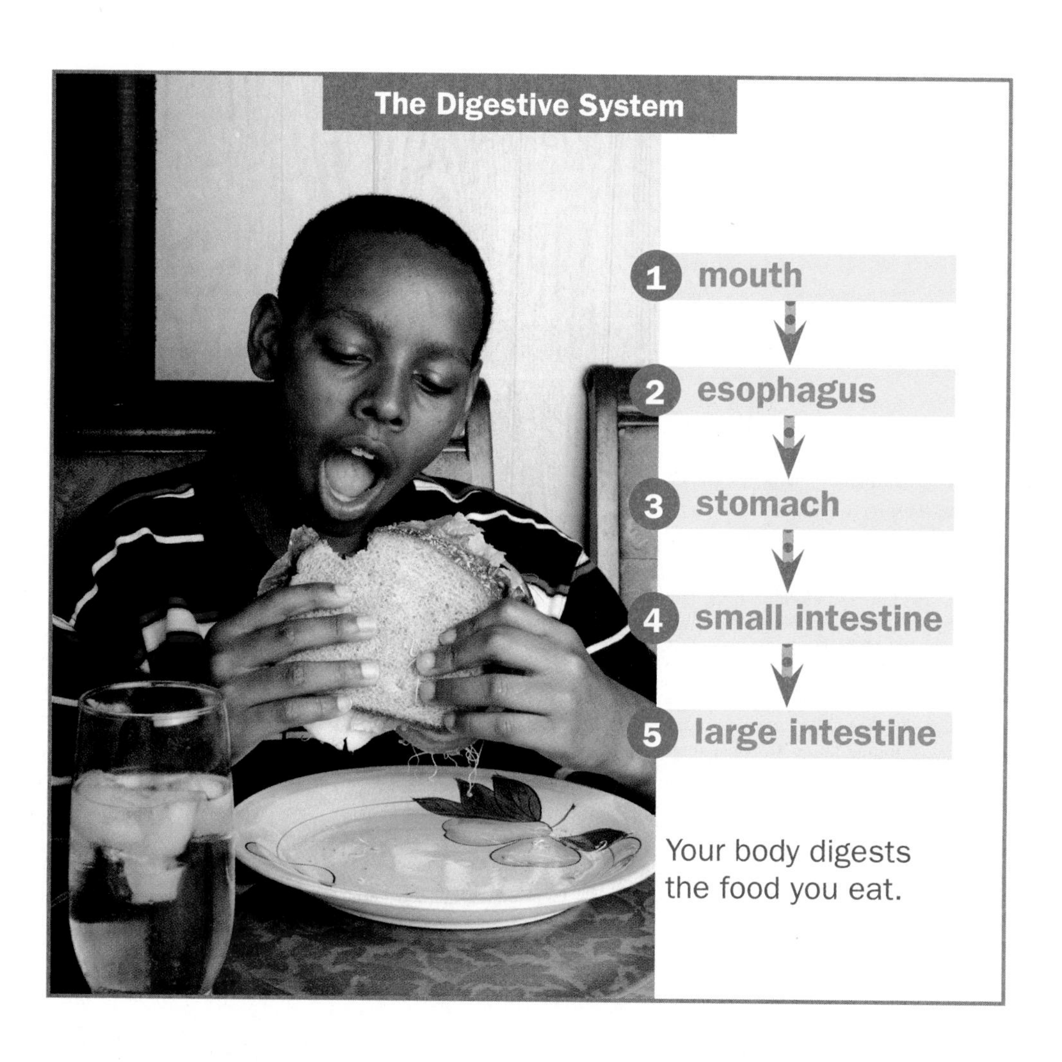

Your body digests the food you eat.

How the Digestive System Works

1 mouth In the mouth, teeth break apart and grind food into smaller bits.

2 esophagus When you swallow, food moves down your esophagus to your stomach.

3 stomach The stomach holds the food for about four hours. Muscles in the stomach break down food into smaller pieces.

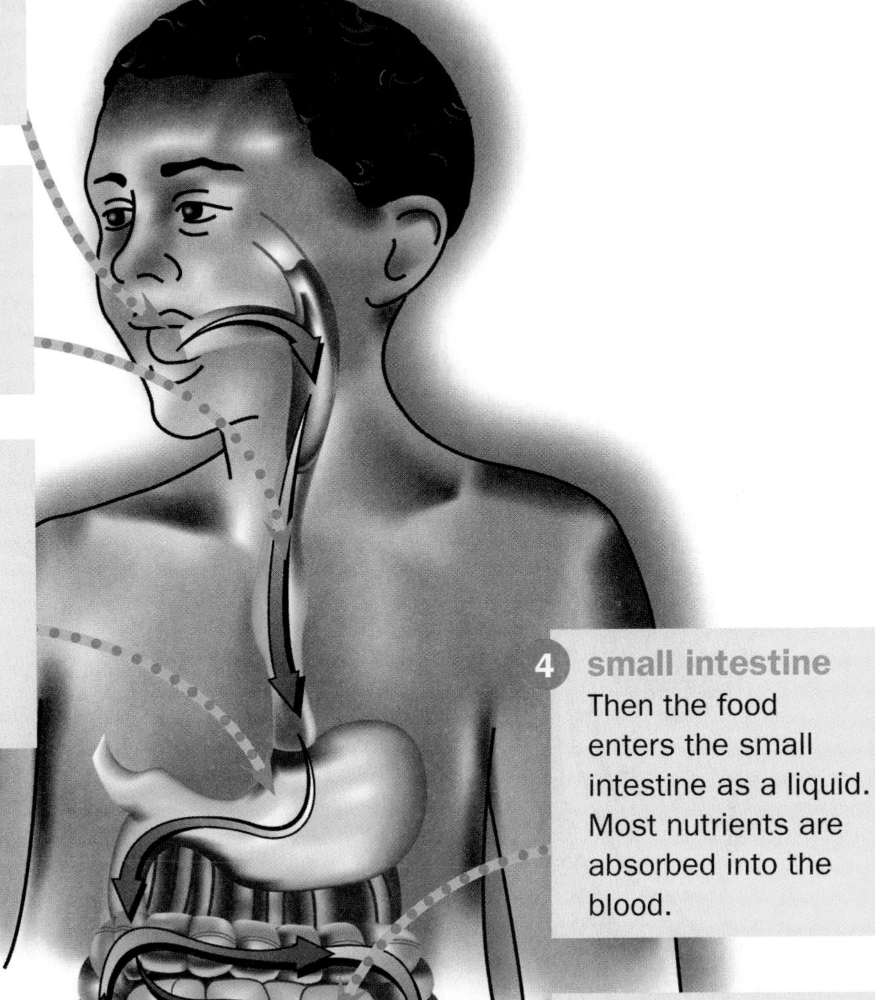

4 small intestine Then the food enters the small intestine as a liquid. Most nutrients are absorbed into the blood.

5 large intestine The digested food goes into the large intestine. Water returns to the body. Solid waste leaves the body.

The Excretory System

To **excrete** means to remove waste from the body. The **excretory system** removes liquid waste, extra water, and extra nutrients from the body.

The major organs in the excretory system are the **kidneys**, **ureters**, **bladder**, and **urethra**.

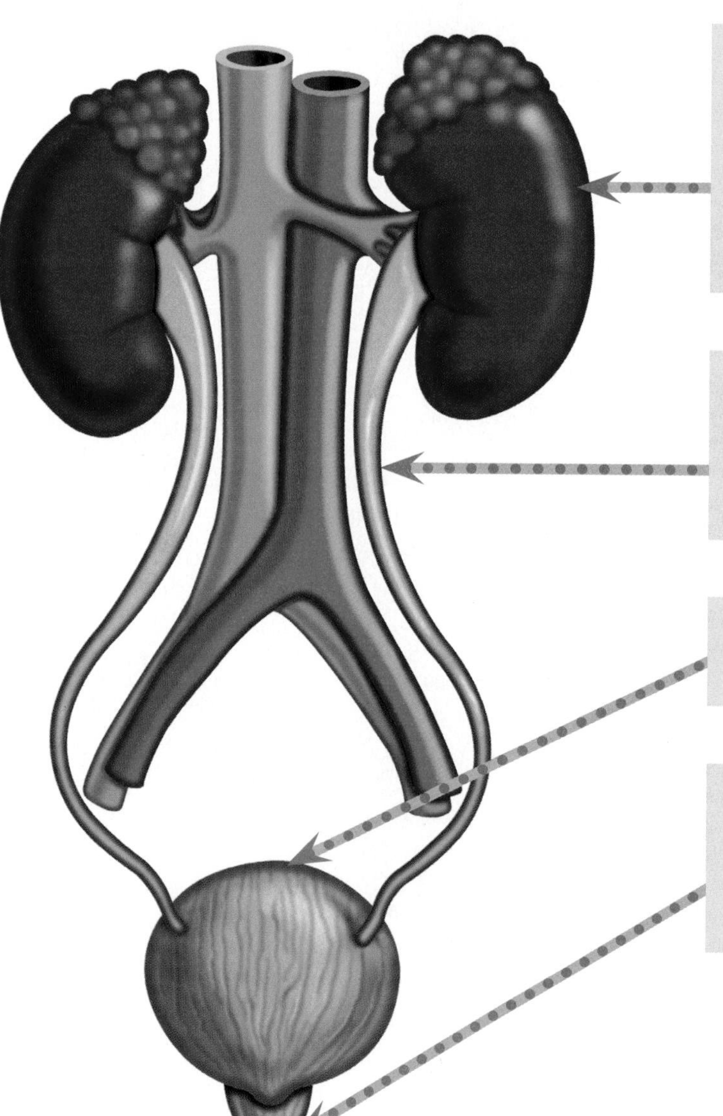

kidneys As blood moves in the body, it passes through the kidneys. The kidneys remove waste from the blood.

ureters The collected waste passes through the ureters to the bladder.

bladder The waste is stored in the bladder.

urethra When the bladder is full, the waste exits as urine through the urethra.

Human Body Systems

system	function
muscular system	allows the body to move
skeletal system	supports and protects the body
respiratory system	lets the body breathe
circulatory system	moves nutrients, gases, and wastes through the body
nervous system	allows parts of the body to communicate
digestive system	breaks down food and helps the body get nutrients
excretory system	removes liquid waste from the body

WHY IT MATTERS

Your body systems work together to help you live.

Keeping Healthy

ESSENTIAL IDEA

A healthy diet, regular exercise, and enough rest are necessary to keep body systems working well.

The main needs of a healthy body are a **balanced diet**, regular **exercise**, and sleep.

A balanced diet provides the body with nutrients. The body needs six main nutrients: **fats**, **proteins**, **carbohydrates**, **vitamins**, **minerals**, and water.

food	nutrients
	fats and proteins Meat is one source of fats and proteins.
	carbohydrates Bread is one source of carbohydrates.
	vitamins Oranges have lots of vitamin C.
	minerals Milk has calcium, which is a mineral your body needs.
	water All of your body systems rely on water.

Exercise makes all your body systems work harder, and it helps keep them working properly. Your bones and muscles need exercise to be strong and healthy.

Your body repairs itself while you are sleeping. If you fall asleep during the day, your body is telling you to sleep more at night.

sleep

WHY IT MATTERS

- You are responsible for keeping your body healthy.
- Your body tells you when you need food or sleep.

Heredity and Traits

ESSENTIAL IDEA

Parents pass on genes to their offspring. Genes have different forms, and the way they combine determines your traits.

The nucleus of each cell contains **chromosomes**. Chromosomes are made up of small parts called genes. Each **gene** contains information about traits. Eye color and body shape are examples of **traits**.

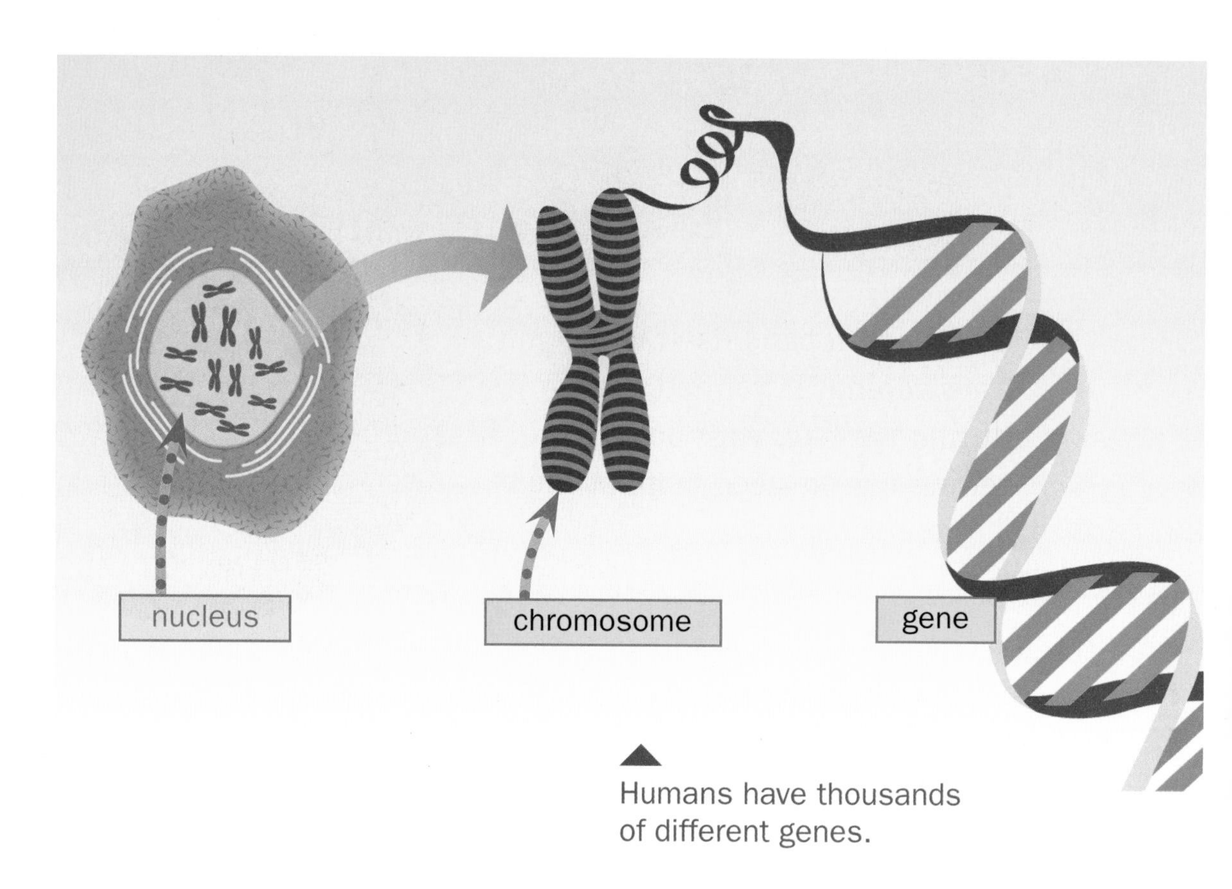

Humans have thousands of different genes.

Heredity is the passing of traits from parents to children.

A child **inherits** chromosomes from each parent. For each trait, a child has two genes.

Some genes are **dominant**, and others are **recessive**. Genes for brown eyes are dominant. Genes for blue eyes are recessive. If a child is born with one gene for brown eyes and one gene for blue eyes, the child's eyes will be brown.

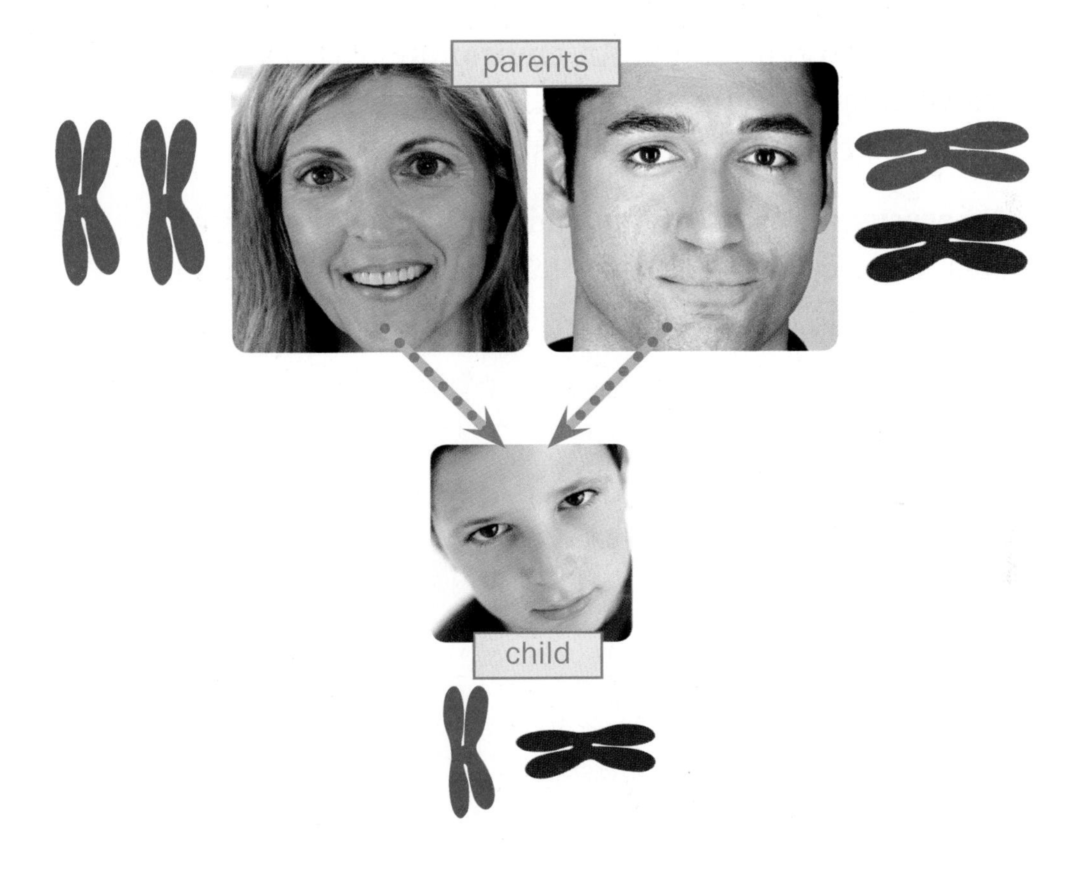

WHY IT MATTERS

- You inherited your traits from your parents.
- Genes in your body contain many dominant and recessive traits.

LIFE SCIENCE

Ecosystems

ESSENTIAL IDEA

An ecosystem includes all the living and nonliving things in an environment.

Plants, animals, and other organisms live together to form a **community**, or group. An **environment** is the place where animals and plants live. Environments have nonliving things, such as rocks and soil.

An **ecosystem** is the living and nonliving things in an area, or place. An ecosystem may be as small as a puddle or as large as a forest.

The living and nonliving things in an ecosystem **interact** with one another in many ways. The living organisms get what they need, such as food and shelter, from the ecosystem.

squirrel

interactions The plants get what they need from nonliving things in the environment, such as water and minerals. Birds and other animals use the plants for shelter and food.

ecosystem

deer

raccoon

rock

The Sun is the main source of **energy** for ecosystems. Plants are **producers**. They can use the Sun's energy. Plants use a process called photosynthesis to produce their own food.

Consumers cannot produce food directly from the Sun's energy. They must eat other organisms, such as plants and animals, to get energy.

The plants in a forest use the Sun's energy to produce food.

This squirrel gets its energy from eating parts of plants.

When organisms die or produce waste, **decomposers** break them apart into nutrients. The nutrients enter the soil so they can be used again. Some of the Sun's original energy remains in the nutrients. Examples of decomposers are bacteria, worms, and mushrooms.

These decomposers are breaking up a dead tree. As the tree crumbles away, nutrients return to the soil.

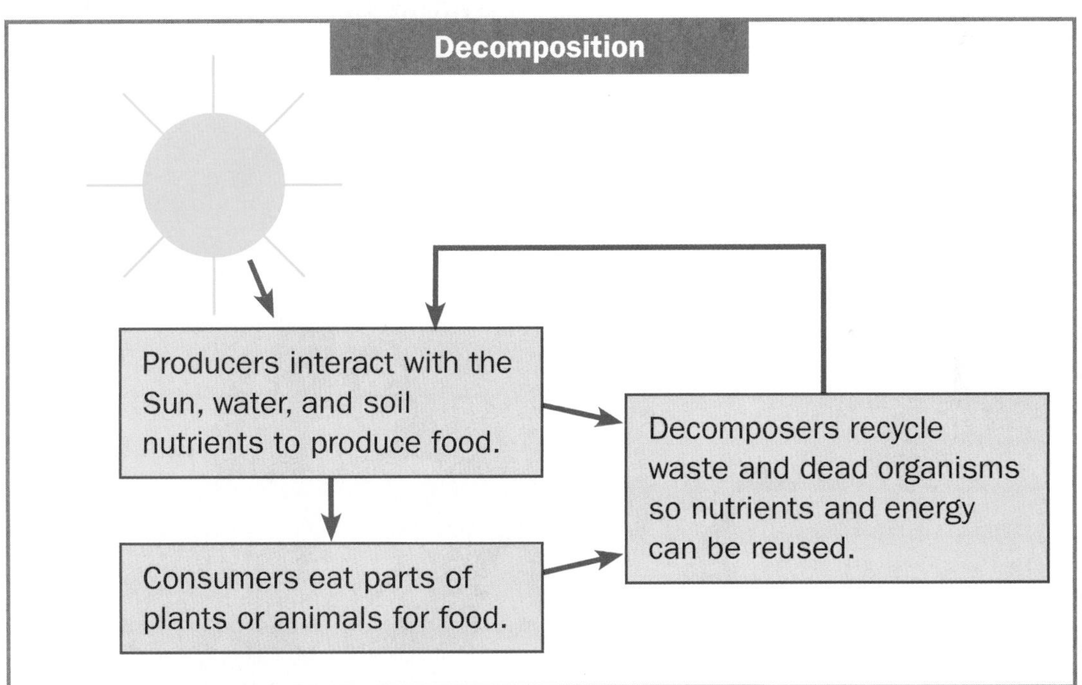

WHY IT MATTERS

- You are part of an ecosystem.
- You interact with your ecosystem. It helps you get the things you need to live.

LIFE SCIENCE

Interactions of Living Things

ESSENTIAL IDEA

Living things in an ecosystem interact with each other and with their environment.

An **individual** organism, such as a plant or animal, lives in an **environment.** When organisms live in the same environment, they form a **community**. Living things **interact** when they have an effect on, or change, one another.

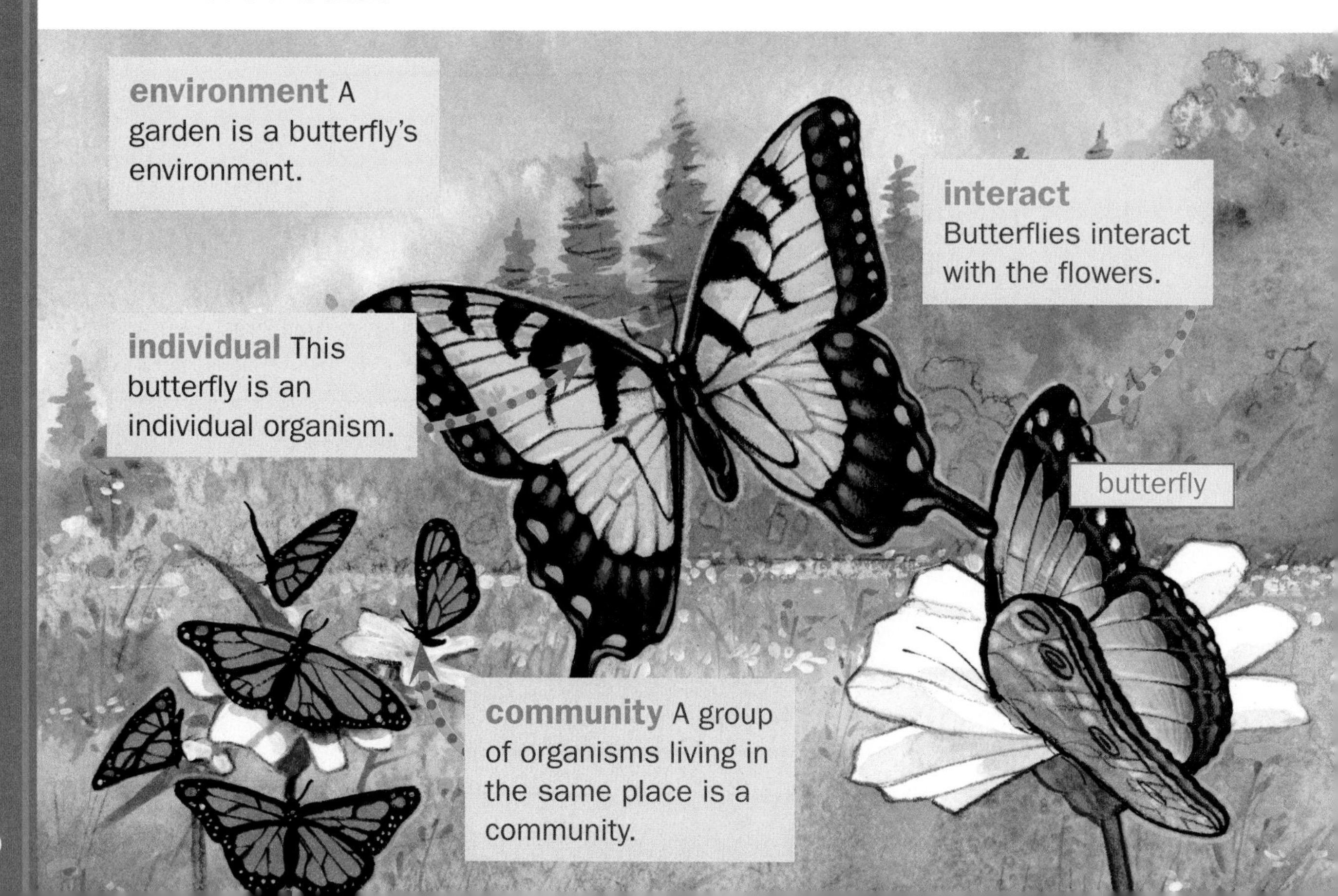

Interactions are often about physical needs, such as getting food, clothing, or shelter. Interacting with others also meets social needs. For example, when you pet a dog or cat, the interaction makes both you and the animal feel good.

This boy interacts with an individual organism, a cat.

This girl interacts with flowers in her environment.

WHY IT MATTERS

- You interact with plants and animals in your environment.
- Interactions with living things help you meet many of your needs.

The Nitrogen Cycle

ESSENTIAL IDEA

Nitrogen is a gas in the air that living things need. Nitrogen continually moves through living things and the environment.

Plants need **nitrogen** to grow, and animals depend on the nitrogen in plants. About 78 percent of the air is nitrogen gas, but plants and animals cannot use this nitrogen. First the nitrogen needs to be converted, or changed.

Nitrogen **fixation** is a process that **converts**, or changes, nitrogen. Fixation changes nitrogen into something useful.

Lightning and bacteria change nitrogen. Nitrogen helps plants grow.

The Nitrogen Cycle

Nitrogen can be converted in two ways. Lightning can change nitrogen into a form that plants use to grow. Animals eat the plants, and the nitrogen becomes part of their cells.

Bacteria and molds in the soil can also change nitrogen. When plant and animal waste decomposes, the bacteria and molds convert nitrogen.

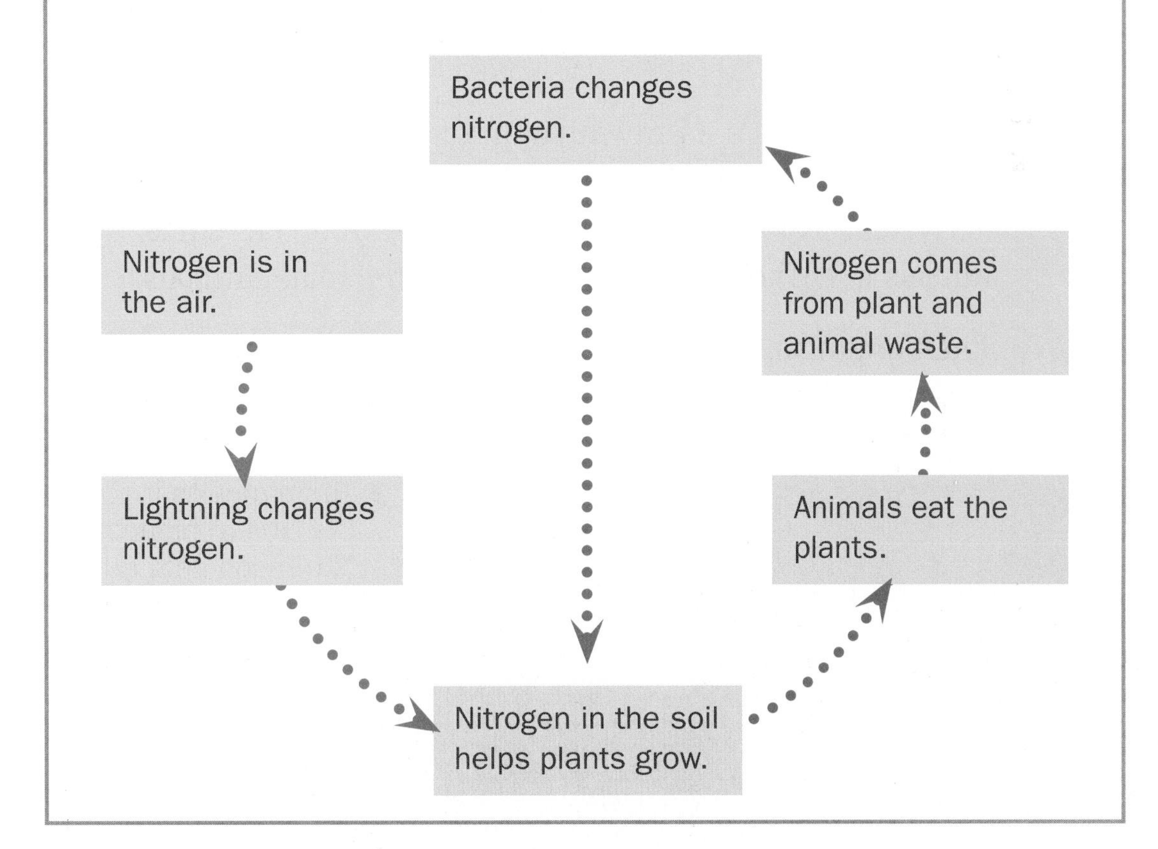

WHY IT MATTERS

You need nitrogen to build the cells of your body.

You get nitrogen by eating plants and animals.

LIFE SCIENCE

Symbiosis and Competition

ESSENTIAL IDEA

Some organisms support each other's needs. Other organisms compete with each other for resources.

A **habitat** is the area in which an organism lives. Each organism has a **niche**, or role, that it plays in the ecosystem. For example, plants produce food that some animals eat. They also provide shelter for some animals.

When organisms interact, they affect one another in different ways. **Symbiosis** is an interaction that **benefits** both organisms.

The bird eats insects that live on the hippopotamus. The hippo gets rid of insects, and the bird gets food.

In any habitat, resources such as food, water, and shelter are limited. Organisms must sometimes **compete** for the same resources.

Eagles and jaguars are both **predators**. They compete because they sometimes hunt the same **prey**.

Eagles can swoop down on the prey from above.

The jaguar can climb up into trees to reach its prey.

WHY IT MATTERS

- You sometimes compete with others for your needs.
- You work in symbiotic, or helpful, ways with other students.

Feeding Relationships

ESSENTIAL IDEA

Consumers eat other organisms to get energy to live.

The animals in a habitat are consumers. They feed on other organisms to get the energy they need to live.

Herbivores are consumers that eat only plants. **Carnivores** eat only other animals. **Omnivores** eat both plants and animals. **Scavengers** eat dead or decaying plants and animals.

A freshwater pond is the habitat of many animals.

The pictures show some feeding relationships around a freshwater pond habitat.

Herbivore

Some fish, such as this carp, are herbivores. They eat water plants and algae.

Carnivore

The great blue heron is a carnivore. It feeds mainly on small fish. The heron also eats insects, crayfish, snakes, and mice.

Omnivore

The raccoon is an omnivore. It eats fruits, vegetables, and mice. Raccoons also eat crayfish, frogs, worms, and fish.

Scavenger

The crab is a scavenger. It eats dead animals and plants that fall to the bottom of the pond.

WHY IT MATTERS

- You are an omnivore if you eat both plants and animals.
- You are an herbivore, or vegetarian, if you eat only fruits, vegetables, and other plants such as grains.

Food Chains

ESSENTIAL IDEA

A food chain shows the path of energy as it travels from one organism to another.

Energy from the Sun passes from plants to animals, and then on to other animals and plants. This movement of energy is called a **food chain**.

Herbivores, or plant eaters, are **primary** consumers. They are the first consumers to eat producers, or plants.

A **secondary** consumer eats a primary consumer. Larger animals are usually **tertiary** consumers, or third in line. When consumers die, decomposers return the energy to the soil.

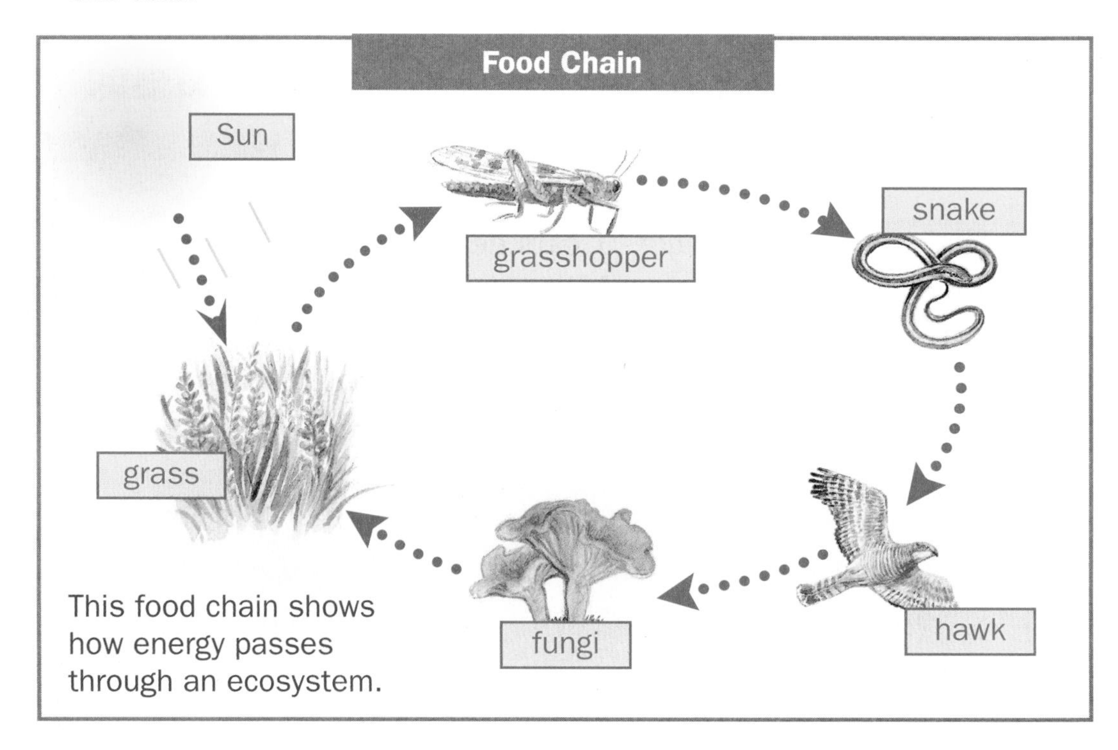

This food chain shows how energy passes through an ecosystem.

An **energy pyramid** shows the many organisms of a food chain. Consumers use more energy than producers, so there must be more producers than consumers.

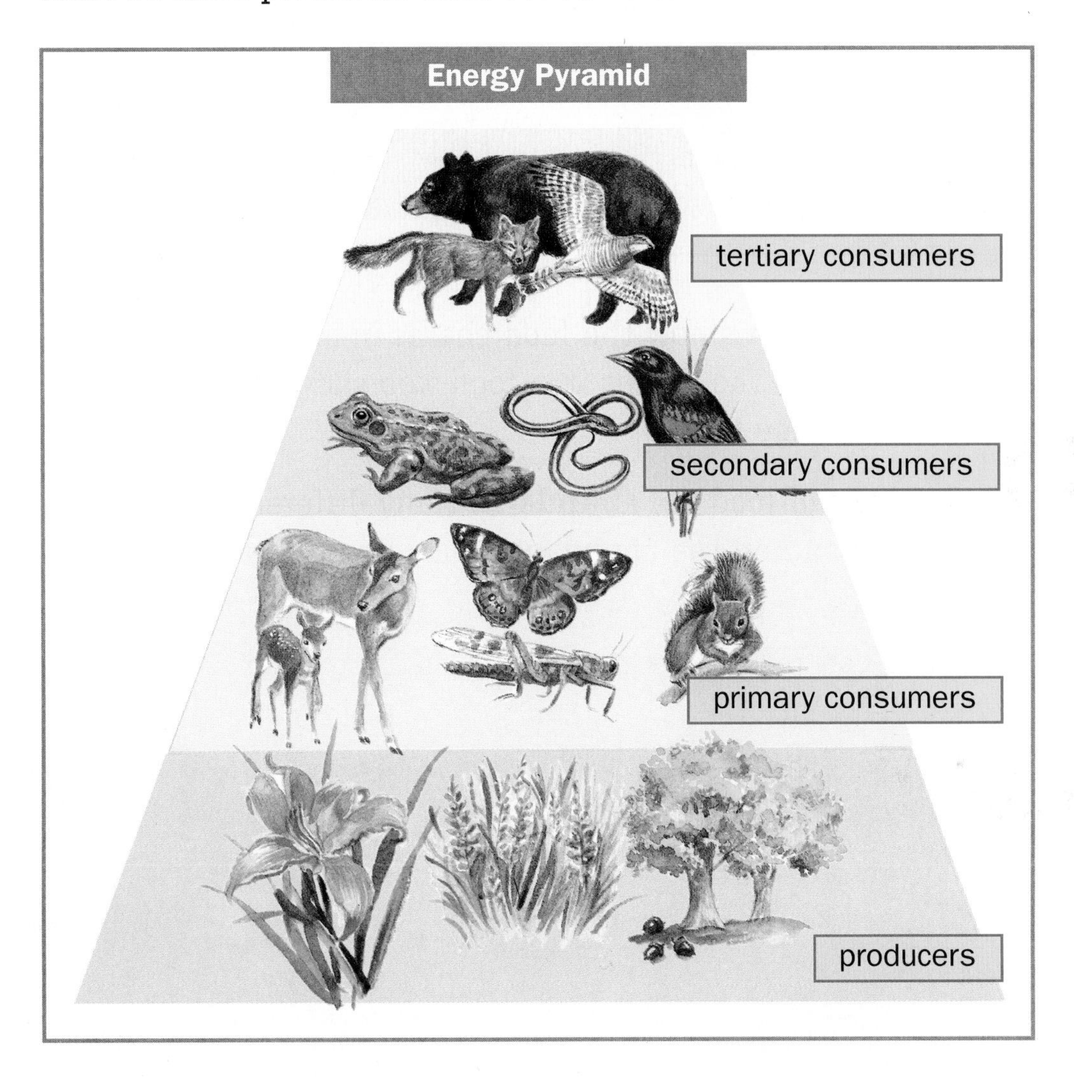

WHY IT MATTERS

- You are a primary consumer when you eat fruits and vegetables.
- You are a tertiary consumer when you eat meat or fish.

LIFE SCIENCE

Food Webs

ESSENTIAL IDEA

One organism can be part of many different food chains. When food chains overlap, they form a system called a food web.

A **food web** shows how the food chains in an ecosystem are connected. The arrows in a food web show the direction in which energy travels.

Some types of food are **abundant**. Many different species might **depend** on the abundant organism for food.

Deer depend on plants and parts of trees for food.

Food Web

An ecosystem usually has several kinds of **predators** and **prey**. A mouse might be prey for owls or foxes. This makes the mouse part of several different food chains.

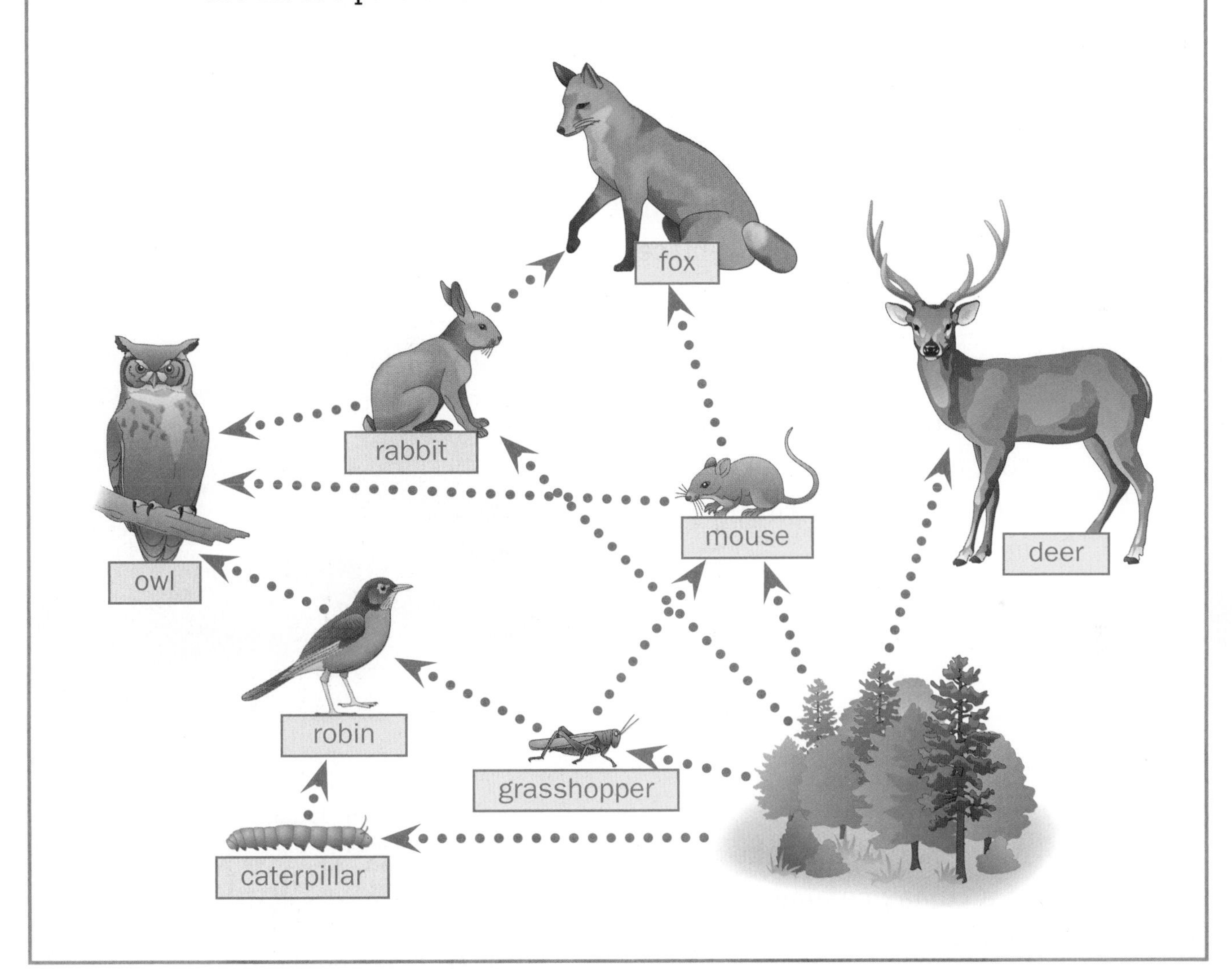

WHY IT MATTERS

You are part of a food web.

Ecological Succession

ESSENTIAL IDEA

Over time, the communities in an area change.

When plants have been growing in an area for many years, they form a **climax community**. **Ecological succession** is a process in which communities of plants and animals **gradually**, or slowly, replace one another.

The plants in a climax community are best adapted for that area. They will continue to grow until the area is disturbed, or changed.

A fire can destroy the plants in a climax community. Consumers, or animals, then leave the area because there is no food.

After the fire, some roots and seeds remain below the ground. Grasses and small shrubs are the first plants to grow back. They are called **pioneer plants**.

As trees and plants grow, animals that use those plants for food and shelter return. The ecological succession can take more than 100 years in some ecosystems.

WHY IT MATTERS

You can see different stages of ecological succession in habitats around you.

Biomes

ESSENTIAL IDEA

Earth's biomes are different according to the climate. Plants and animals in a biome are adapted to living in that climate.

A **biome** is an entire community of plants and animals that live in a large **region**, or area. Scientists group biomes by their **climate**. Climate includes the amount of rain or snow a region receives. Climate also includes the range of temperature.

Each biome has a variety of plants and animals that are best adapted to that climate.

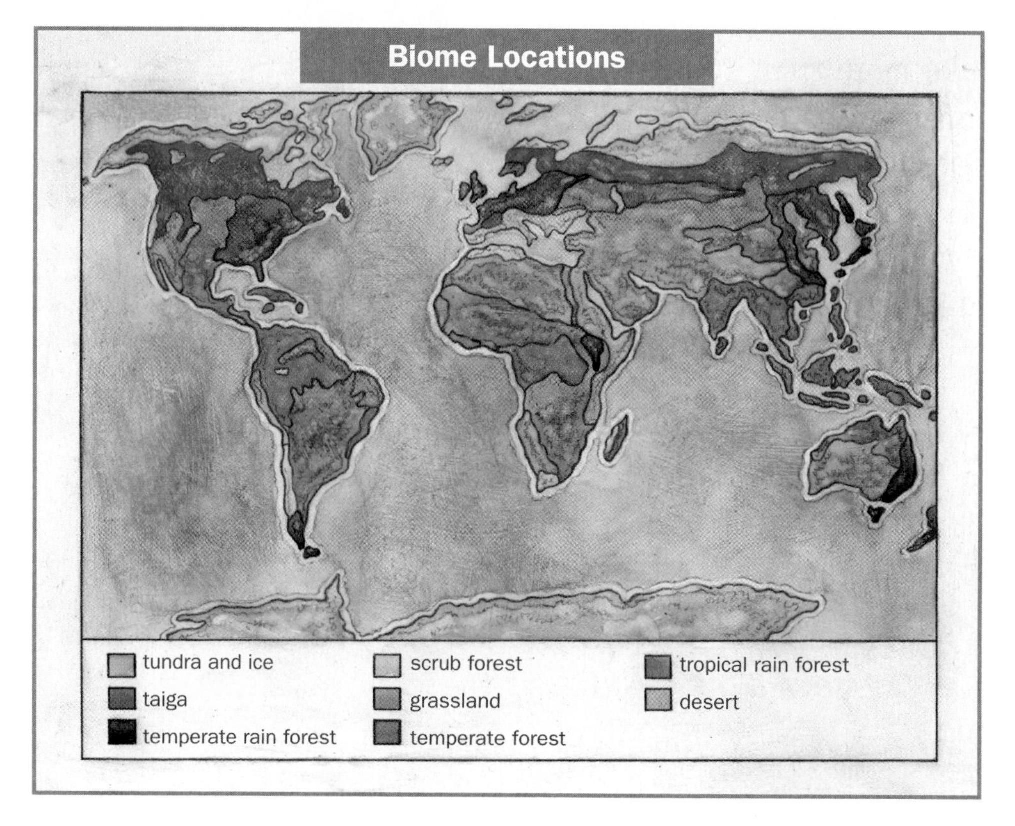

The **tundra** is a treeless biome where it is cold and dry all year. The **taiga** is a moist, coniferous forest biome. The taiga begins where the tundra ends, so it is still cold in the taiga.

Temperate forests are below the taiga and can be moist or dry. The temperate forests have four different seasons. The **grassland** biome has grasses instead of trees. It has a warm and wet season and a warm and dry season.

Deserts are the driest biome. They get very little moisture. Some deserts are very hot in the daytime and very cold at night. Other deserts are very cold.

Unlike deserts, **tropical rain forests** get a lot of moisture. Tropical rain forests have hot temperatures.

The **oceans** are a marine biome, or water environment. Oceans are the home of plants and animals that have adapted to spending their entire lives in water.

Biome Climates

biome	climate
tundra	cold and dry
taiga	cold and moist
temperate forest	dry or moist with four seasons
grassland	warm with wet and dry seasons
desert	dry with hot or cold temperatures
tropical rain forest	hot and moist
oceans	water

WHY IT MATTERS

The animals and plants you see live in your biome.

LIFE SCIENCE

Preserving Life

ESSENTIAL IDEA

Humans can protect species from extinction.

Extinction takes place when all the members of a species disappear from Earth. Many species become extinct because of human activity, such as the **destruction** of habitat. As a habitat gets smaller, the **population** of a species **declines**.

The moa was a huge bird that lived in New Zealand. Humans hunted the moa and destroyed its habitat. Within 100 years, the moa became extinct.

To survive, a species must be able to keep or add to its population size. A species is **threatened** when its population size decreases. A threatened species still has enough members to **maintain**, or keep, its population.

A species is **endangered** when the population may not be large enough to produce enough offspring, or babies.

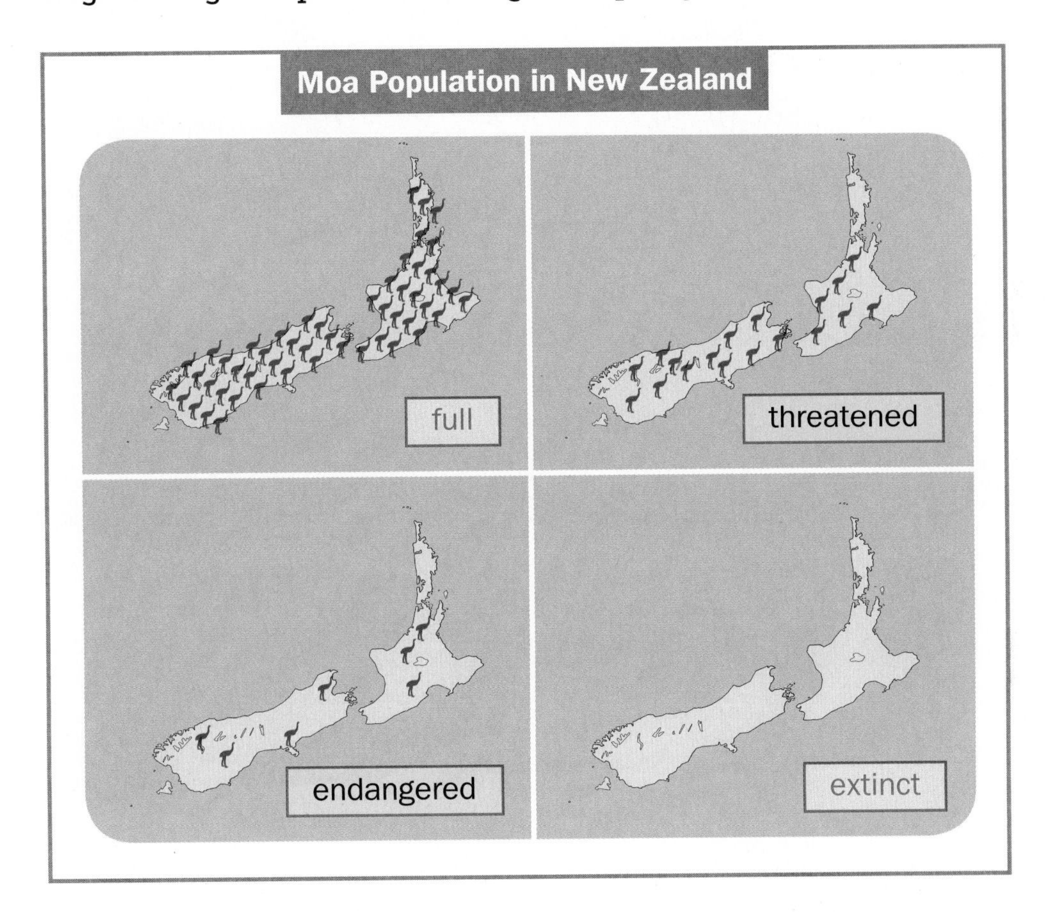

WHY IT MATTERS

- You can be affected if organisms in your environment become extinct.
- You can help threatened and endangered species survive by protecting their habitats.

Earth Science

Earth's Layers

ESSENTIAL IDEA

Earth is made of different layers.

Earth is not the same the whole way through. It has different **layers**.

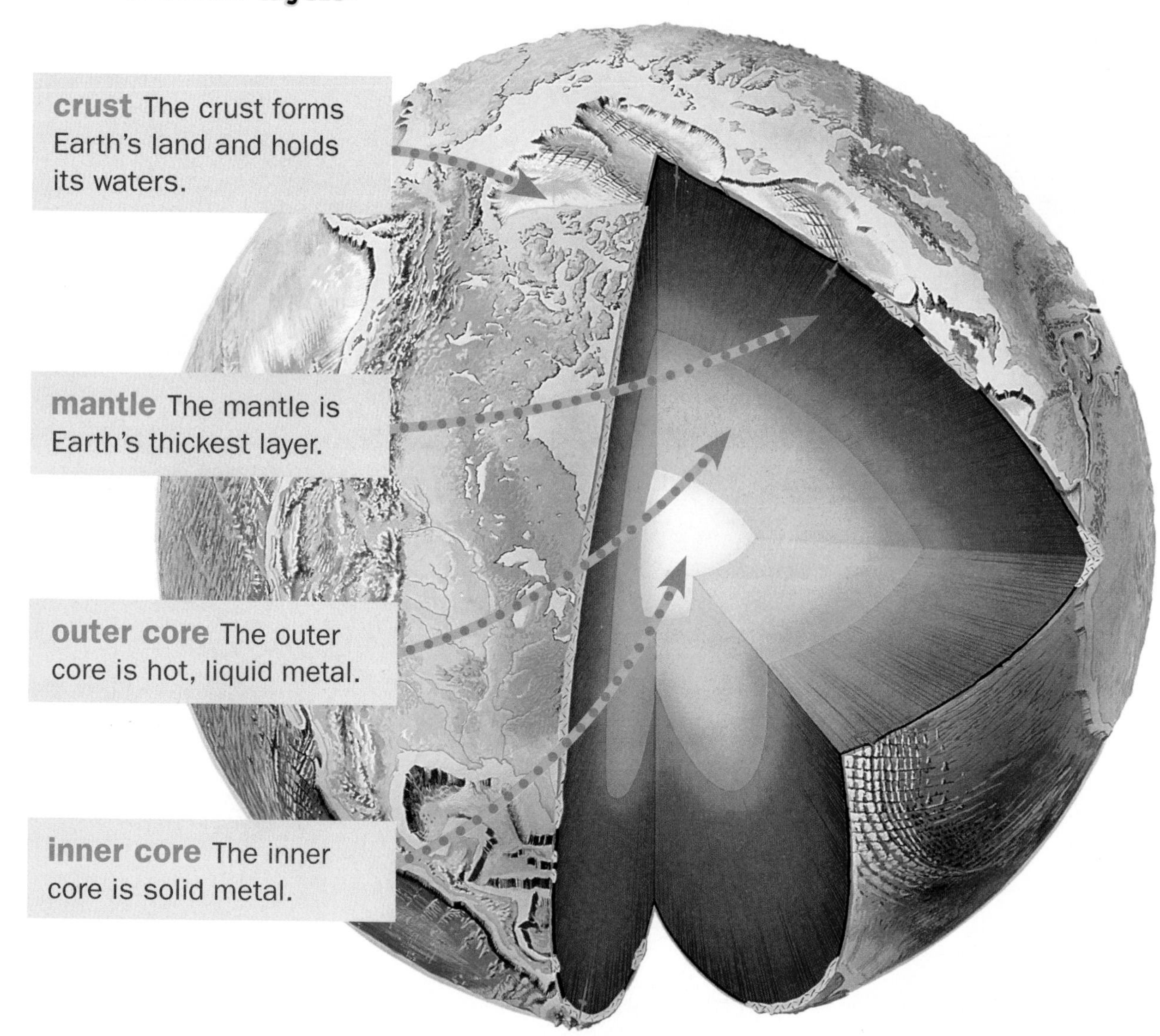

The **crust** is the rocks and soil that cover Earth. The crust forms the land. It also holds lake and ocean waters.

Under the crust is the **mantle**. Most of the mantle is solid rock. Some of the mantle is hot, melted rock that flows slowly.

Deep inside Earth is its core. The **outer core** is hot, liquid metal. The **inner core** is a hot, solid ball of metal.

What Makes Up Earth

layer	made of
crust	rocks and soil
mantle	solid and melted rock
outer core	liquid metal
inner core	hot, solid metal

WHY IT MATTERS

You know living and nonliving things are on Earth's crust.

Earth's Plates

ESSENTIAL IDEA

Earth's crust is slowly moving.

Earth's **lithosphere** is the crust and upper mantle together. The lithosphere is broken into huge pieces called **plates**.

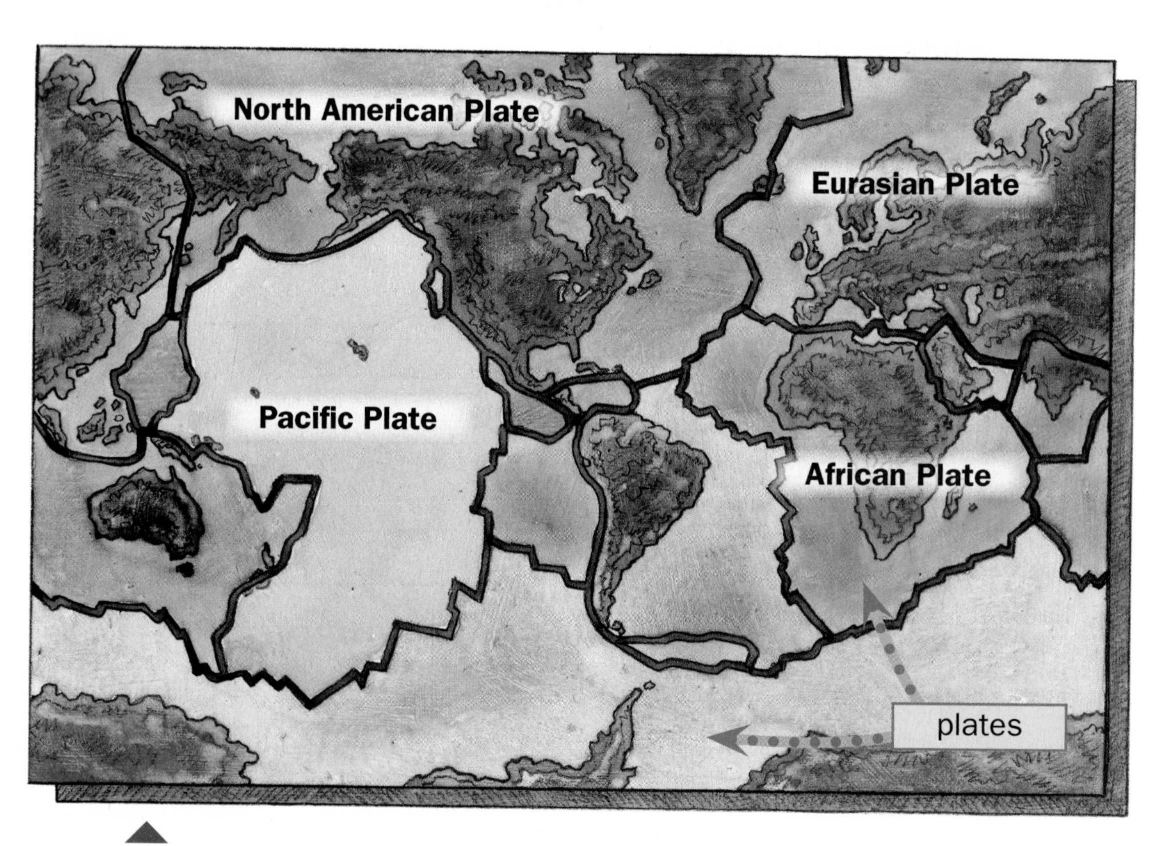

Many plates include both land and ocean.

Earth's lithosphere floats on the heavy, thick material of the lower mantle. As material in the lower mantle moves, the plates interact. Some plates **collide**, or hit one another. Other plates move apart or slide past one another.

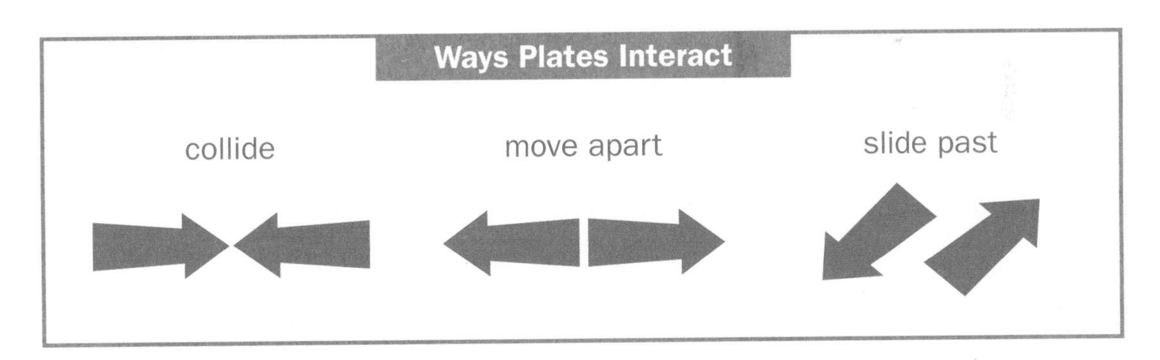

WHY IT MATTERS

- You live on one of Earth's plates.
- Plate movement can cause earthquakes or volcanoes that might affect your life.

Earth's Changing Surface

ESSENTIAL IDEA

Earth's plates move and interact. Mountains form when plates push together. Rift valleys form when plates pull apart.

The place where Earth's plates meet is called a **boundary**. As the plates collide or pull apart, the **surface** of Earth changes.

When **continental plates** collide, land is pushed up. Mountain ranges form at the boundary.

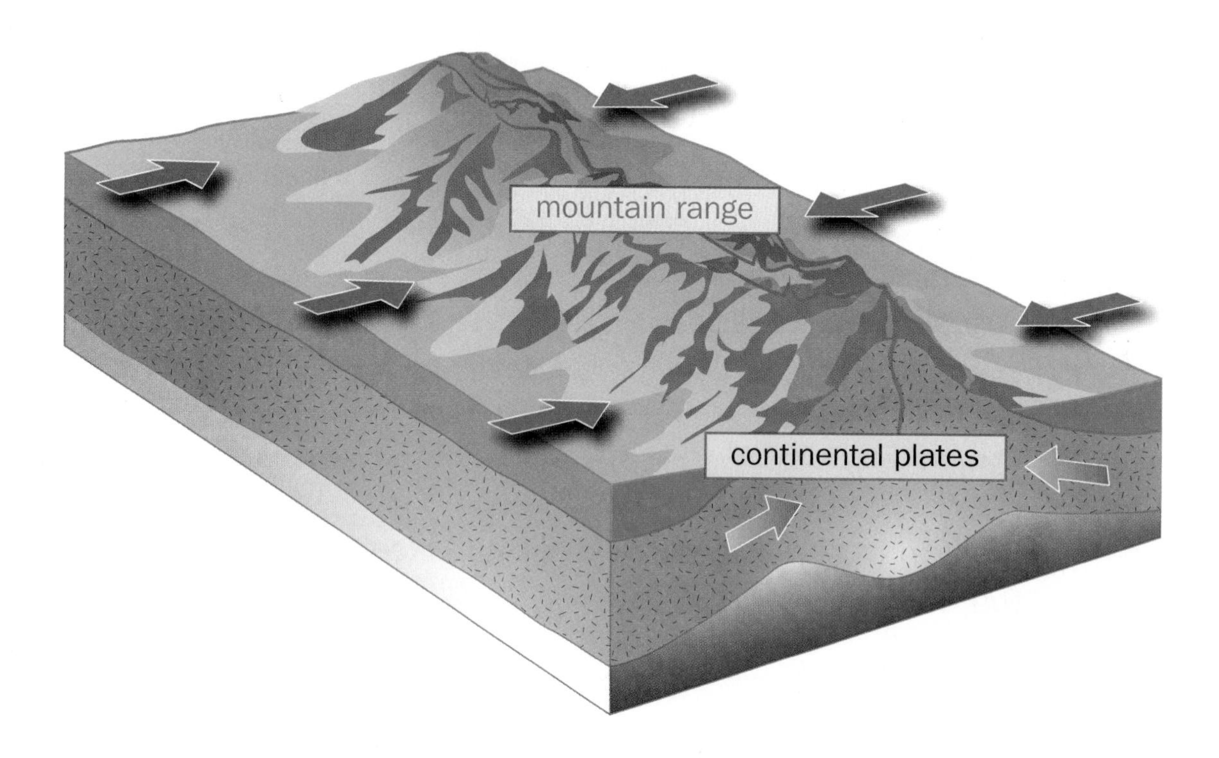

Where plates pull apart, a rift valley forms. **Rift valleys** can form on land and on the ocean floor. Some rift valleys are long and narrow. They have sides that are very steep.

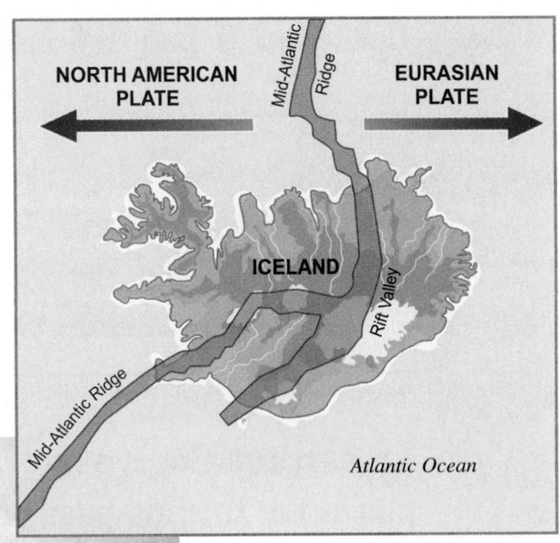

This is one of Iceland's rift valleys. The valley is widening, or moving apart, by 1 to 2 inches each year.

WHY IT MATTERS

Because of plate movements, the surface of Earth around you is always changing.

Earthquakes

ESSENTIAL IDEA

Earthquakes are caused by a sudden release of energy in Earth's crust.

An **earthquake** is a shaking of Earth's crust. As Earth's plates try to slide past one another, pressure builds up. When the pressure gets too great, the plates move all at once. A **fault** is a break in the rock where plates move.

Earthquakes can cause damage to land, roads, and buildings.

How Earthquakes Form

The **focus** of the earthquake is underground. The earthquake starts at the focus when two plates suddenly move against each other. Directly above the focus is the epicenter. The **epicenter** is on Earth's surface.

Waves spread out from the focus. Earthquake waves travel both underground and along Earth's surface.

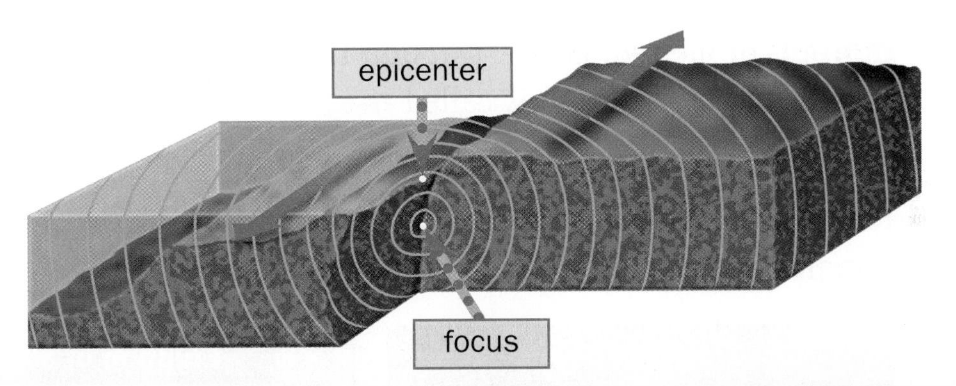

WHY IT MATTERS

Knowing where earthquakes are likely to happen can help you prepare for an earthquake.

Volcanoes

ESSENTIAL IDEA

Volcanoes form when magma forces its way through Earth's surface.

A **volcano** is an opening in Earth's crust. Rock that is **molten**, or melted, comes through the opening. Molten rock inside the volcano is called **magma**.

Magma, gases, and ash all **erupt** from a volcano. Ash is rock broken into tiny pieces. Wind can carry the ash hundreds of miles.

Lava is magma that flows out of a volcano. As the lava cools, it forms new layers of rock.

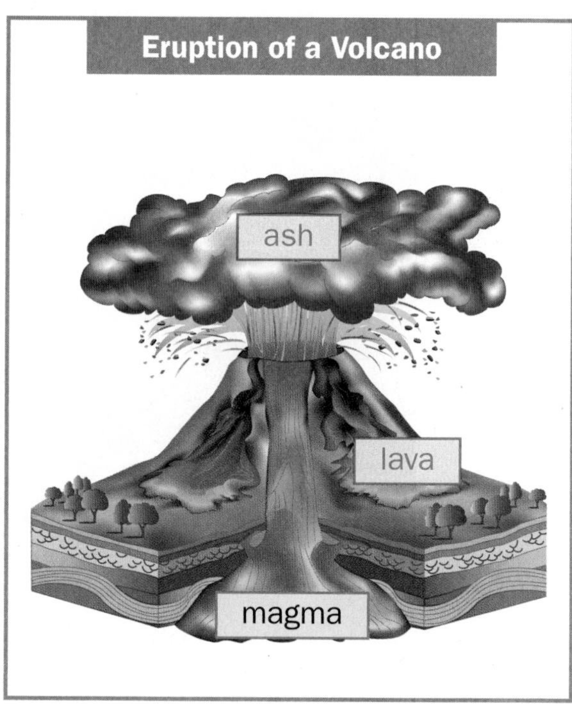

Ways Volcanoes Form

Volcanoes can form in three ways.

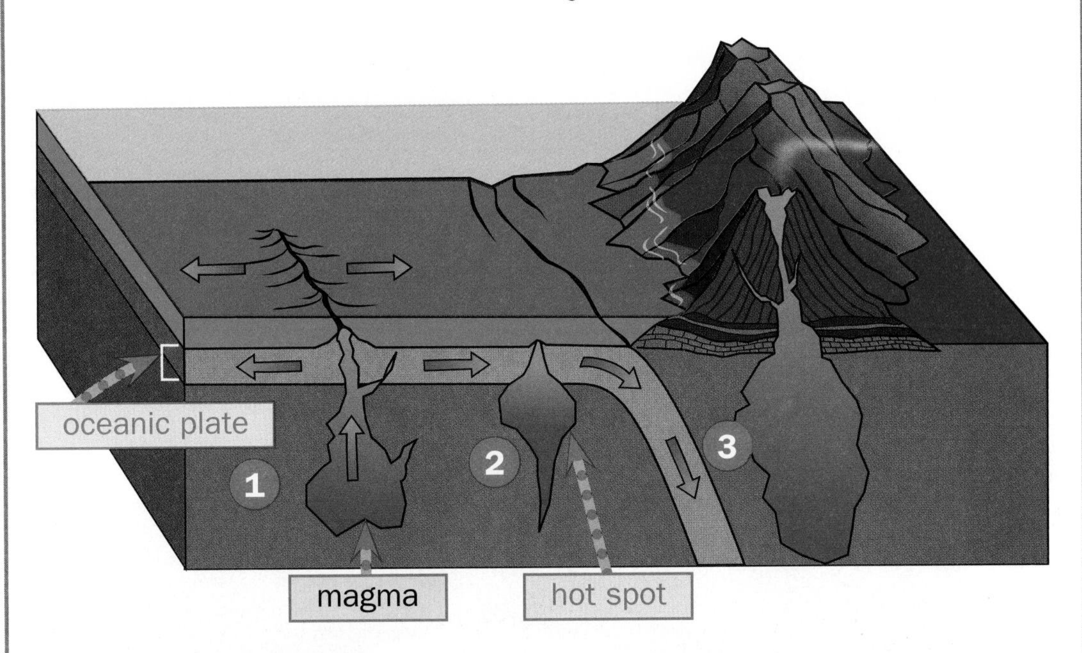

1. Volcanoes can form under water when oceanic plates move apart.

2. Volcanoes can form under water or on land when a plate moves over a hot spot. This causes magma to escape through Earth's crust.

3. Volcanoes can form on land or in the ocean when oceanic plates slide under other plates.

WHY IT MATTERS

An erupting volcano can affect you, even if you live hundreds of miles away.

Weathering

ESSENTIAL IDEA

Weathering is the process that changes the rocks on Earth's surface.

Weathering is the natural breakup of rock at Earth's surface. **Mechanical weathering** happens when rocks split or break into smaller pieces. Ice, water, wind, plants, and animals can cause mechanical weathering.

Plants can cause mechanical weathering by breaking rocks apart.

To form the shape of this land, sediment was carried away by water when it rained.

Weathering breaks rocks into small pieces called **sediment**. Wind and water **transport**, or carry, the sediment away. The process of moving sediment is called **erosion**. When the sediment stops moving, **deposition** takes place.

WHY IT MATTERS

The surface of Earth around you is constantly changing because of weathering.

Landforms

ESSENTIAL IDEA

The physical features on Earth's surface are the result of natural processes.

Earth has different **physical features**. A **landform** is a physical feature of Earth with a particular shape. Different natural processes create landforms. Here are some examples of landforms.

A **valley** is a flat area of land. Around a valley are hills or mountains. Valleys are formed by erosion, or the wearing away of land.

A **canyon** is a deep valley with very steep sides. Running water, such as a river, causes erosion and forms the canyon.

Sand **dunes** are hills of loose sand grains shaped by the wind. Dunes are often found in deserts or near beaches. Dunes are formed by deposition, or dropping, of sand.

A **delta** is a fan-shaped area of land. Deltas form where a river meets an ocean. The land is formed by deposition.

Natural Processes That Cause Landforms

erosion	deposition
valley	dunes
canyon	delta

WHY IT MATTERS

The landforms where you live were created by natural processes.

EARTH SCIENCE

Oceans

ESSENTIAL IDEA

Oceans cover most of Earth's surface and surround the continents.

Oceans cover more than 70 percent of Earth's surface. Most ocean water covers the oceanic crust. When an ocean meets land, water covers part of the continental crust. The **continental margin** is the underwater part of the continental crust.

The continental margin is made up of the continental **shelf** and the continental **slope**. The shelf is closest to land and not very deep. The slope connects the continental crust to the oceanic crust.

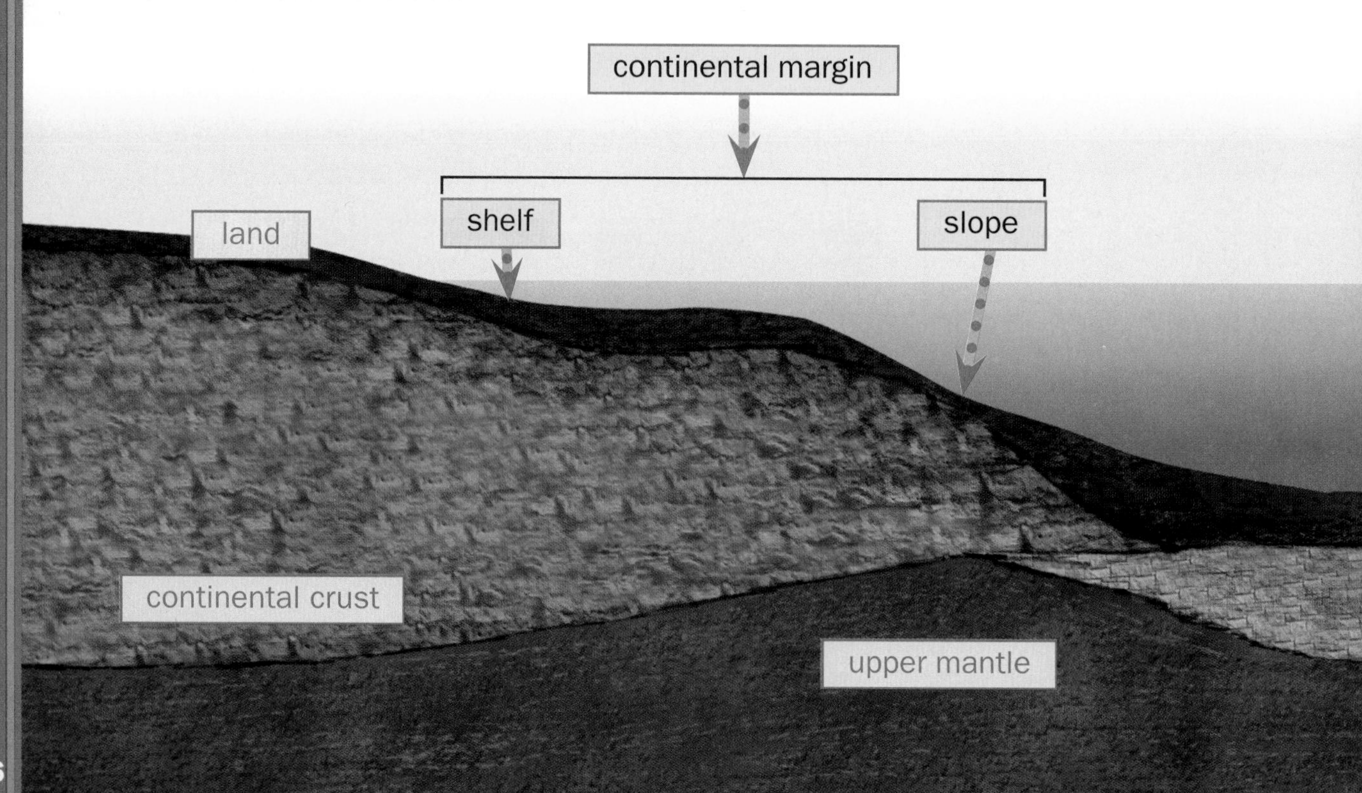

The ocean floor has many landforms.

The **abyssal plain** is the deep ocean floor. It is the flattest part of Earth's surface.

An **oceanic ridge** is an underwater mountain range. An oceanic ridge forms when two oceanic plates move apart. Lava rises from below the crust and forms new ocean floor.

A **trench** is a deep crack in Earth's crust. Underwater trenches can be as deep as the height of mountains.

WHY IT MATTERS

The land you live on is surrounded by oceans.

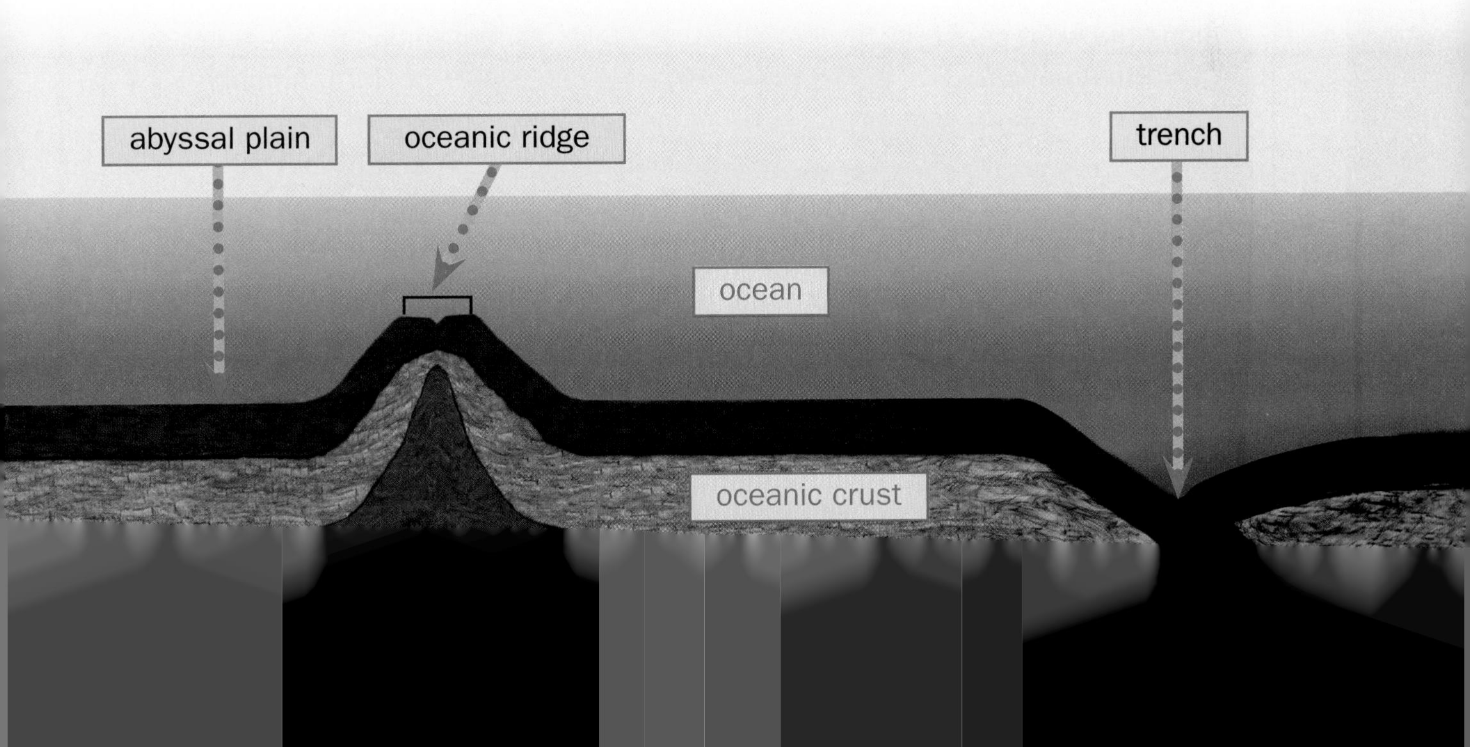

EARTH SCIENCE

How Ocean Waters Move

ESSENTIAL IDEA

Ocean water is always moving.

Ocean waters move in many different ways. Wind causes the **surface current** to move all the time. The temperature of a surface current depends on whether the water comes from warm places or cold places.

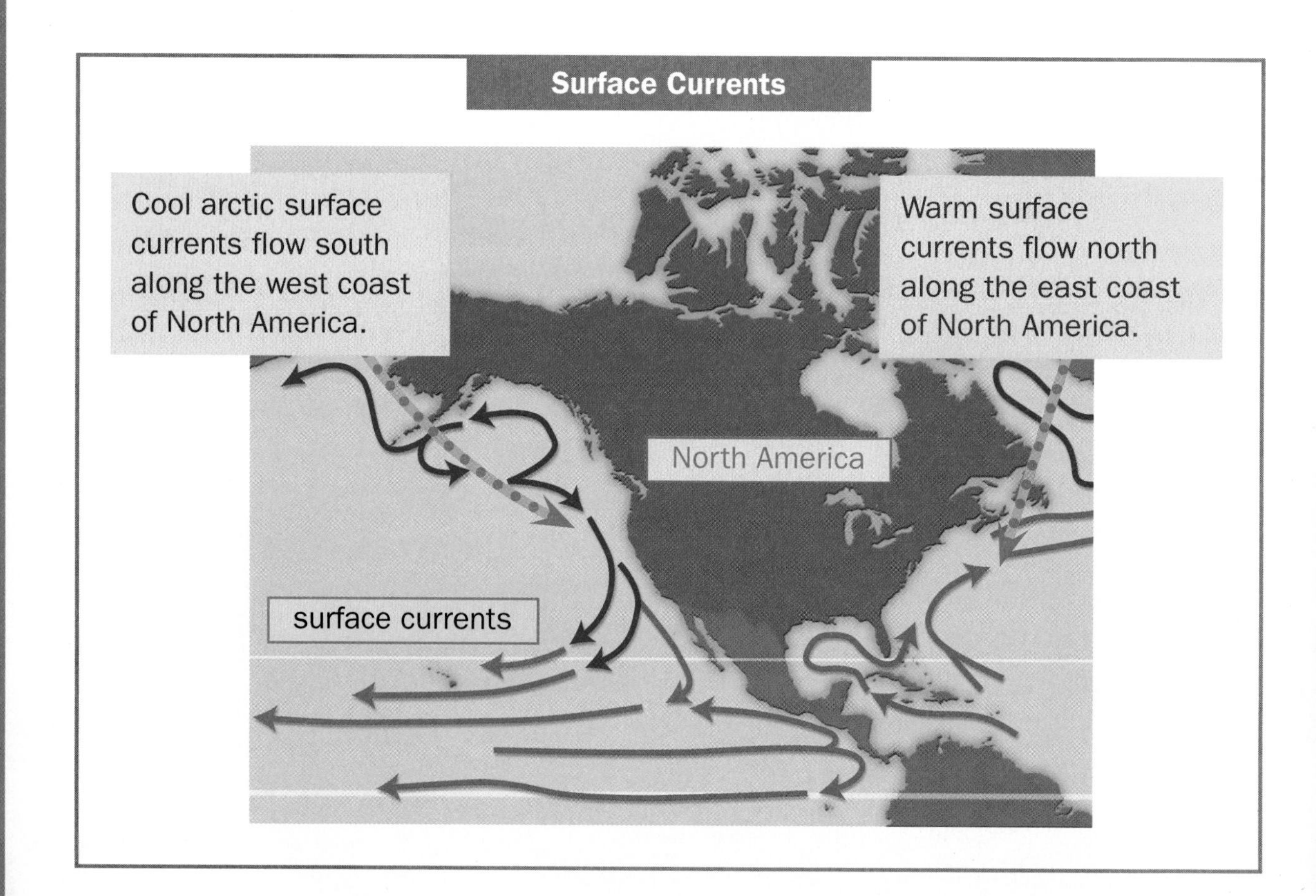

Subsurface water has an up and down current. This current carries water around the entire Earth. It is called the **great ocean conveyor belt** because it is always moving. The deeper water is colder and more salty than water at the surface.

Great Ocean Conveyor Belt

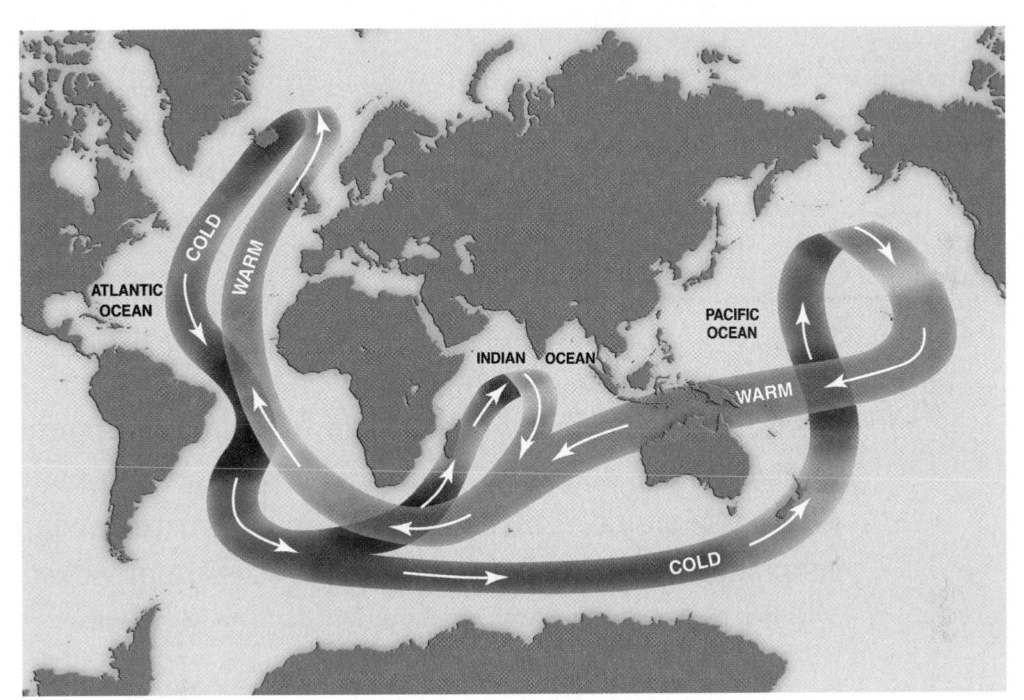

Subsurface water rises and falls as it circles Earth. It takes a thousand years to make the whole trip.

WHY IT MATTERS

The movement of ocean waters affects the weather and climate where you live.

EARTH SCIENCE

Exploring the Ocean

ESSENTIAL IDEA

Scientists use technology to explore and make discoveries in the ocean.

Scientists explore the ocean using different types of **technology**. **Satellites** in the sky can measure many properties of oceans, such as ocean temperature, wave height, and direction of current.

How Sonar Works

Ships on the surface of the water use **sonar** to bounce a signal off the ocean bottom. This is called **echo sounding**. When the signal returns to the ship, it creates a map. The map shows what the bottom of the ocean looks like.

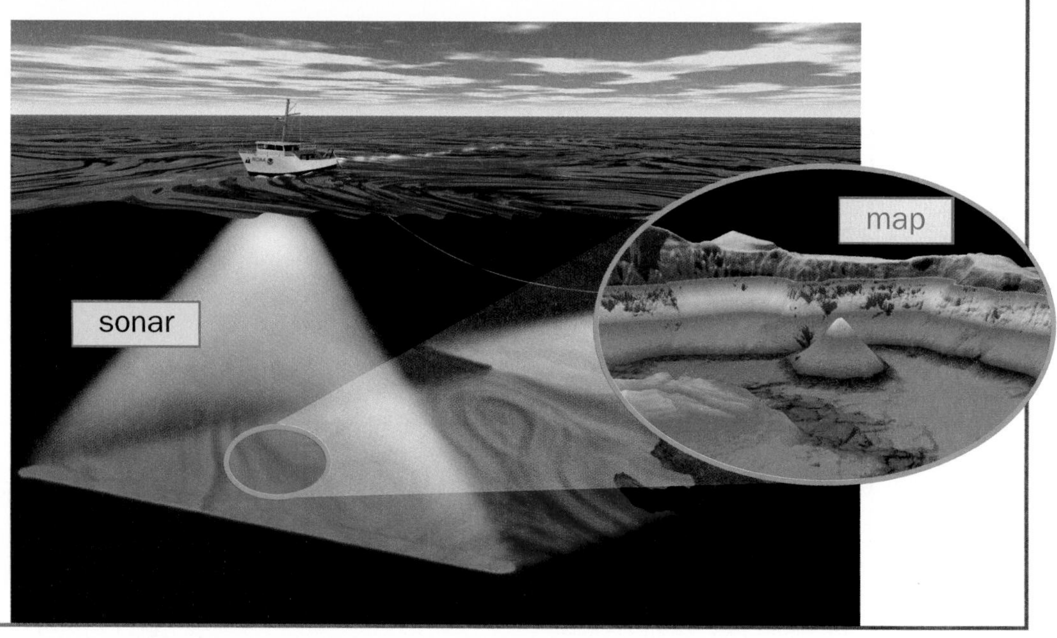

Submersibles are small submarines. Scientists use submersibles to explore and make **discoveries** about the deepest parts of the ocean.

Submersibles help scientists study life under the ocean.

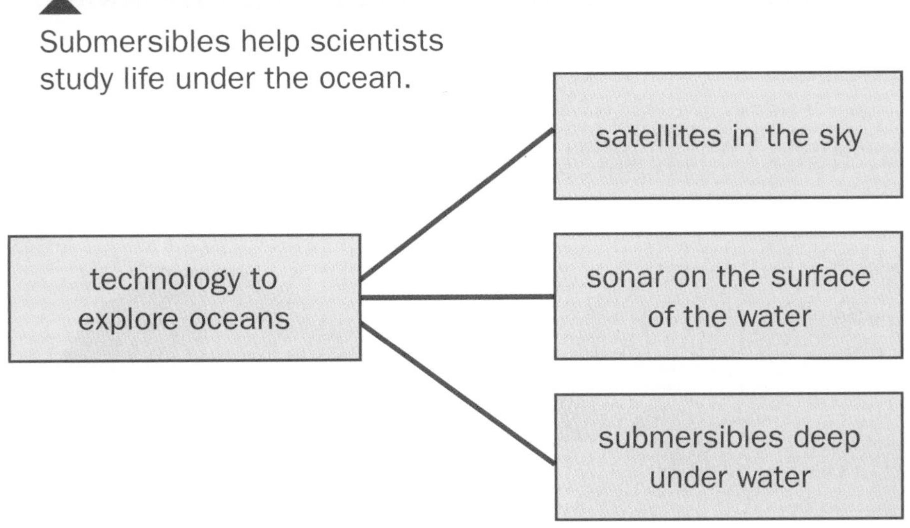

WHY IT MATTERS

Technology helps you understand what happens in the oceans.

EARTH SCIENCE

Salt Water and Freshwater

ESSENTIAL IDEA

Only about 3 percent of Earth's water is freshwater.

About 97 percent of all Earth's water is **salt water**. Oceans are made of salt water. Because of the **salinity**, or amount of salt, water from the oceans cannot be used for drinking or watering crops.

The other 3 percent of Earth's water is called **freshwater**. Freshwater does not have salt.

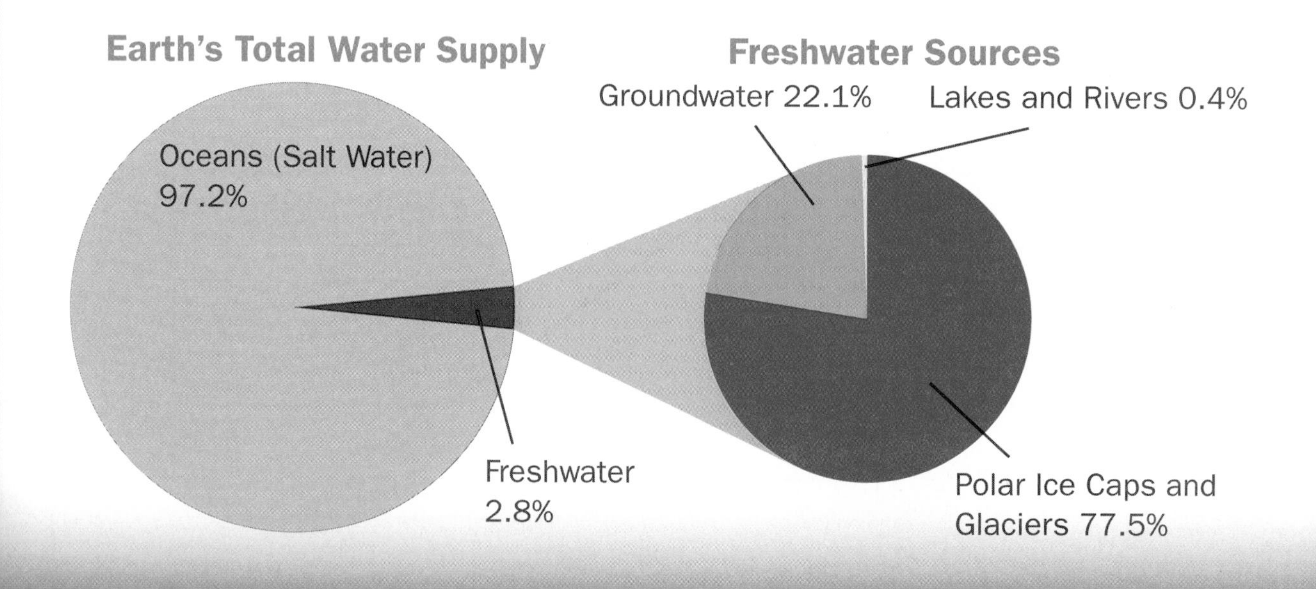

Most of Earth's freshwater is frozen in **ice caps** and **glaciers** near the north pole and the south pole. People are not able to use this water because it is frozen.

Groundwater

Most freshwater that is not frozen is stored under the ground. This **groundwater** is stored in spaces between soil particles and rocks. There is much more water in the ground than in lakes and rivers.

WHY IT MATTERS

- You could not survive without freshwater.
- Most of the water you use comes from lakes, rivers, or groundwater.

EARTH SCIENCE

The Water Cycle

ESSENTIAL IDEA

Earth's water moves in a cycle.

A **cycle** is a series of events that repeats over and over. Earth's **hydrosphere** contains all the water in the oceans, rivers, lakes, air, and ground. Water moves through the hydrosphere in a cycle.

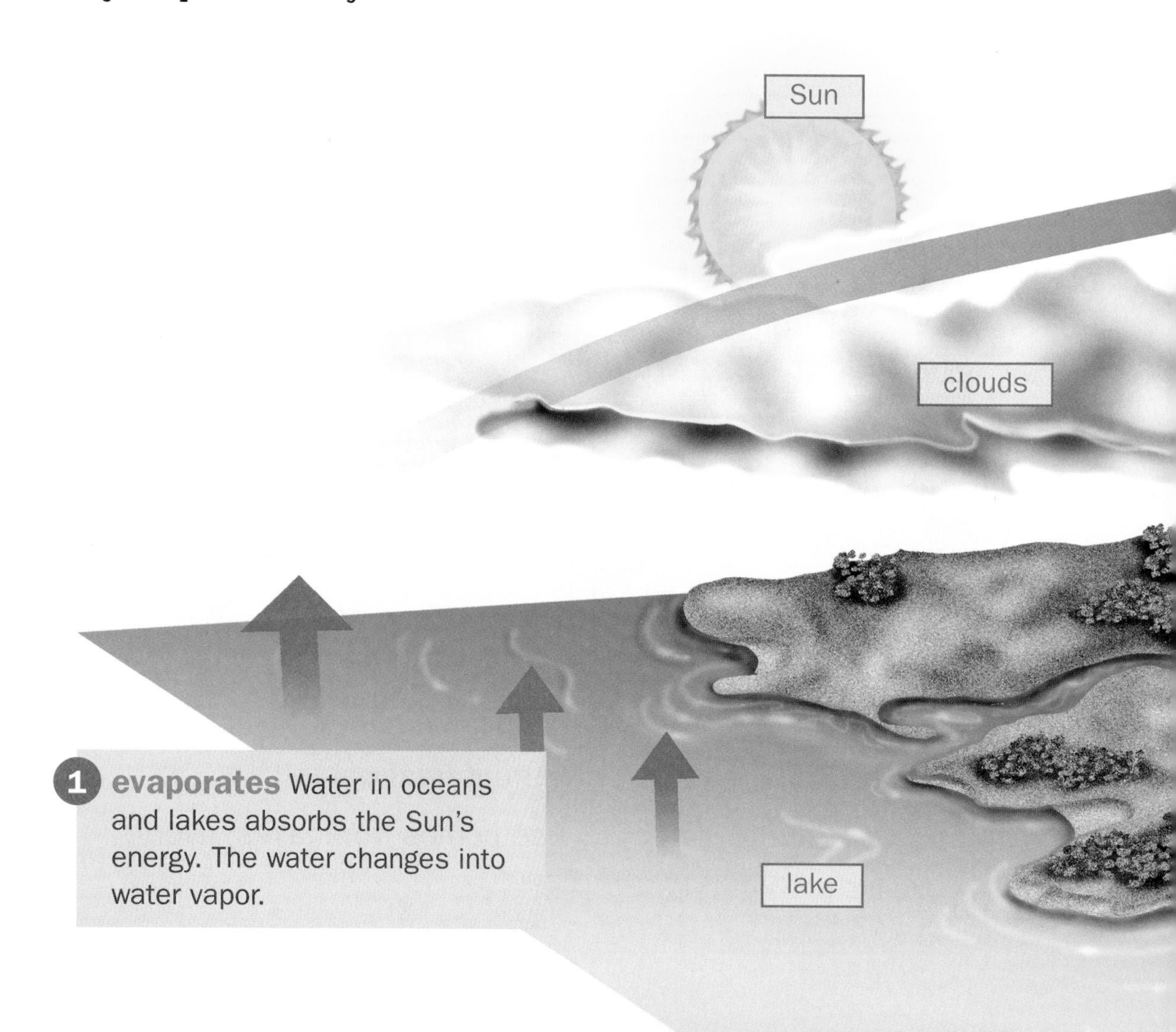

1 evaporates Water in oceans and lakes absorbs the Sun's energy. The water changes into water vapor.

First, water **evaporates**, or changes into a gas called water vapor. Next, the water vapor cools and **condenses**, or changes into tiny water droplets that form clouds. Then, the water **precipitates**, or falls to Earth as rain or snow. Finally, water collects on the surface or as **groundwater**.

WHY IT MATTERS

Water you use has moved through the water cycle many times.

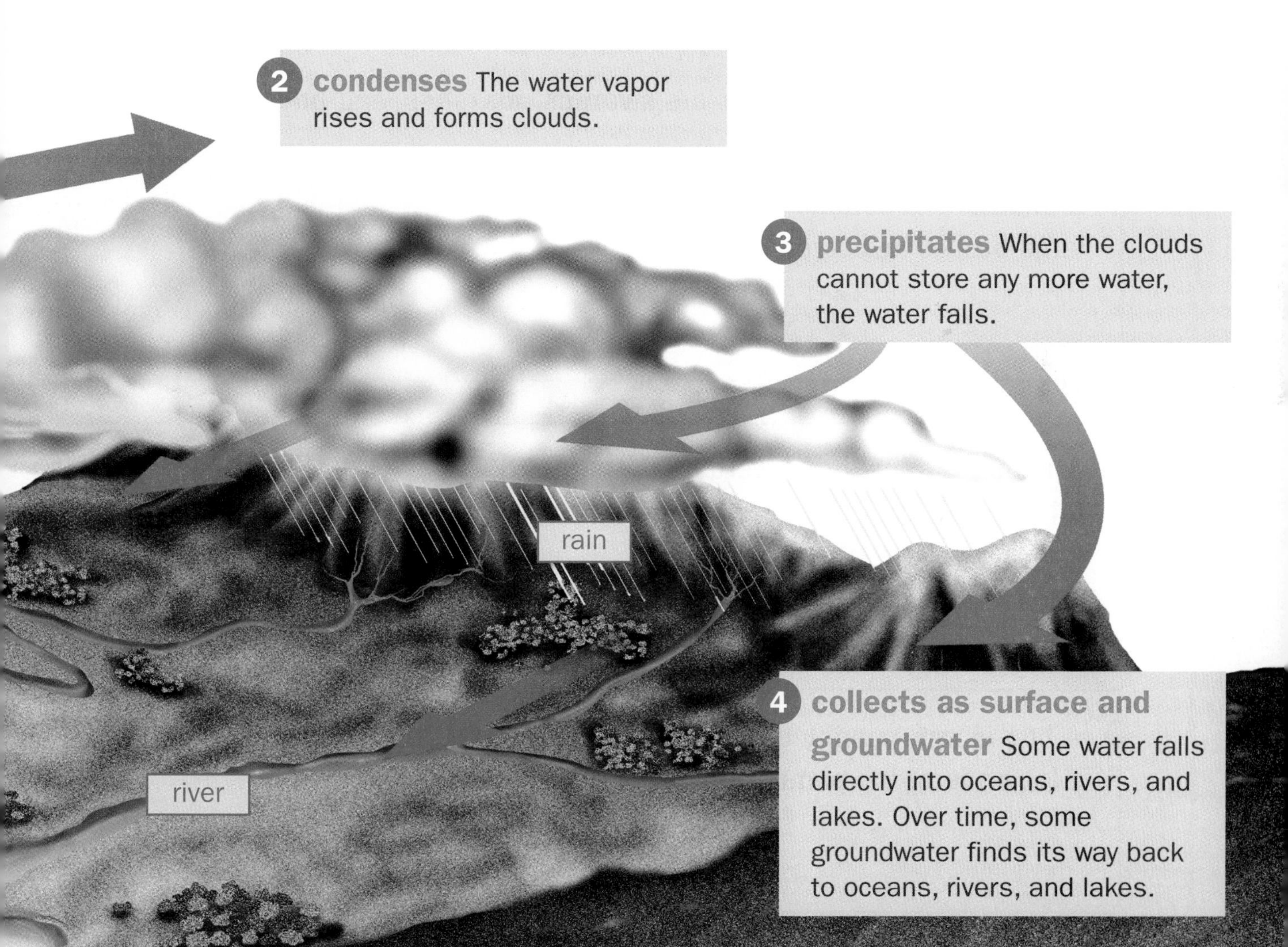

What Wetlands Do

ESSENTIAL IDEA

Wetlands are important because they filter and clean the water. Wetlands also provide habitats for many types of organisms.

In **wetlands**, water is near the surface. Wetlands can have water for all or part of the year. Wetlands are habitats for many species of animals and plants.

Three types of wetlands are **swamps**, **marshes**, and **bogs**.

A swamp is a wetland that has many large bushes and trees.

A marsh is a low-lying wetland with lots of grasses.

A bog is wet, spongy ground with a lot of decaying plants.

Wetlands **filter**, or clean, water. Wetlands take out the **excess** nutrients, harmful chemicals, and sediment that could hurt fish and other animals.

The plants and bacteria that live in wetlands help clean the water.

Wetlands can also prevent floods. A **flood** happens when water fills land that is normally dry. When there is a lot of rain, wetlands act like sponges. Wetlands hold extra water that might flood cities or farmland.

WHY IT MATTERS

Wetlands help filter freshwater that you use.

EARTH SCIENCE

Earth's Atmosphere

ESSENTIAL IDEA

Earth is surrounded by layers of gases called the atmosphere. Earth's weather changes because of changes in the layer closest to Earth.

Earth's **atmosphere** is made up of mostly nitrogen and oxygen gases. It has several layers, or levels.

The layer closest to Earth is called the **troposphere**. All of Earth's weather forms in the troposphere. Changes in temperature, air pressure, and amount of moisture in the troposphere can create clouds, rain, or wind.

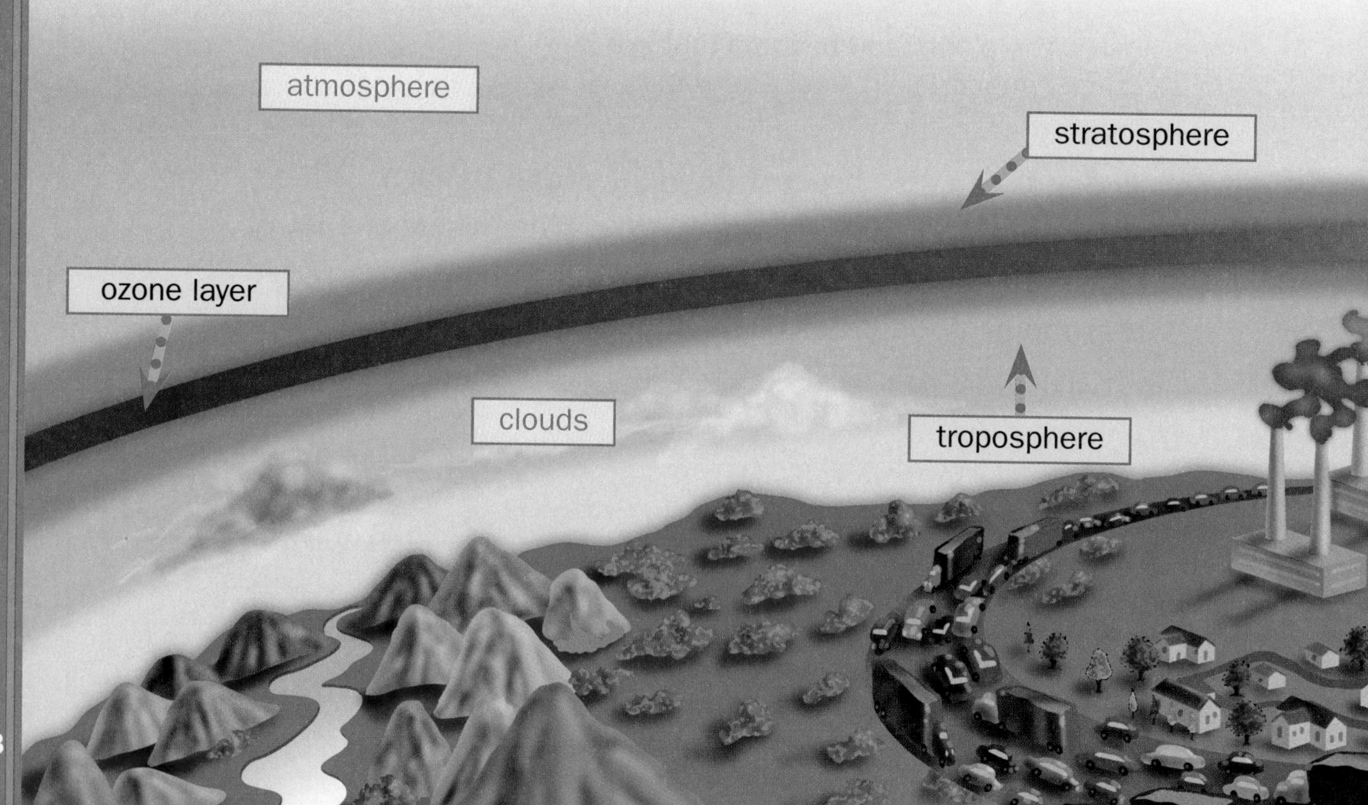

The **stratosphere** is the layer above the troposphere. The stratosphere has a band of gas called the **ozone layer**. The ozone layer absorbs many of the Sun's **ultraviolet rays**. These harmful rays can sometimes cause skin cancer or blindness.

WHY IT MATTERS

- You live in the troposphere.
- You rely on the atmosphere for the oxygen you breathe.
- All of the weather you feel begins in the troposphere.

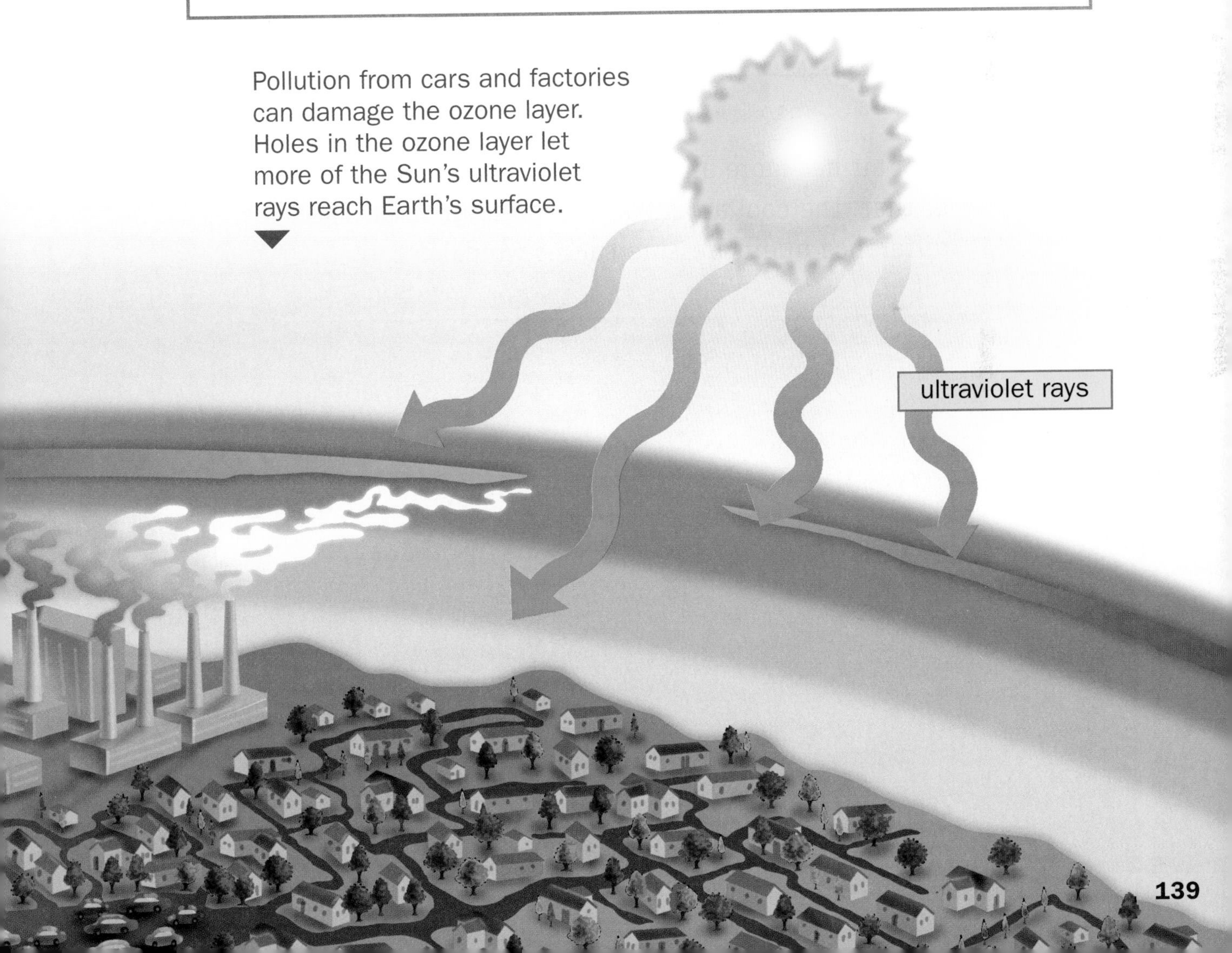

Pollution from cars and factories can damage the ozone layer. Holes in the ozone layer let more of the Sun's ultraviolet rays reach Earth's surface.

What Causes Wind

ESSENTIAL IDEA

Winds are caused by the uneven heating of Earth's surface by the Sun.

The weight of air is called **air pressure**. Air flows from areas of high pressure to areas of low pressure. **Wind** is air moving from areas of high air pressure to areas of low air pressure.

How Wind Forms

Cool air has more air pressure than warm air. Because of that, the cool air sinks and warm air rises. The difference in air pressure causes wind.

Wind moves from cool to warm air.

Air rises over hot areas of Earth, such as the equator. As the air moves, it cools. The cooler air then sinks back to Earth. This forms wind patterns over Earth's surface.

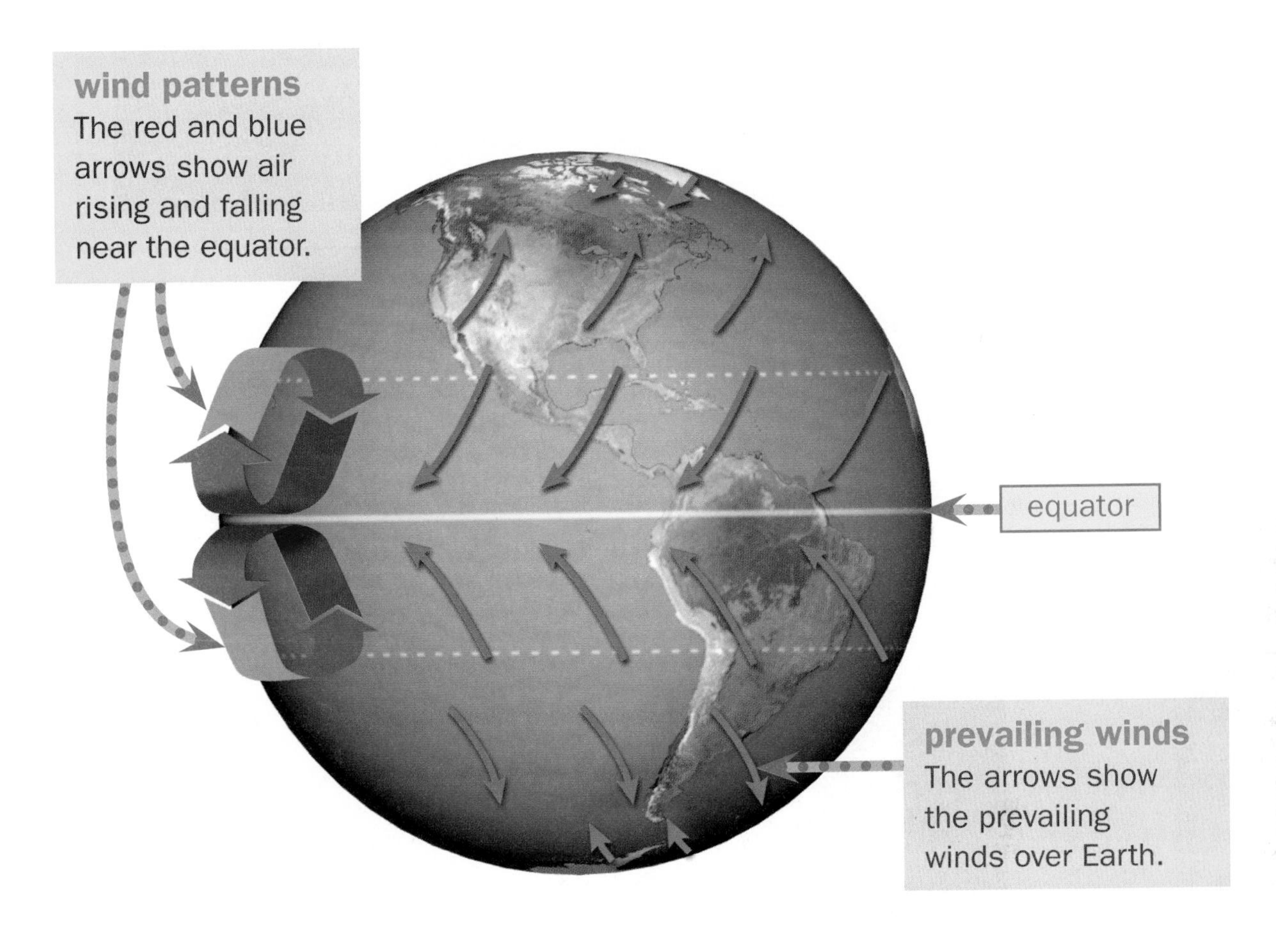

Winds over different parts of Earth usually blow from the same direction. These are called **prevailing winds**.

WHY IT MATTERS

- You feel the wind moving from place to place.
- The prevailing winds in your area come from the same direction.

EARTH SCIENCE

Thunderstorms

ESSENTIAL IDEA

When warm, moist air rises rapidly, it can form a thunderstorm. Thunderstorms can produce lightning, rain, wind, thunder, and hail.

A **thunderstorm** is a storm with lightning, thunder, strong wind, and rain. Thunderstorms form where cold and warm air masses meet.

An **air mass** is a body of air with the same temperature and **humidity**, or amount of water. A **front** forms where different air masses meet. The cold air pushes up the warm air. As the warm air cools, large thunderclouds form.

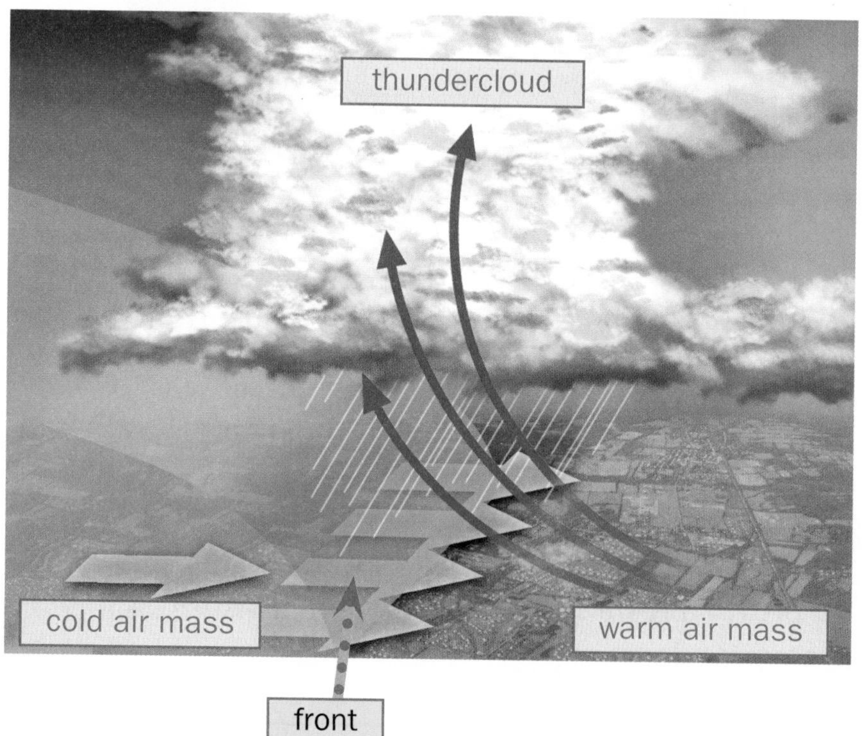

Thunderstorms produce **lightning**. As clouds move, they form static electricity. Lightning is the **discharge**, or release, of static electricity. Thunderstorms can also produce **hail**, or balls of ice.

Lightning can move from a cloud to another cloud or from a cloud to the ground.

Hail can fall during a thunderstorm. Hail usually occurs in the summer.

WHY IT MATTERS

- You should stay inside during thunderstorms.
- You should protect yourself from lightning and hail.

Tornadoes

ESSENTIAL IDEA

Tornadoes can appear after thunderstorms. They form a fast spinning column of air that often touches the ground.

Tornadoes can occur anywhere in the world, but most occur near the middle of the United States. A tornado sometimes forms on land after a violent thunderstorm. Fast spinning winds from a tornado can destroy houses and lift cars.

The places where houses were destroyed show the path of the tornado.

How Tornadoes Form

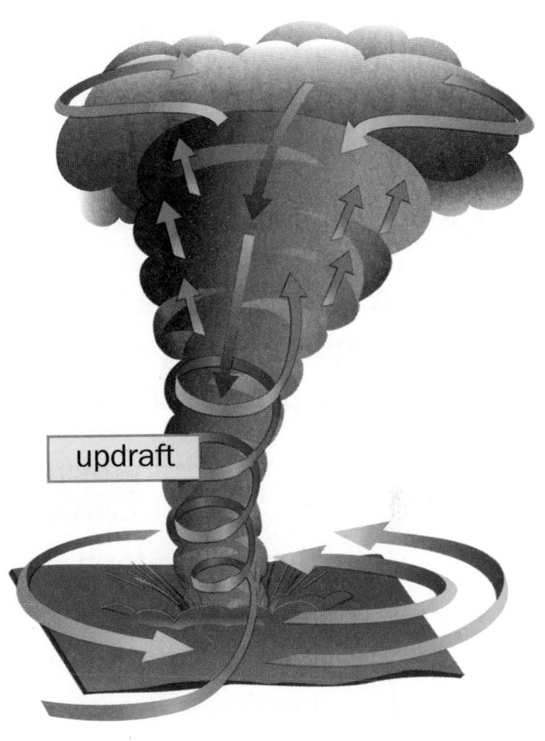

Tornadoes are caused by an **updraft**, or air moving up. Tornadoes form when winds close to the ground blow at different speeds and in different directions from winds higher up.

WHY IT MATTERS

You should learn how to protect yourself if a tornado approaches.

Hurricanes

ESSENTIAL IDEA

Hurricanes, typhoons, and cyclones are tropical windstorms that form over water.

A **hurricane** is a large storm that forms over the warm, **tropical** waters of the Atlantic Ocean. The same storms in other parts of the world are called **typhoons** or **cyclones**.

How Hurricanes Form

Hurricanes form over the ocean when warm, humid air rises. As the air rises, the air cools and releases heat. Clouds and rain form. As the hurricane grows, Earth's rotation makes the air spin. This fast spinning turns into a fierce storm.

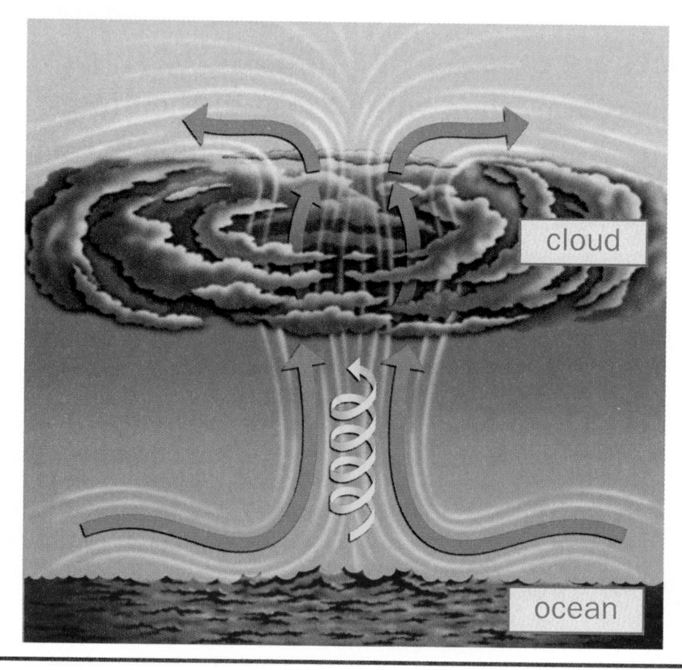

A hurricane spins around the eye of a storm. The **eye**, or center, of a hurricane is calm.

A **storm surge** is ocean water that moves to the shore during a hurricane. Strong hurricane winds cause ocean water to rise up. Strong winds and rising water from a hurricane can damage trees and buildings.

WHY IT MATTERS

- If you are near the Atlantic Ocean, you might be affected by a hurricane.
- Hurricanes can cause severe damage, so people affected by them may need your help.

EARTH SCIENCE

Blizzards

ESSENTIAL IDEA

A blizzard is a severe winter storm with blowing snow, cold temperatures, and high winds.

A **blizzard** is a severe winter storm. Winter storms occur when cold, **polar** air masses move toward the equator. When the cold air meets warmer, **tropical** air, a large winter storm may form.

Like thunderstorms, winter storms have precipitation. **Precipitation** in a winter storm may be rain, freezing rain, **sleet**, or snow. The type of precipitation depends on the air temperature.

Precipitation

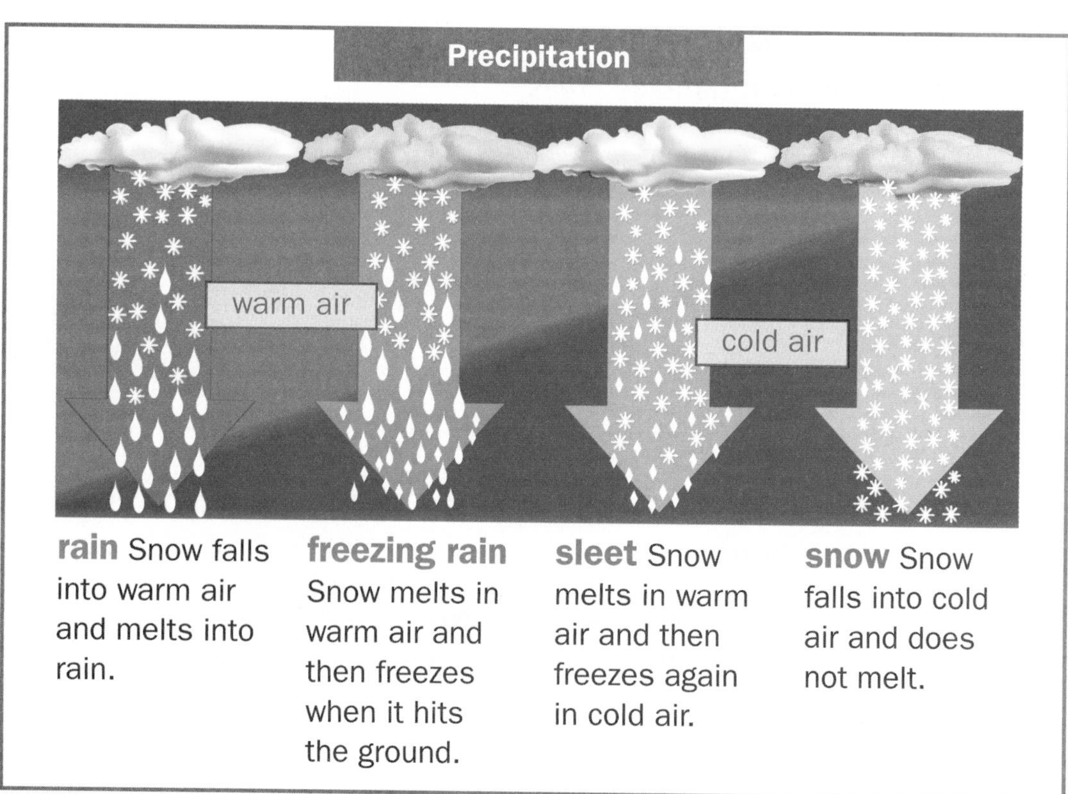

rain Snow falls into warm air and melts into rain.

freezing rain Snow melts in warm air and then freezes when it hits the ground.

sleet Snow melts in warm air and then freezes again in cold air.

snow Snow falls into cold air and does not melt.

A blizzard has winds over 35 miles per hour and temperatures less than 19°F. In a blizzard, falling and blowing snow **decrease visibility**, or make it hard to see.

A blizzard lasts for at least three hours, but a severe blizzard can last for several days. Several feet of snow may fall. Winds can blow the snow into huge **snow drifts** that cover cars, roads, and buildings.

WHY IT MATTERS

- Winter storms can bring different kinds of precipitation.
- You should know how to stay safe and protect yourself if a blizzard hits your area.

EARTH SCIENCE

Predicting Weather

ESSENTIAL IDEA

Scientists use data collected by radar and satellites to predict the weather.

Weather forecasting means using science and technology to predict future weather. Scientists who predict the weather are called **meteorologists**.

Meteorologists track the size, direction, and **intensity**, or strength, of a storm using **radar**. The radar sends out radio waves. When the waves bounce off objects, such as raindrops, the waves return to the radar. Then scientists can tell where the rain is and how big storms are.

A weather **satellite** is an object placed in space. Satellites **orbit**, or move around, Earth. Weather satellites take photographs that help meteorologists predict the weather. Some satellite photographs show how much heat is in an area.

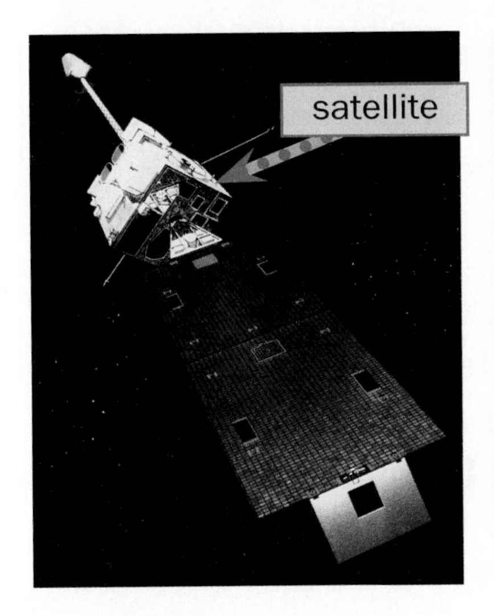

Satellites send photographs back to Earth.

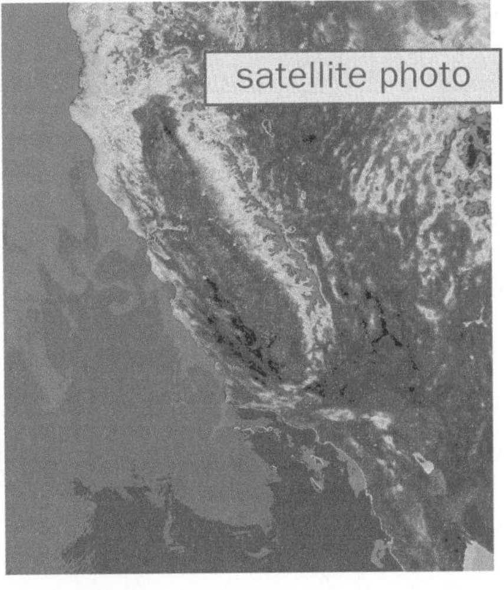

This satellite photograph shows temperatures in California.

Technology for Predicting Weather

technology	uses
radar	radio waves
satellite	photographs

WHY IT MATTERS

- A weather forecast tells you what to expect and helps you decide what to wear.
- Forecasts can help you prepare for the weather.

Climate

ESSENTIAL IDEA

Climate is a long-term pattern of weather for a region.

Weather changes almost every day. **Climate** is the average weather over a long time, or at least 30 years. Different climates have different temperatures and different amounts of rain and snow. An area's climate is controlled by its **elevation** and **latitude**.

elevation
Temperatures are colder and air is drier at higher elevations.

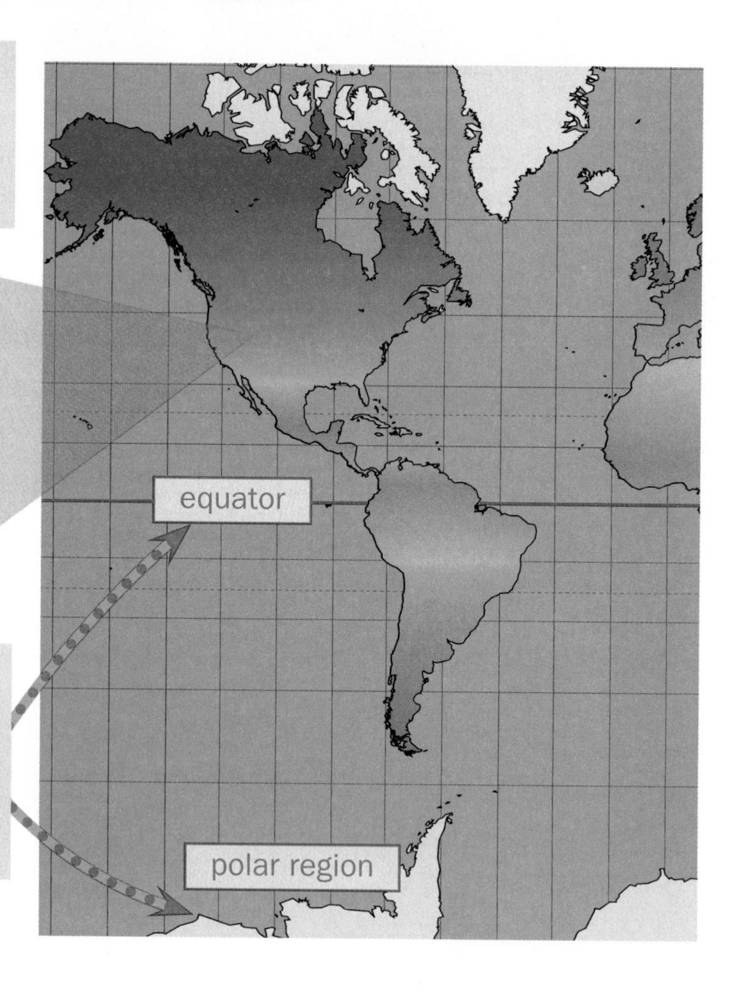

latitude
Temperatures are warmer near the equator and cooler in polar regions.

The amount of **vegetation** and nearby bodies of water can strongly affect the climate. Each type of climate can have several different conditions. A tropical climate may be dry or wet. A dry climate may be cold or hot.

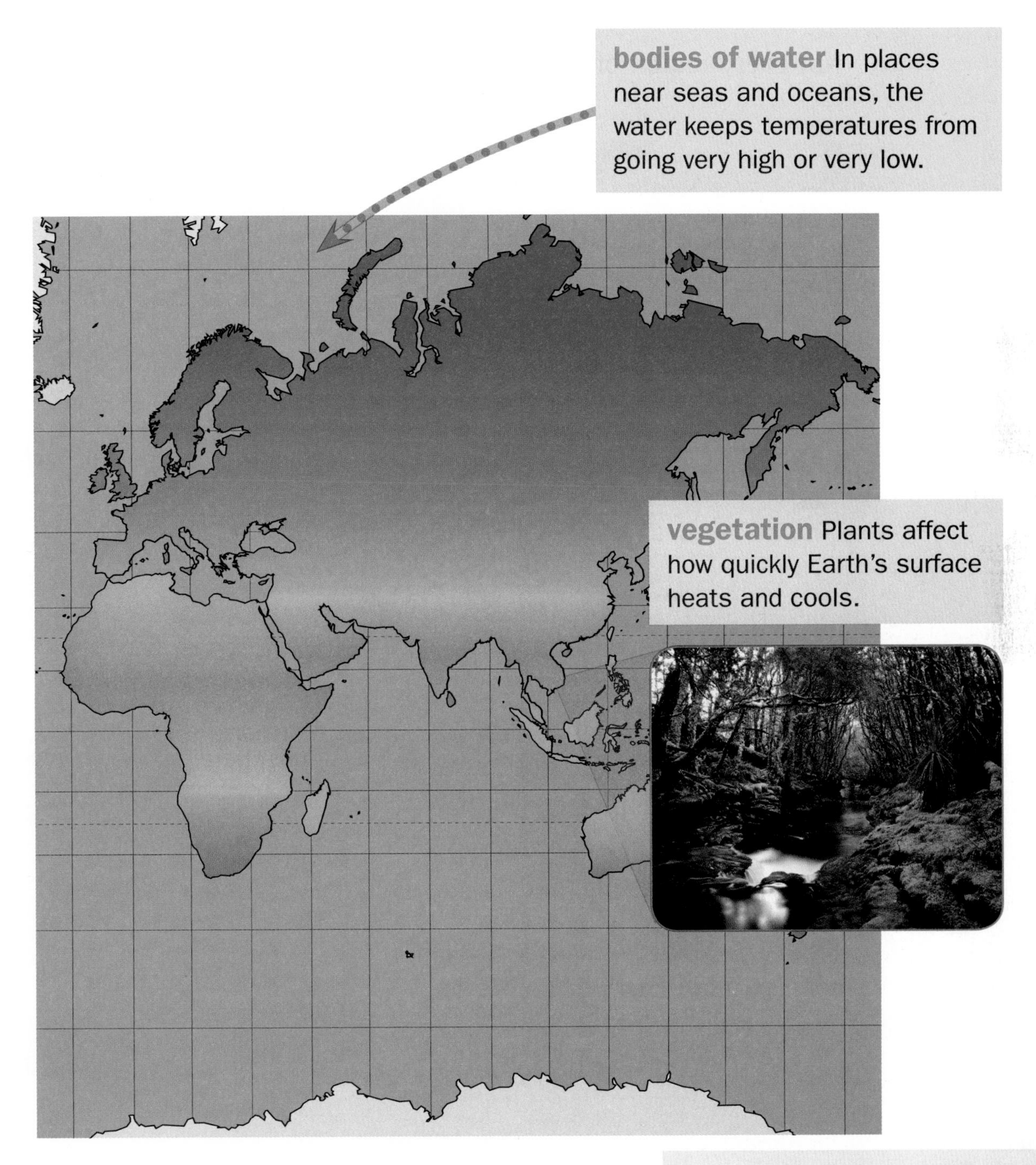

Seasons

A **season** is a major division, or part, of the year. Temperate climates have four seasons: spring, summer, **autumn** (or fall), and winter.

Not every region of Earth has four seasons.

Tropical regions may be hot all year.

Polar regions are cold all year.

Earth can be divided into hemispheres. The half of Earth north of the equator is called the **northern hemisphere**. The half south of the equator is the **southern hemisphere**.

As Earth circles the Sun during the year, parts of Earth get more or less direct sunlight because of the tilt, or slant, of Earth's **axis**.

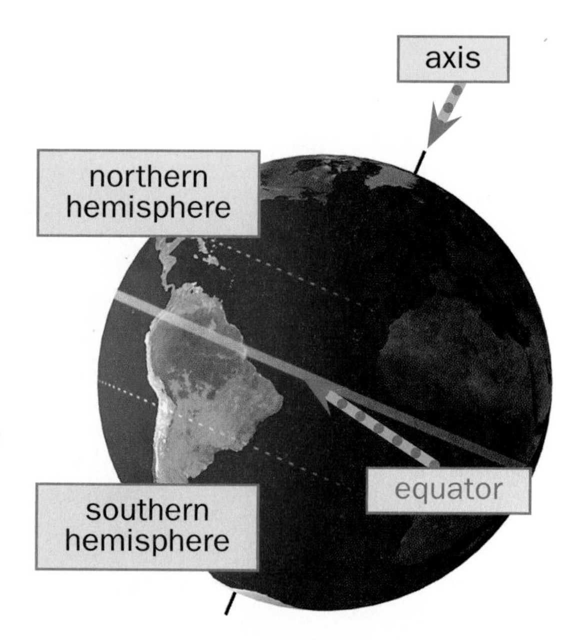

Seasons in the Northern Hemisphere

During summer, the Sun's rays hit the northern hemisphere more directly. This is because the northern hemisphere tilts toward the Sun. In winter, the Sun's rays hit less directly, so the northern hemisphere is not as warm.

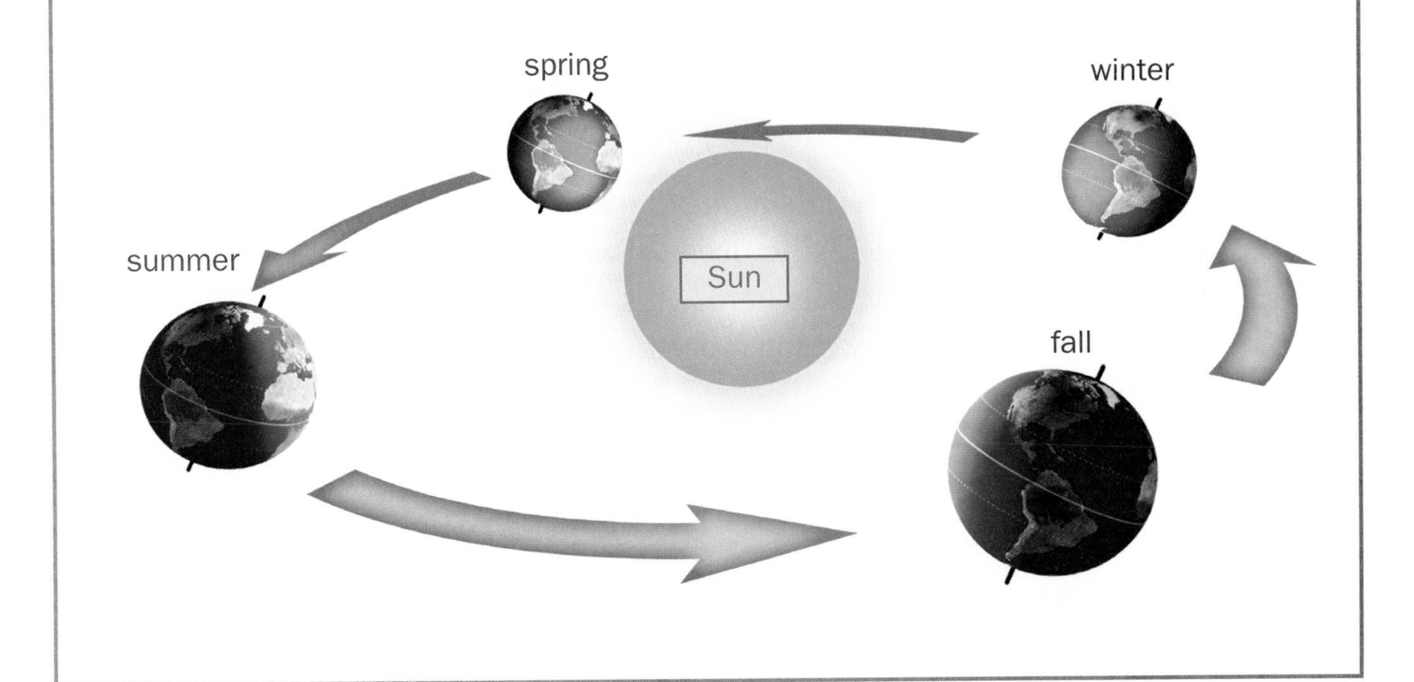

WHY IT MATTERS

- The area where you live has its own climate.
- The tilt of Earth's axis causes you to feel different temperatures in each season.

Climate Change

ESSENTIAL IDEA

Natural events can cause a climate to change. Human activities can also cause climate change.

Climate changes over time. Some climate changes repeat. This sort of climate change is part of a **natural cycle**.

For example, **trade winds** along the equator affect temperatures in the Pacific Ocean. Every few years, the trade winds don't blow as hard. This causes an event called **El Niño**. El Niño causes some parts of Earth to be wetter or drier than normal.

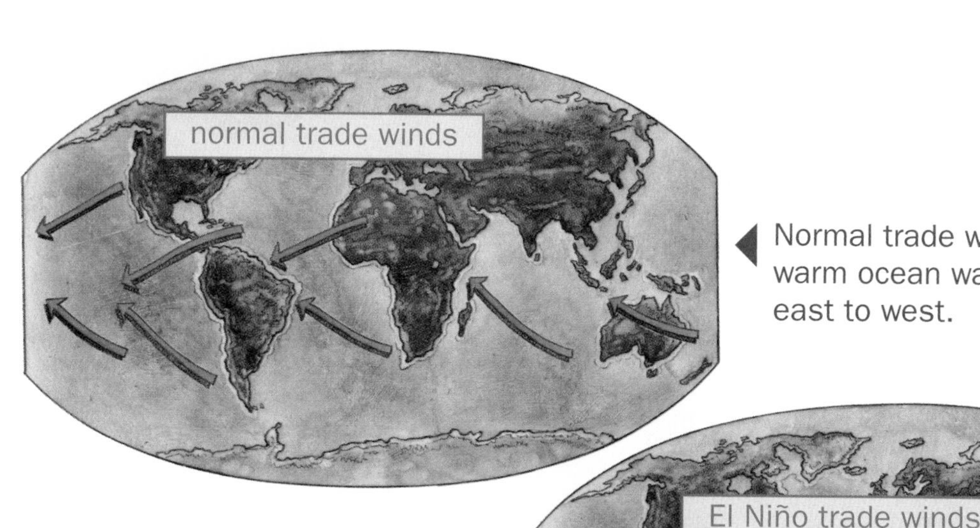

Normal trade winds push warm ocean water from east to west.

Every three to seven years, trade winds are less strong.

Many scientists think that people also cause climate change. The fuel people burn adds **greenhouse gases** to the air. Greenhouse gases help keep Earth warm. When greenhouse gases increase, they can cause **global warming**.

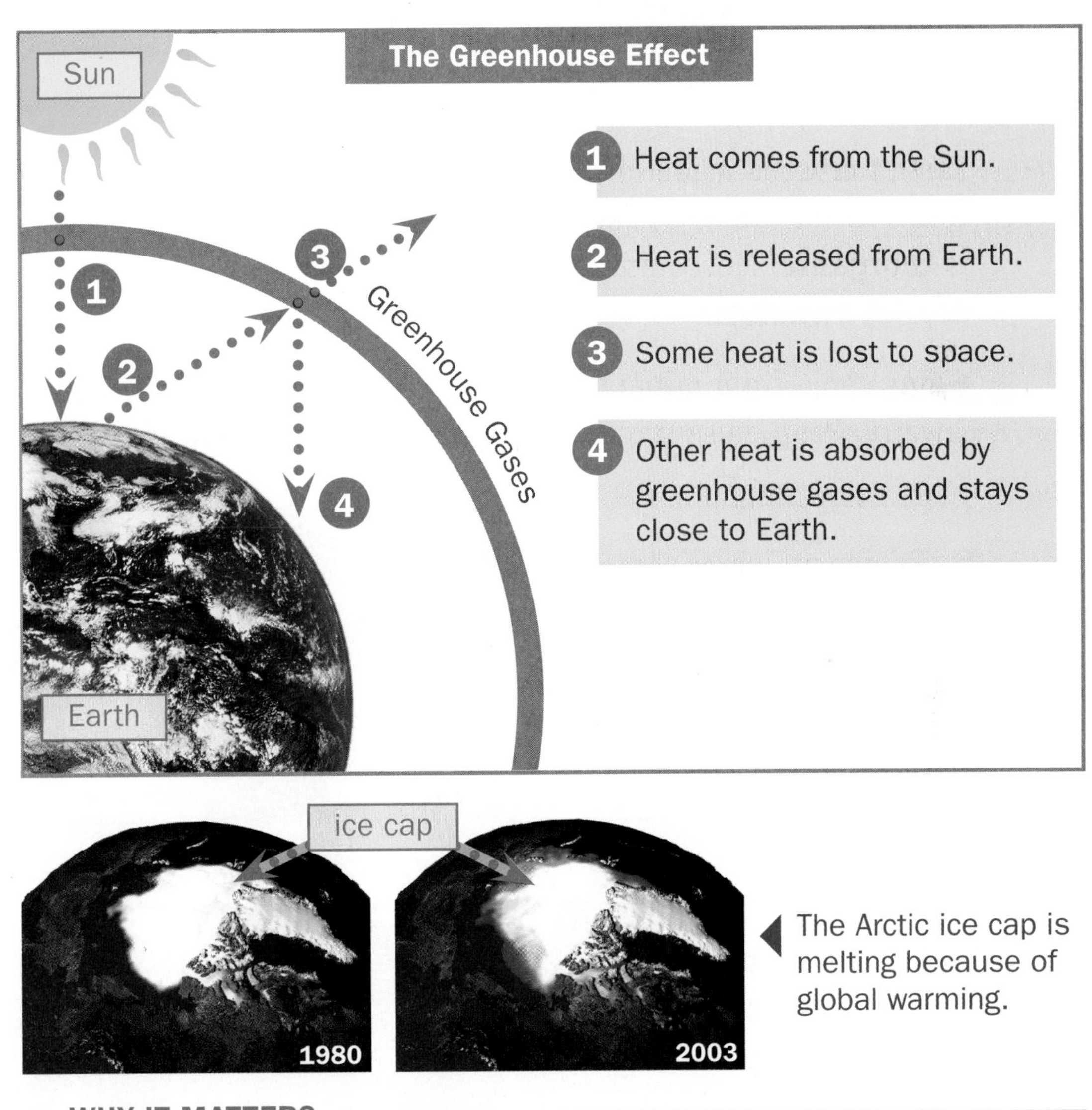

The Arctic ice cap is melting because of global warming.

WHY IT MATTERS

If global warming continues, the climate where you live may change.

Minerals

ESSENTIAL IDEA

Minerals are nonliving substances that are made in Earth. People use minerals to make things.

Earth's crust is made of rocks and minerals. A **mineral** forms in nature and is solid. A mineral was never alive—it is **inorganic**. Most minerals have a regular pattern called a **crystal structure**.

Gems come from minerals. People use gems to make jewelry. People use minerals to make many different things.

- Rubies are gems. Rubies come from a mineral called corundum.

- Quartz is a mineral people use to make glass and sandpaper. Quartz crystals are used in watches and computers.

Many useful metals, such as aluminum and iron, come from minerals. You can find minerals in your home.

This rock is called bauxite. It contains several minerals. Aluminum comes from bauxite.

Iron is used to make steel, which is in cars and nails. Most iron comes from a mineral called hematite.

Granite is a rock made of several minerals. People often use it to make floors and countertops.

WHY IT MATTERS

Many things you use or can find in your home are made from minerals.

EARTH SCIENCE

How Rocks Form

ESSENTIAL IDEA

Rocks are mixtures of minerals joined together. Rocks form in several different ways.

A rock is made of minerals that mix and join together. Rocks usually form very slowly over many thousands of years.

Rock Types

Rocks form in three ways. **Igneous rocks** form when magma cools. **Metamorphic rocks** form under high heat and pressure. **Sedimentary rocks** form when small particles of rocks and minerals are pressed together in layers.

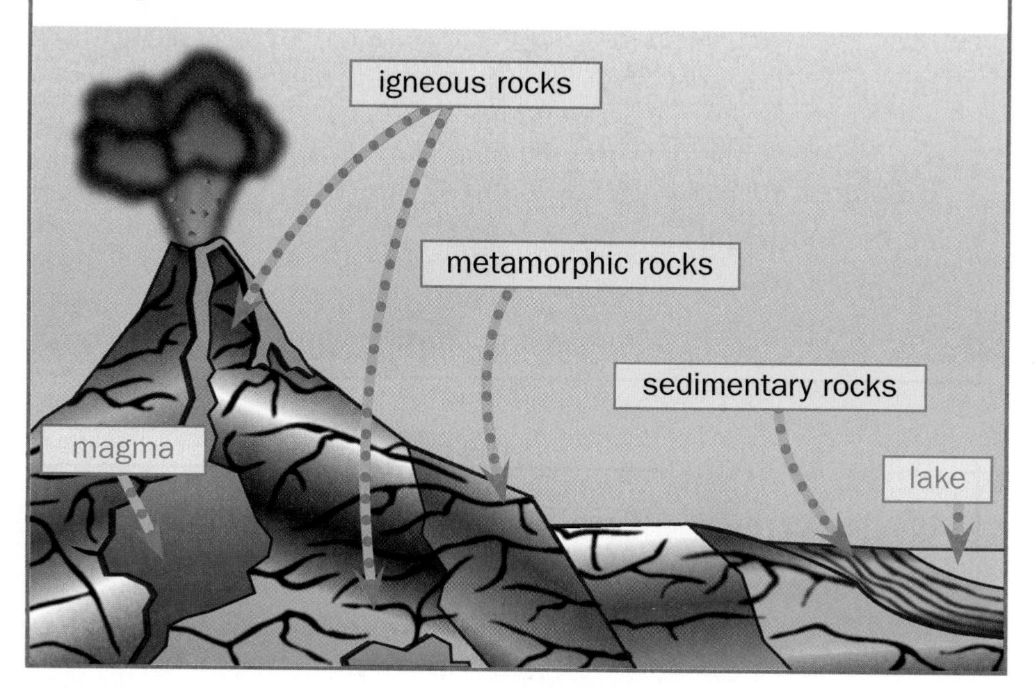

Many rocks form underground. Other rocks form on the surface.

Igneous Rocks

When igneous rocks form, minerals join together as magma cools. Igneous rocks can form inside Earth or on Earth's surface.

Metamorphic Rocks

Metamorphic rocks form deep inside Earth. They also form where Earth's plates collide or slide past each other.

Sedimentary Rocks

Sedimentary rocks form at the bottom of lakes and oceans. Over time, layers of **sediment** press together and turn into sedimentary rock.

WHY IT MATTERS

Most of the rocks you see are sedimentary rocks.

EARTH SCIENCE

The Rock Cycle

ESSENTIAL IDEA

Rocks constantly change their form and structure. This process is called the rock cycle.

In the **rock cycle**, rocks change from one kind to another. This can happen over a long time through weathering, pressure, and heat. All three types of rocks can become any other type of rock.

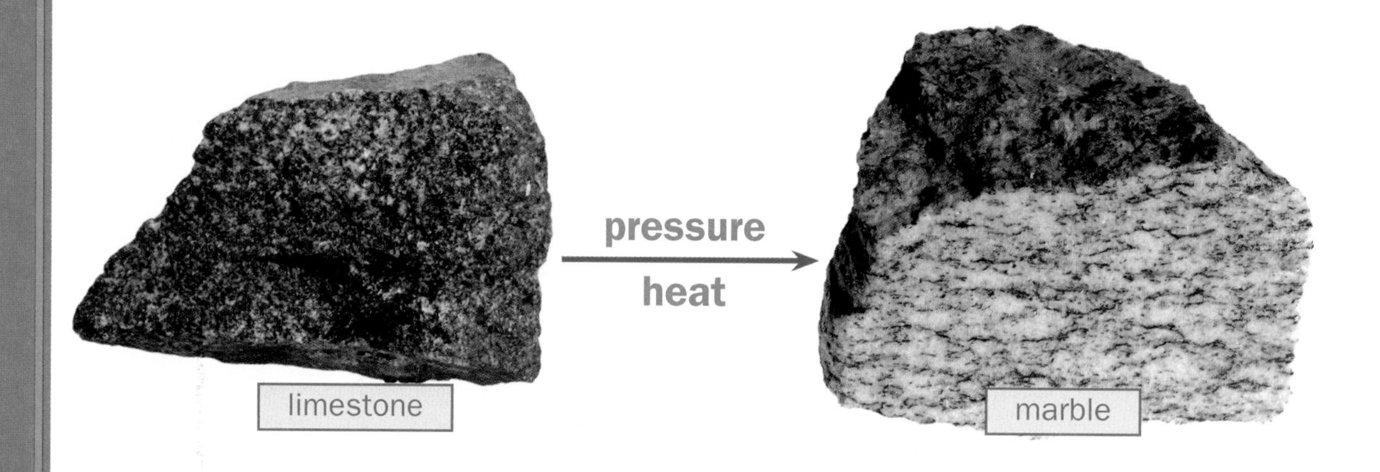

Heat and pressure can change limestone, a sedimentary rock, into marble, a metamorphic rock.

Weathering, pressure, and heat change one kind of rock into another kind of rock.

Weathering

Weathering helps igneous and metamorphic rocks turn into sedimentary rocks. Weathering breaks rocks into tiny particles called sediment. Water and wind move the sediment into layers. The pressure on the layers then forms sedimentary rocks.

Pressure

Pressure **compresses**, or pushes together, layers of rock. Pressure can **cement** particles of sediment together to form sedimentary rocks. Pressure also helps form metamorphic rocks.

Heat

Heat inside Earth can also melt any kind of rock into magma. When magma cools, igneous rocks form. Combined with pressure, heat can turn igneous and sedimentary rocks into metamorphic rock.

WHY IT MATTERS

The rocks around you are constantly changing.

EARTH SCIENCE

Soil

ESSENTIAL IDEA

Soil is made of rocks, minerals, and organisms. Soil takes thousands of years to form.

Over time, **weathering** breaks down rocks and minerals. Dead organisms also **decay**, or break down. Soil is a mixture of broken rocks, minerals, and organisms.

Steps in Soil Formation

Soil forms very slowly. First, weathering breaks down solid rock. Then, plants begin to grow. The plants decay and help form **humus** in the ground. New plants use nutrients in the humus. The plant roots break rock apart even more.

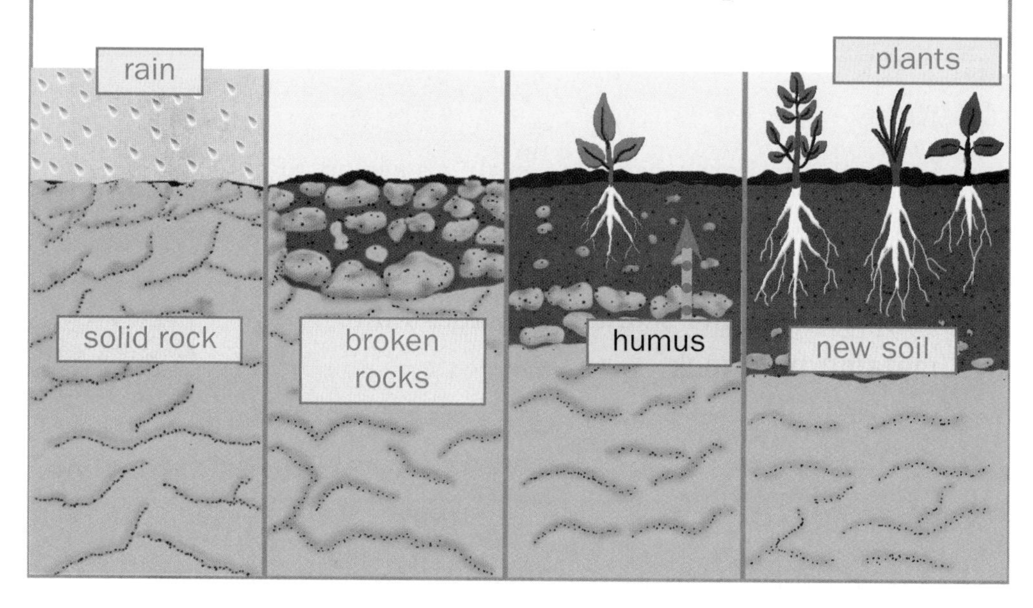

Growing plants take nutrients from the soil. Sometimes farming can **overuse** the soil. Soil **depletion** means the soil does not have enough nutrients for new plants to grow.

Erosion also affects soil. Water and wind can move soil and cause erosion. When soil is overused, erosion can happen more quickly than normal.

Soil is a renewable resource, but it takes thousands of years to replace.

WHY IT MATTERS

- The fruits and vegetables you eat grow in soil.
- The plants and trees you see every day need soil to grow.

Fossils

ESSENTIAL IDEA

Fossils are the evidence of past life found in rock. Fossils form in many ways.

Fossils are the evidence of plants and animals that lived long ago. You can see fossils a long time after an animal dies. Fossils show us what **ancient**, or very old, organisms once looked like.

A fossil may come from the hardened **remains** of an organism. The remains are usually the hard parts of an animal, like bones or shells.

People study fossils to learn about ancient animals.

Dinosaurs were sometimes buried under layers of sedimentary rock. Over time, minerals replaced the bones to form fossils in the rock.

As the shell of this organism decayed, it left a **mold**. The mold was a hole shaped like the shell. Minerals filled the mold and created a **cast fossil**.

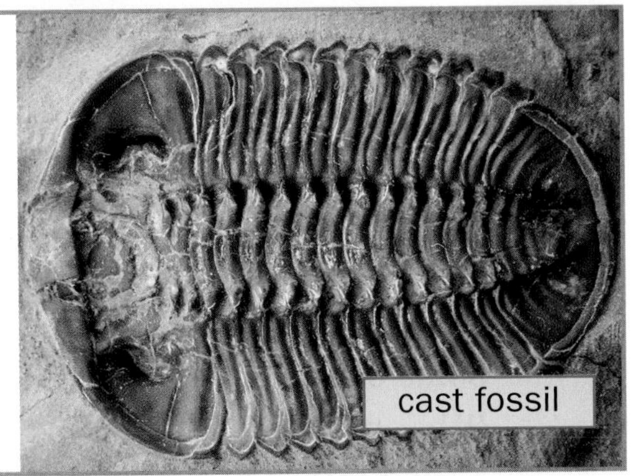

Footprints are an example of **trace fossils**. Trace fossils can show how an animal moved or lived.

WHY IT MATTERS

- Fossils let you see what early organisms looked like.
- Some fossils show you how and where early animals lived.

Fossil Fuels

ESSENTIAL IDEA

Fossil fuels formed from organisms that lived millions of years ago. They are important resources, but they cannot be replaced.

Fossil fuels formed from plants and animals that lived up to 400 million years ago. **Oil** and **natural gas** formed from organisms that were buried under ocean or river sediments. **Coal** formed from plants that were buried under swamps.

Places where you find fossil fuels are called **deposits**. Some oil and gas deposits are under the ocean floor. Other deposits are on land where ancient oceans have been covered by land.

Fossil Fuel Formation

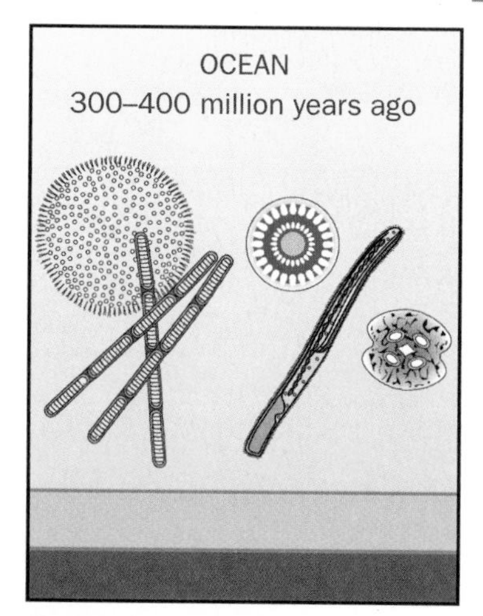

Organisms lived long ago.

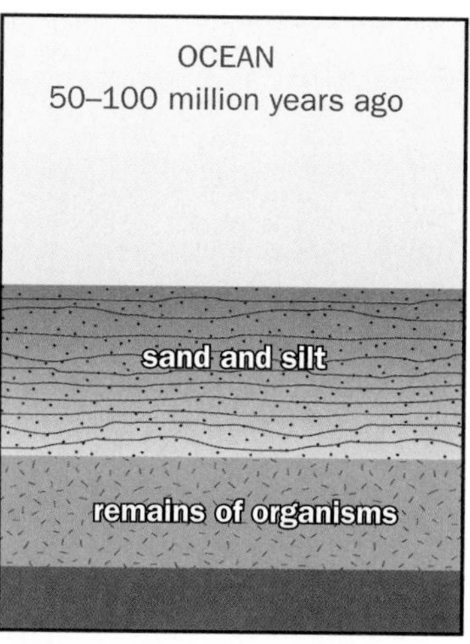

They died and were covered by sand and silt.

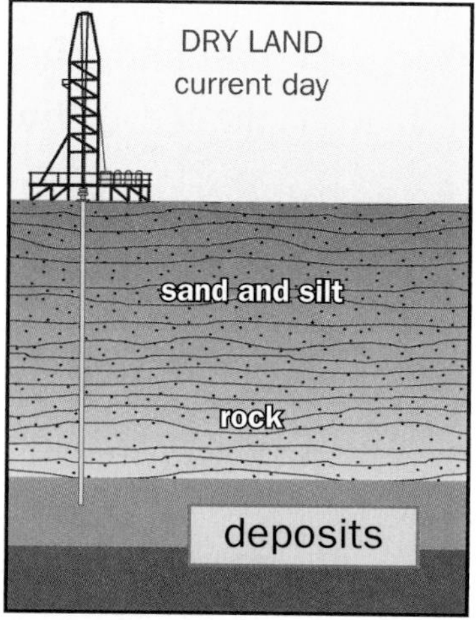

Their remains turned into fossil fuels.

Oil

The United States **imports**, or brings in, a lot of oil from other countries.

Natural Gas

Natural gas has no color or smell. It burns very easily.

Coal

It took ten feet of dead plants to produce one foot of coal.

WHY IT MATTERS

- Fossil fuels produce the energy that heats your home.
- Fossil fuels provide the energy for cars and school buses.

Earth's Resources

ESSENTIAL IDEA

Natural resources help meet people's needs. Some resources can be replaced after they are used. Other resources are gone forever.

A **natural resource** is anything in nature that humans use. Some resources, such as water, trees, sunlight, and wind, can be replaced. They are **renewable resources**.

Renewable Resources

Some renewable resources, such as soil and trees, take a long time to replace.

Renewable resources

water, trees, sunlight, wind

Many resources cannot be replaced. Fossil fuels and the minerals in Earth's crust are **nonrenewable resources**. They are **limited** resources.

Nonrenewable Resources

Nonrenewable resources		
oil	coal	gravel

Oil, coal, and gravel come from Earth's crust. They are not renewable.

WHY IT MATTERS

- You use both renewable and nonrenewable resources.
- You can help the environment by using fewer resources.

Conserving Resources

ESSENTIAL IDEA

People can make choices that conserve Earth's natural resources.

To **conserve** resources means to not waste them. Some natural resources are limited. It is important to use resources **efficiently** so that they will last longer.

One way to conserve resources is to find new ways to make energy. Sunlight and wind are **alternative resources**. They can be changed to electricity.

Solar panels change the Sun's energy into electricity.

Windmills change wind into electricity.

Another way to conserve resources is to use less of them. Walk instead of riding in a car. Try not to waste water. **Recycle** or reuse paper and plastic bags, glass, and aluminum or steel containers.

Recycling Is Conservation

▲ Things you recycle can be made into new products.

WHY IT MATTERS

- You can do many things to help conserve resources.
- When you conserve, you help the environment.

The Sun

ESSENTIAL IDEA

The Sun is a huge ball of hot matter.
Most of Earth's energy comes from the Sun.

All life on Earth needs the Sun. The Sun is Earth's **primary**, or most important, source of energy.

The Sun is a huge ball of hot matter. A million Earths could fit inside the Sun. It is about 93 million miles away.

Sunglasses can help protect your eyes from the Sun's rays. You should never look directly at the Sun.

Like Earth, the Sun has layers. The **core**, or center, is where the Sun produces energy. The part of the Sun you see is called the **photosphere**. This is where the Sun's energy escapes into space.

The inner part of the Sun's atmosphere is the **chromosphere**. The outer part is the **corona**.

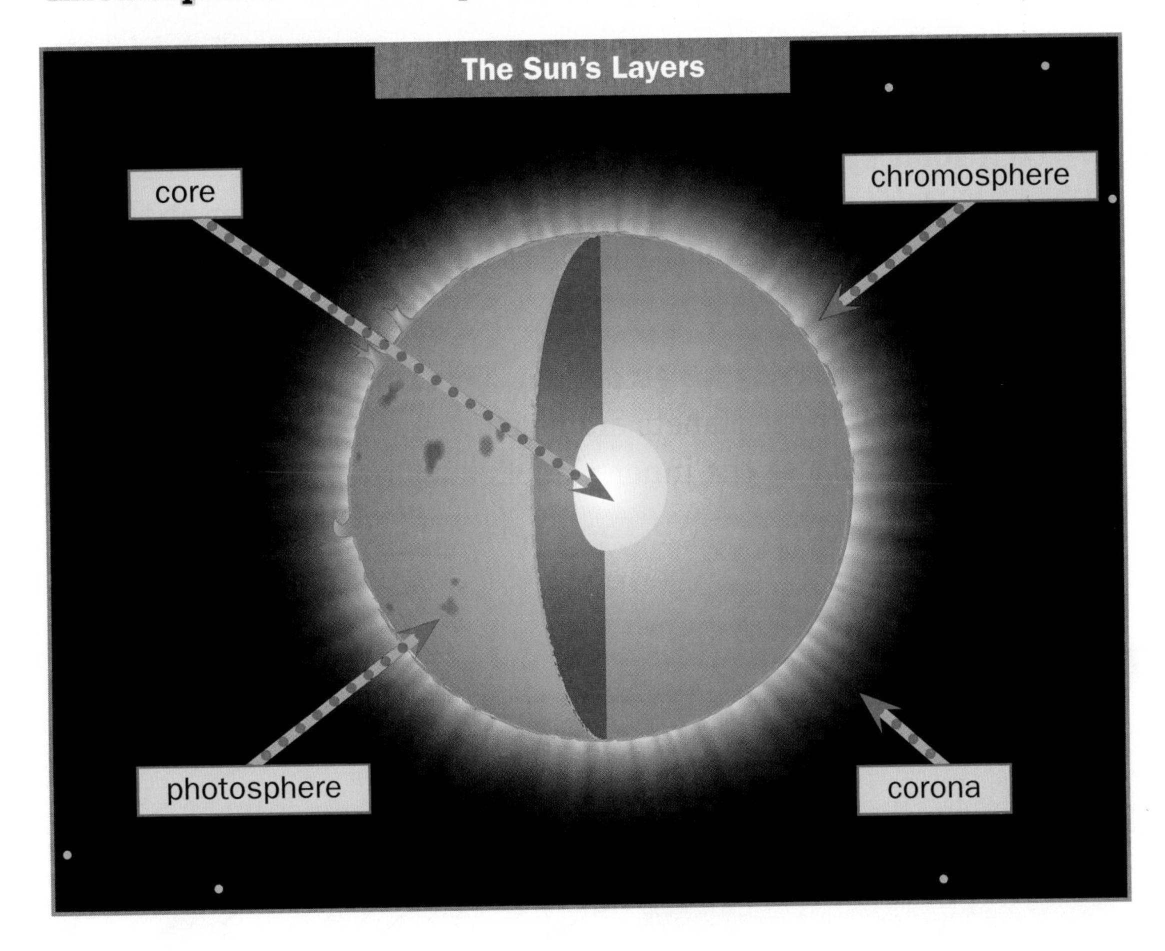

WHY IT MATTERS

- You could not survive without energy from the Sun.
- The Sun's energy gives you light and heat.

EARTH SCIENCE

The Solar System

ESSENTIAL IDEA

Earth, other planets, and many smaller objects orbit the Sun. It takes Earth one year to complete its orbit around the Sun.

A **solar system** is made up of a star and the objects that **orbit**, or move around, the star. The Sun is the star at the center of our solar system. Our solar system contains eight main **planets**.

The Sun's **gravity**, or attraction, holds objects in orbit around it. Inner planets are much warmer than outer planets because the inner planets are closer to the Sun.

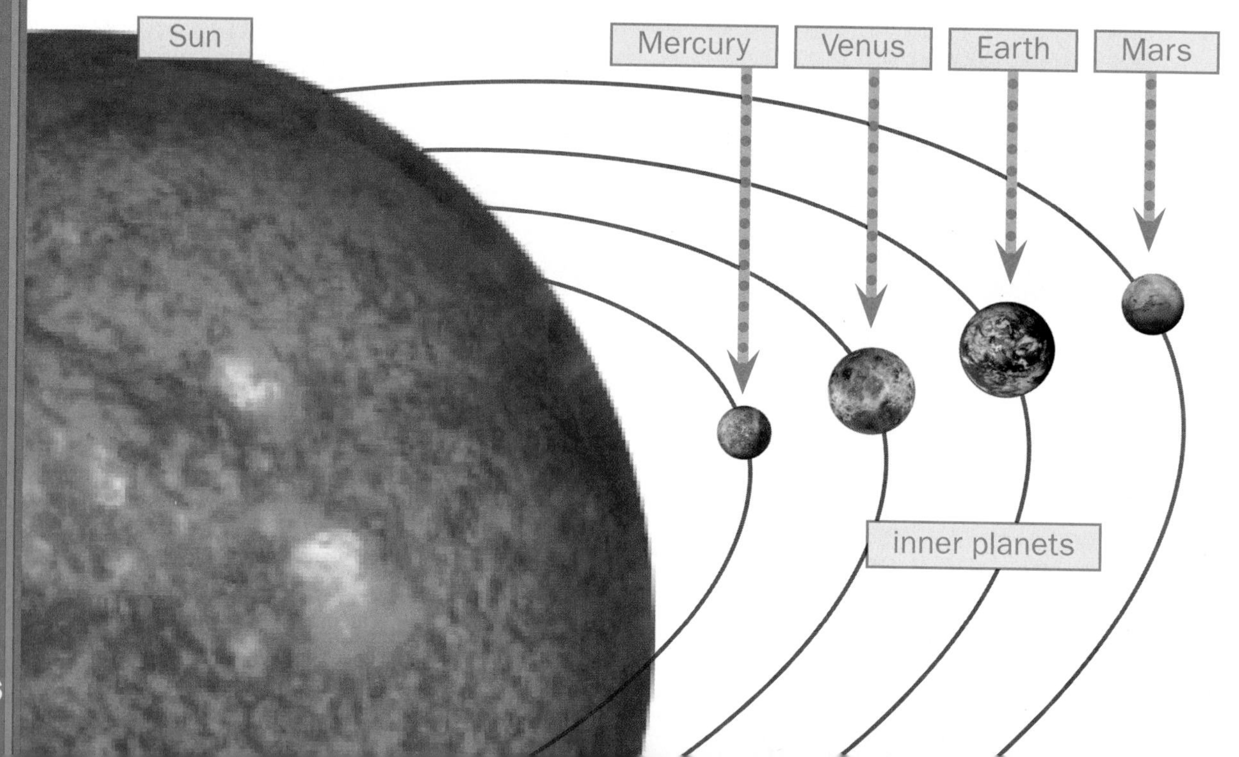

Scientists have not agreed on what makes an object a planet. For a long time, scientists called Pluto a planet, but it is much smaller than the other planets. It is even smaller than some **moons** that orbit other planets. Pluto, which is near Neptune, is now called a **dwarf planet**.

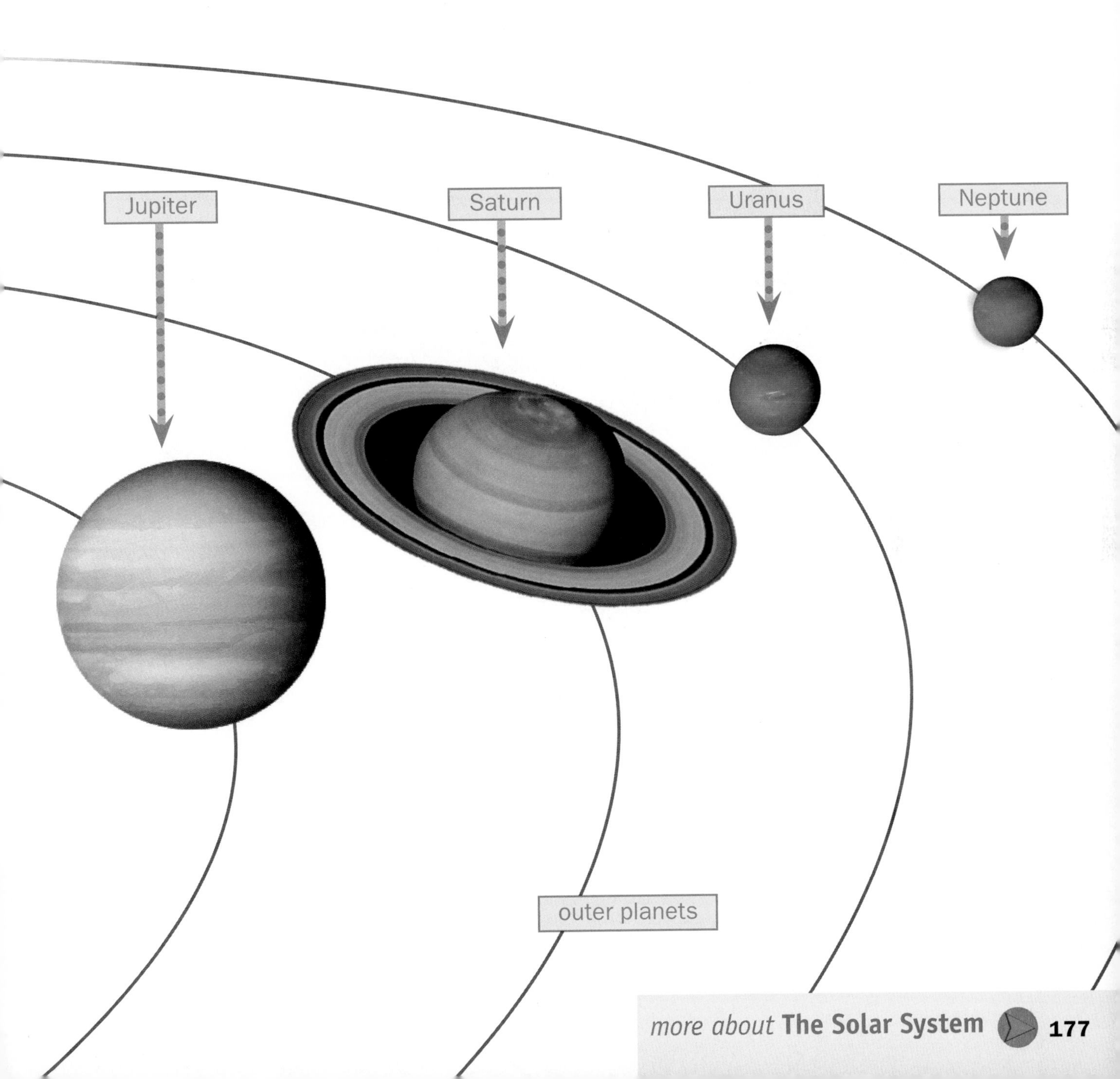

Years

A year is the time it takes a planet to orbit the Sun once. This is called one **revolution**. To **revolve** means to move around another object.

Length of Years

Planets that are far away from the Sun have longer years. Outer planets have to travel a lot farther to circle the Sun.

The length of a year increases as you move away from the Sun.

planet	length of year (in Earth years)
Mercury	0.24
Venus	0.61
Earth	1.00
Mars	1.88
Jupiter	11.86
Saturn	29.46
Uranus	84.07
Neptune	164.82

Days

As planets revolve around the Sun, they also turn, or **rotate**, on their axis. One day is the time it takes a planet to make one full turn. Planets rotate at different speeds. On Earth, one day is 24 Earth hours. It takes Venus 243 Earth days to make one full turn.

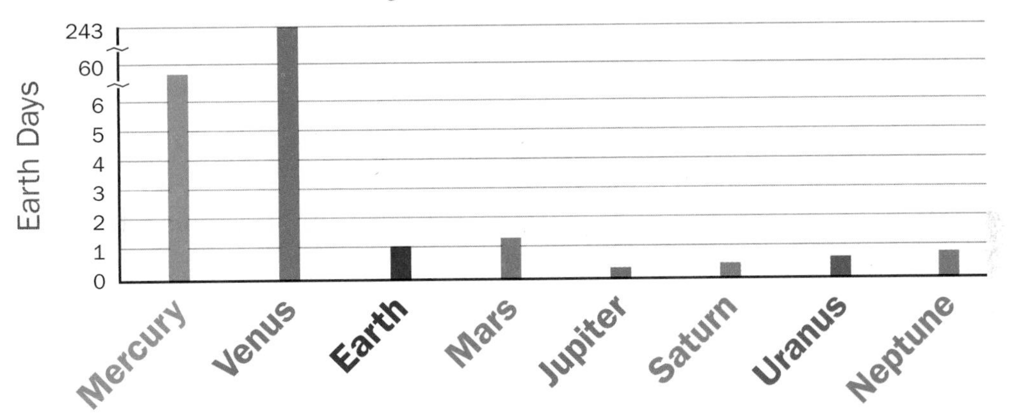

A Day on Mars

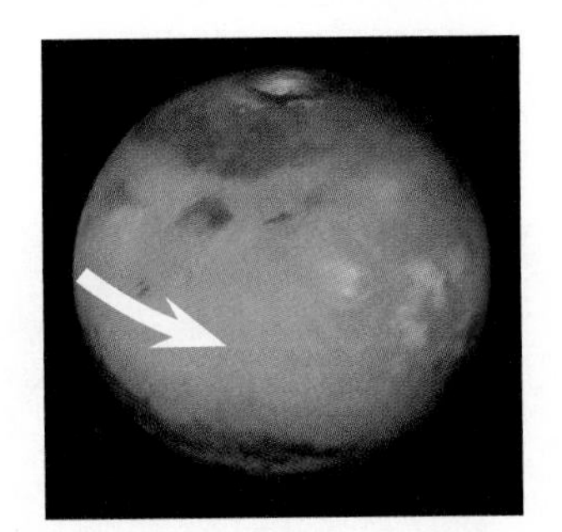

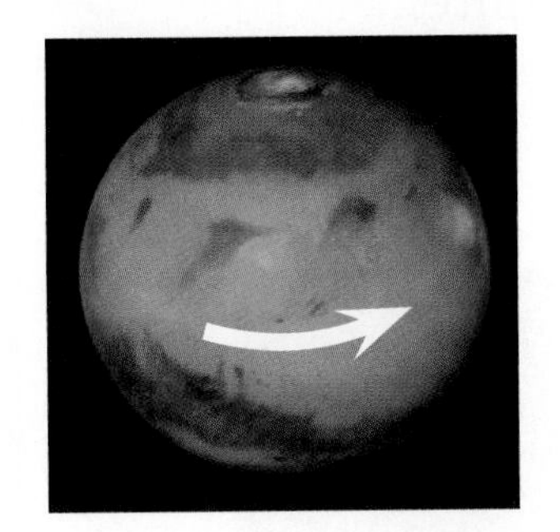

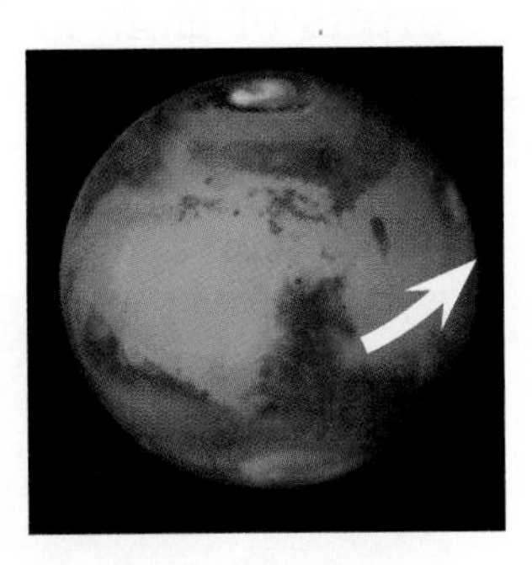

A day on Mars is just 37 minutes longer than a day on Earth.

WHY IT MATTERS

- You live on the third planet from the Sun.
- You live on one of the inner planets in the solar system.

Asteroids, Comets, and Meteors

ESSENTIAL IDEA

Objects in the solar system include asteroids, comets, and meteors.

Asteroids, comets, and meteors are small chunks of rock or ice. They formed at the same time as the solar system.

Asteroids are made of rock and metal. They orbit the Sun like planets. Most asteroids are in the **asteroid belt** between the orbits of Mars and Jupiter.

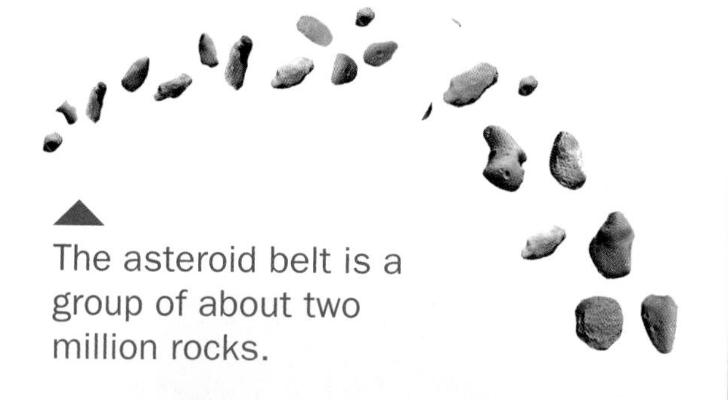

The asteroid belt is a group of about two million rocks.

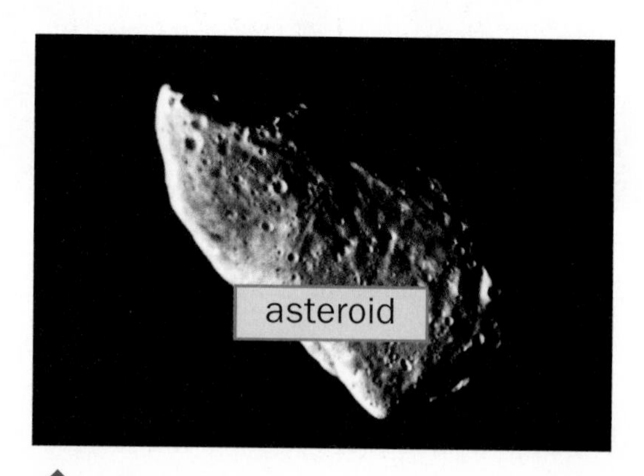

Many asteroids are small and have an irregular shape.

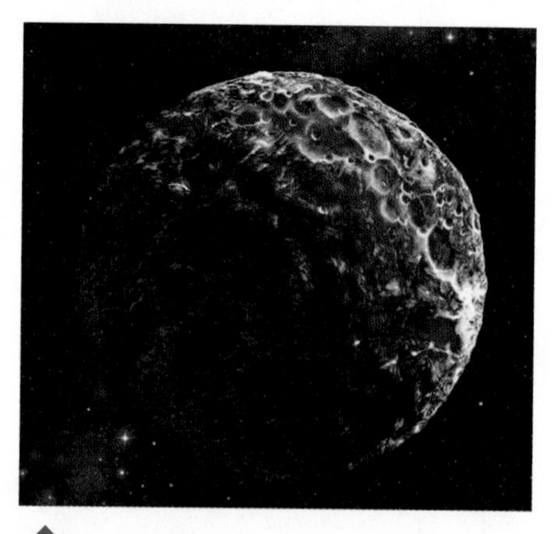

Ceres, the largest asteroid, is about 1,000 kilometers long.

Comets are chunks of ice and rock. When the comet's orbit brings it near the Sun, the heat changes some of the ice to gases. Gases and dust form a tail behind the comet.

Meteors look like streaks of light in the sky. When small bits of rock enter Earth's atmosphere, the rocks get so hot that they burn. The light you see is burning rock.

Sometimes the rocks **impact**, or hit, Earth's surface. A rock that impacts Earth this way is called a **meteorite**. When a meteorite falls, it forms a **crater** on Earth's surface.

WHY IT MATTERS

- You sometimes see meteors in the night sky.
- You may see a comet during your lifetime.

Earth and the Moon

ESSENTIAL IDEA

As the Moon revolves around Earth, you see the part of the Moon in sunlight. Phases of the Moon are the different shapes that you see.

The Moon revolves, or goes around, Earth in about a month. From Earth, you can only see the part of the Moon that receives the Sun's light. The changes you see are called the Moon's **phases**.

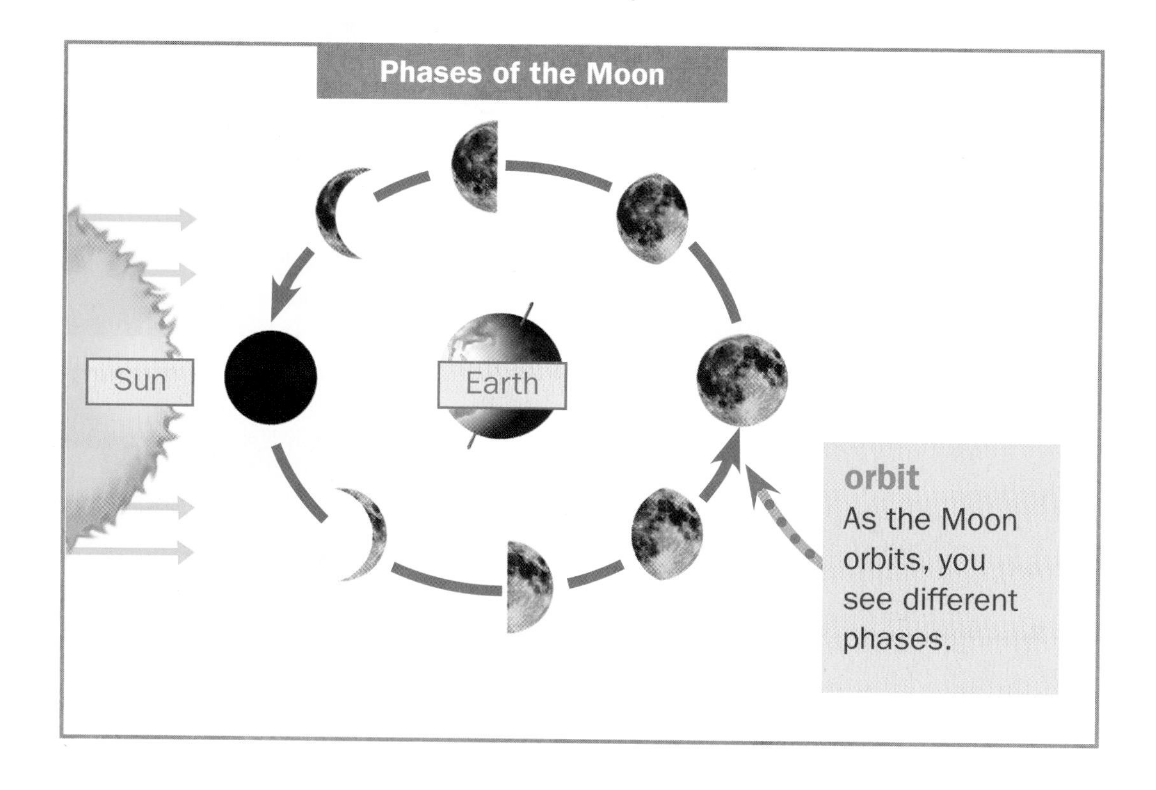

As the Moon revolves around Earth, more and more of it becomes visible. The Moon is **waxing** when you can see more of it each night.

After the full moon, the amount of the Moon that is visible gets smaller. The Moon is **waning** when you can see less of it each night. The Moon then changes from a **gibbous moon** to a quarter moon and then a **crescent moon**.

full moon

gibbous moon

quarter moon

crescent moon

WHY IT MATTERS

- You see different phases of the Moon each night.
- You can sometimes see the Moon in the daytime.

The Surface of the Moon

ESSENTIAL IDEA

You can see different features on the Moon.

Like Earth, the surface of the Moon has different features. Meteorites and ancient volcanoes created many of the Moon's features. Some of the Moon's features are **maria**, **rilles**, **highlands**, **craters**, and **rays**.

maria Lunar maria are flat plains. Maria formed when lava flowed over the surface of the Moon.

rilles Rilles are trenches or ditches across maria. Rilles may have formed when molten lava flowed along the surface of the Moon.

Moon

WHY IT MATTERS

You can see maria, craters, and highlands when you look at the Moon.

highlands Rocks in the highlands reflect more sunlight than the maria. Scientists believe that these rocks were the original lunar crust.

Earth

craters Craters formed by the impact of meteorites. The biggest crater on the Moon is more than 480 kilometers long.

rays Some craters have rays. The rays may be dust and rock that splashed out of the crater when the meteorite hit.

Life on Mars?

ESSENTIAL IDEA

Scientists have sent spacecrafts to explore Mars. They look for an answer to the question: Is there life on Mars?

Mars is the planet that is most like Earth. It is about the same size, but it is farther from the Sun. Scientists want to know if life ever existed on Mars.

Unmanned missions, or **spacecrafts** with no people, have gone to Mars. Scientists try to figure out how the Mars climate has changed. They also want to know if water existed on Mars. Scientists believe that life is more likely to exist where there is water.

This robot was sent to explore Mars.

This image of the surface of Mars is made of hundreds of pictures taken by robots.

Searching for Life

Many scientists believe there may have once been water on Mars.

Scientists call tiny spheres found on Mars "blueberries." They are made of iron. Similar objects are also in the desert of Utah. Water that once flowed in Utah left the objects behind.

The white patches dug up by the robot's wheel are salt **deposits** on Mars. On Earth, similar deposits form when water evaporates.

WHY IT MATTERS

Knowing how life could have developed on Mars can help you understand how life developed on Earth.

Galaxies

ESSENTIAL IDEA

The universe includes billions of galaxies. Each one is made up of billions of stars and the objects that revolve around them.

The **universe** is everything that exists. Look into the sky at night, and you see many stars. Some of those stars are really galaxies. **Galaxies** are clusters of millions or billions of stars. Our solar system is part of the Milky Way galaxy.

Scientists measure galaxies in **light-years**. A light-year is the distance that light travels in one year.

Milky Way Galaxy

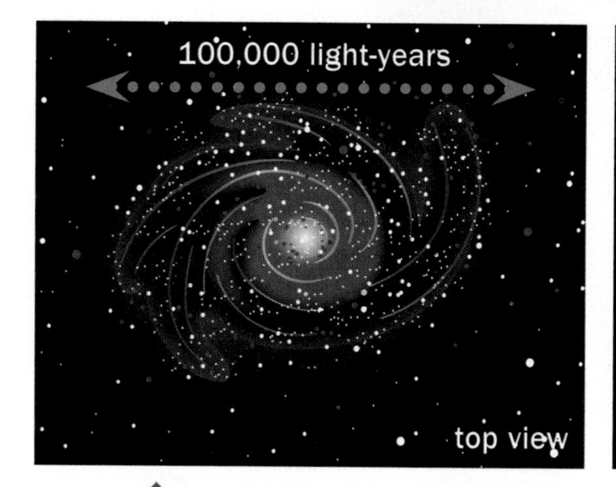

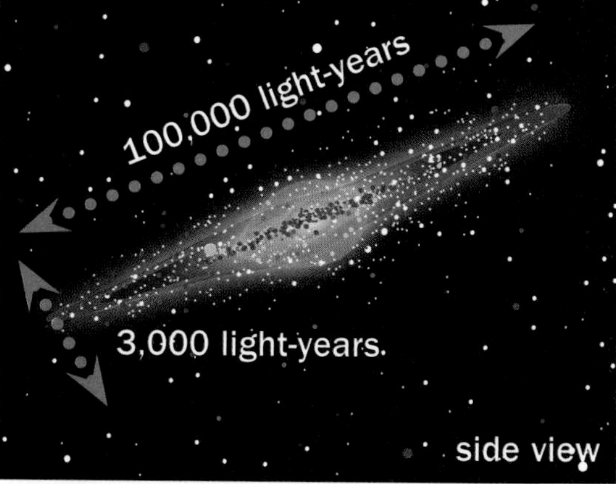

The Milky Way is 100,000 light-years long. It is 3,000 light-years thick.

Galaxies come in different shapes. The Milky Way is a **spiral galaxy**. It has a bright center. The outer parts of the spiral are made of younger stars.

This image of a spiral galaxy is made of many different pictures taken from Earth and space. Light from this galaxy took 25 million years to reach Earth.

Some galaxies look like clouds of stars. The smaller galaxies may later combine to form a large galaxy.

WHY IT MATTERS

You live on a planet in the Milky Way galaxy.

Constellations

ESSENTIAL IDEA

The stars in the night sky appear to be in groups called constellations. Ancient people named these groups and told stories about them.

When you look at the night sky, you see between 1,000 and 1,500 stars. The nearest star to the **solar system** is four **light-years** away. That means that you are seeing light that the star made four years ago!

When people look at the night sky, they see groups of stars. These groups of stars are called **constellations**.

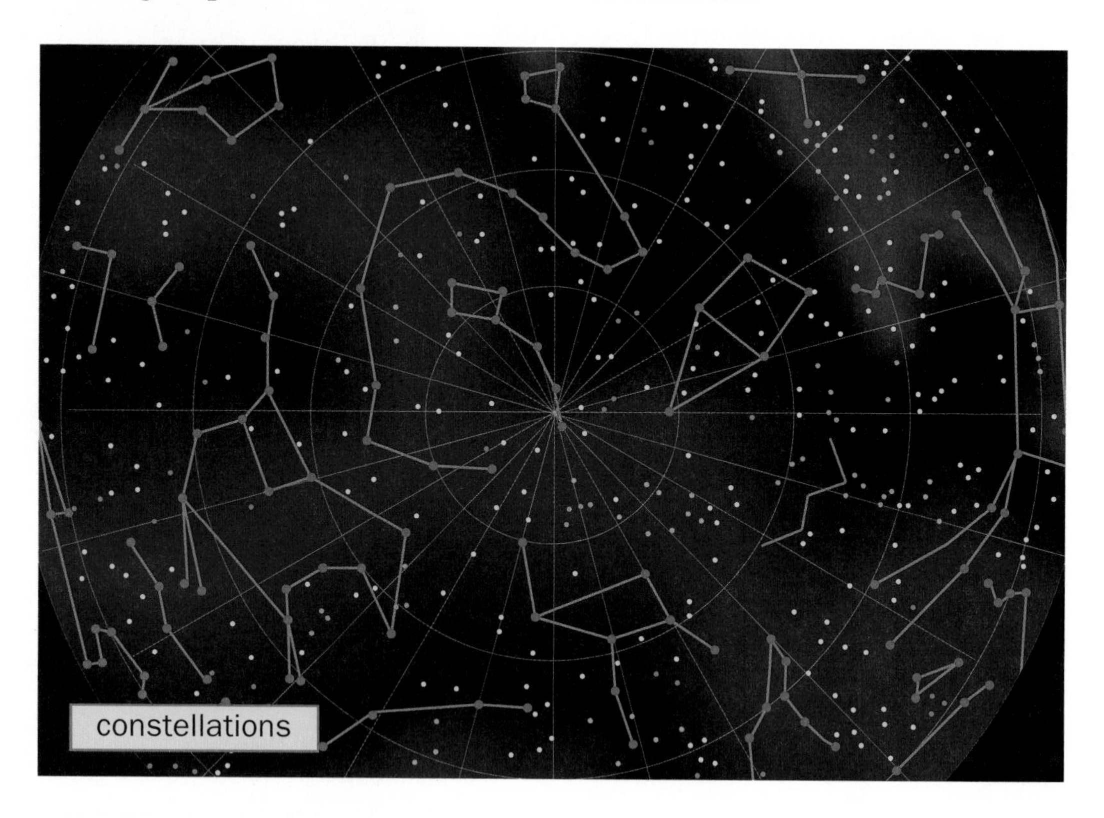

Ursa Minor Ancient people saw gods, heroes, and animals in the stars. This constellation is called Ursa Minor, which means Little Bear.

Draco Some ancient people saw this constellation as a dragon.

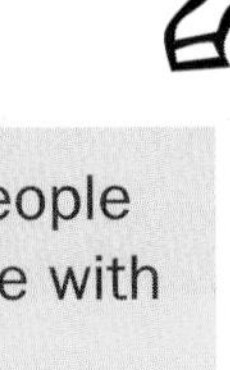

Pegasus Ancient people saw Pegasus, a horse with wings, in the stars.

WHY IT MATTERS

You can learn the names and locations of stars by recognizing constellations.

Exploring Space

ESSENTIAL IDEA

Advances in technology help scientists explore space.

Technology means using science to meet people's needs. Many new types of technology help scientists explore space. **Rockets** send **astronauts**, **spacecrafts**, and **satellites** into space.

Astronauts on the Space Shuttle *Endeavor* helped fix a broken satellite.

astronauts

Telescopes help scientists see things that are very far away. Some telescopes search the sky for radio waves.

The Hubble Space Telescope is also a satellite because it orbits Earth. The Hubble takes pictures of distant objects and sends them back to Earth.

WHY IT MATTERS

Technology helps you learn more about outer space.

Physical Science

Properties of Matter

ESSENTIAL IDEA

Matter has physical and chemical properties. You can observe physical properties with your senses.

Matter is anything that takes up space and has **mass**. All matter has **properties**, or things that help you identify it.

A **physical property** is something you observe with your senses. Some physical properties are color, shape, and texture.

Physical properties of charcoal

black color
sometimes shaped like a stick
smooth texture
breaks when you hit it
leaves black marks on paper

A **chemical property** can be seen when a substance is changed into a new substance. For example, iron changes to **rust** when it is exposed to air over a long period of time.

Rust forms because of a chemical property of iron.

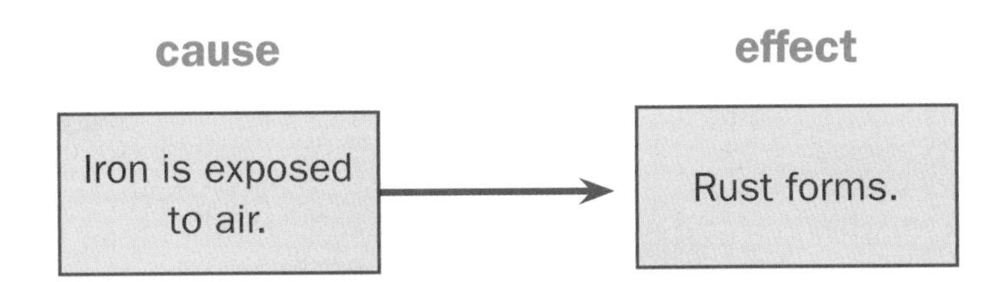

WHY IT MATTERS

- You identify things by their physical properties.
- You see the effect of a chemical property when you see rust.

PHYSICAL SCIENCE

States of Matter

ESSENTIAL IDEA

Matter exists in different states.

The **state** of matter is a physical property. Three states of matter are **solid**, **liquid**, and **gas**.

Water is unusual. It can exist in three states of matter at the same time. Snow is a solid, water is a liquid, and steam is a gas.

This picture shows water in three states of matter.

All matter is made of **particles**, or tiny pieces. In different states, particles have different amounts of motion.

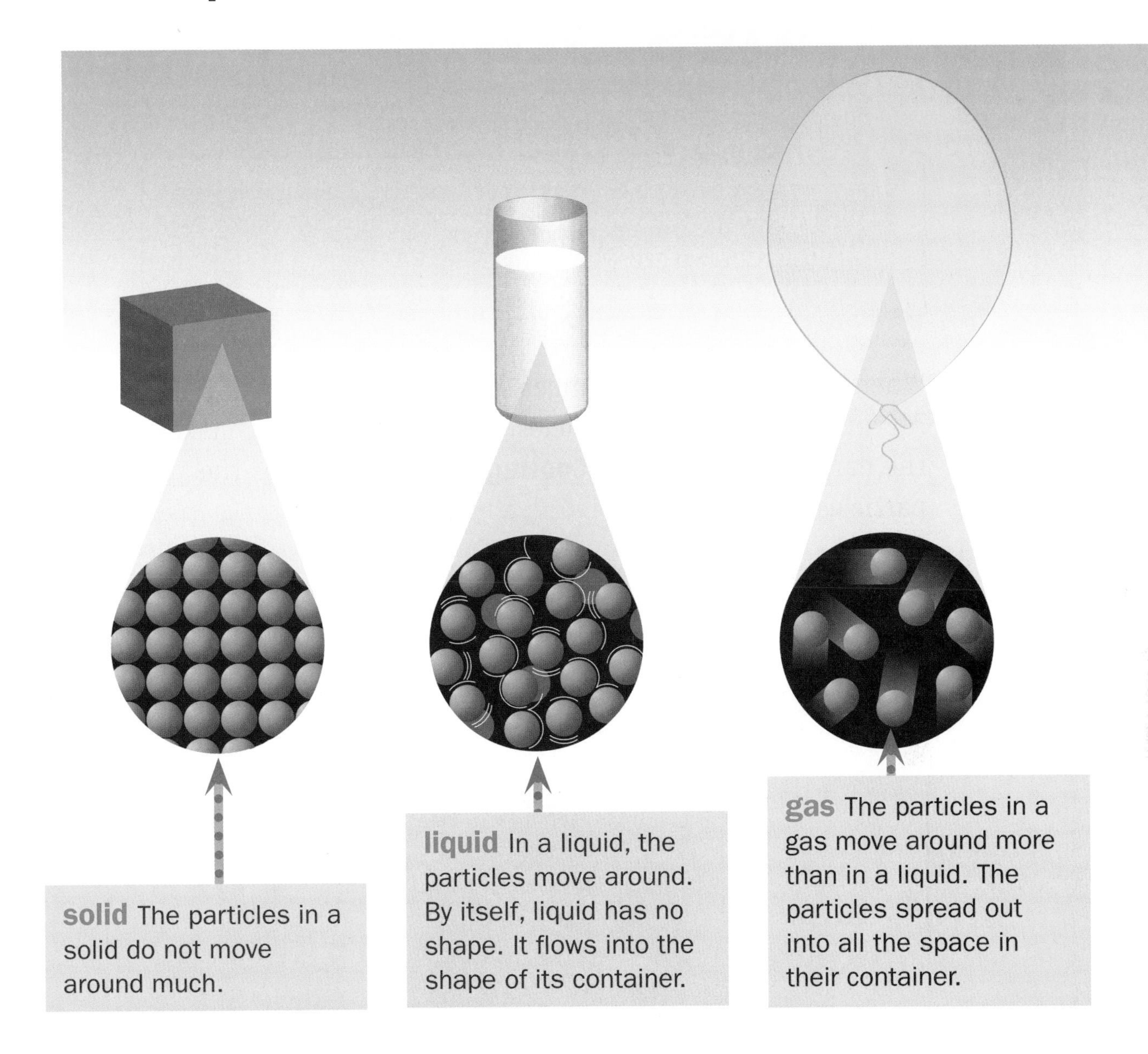

WHY IT MATTERS

All the things you eat and drink are solids and liquids.

The air you breathe is a gas.

PHYSICAL SCIENCE

How Matter Changes State

ESSENTIAL IDEA

The state of matter can change when the temperature changes.

When the temperature changes, matter changes. All matter has moving particles. **Heating** something makes the particles move faster. **Cooling** something makes the particles move slower.

How Water Changes State

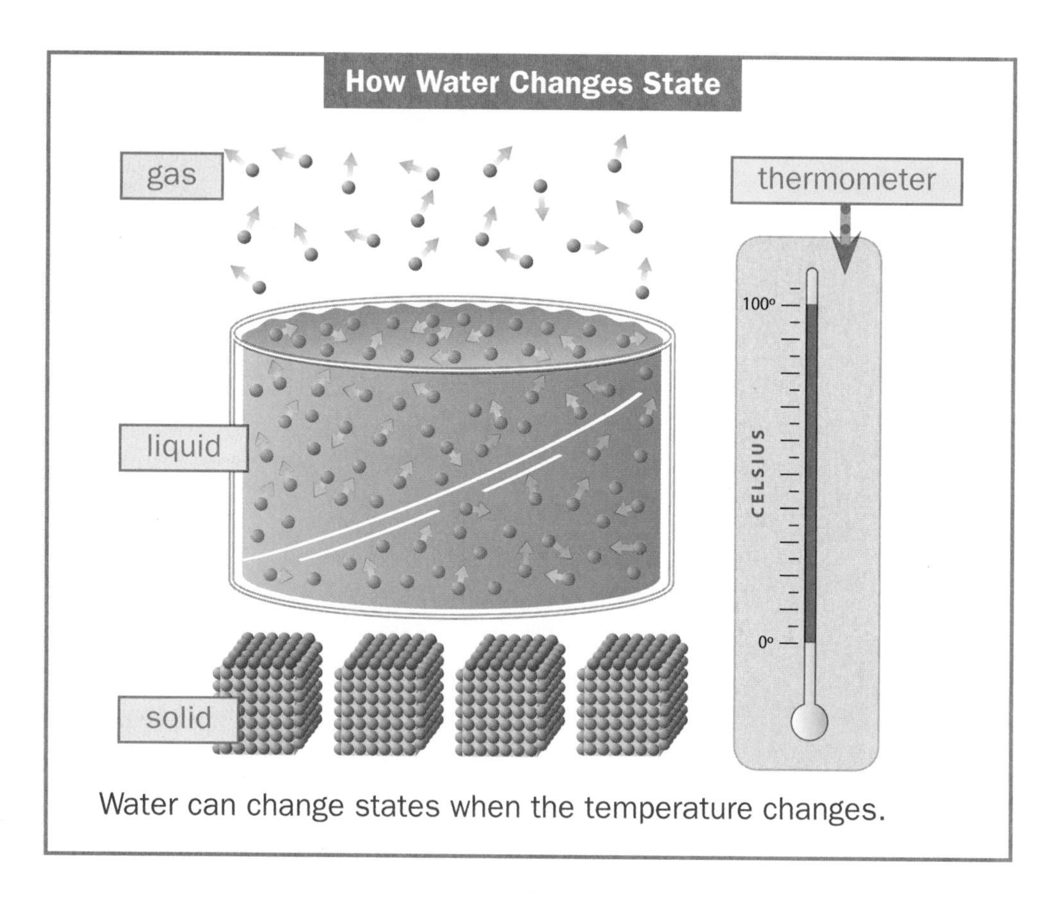

Water can change states when the temperature changes.

If a solid is heated, the particles move faster. When something melts, the particles in it break away from each other and move apart enough to become a liquid.

If a liquid is heated, the particles move faster. If the particles move fast enough, the liquid becomes a gas. The change from a liquid to a gas is called **evaporation**.

As a gas cools, the particles move slower. The gas changes into a liquid. A change from a gas to a liquid is called **condensation**. As a liquid cools, the particles slow down. The liquid freezes and becomes a solid.

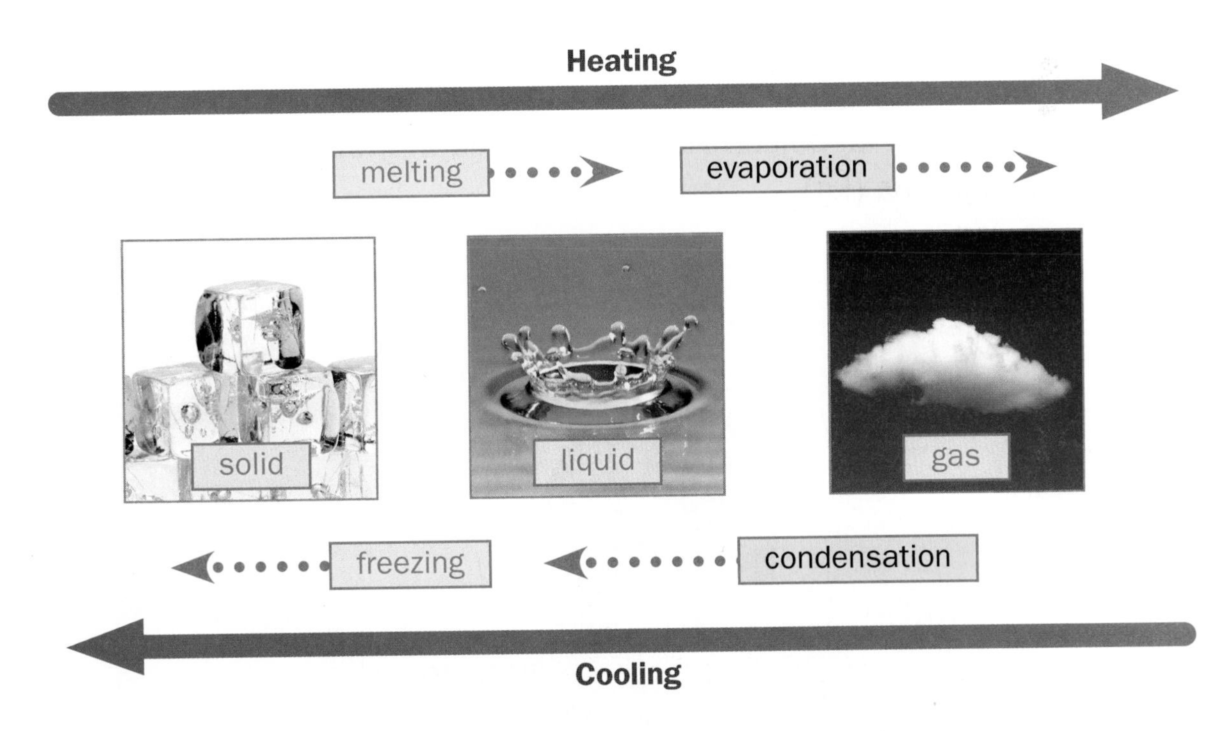

WHY IT MATTERS

You see water change its state when snow or ice melts.

When you boil water to cook food, some of the water changes to a gas.

Measuring Matter

ESSENTIAL IDEA

You can use different tools to measure physical properties of matter.

You can measure some properties, like mass, volume, and density, with tools.

Mass

You use a balance to measure the **mass**, or amount of matter, in an object. Mass is measured in **grams** (g) or **kilograms** (kg).

Volume

You sometimes have to **calculate** measurements. The **volume** of an object is how much space it **occupies**. The volume of a **rectangular solid** is length times width times height.

$$V = \ell \times W \times H$$

When you measure an object in centimeters, the volume is in cubic centimeters (cm^3 or cc).

You can measure the volume of a liquid using a measuring cup or graduated cylinder. The volume of a liquid is measured in liters (L) or milliliters (mL).

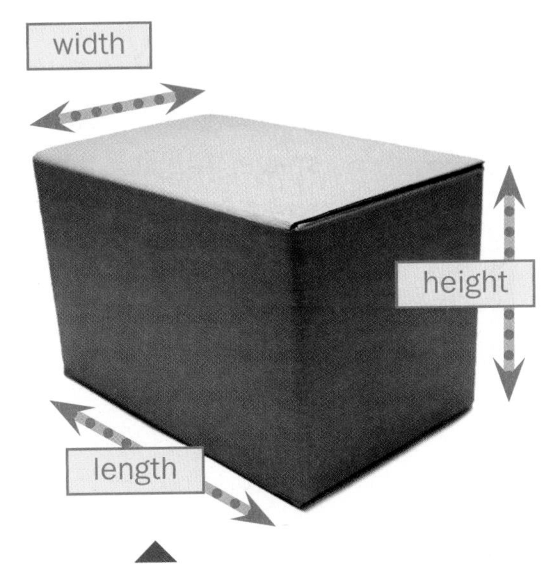

You can measure the volume of solid objects in cubic centimeters (cm^3).

You can use milliliters (mL) to measure the volume of liquids.

Density

Density is a measure of how much mass is packed in a given space. A brick has more mass packed into the same space than a wood block, so the brick has a higher density than wood. Density (D) equals mass (M) divided by volume (V).

$$D = M \div V$$

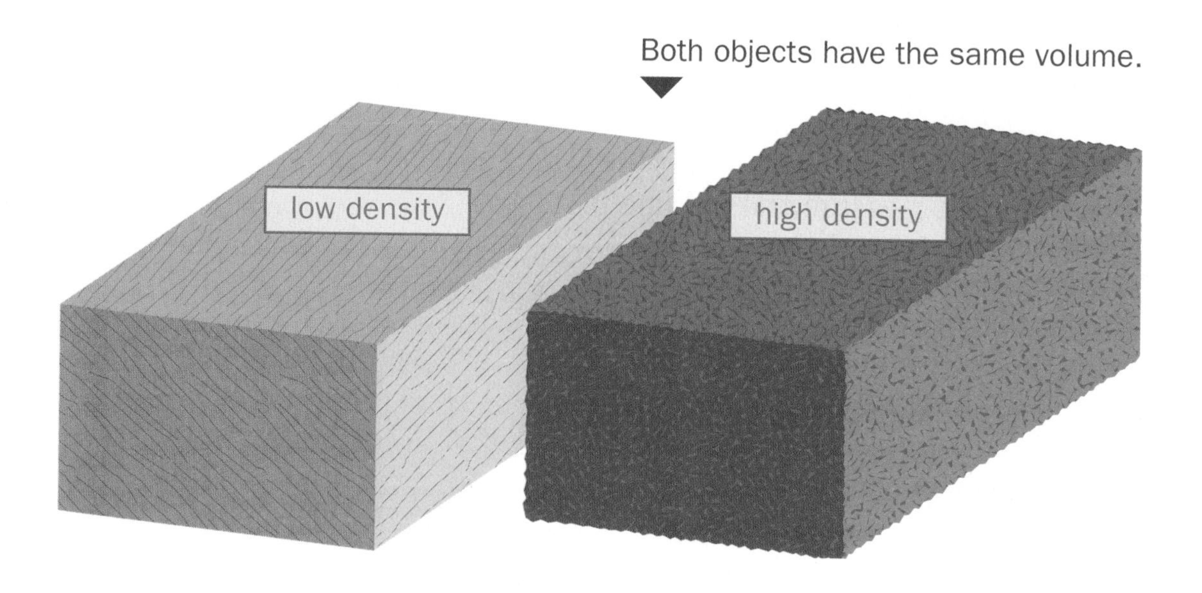

Both the brick and the wood block have a volume of 855 cm^3. The wood block has a mass of 280 grams. It has a density of .327 g/cm^3.

$$.327 = 280 \div 855$$

The brick has a mass of 2,380 grams. It has a density of 2.78 g/cm^3.

$$2.78 = 2{,}380 \div 855$$

The density of a substance determines if it will float or sink in water. Substances with a density greater than the density of water will sink. Substances with a density less than the density of water will float.

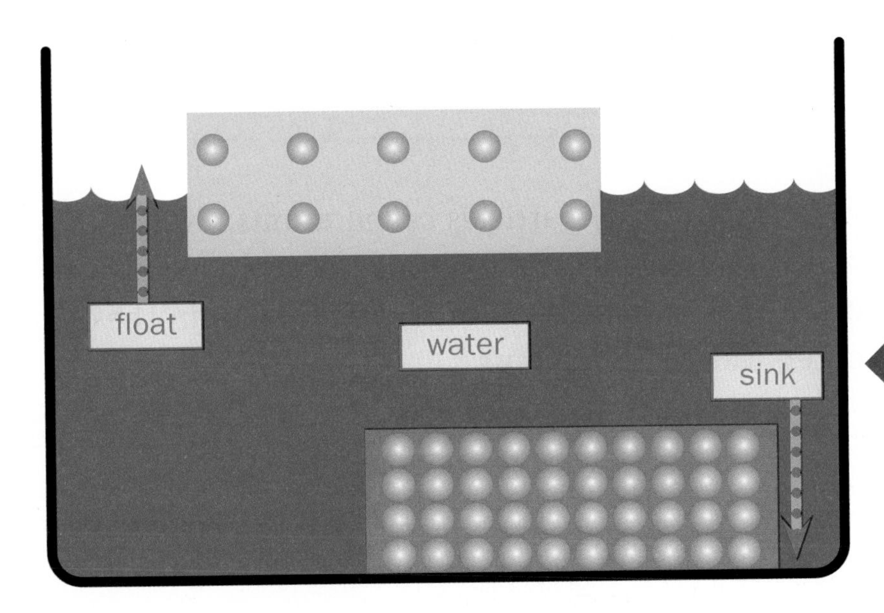

The object at the bottom has greater density. It has particles that are closer together.

Different Measures of Matter

measurement	definition
mass	amount of matter
volume	amount of filled space
density	amount of mass in a known volume

WHY IT MATTERS

- You can read the amount of matter in drinks and foods on their labels.
- You can see objects sink and float in water.

Atoms

ESSENTIAL IDEA

All matter is made up of atoms. All atoms have the same kinds of parts.

All matter is made of tiny particles called **atoms**. Every atom contains the same parts—**protons**, **neutrons**, and **electrons**. Protons and neutrons are held together in the atom's center, called the **nucleus**.

Parts of an Atom

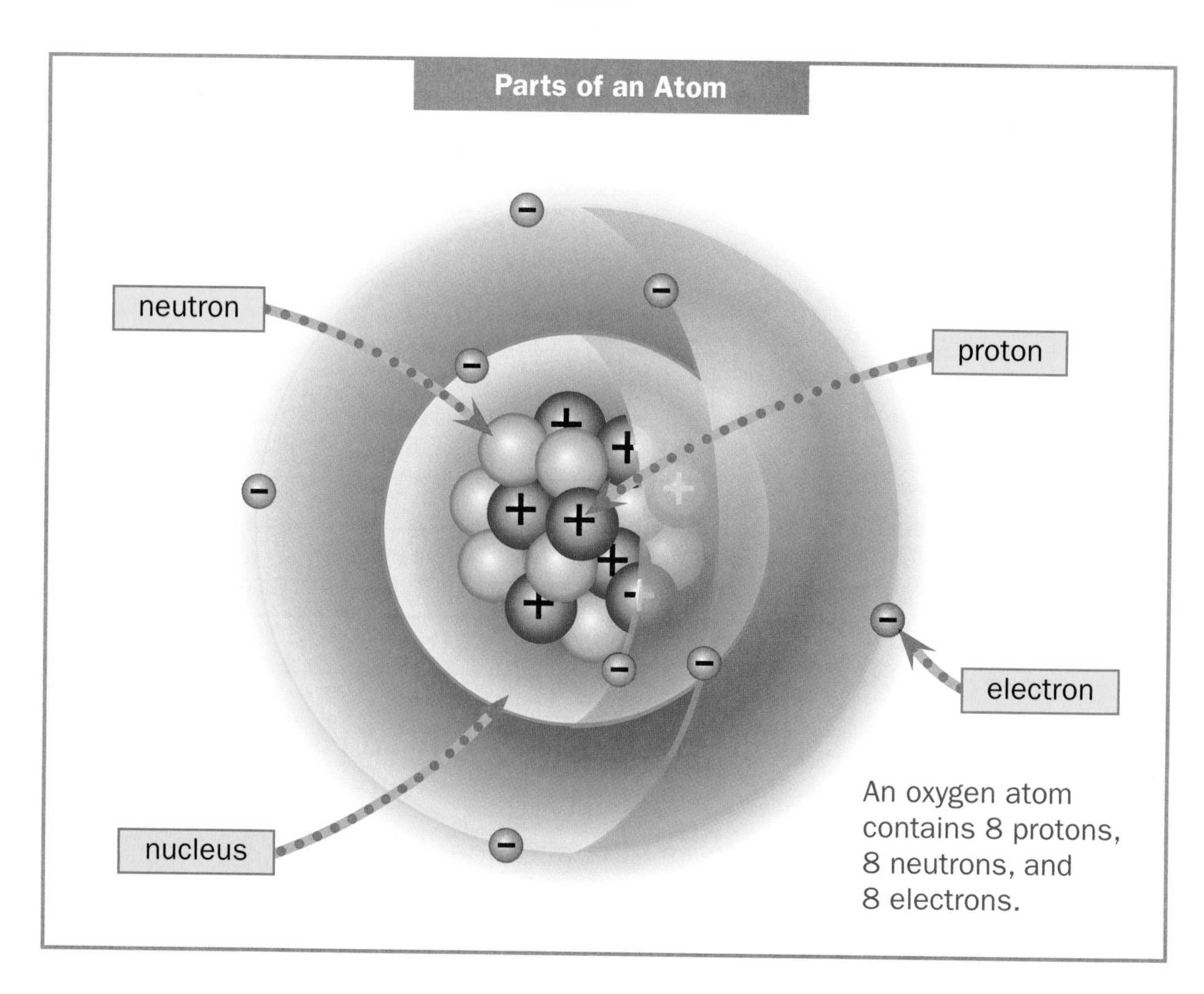

An oxygen atom contains 8 protons, 8 neutrons, and 8 electrons.

Charges in an Atom

Protons and neutrons have about the same mass. Protons have a **positive charge** (+). Neutrons have no charge.

Electrons move around the outside of the nucleus. Electrons have a **negative charge** (–) and very little mass.

part of an atom	type of charge
proton	positive charge
neutron	no charge
electron	negative charge

An oxygen atom is different from an atom of gold or an atom of iron. Different kinds of atoms have different numbers of protons, neutrons, and electrons.

WHY IT MATTERS

- You are made of atoms.
- Everything you use, see, or touch is made of atoms.

Elements

ESSENTIAL IDEA

Elements are types of matter made up of only one kind of atom.

Some substances contain only one kind of matter. They are called **pure substances**. **Elements** are the simplest kind of pure substance. They are made up of only one kind of atom. All the atoms of an element are alike.

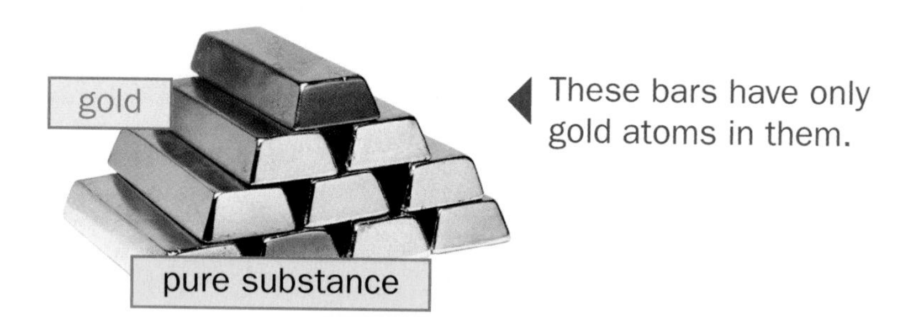

These bars have only gold atoms in them.

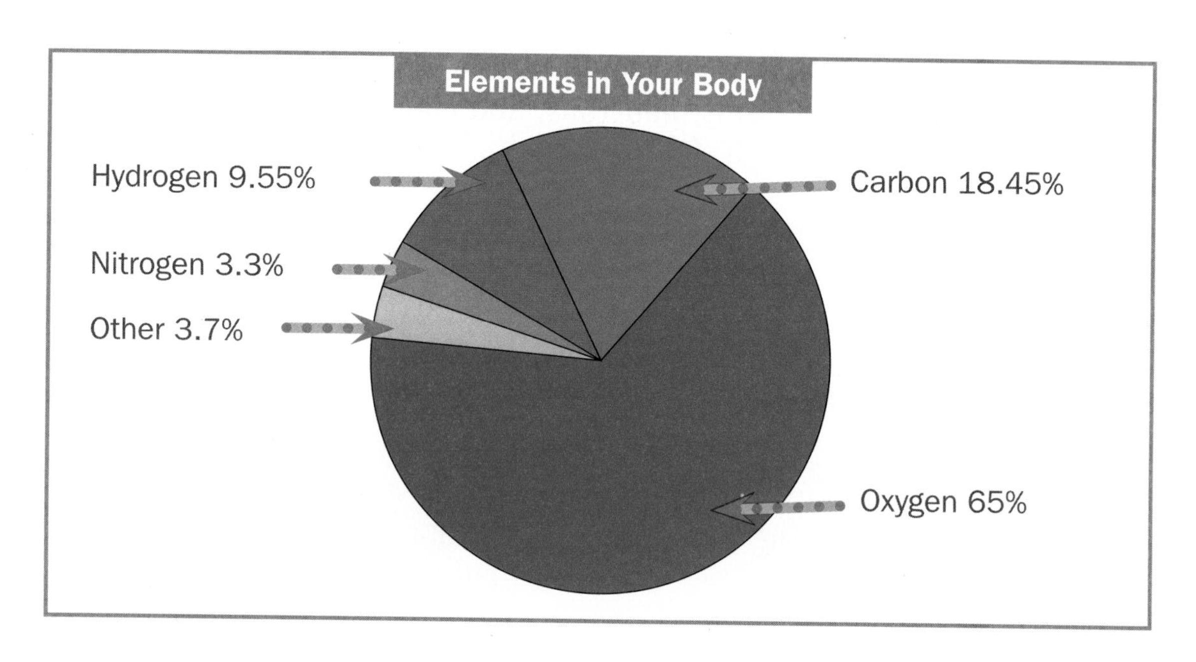

Symbols are often used instead of the name of the element. Each element has its own symbol.

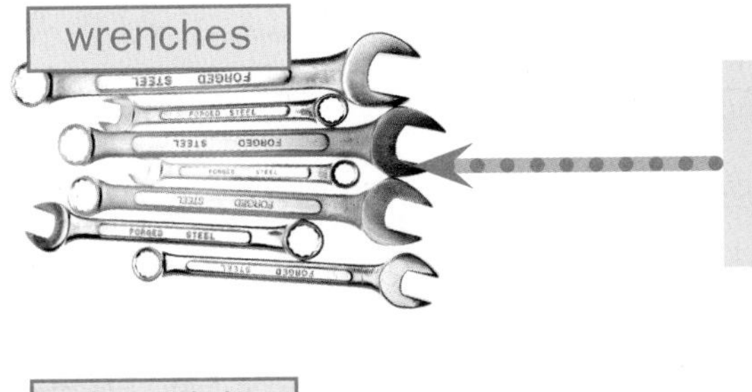

Fe The symbol for iron is Fe. Iron is used to make steel.

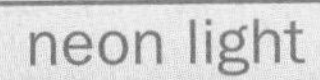

Ne The symbol for neon is Ne. Neon is a gas that glows in clear tubes.

He The symbol for helium is He. Helium is a gas that makes balloons rise.

WHY IT MATTERS

- Everything you touch is made of elements.
- Oxygen is an element from air that you breathe to stay alive.

PHYSICAL SCIENCE

Metals

ESSENTIAL IDEA

Most of the elements are metals.

Metals are elements that have many properties in common. They usually have a higher density than other elements.

Most metals are good **conductors** of heat and electricity. Conductors allow heat and electricity to pass through them easily.

Metals are used to make pots and pans. The metal allows heat to reach the food and cook it.

Most metals have a **luster**, or shininess. Gold and silver are metals. Because of their luster, people throughout history have worn metals as jewelry.

Some metals change when they are exposed to air for a while. Metals like silver **tarnish**, or form a dark coating. Other metals, like iron, **rust**.

WHY IT MATTERS

- You use objects that are made of metal, like paper clips and coins.
- Cars you ride in contain a lot of different metals.

PHYSICAL SCIENCE

Compounds

ESSENTIAL IDEA

In nature, most elements combine with other elements to form compounds.

A **compound** is a substance made of two or more elements. Water is a compound. The elements hydrogen and oxygen combine to form the compound water.

Chemical **bonds** hold the elements together. A **molecule** is the smallest unit of compounds such as water.

The compound water is a liquid.

A **formula** is used to represent the **composition** of a compound. Compounds always have the same composition, or number and kinds of atoms. The formula shows which elements are in the compound. It also shows how many atoms of each element are in it.

Water's Formula

Every water molecule has two atoms of hydrogen (H) and one atom of oxygen (O). The formula for water is H_2O.

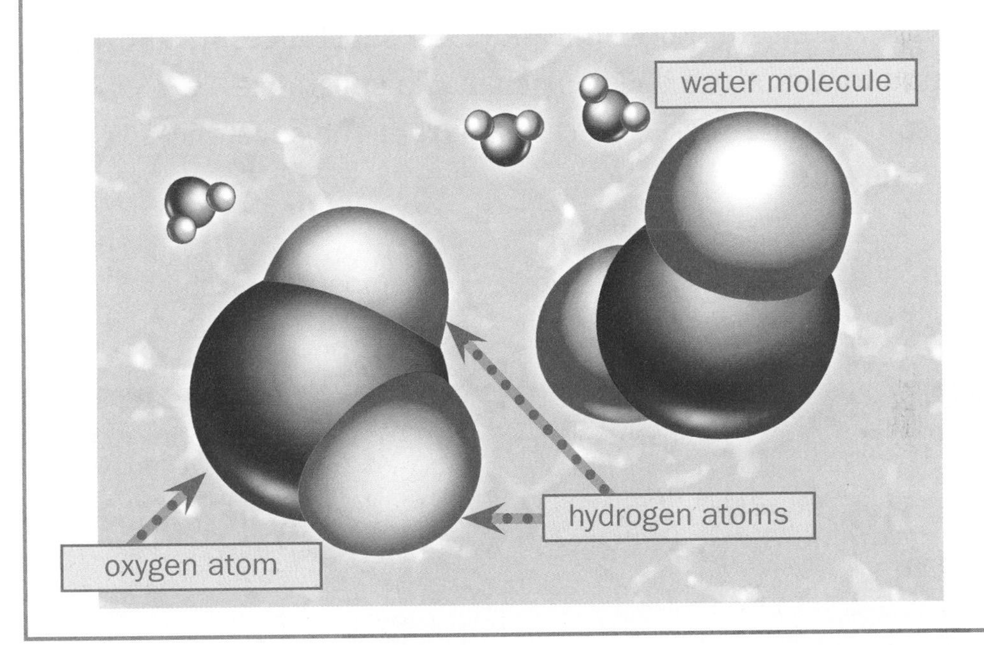

WHY IT MATTERS

- Your body is made up of many different compounds.
- Your body uses many compounds, such as water and sugar.

Mixtures and Solutions

ESSENTIAL IDEA

A mixture is made of two or more substances. A solution is a special mixture in which one substance is evenly spread in another substance.

A **mixture** contains two or more substances. You can see the different substances in some mixtures.

Soil is a mixture. Rocks and sand are substances in soil. Being in a mixture does not change a substance—a rock in soil is still a rock. You can **separate** the substances in a mixture.

You can use properties, such as color or size, to separate a mixture.

A **solution** is a mixture that looks like one substance. One of the substances in a solution is evenly spread in the other and cannot be seen. When salt **dissolves** in water, it seems to disappear.

Even though a solution looks like one substance, you can separate the substances in a solution. For example, if you boil a solution of salt water, the water will boil away and leave the salt in the pan.

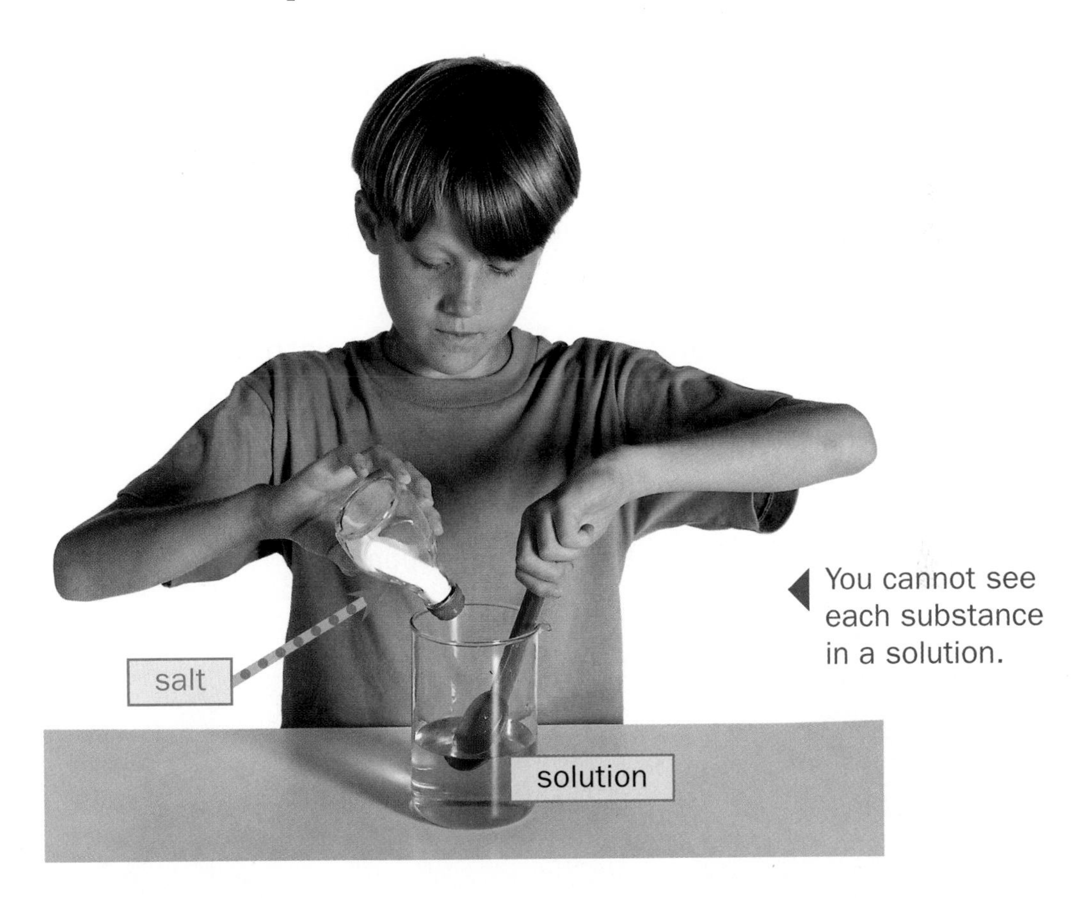

You cannot see each substance in a solution.

WHY IT MATTERS

- Your body is a mixture of many different substances.
- You make a solution when you make lemonade.

PHYSICAL SCIENCE

How Matter Reacts Chemically

ESSENTIAL IDEA

In chemical reactions, new substances form.

Elements can combine to make compounds. Compounds can also break apart to form elements or other compounds. A **chemical reaction** takes place when bonds are made or broken. When matter **reacts**, or changes chemically, new substances form.

The elements or compounds you start with in a chemical reaction are called **reactants**. The substances that form during the reaction are called **products**.

Fire is a chemical reaction.

Chemical Reactions

1 Reactants change into products. Products have properties that reactants do not have.

Baking soda is a powder. Vinegar is a liquid. When you mix them, they react. A gas is produced.

2 Heat and light are sometimes produced in a chemical reaction.

When the elements in fireworks react with oxygen in the air, they make different colors of light.

WHY IT MATTERS

- Your body burns food to produce heat that keeps you warm.
- Chemical reactions happen when you cook food.

Force

ESSENTIAL IDEA

A force is a push or a pull on something. Forces have both strength and direction.

A **force** is a push or a pull. The wind pushes the leaves of trees. Earth and the Moon pull on each other. You push on the pedals of your bicycle. These are all forces.

When you **exert** a force on an object, you use energy. **Energy** is the ability to change something. Forces can move or change the shape of an object.

Forces

Forces pull in different directions.

The skier feels many forces. The boat pulls the skier forward. Gravity pulls him down. The water pushes him up. Air pushes against him.

A force has both a strength and a direction. The strength of a force is measured in a unit called a **newton** (N). Forces are often shown as arrows. The length of the arrow shows the strength of a force. The arrow points in the direction of the force.

When an object is **stationary**, or not moving, all the forces are **balanced**, or equal.

The forces are equal in strength, but opposite in direction. The forces are balanced, so the students are not moving.

WHY IT MATTERS

- You use forces to move or change objects.
- The wind you feel is a force.

Gravity

ESSENTIAL IDEA

Gravity is the force that makes objects pull toward each other.

Gravity is a force that makes objects **attract**, or pull toward, each other. Gravity keeps the Moon in orbit around Earth.

The strength of the **gravitational force** depends on the masses of the objects and the distance between them. As the mass of the objects increases, the attraction increases.

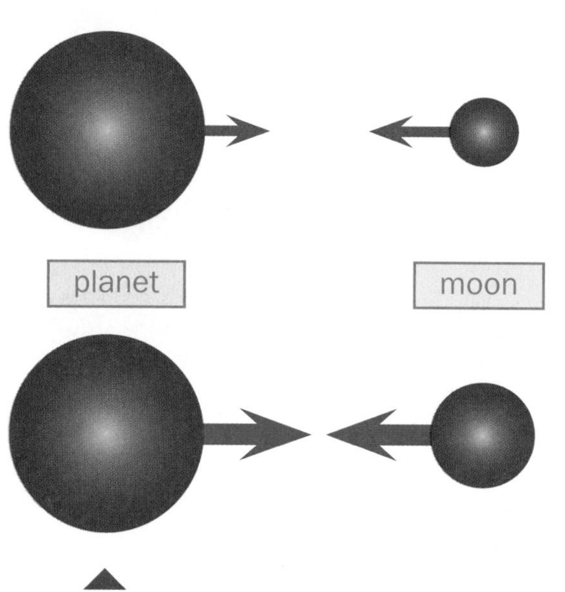

Bigger planets and moons have more gravitational force.

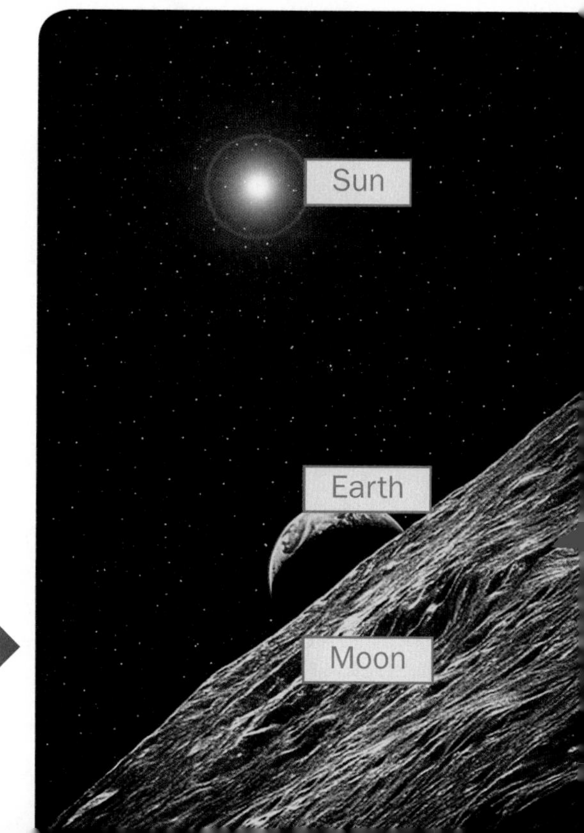

The Sun has more mass than the Earth. Earth has more mass than the Moon.

As objects get farther apart, the attraction decreases.

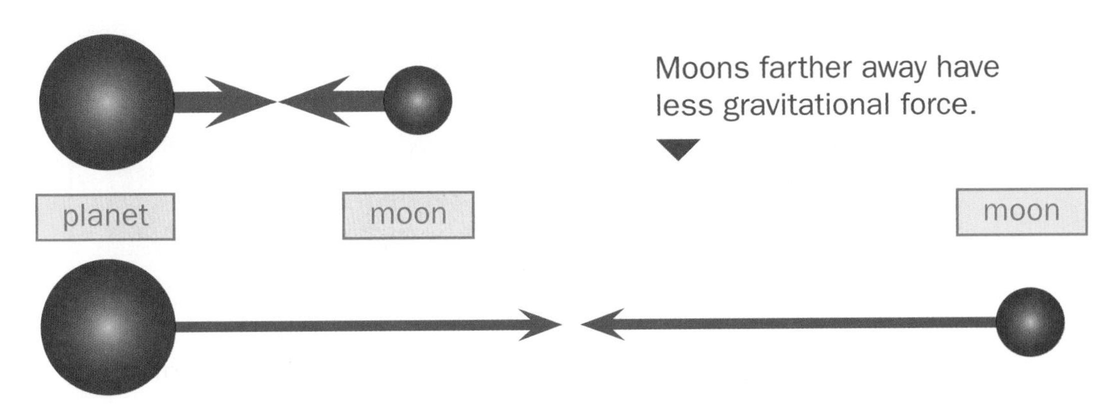

Moons farther away have less gravitational force.

Weight measures the force of gravity on an object. Astronauts in the Space Shuttle are so far away from Earth that they don't feel Earth's gravity.

Astronauts have very little weight in space.

WHY IT MATTERS

- The force of gravity holds you on the surface of Earth.
- When you throw a ball into the air, gravity makes it fall back to Earth.

Friction

ESSENTIAL IDEA

Friction is a force that slows the movement of objects. Wheels are used to reduce friction.

Friction is a force that **resists**, or works against, the motion of objects. To push something across a surface, the force of the push must be greater than the force of friction.

A **rough** surface, like gravel, has more friction than a **smooth** surface, like ice. Also, a heavier object has more friction than a lighter object. You need to push harder to move an object across a rough surface or to move a heavy object.

To move a couch, you push against the force of friction.

Working with Friction

Wheels or rollers make it easier to move something across a surface. As an object is pushed across rollers, there is less friction. People can move very heavy objects by using wheels or rollers.

Wheels and rollers decrease friction.

Sometimes friction helps you. The brakes on your bicycle apply friction to help you stop.

Brakes increase friction.

WHY IT MATTERS

- Using wheels makes it easier for you to move things.
- Friction keeps you from falling down when you walk.

Motion

ESSENTIAL IDEA

Motion is a change in position of an object.

Something is in **motion** when it changes **position**, or location. You see the motion of an object from your **frame of reference**.

For example, if you are standing on a street, you can see a bus move past you. If you are riding on a bus, you see things outside the window move past you.

Your frame of reference depends on your position, or where you are.

Objects can move in more than one direction at the same time. When you hit a softball, the ball moves up into the air. The ball also moves away from you. Each motion is separate. The ball looks like it travels in a curve.

WHY IT MATTERS

- You see and react to motion all the time.
- When you run, walk, and bike, you are in motion.

PHYSICAL SCIENCE

Speed

ESSENTIAL IDEA

Speed is the change of position over time.

A **rate** is a measurement of how much something changes over time. **Speed** is a rate. Speed measures how far something moves over time. In other words, speed measures how fast something moves.

In a race, the person with the fastest time wins.

You need to measure two things to figure out speed (S): the **distance** (D) an object moves and the time (T) it takes to go that distance. To find the speed, you divide the distance by the time.

$$S = D \div T$$

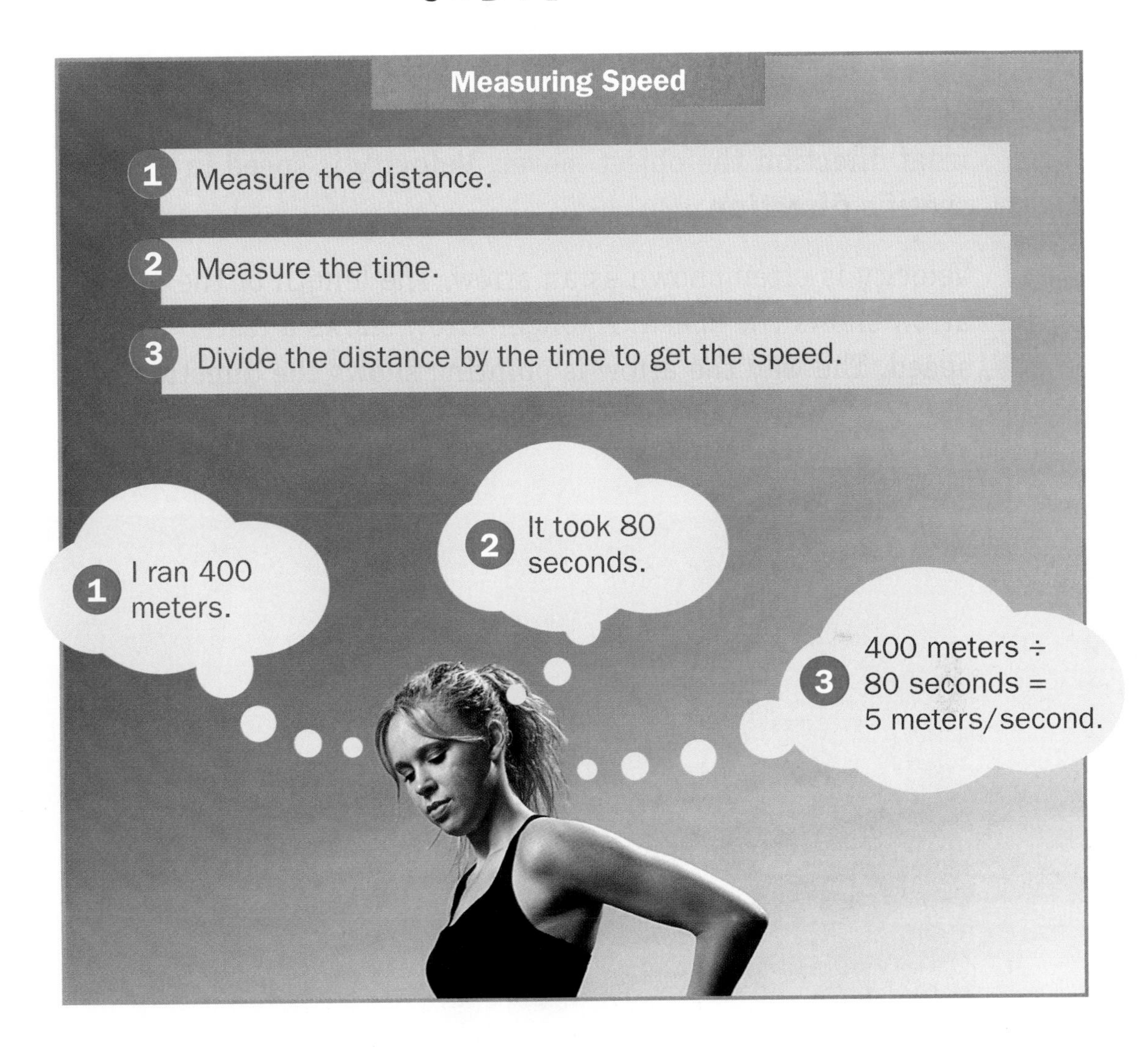

WHY IT MATTERS

You usually walk, run, or bike at different speeds.

Velocity

ESSENTIAL IDEA

Velocity is speed in a specific direction.

Speed tells how fast something moves. Speed does not tell what direction the object moves. **Velocity** is speed in a specific **direction**.

Velocity is often shown as an arrow. The length of the arrow shows the speed. A longer arrow shows a faster speed. The way the arrow is pointing shows the direction.

The arrows show that the cheetah is moving to the right and the rocket is moving up. The rocket has a faster speed.

Velocity and Direction

One car travels at a speed of 50 miles per hour to the west. A second car travels at a speed of 50 miles per hour to the east. Both cars have the same speed, but they have different velocities because they are traveling in different directions.

This car is traveling 50 mph west.

This car is traveling 50 mph east.

WHY IT MATTERS

Your velocity changes as you ride in a bus or car.

Changes in Motion

ESSENTIAL IDEA

Objects that are not moving will stay that way until a force acts on them. Forces can change the way an object moves.

Force is needed to change motion. Without force, an object that is moving will keep moving. An object that is at rest, or not moving, will stay at rest. An object that is moving at a constant speed or is at rest has **inertia**.

The soccer ball is at rest. The ball will move when the player kicks it.

As objects move, their velocity often changes. Objects can move faster, move slower, or change direction. **Acceleration** is a rate that measures change in velocity—that is, any change in speed or direction.

Acceleration and Velocity

When you ride a roller coaster, you accelerate a lot. You move faster when you go down. You move slower when you go up. Your velocity also changes when you go around curves.

WHY IT MATTERS

- You accelerate when you go downhill or make a turn on a bike.
- In science, you accelerate any time you speed up, slow down, or change direction.

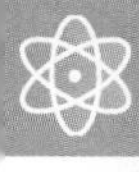

PHYSICAL SCIENCE

Work

ESSENTIAL IDEA

Work is the use of a force to move an object through a distance.

In science, **work** means using force and making something move or change. If something does not move or change, there was no work.

When the basketball player applies a force to the ball, the ball will move through a distance.

When the students are holding phones, they are not moving the phones so there is no work.

Work and Applied Force

Work is done when there is **movement** in the same direction as the **applied force**.

work The student is doing work against gravity. The force she applies to lift the books is in the same direction as the movement of the books.

no work The student does no work against gravity when she holds the books. The books are not moving.

WHY IT MATTERS

- You do work whenever you lift something.
- You do not do work when you push or pull something that does not move.

PHYSICAL SCIENCE

Measuring Work

ESSENTIAL IDEA

You can measure the amount of work applied to an object.

Work is done when a **force** moves an object. You can measure work. You need to know how much force is applied. You also need to know the **distance** the object moved. Then you multiply the force times the distance to measure the amount of work.

Work = Force × Distance

Measuring Work

When you climb stairs, you do work to overcome gravity. It could take a force of 500 newtons to climb a height of 2 meters. That amount of work would measure 1,000 joules.

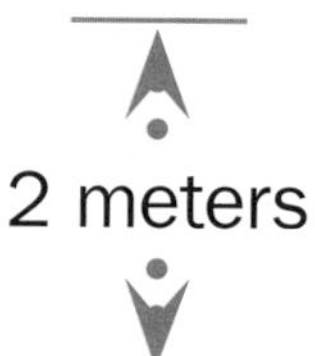

Whether you run or walk up the stairs, the work done is the same. In science, **power** describes how much work is done in a certain time. Power equals work divided by time.

Power = Work ÷ Time

Measuring Power

The amount of work is 1,000 joules whether you walk or run 2 meters. It takes 4 seconds to walk and 2 seconds to run. You use 250 watts of power when you walk and 500 watts when you run.

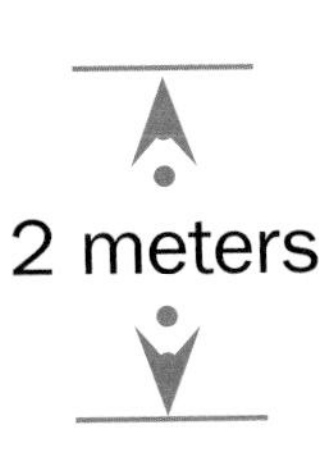

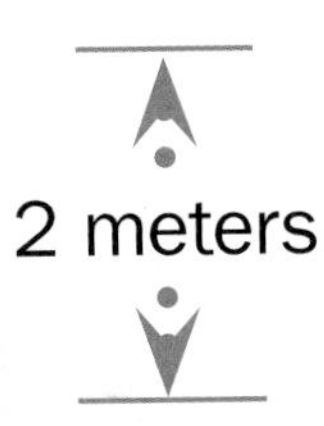

WHY IT MATTERS

- You do the same amount of work whether you walk or run to school.
- You use more power if you run rather than walk.

Simple Machines

ESSENTIAL IDEA

Simple machines make work easier.

You do work when you apply force to an object and the object moves. **Machines** change the size or the direction of a force. Some machines change both size and direction. The amount of work remains the same.

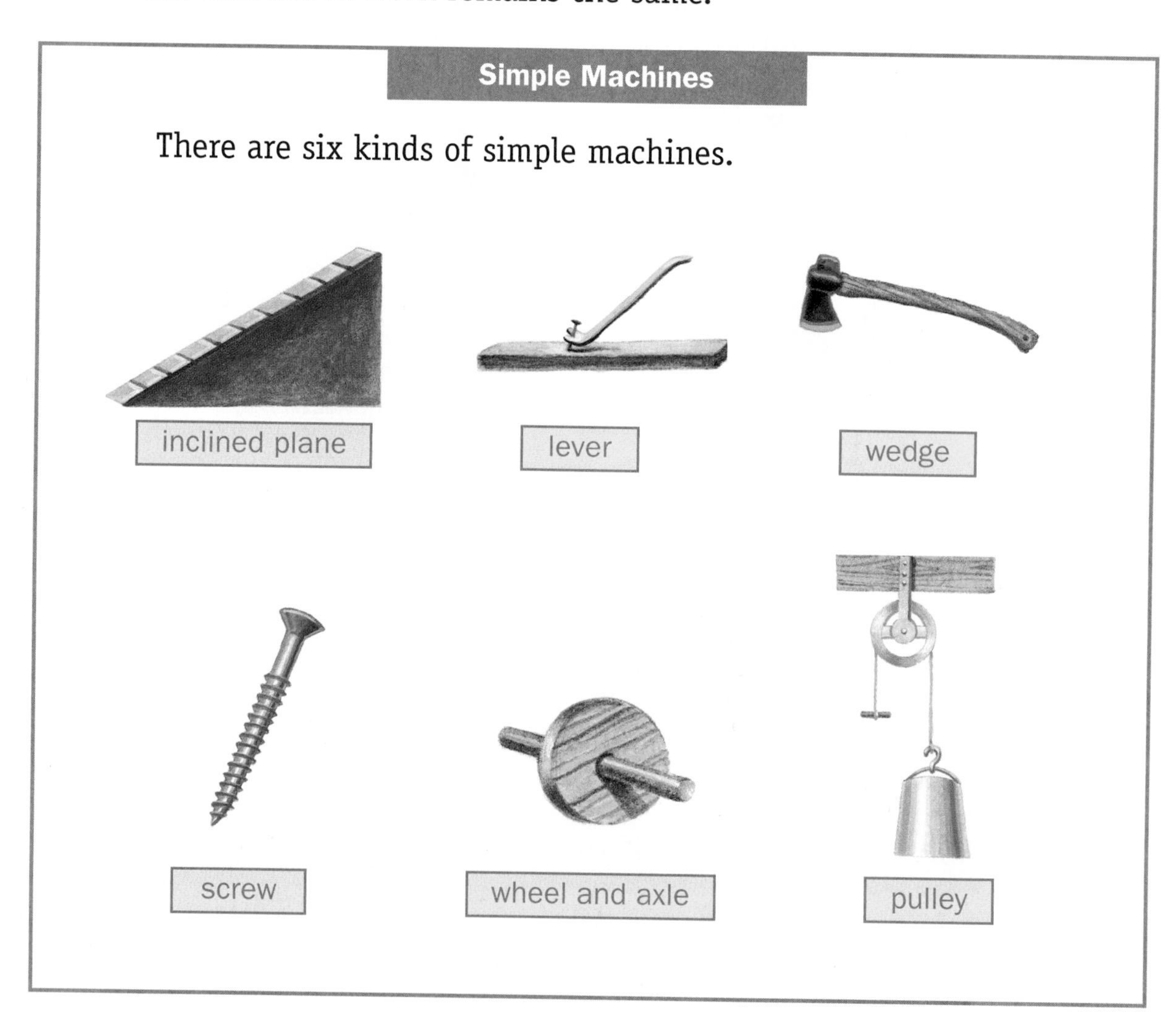

How Simple Machines Work

A bottle opener is an example of one kind of simple machine called a lever.

When you pull the handle, you move the handle farther than if you pull the cap. You apply force over a greater distance, but you use less force.

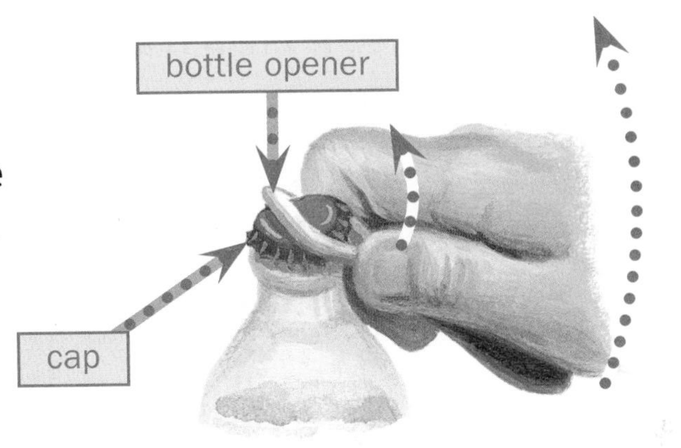

When you use a machine, there are always two forces. The force you apply is called the **effort force**. The force you try to overcome is called the **resistance force**.

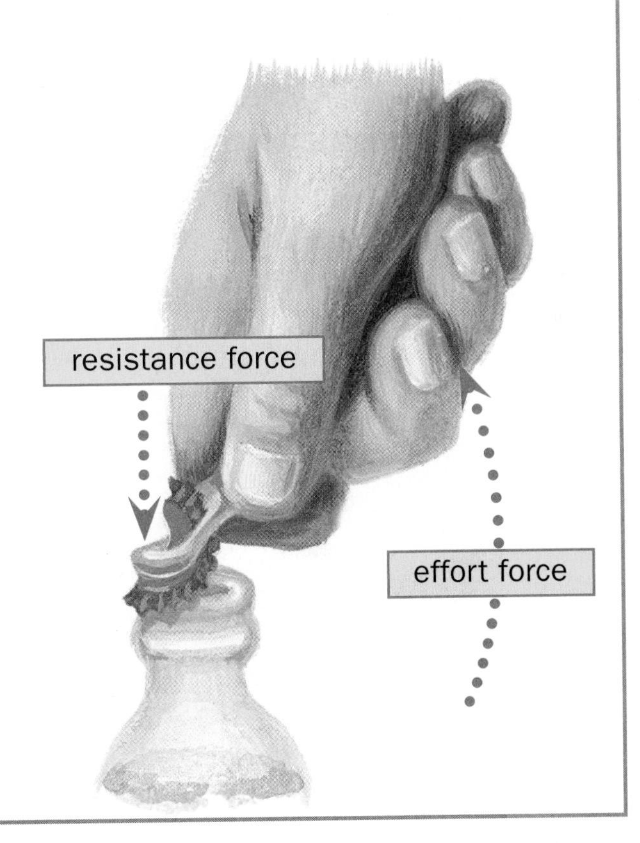

Inclined Plane

A **plane** is a flat surface. An **inclined** plane is a flat surface that is slanted, or angled. The inclined plane makes it easier to move objects from a lower level to a higher level. A **ramp** is an inclined plane that people use every day.

It is easier for wheelchairs and scooters to move up ramps than to move up stairs.

It is easier to push a heavy object up an inclined plane than to lift it onto the truck.

An inclined plane makes work easier by increasing distance and decreasing force. You have to move an object farther, but you do not have to use as much force.

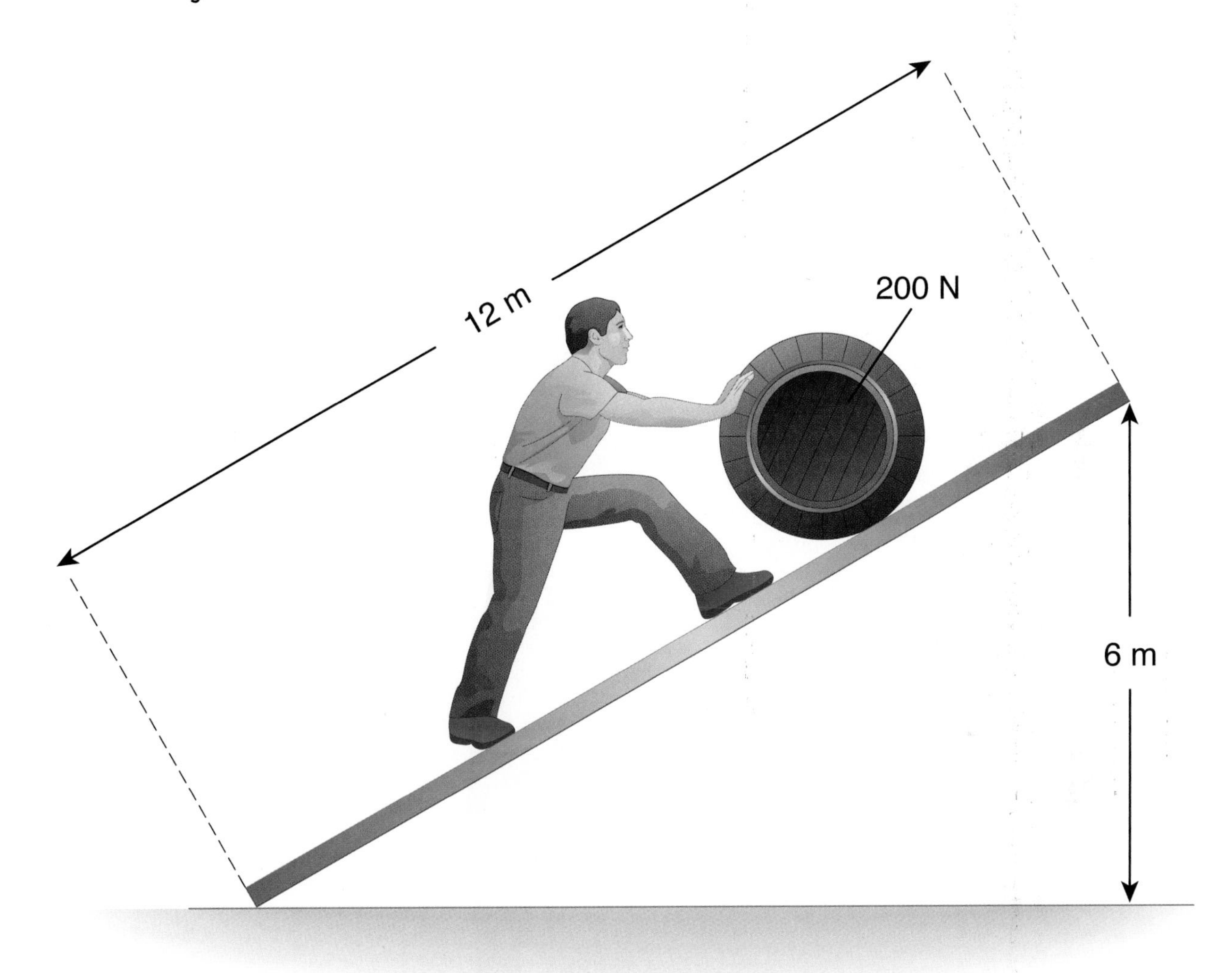

Rolling something a long distance is easier than lifting something a short distance.

Wedge

A **wedge** is an inclined plane that helps push or hold things apart. Many wedges are used to separate or cut something.

A wedge is thin at one end. The effort force is applied to the wide end. The force moves from the wide to the thin end. The wedge **multiplies** the force by moving a large force to a small surface.

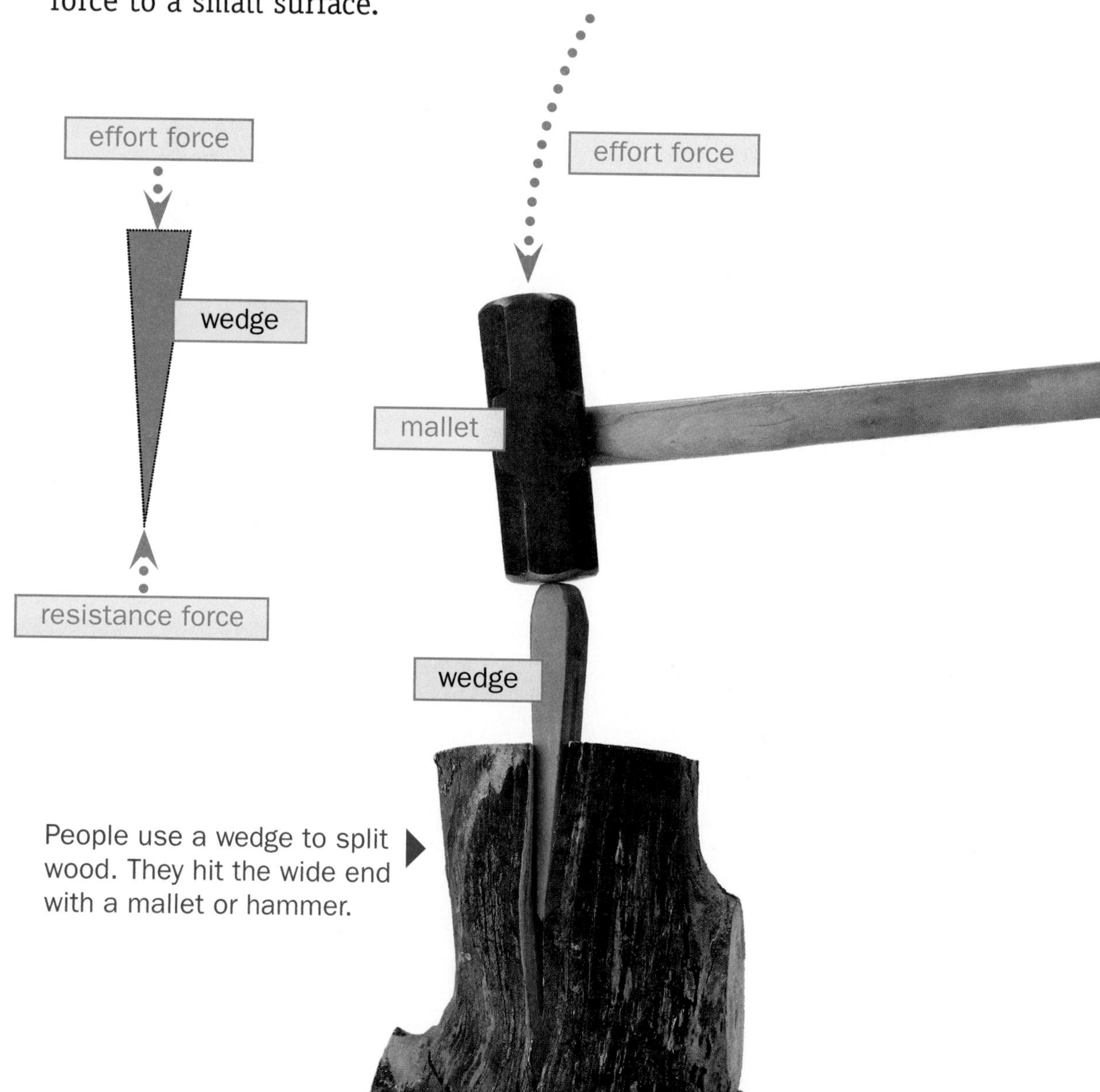

People use a wedge to split wood. They hit the wide end with a mallet or hammer.

Types of Wedges

Long ago people used stone to make arrowheads and spear points.

Pins and thumbtacks are sharp, pointed wedges.

Wedges can be used to keep cars or airplanes from rolling.

Chisels are wedges. They are used to cut and shape things.

Screw

If you could look closely at a **screw**, it would look like an inclined plane. A screw is an inclined plane wrapped around a **cylinder**.

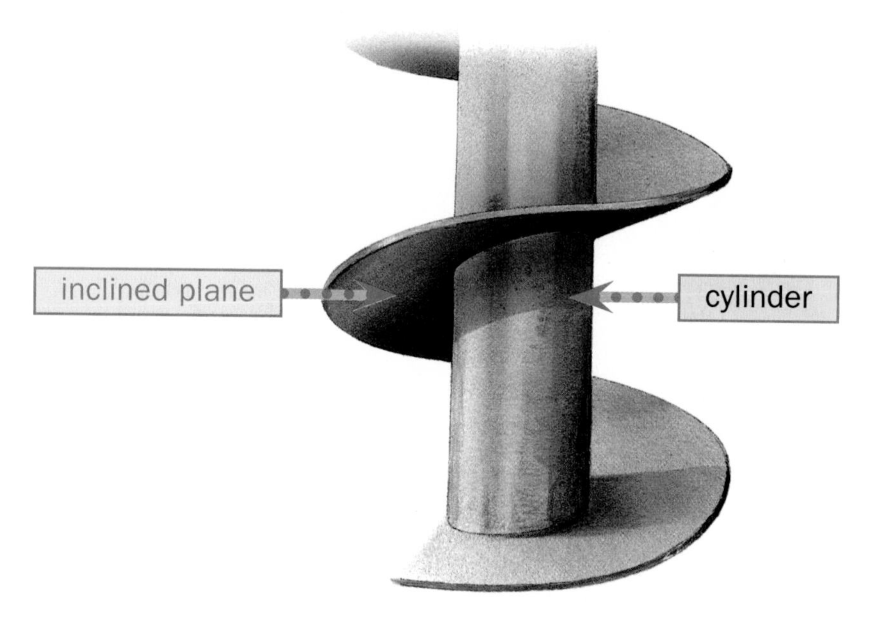

The inclined plane on a screw forms the **threads**, or ridges.

A screw with more threads is easier to turn than a screw with fewer threads. The close threads form a longer inclined plane. When the distance is longer, the force needed to turn the screw is less.

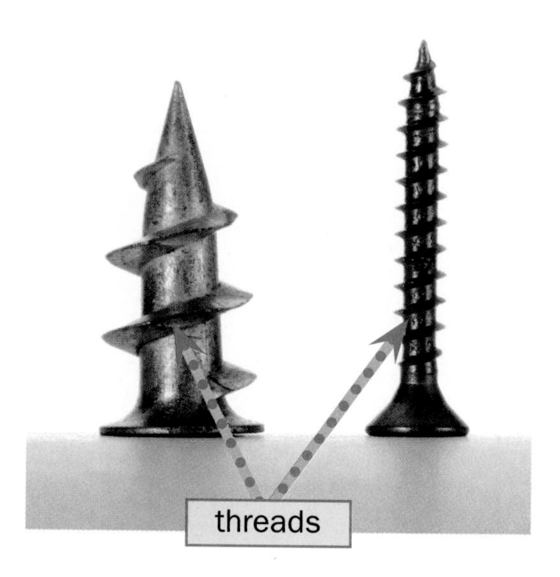

Using Screws

To use a screw, you apply force with a **screwdriver**. As you turn the screwdriver, the screw turns. Screws can hold things together.

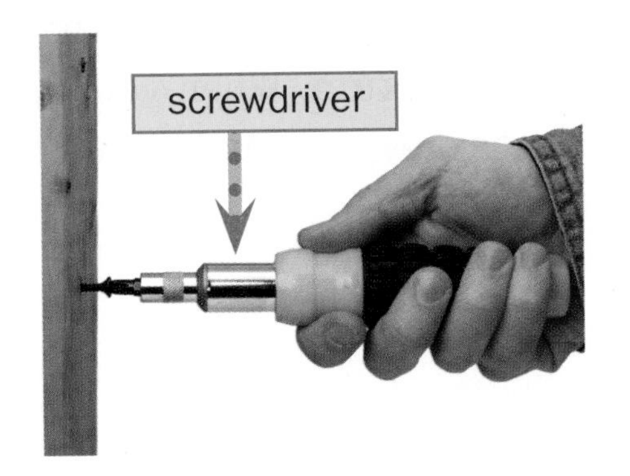

Screws can lift things. In some chairs, you move up or down when you turn. These chairs act like screws.

Screws can move things. Around 250 B.C., a Greek **inventor** used screws to move water out of ships. When a person turned the handle, water moved up the screw.

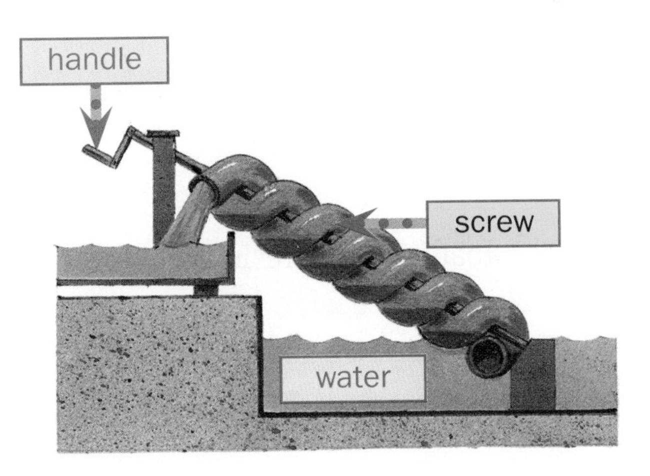

Lever

A **lever** is a stiff bar that moves around a fixed point called a **fulcrum**. When you apply an effort force to one part of the lever, a **load** on another part of the lever moves.

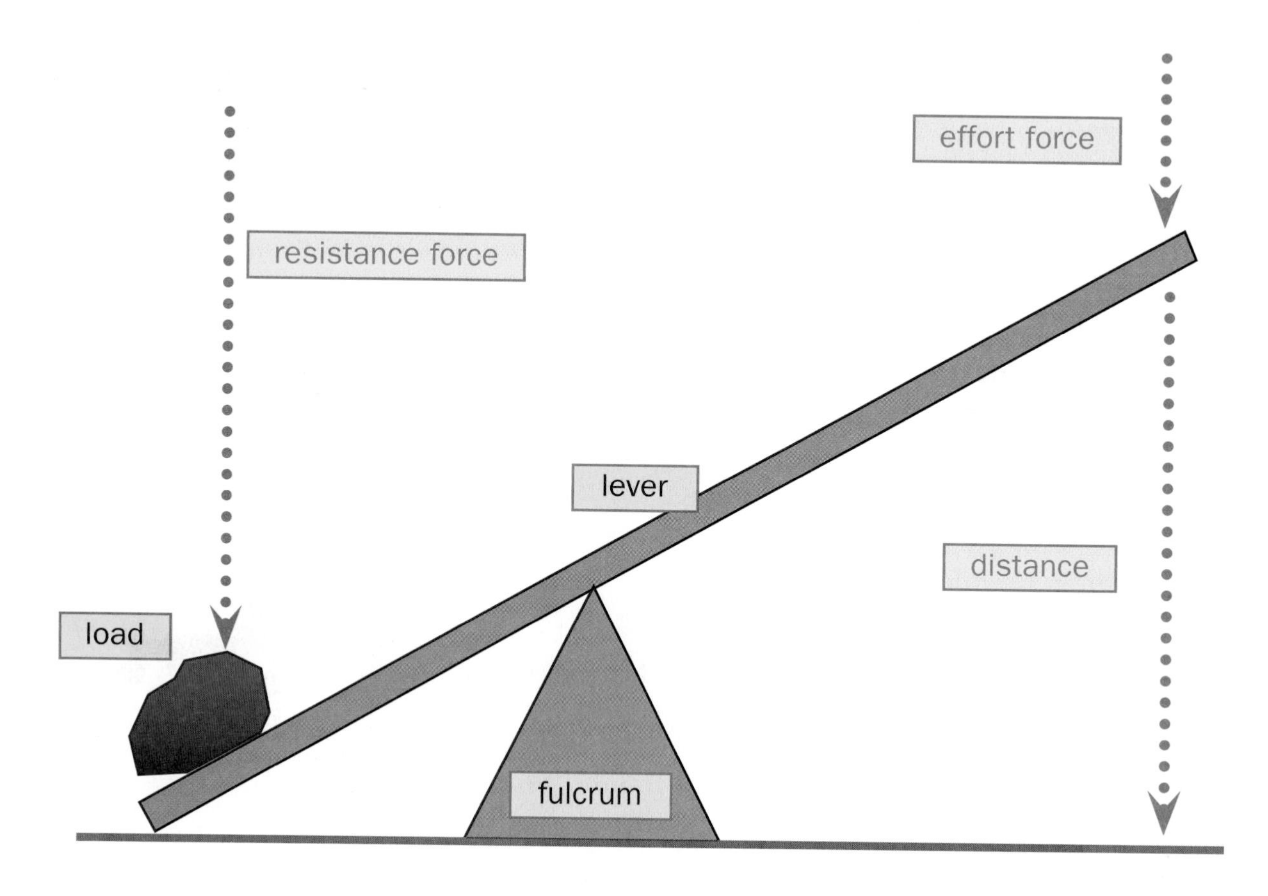

The load offers a resistance force. The length of the lever makes work easier, because work is force times distance. As the distance increases, less effort force is needed.

Kinds of Levers

There are three kinds of levers. They are called **first-class levers**, **second-class levers**, and **third-class levers**. The class of lever depends on where the fulcrum is compared to the effort and load.

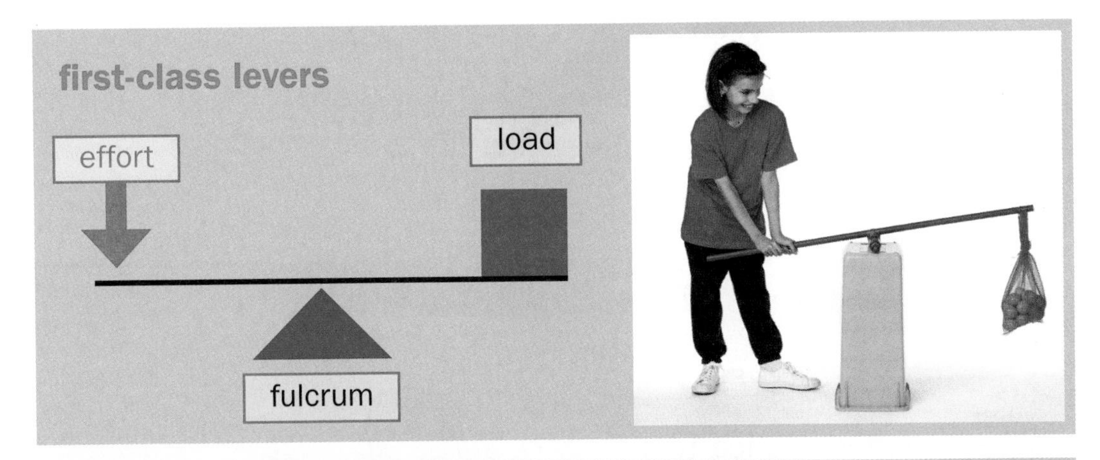

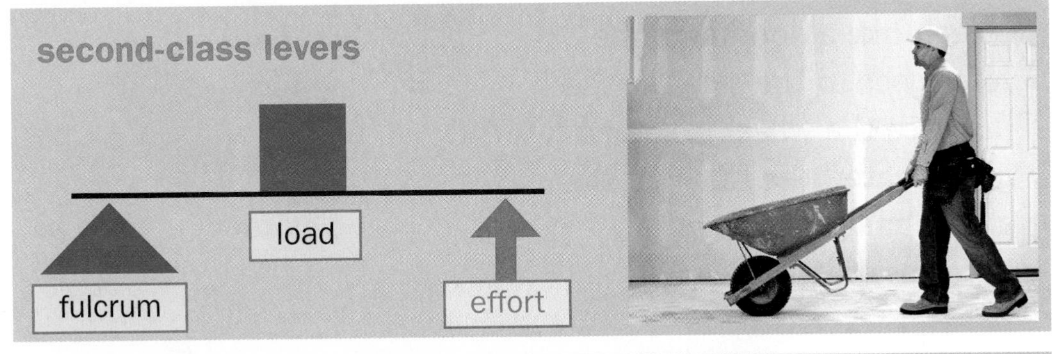

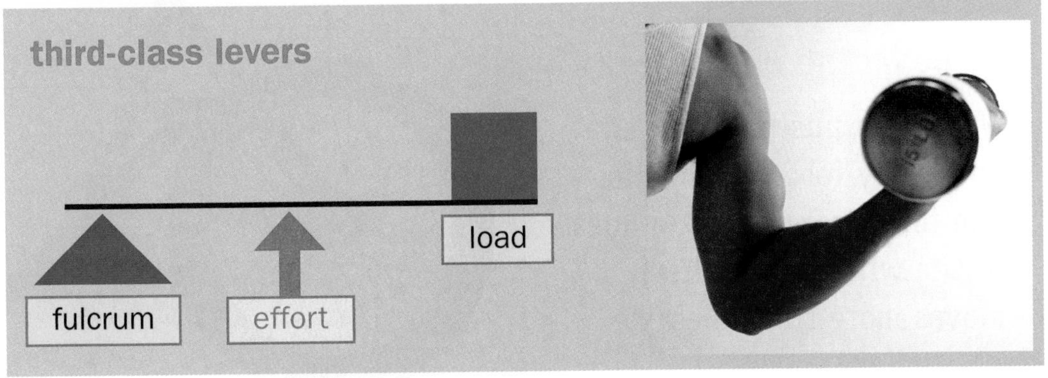

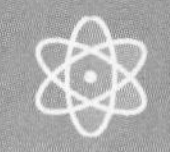

Wheel and Axle

A **wheel and axle** is another simple machine. It is made of a rod or shaft, called an axle, through the middle of a wheel. You can apply force to either the wheel or the axle.

Using a Wheel and Axle

Force on the wheel

When force is applied to a wheel, like a doorknob, the force goes to the axle. As the distance the wheel is turned gets greater, the force on the axle is **magnified**, or becomes greater.

Force on the axle

When you push a bike pedal, you apply force to an axle. The force from the axle goes to the wheel. The wheel moves more than the axle.

Pulley

A **pulley** is a rope or chain wrapped around a wheel. It is used to move or lift things. A pulley can change the direction or the amount of an effort force. There are two types of pulleys.

Types of Pulleys

Fixed pulley

A **fixed** pulley does not move. It is attached to something, such as a ceiling or wall. It only changes the direction of a force.

fixed pulley

Movable pulley

A **movable** pulley is hung on a rope. One end of the rope is tied to something fixed. The pulley moves along the rope as the other end is pulled. Only the amount of effort force changes.

movable pulley

WHY IT MATTERS

- You use simple machines every day.
- Simple machines make work easier for you.

PHYSICAL SCIENCE

Working in Space

ESSENTIAL IDEA

Astronauts use special tools to work in space.

The effects of **gravity** in space are small. **Astronauts** float when they work outside the spacecraft. Astronauts need special tools to work in space.

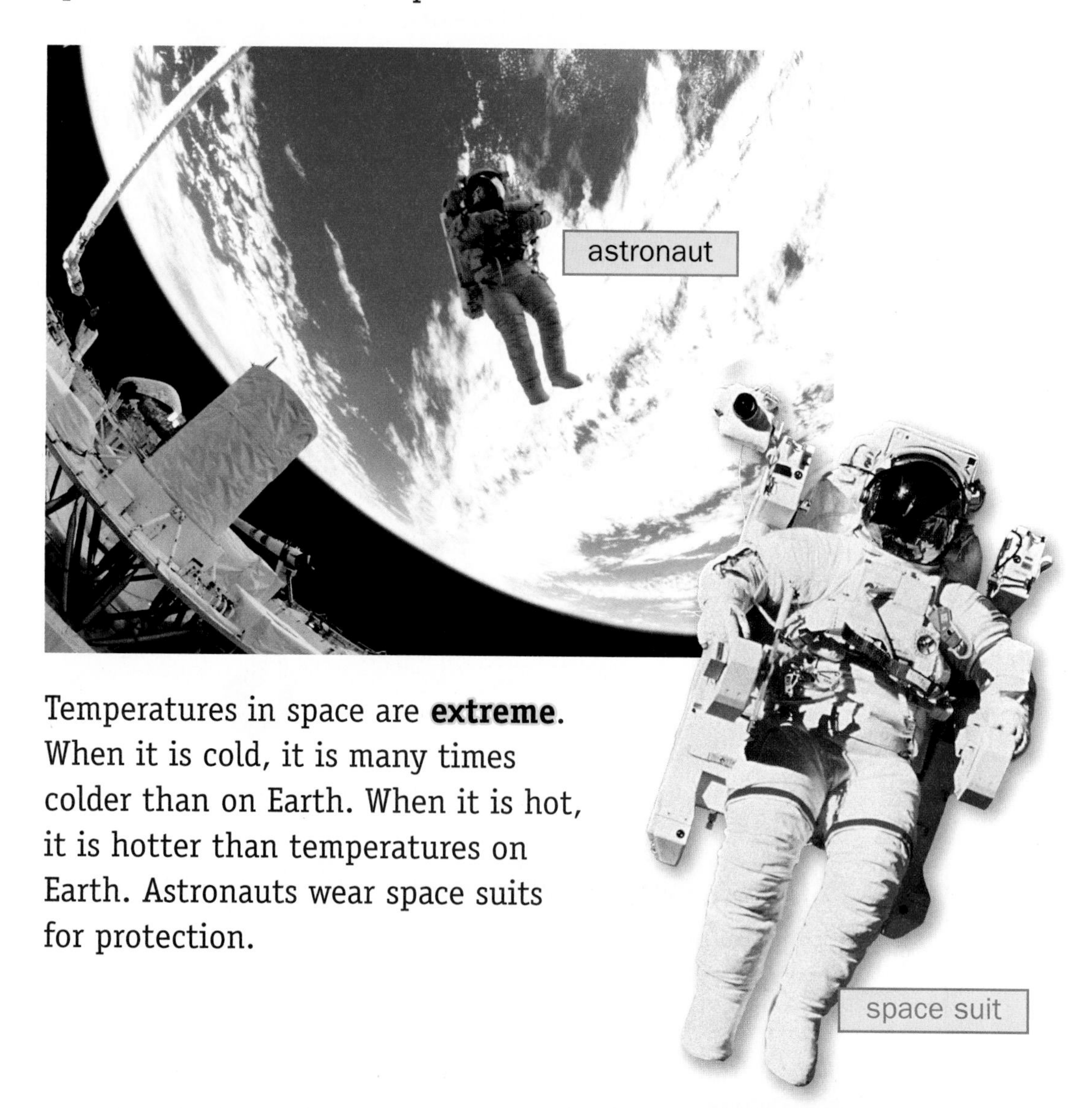

Temperatures in space are **extreme**. When it is cold, it is many times colder than on Earth. When it is hot, it is hotter than temperatures on Earth. Astronauts wear space suits for protection.

Astronauts use **robots** to do work. One kind of robot is called a Canadarm. The Canadarm can grab objects that float away from the spacecraft.

The Canadarm works like a human arm.

Space **technology** has led to many new tools and new kinds of jobs. Cell phones are better because of space technology. Doctors have better medical tools to help save human lives.

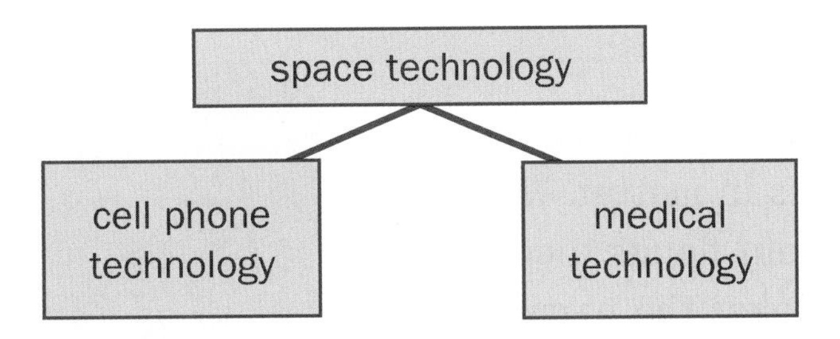

WHY IT MATTERS

The tools made for use in space have led to better tools that help you on Earth.

PHYSICAL SCIENCE

Forms of Energy

ESSENTIAL IDEA

Energy is the ability to move or change things. There are many forms of energy.

Energy is a property of matter. All matter has energy. Energy gives things the power to do work. Energy from the Sun gives plants the power to make food. Energy from gasoline makes a car move.

Mechanical energy is the energy of moving objects. The energy of a bowling ball comes from its motion.

Thermal energy is the motion of particles in matter. When you rub your hands together, friction makes the particles in your skin move faster. Your hands feel warmer.

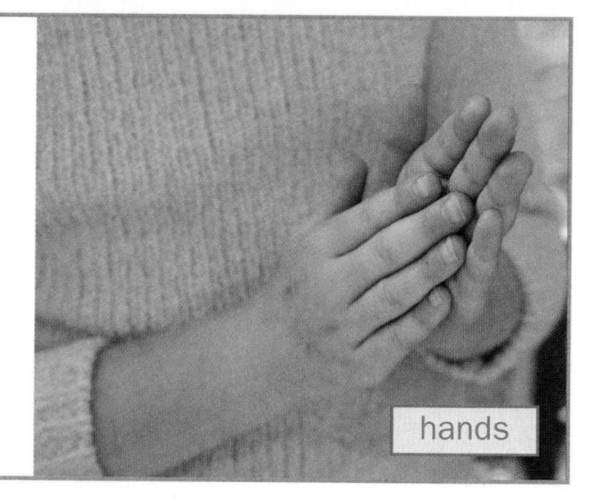

Chemical energy is the energy that holds atoms together in matter. When chemicals react, energy is released. As wood burns, chemical energy is released as heat.

Electromagnetic energy has several forms. Light, radio waves, and electricity are examples of electromagnetic energy. Electromagnetic energy carries the messages from a cell phone.

Nuclear energy is stored in the nucleus of an atom. In a power plant, energy is released when the nucleus changes. This energy can provide heat and light for millions of people.

WHY IT MATTERS

- You transform energy when you eat and digest your food.
- You use several different kinds of energy every day.

PHYSICAL SCIENCE

Mechanical Energy

ESSENTIAL IDEA

Potential energy and kinetic energy are two types of mechanical energy.

All matter has energy. **Energy** is the ability to move or change things. **Mechanical energy** comes from the **motion** or **position** of matter. There are two kinds of mechanical energy.

Something that moves has **kinetic energy**, or the energy of motion. The faster the people ride, the more kinetic energy they have.

kinetic energy

When the biker is stopped, her energy is stored. She has **potential energy**.

potential energy

Potential and kinetic energy change into each other. The water at the top of a waterfall has potential energy. As the water falls down, the potential energy changes to kinetic energy.

The energy in matter is never lost. Energy changes all the time, but the total amount of energy remains the same.

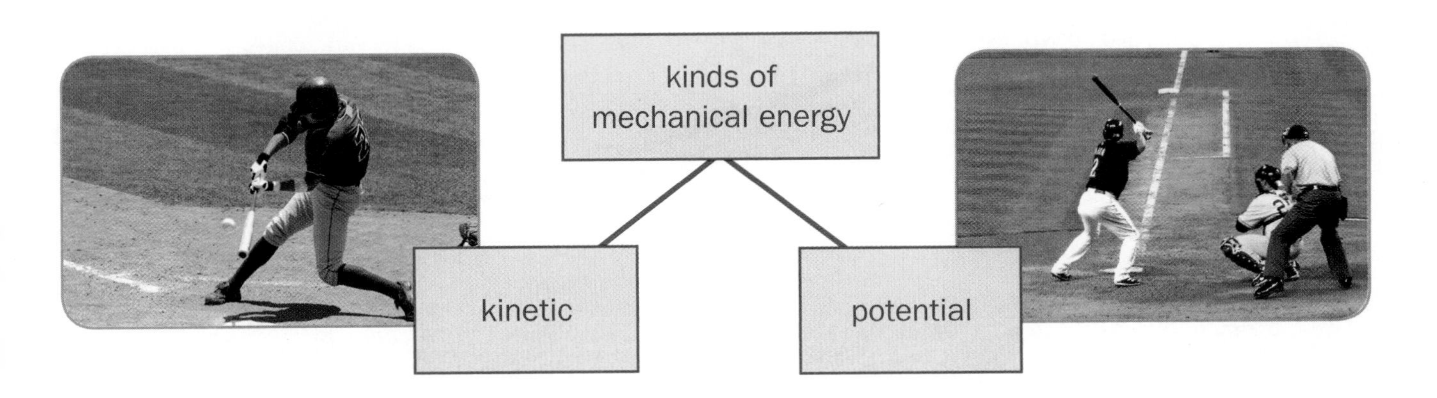

WHY IT MATTERS

- A ball has potential energy when you hold it in your hand.
- A ball has kinetic energy after you throw it and the ball moves through the air.

PHYSICAL SCIENCE

Energy Resources

ESSENTIAL IDEA

Energy comes from many resources.

Energy **resources** provide humans with the energy they need to live. The Sun is an energy resource that provides heat and light.

The Sun is a **renewable** energy resource because its supply is replaced easily. **Solar energy** comes from the Sun. Solar panels change energy from the Sun into electricity.

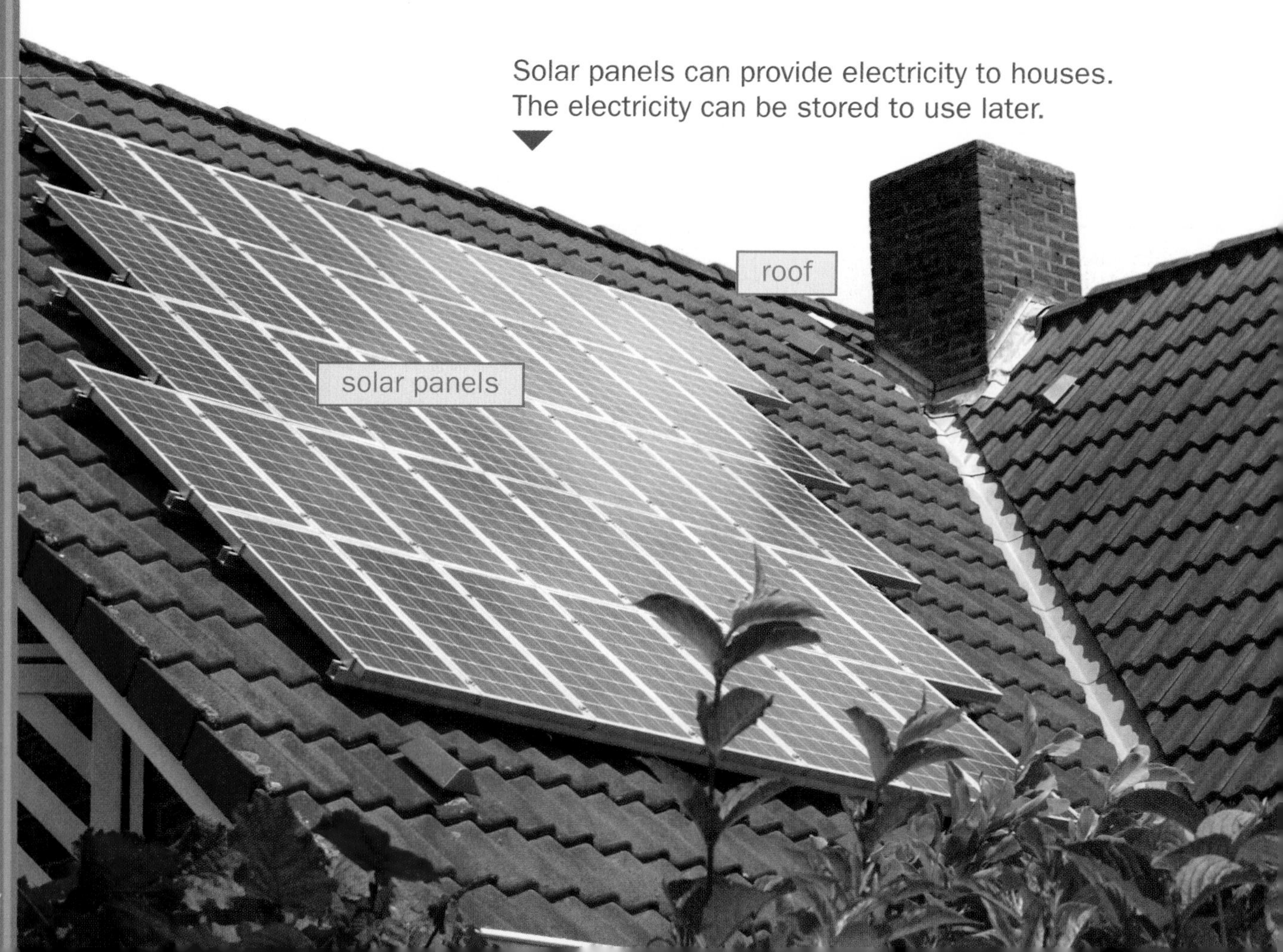

Solar panels can provide electricity to houses. The electricity can be stored to use later.

Humans burn **fossil fuels** for energy. Oil, coal, and natural gas are fossil fuels. They come from the fossil remains of dead plants and animals. Fossil fuels are **nonrenewable** resources because they take millions of years to form.

People use oil platforms to find oil under the ocean.

Types of Resources

renewable resources	nonrenewable resources
solar energy	oil
wind energy	coal
energy from moving water	natural gas

WHY IT MATTERS

- Most of your electricity comes from fossil fuels.
- Solar energy may become more widely used in your future.

Thermal Energy

ESSENTIAL IDEA

Thermal energy is the total energy of the particles in matter.

All matter is made of particles. The particles in matter **vibrate**, or move back and forth. The motion is **kinetic energy**. **Thermal energy** is the total kinetic energy of the particles in a substance.

When water boils, its thermal energy increases. The water moves because of kinetic energy.

Temperature measures the average kinetic energy of the particles. As the particles move faster, the temperature increases.

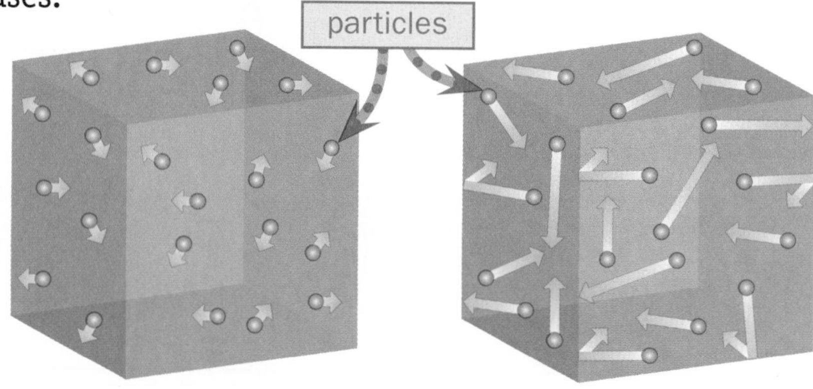

Heat is the flow, or movement, of thermal energy. Heat always flows from hot to cool areas. When you touch something hot, heat flows from the object to your hand. The particles in your hand move faster so your hand feels hot.

You feel heat as thermal energy flows from something hot (cup) to something cool (your hands).

WHY IT MATTERS

- The particles in your body move because of thermal energy.
- You can feel the flow of heat when you get hot or cold.

PHYSICAL SCIENCE

How Heat Moves

ESSENTIAL IDEA

Heat flows in three main ways: conduction, convection, and radiation.

Heat **transfers**, or flows, from one place to another in three main ways: **conduction**, **convection**, and **radiation**.

Conduction is the transfer of heat between objects that are touching. The particles move by direct contact.

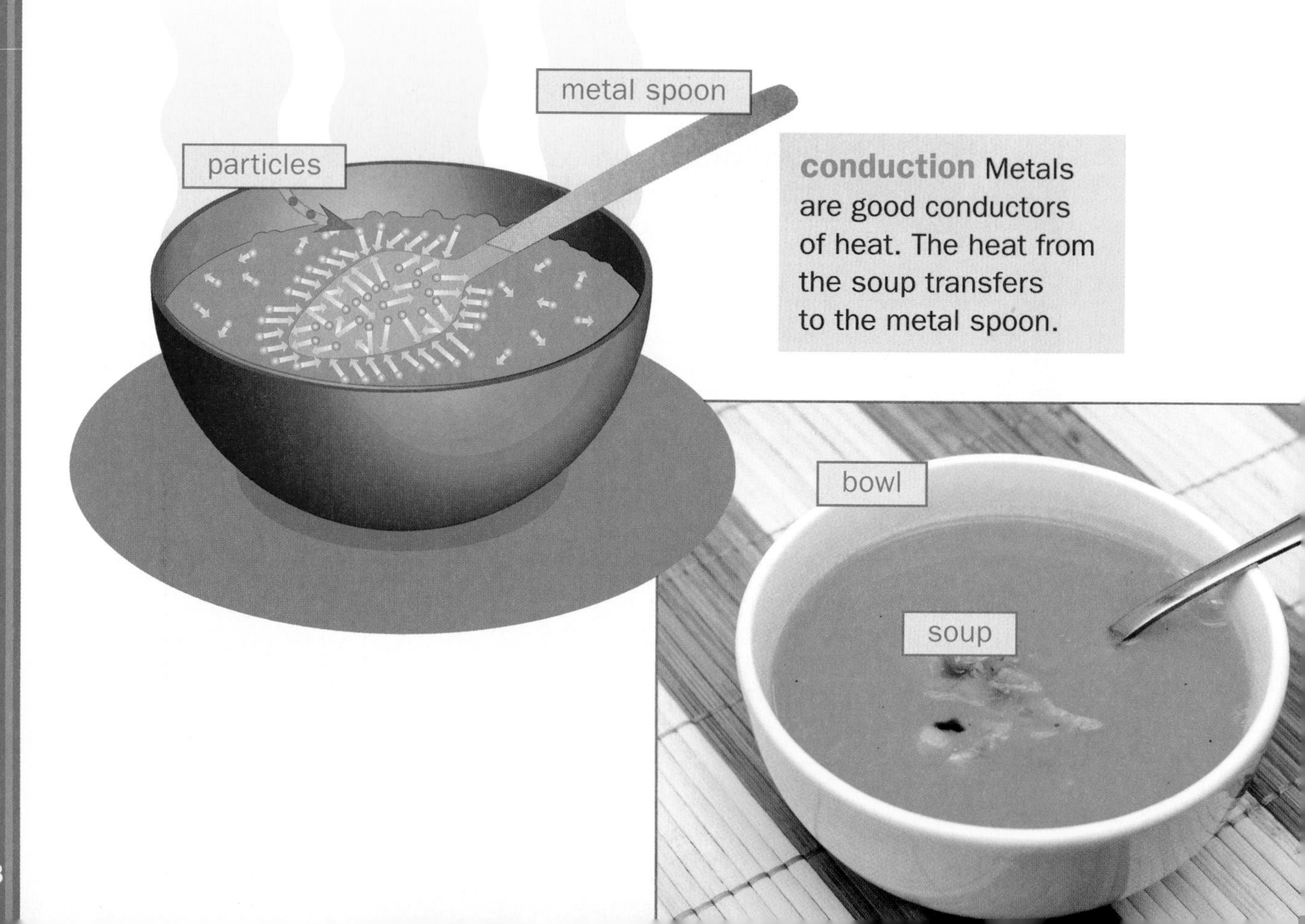

conduction Metals are good conductors of heat. The heat from the soup transfers to the metal spoon.

Convection

Convection is the transfer of heat in liquids and gases. Particles in the liquid or gas carry the energy from one place to another.

convection
As a liquid is heated, the particles move faster. They also move farther apart. Then the warm liquid rises.

Radiation

Radiation is the transfer of heat in waves. Thermal energy from the Sun reaches Earth by radiation.

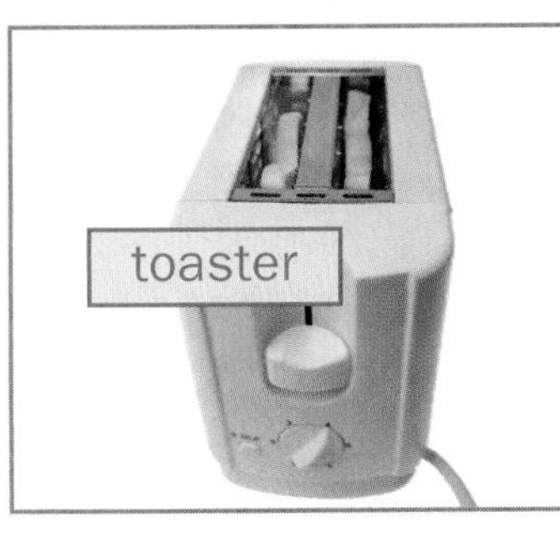

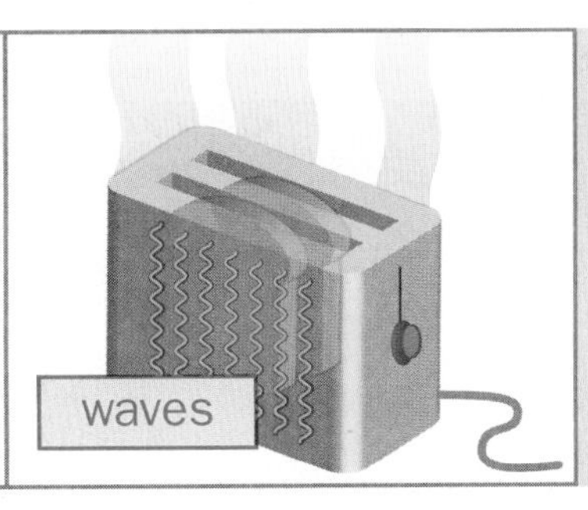

radiation
The toaster transfers heat to the bread by radiation.

WHY IT MATTERS

- Heat from the Sun reaches you by radiation.
- It is warmer near the ceiling of your room and cooler near the floor because of convection.

Static Electricity

ESSENTIAL IDEA

Static electricity is energy produced by moving charges from one place to another.

Atoms contain **electric charges**. In atoms, protons have a positive, or plus, charge. Electrons have a negative, or minus, **charge**. An atom that has the same number of protons and electrons is **neutral**, or has no charge. An atom with extra electrons is negative. An atom that loses electrons is positive.

An atom with a negative charge and an atom with a positive charge **attract**, or pull toward, one another. Atoms that have the same charge **repel**, or push away, one another.

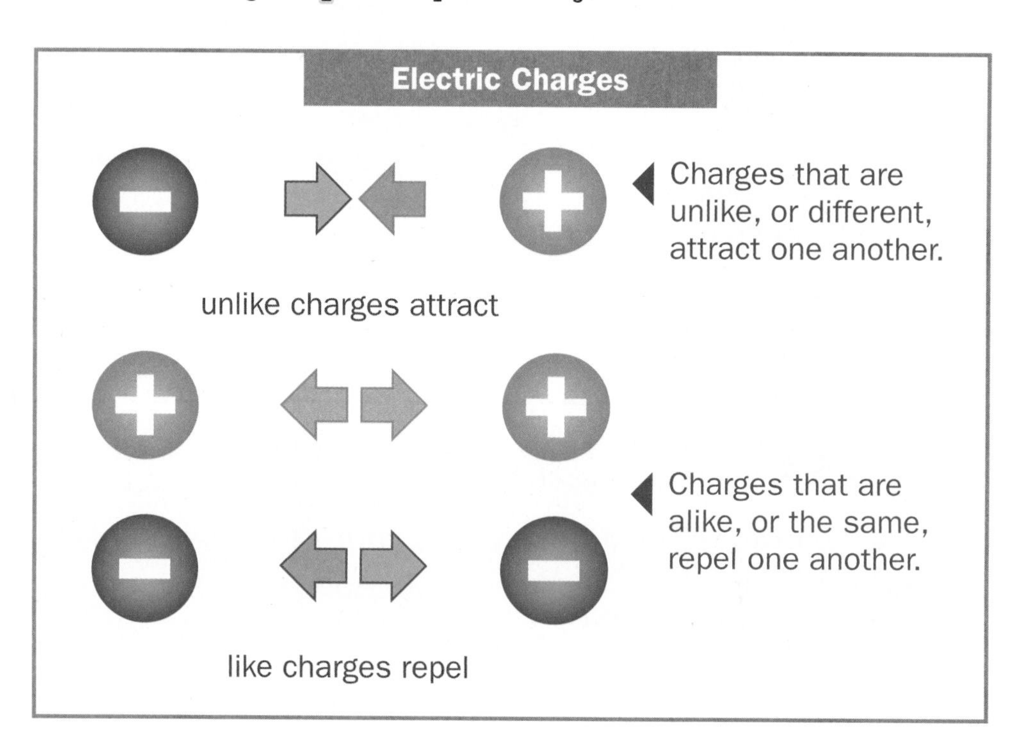

Sometimes electrons build up on a surface. The built-up negative charges are called **static electricity**. The surface becomes neutral again when it **discharges**, or releases, the extra electrons.

When you rub a balloon on your head, the balloon removes electrons from your hair. Your hair then has a positive charge. The balloon has a negative charge. Your hair sticks to the balloon because unlike charges attract.

The boy's hair sticks up because of static electricity.

WHY IT MATTERS

- You see huge discharges of static electricity when you see lightning.
- You see the effects of static electricity when clothes stick together in the dryer.

PHYSICAL SCIENCE

Current Electricity

ESSENTIAL IDEA

Electricity can flow through an electric circuit.
Electricity can change into other types of energy.

Electricity that flows along a wire is called **current electricity**. An electric **circuit** carries current electricity. There are two types of electric circuits.

A Series Circuit

A **series circuit** has one path. The lightbulbs go on as electrons from the battery flow through them. If one lightbulb burns out, the path is broken. All the lightbulbs would go out. Opening the switch also breaks the path.

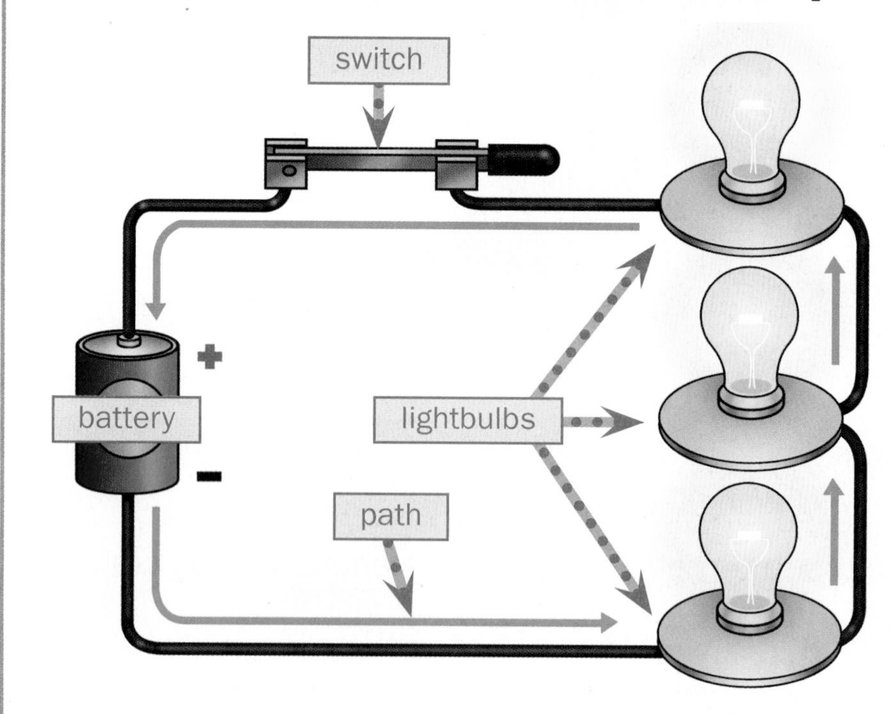

A Parallel Circuit

A **parallel circuit** has several paths. If one lightbulb burns out, the others stay lit. Each lightbulb in a parallel circuit can be turned off and on individually with a switch.

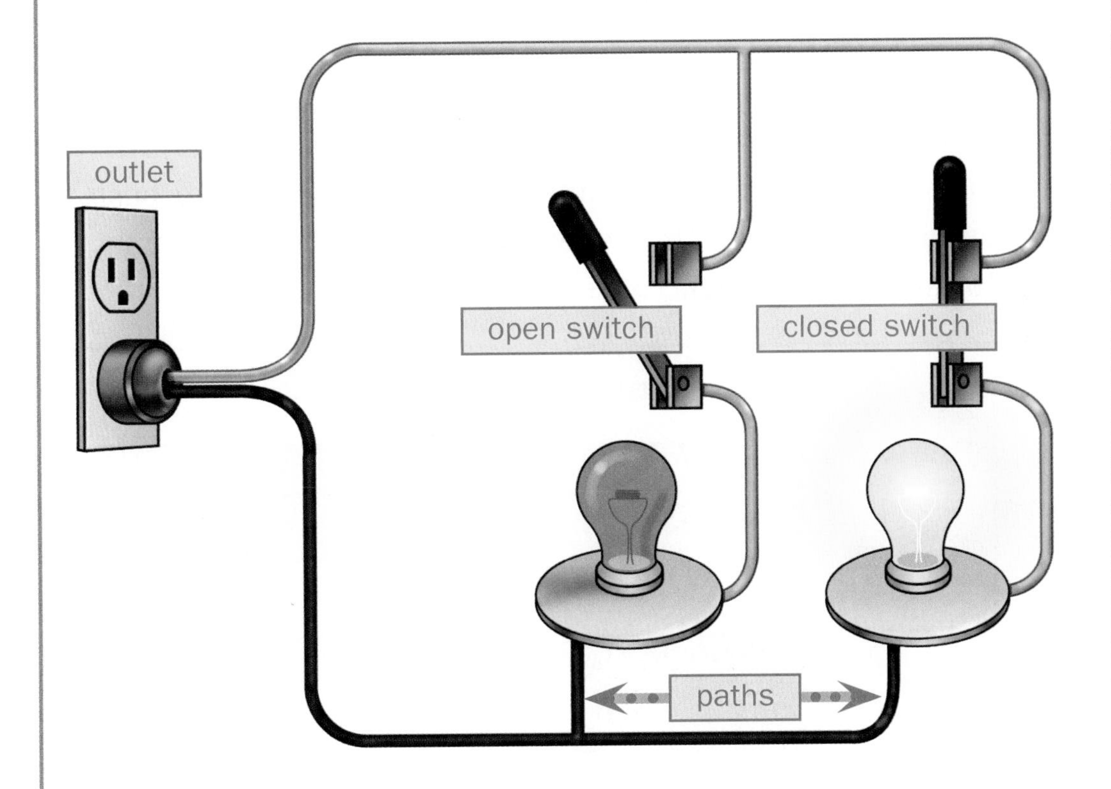

The electric circuits in many homes are parallel circuits.

WHY IT MATTERS

The electricity that you use flows in a current.

PHYSICAL SCIENCE

Magnets

ESSENTIAL IDEA

Magnets are made of special materials and have special properties.

Every **magnet** has a north pole (N) and a south pole (S). Like poles of a magnet (S and S or N and N) **repel**, or push away, one another. Unlike poles (S and N) **attract**, or pull toward, one another.

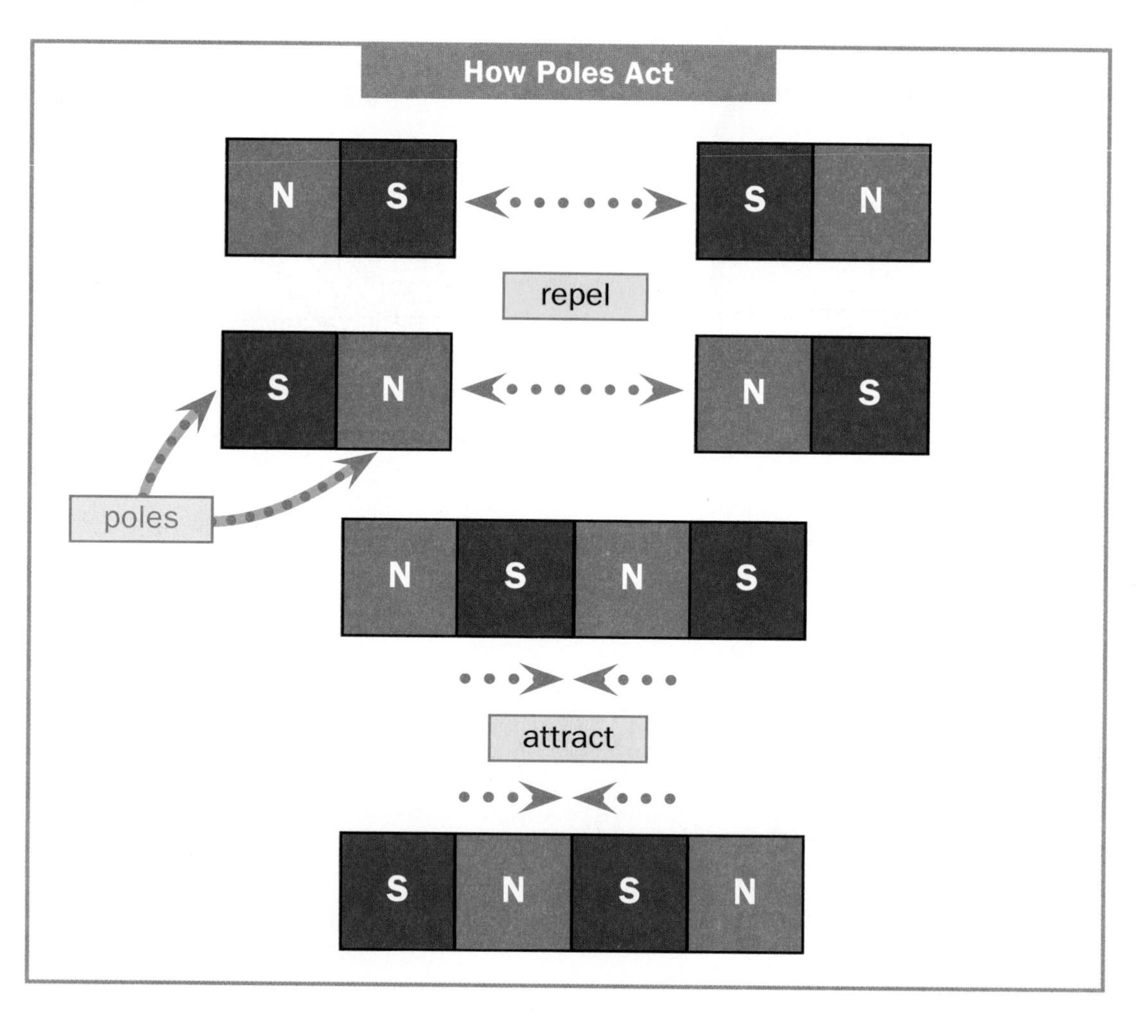

A magnet has a **magnetic field** around it. The lines of a magnetic field show the direction and strength of the force between two poles. The lines in a magnetic field always connect the north and south poles.

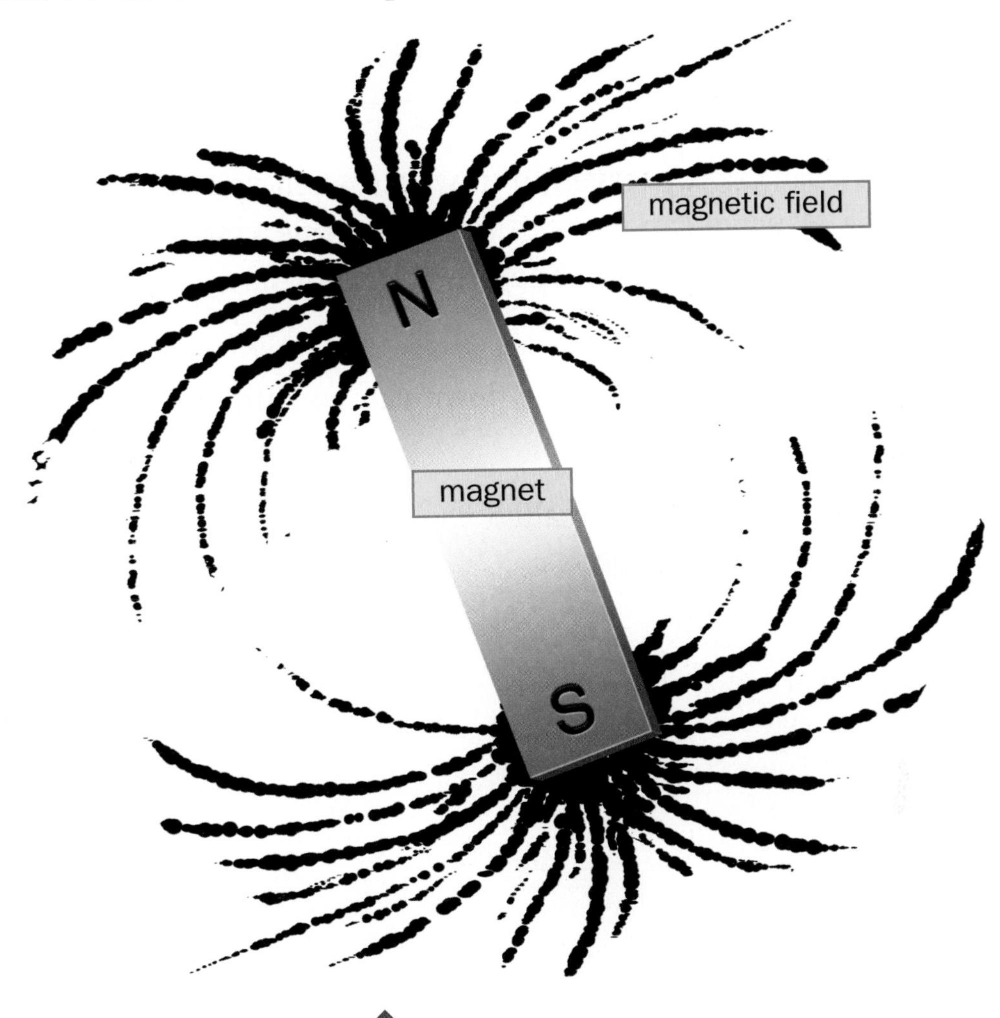

When you place small pieces of iron near a magnet, you can see the magnetic field.

WHY IT MATTERS

- You use magnets in everyday life.
- You can attach messages to a refrigerator with a magnet.

Waves

ESSENTIAL IDEA

Waves move energy. There are two kinds of waves.

You see energy traveling in waves when you look at the sea. A **wave** can move in two ways. One kind of wave moves up and down. The other kind of wave moves back and forth.

Waves that move up and down can go through matter or through empty space.

The top of a wave is called the **crest**. The bottom of a wave is called the **trough**.

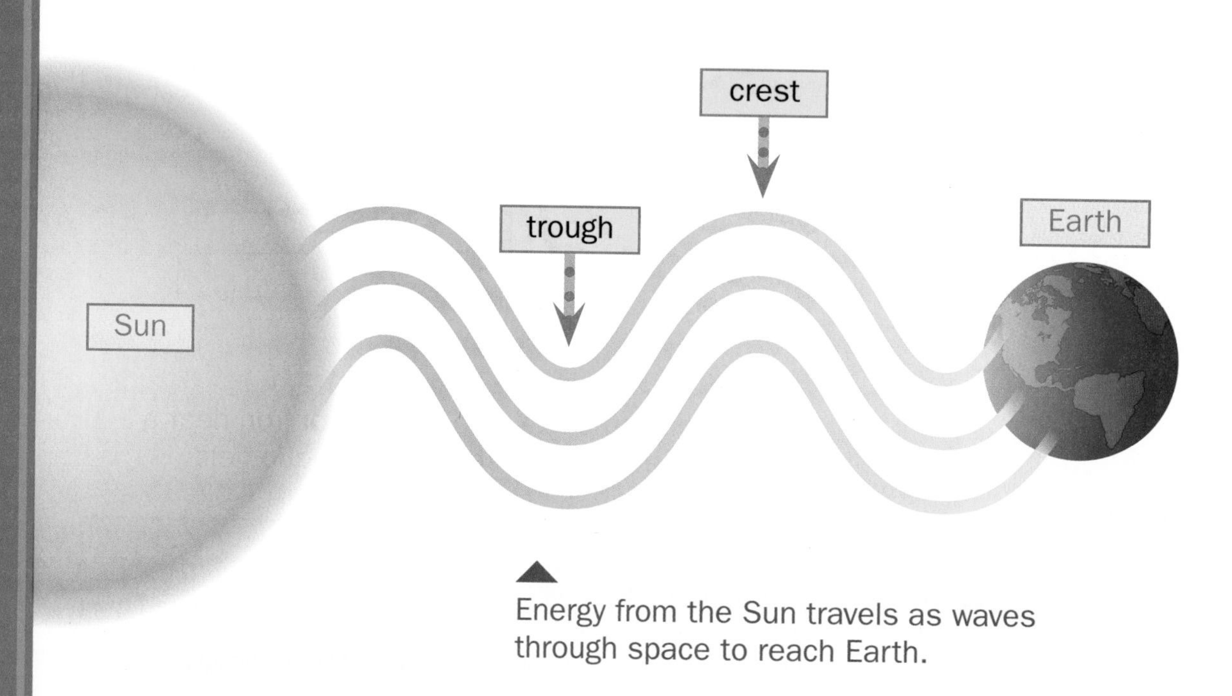

Energy from the Sun travels as waves through space to reach Earth.

Waves that move back and forth can only go through matter. These waves need particles to push back and forth.

Sound energy moves through air, water, and solid materials in waves.

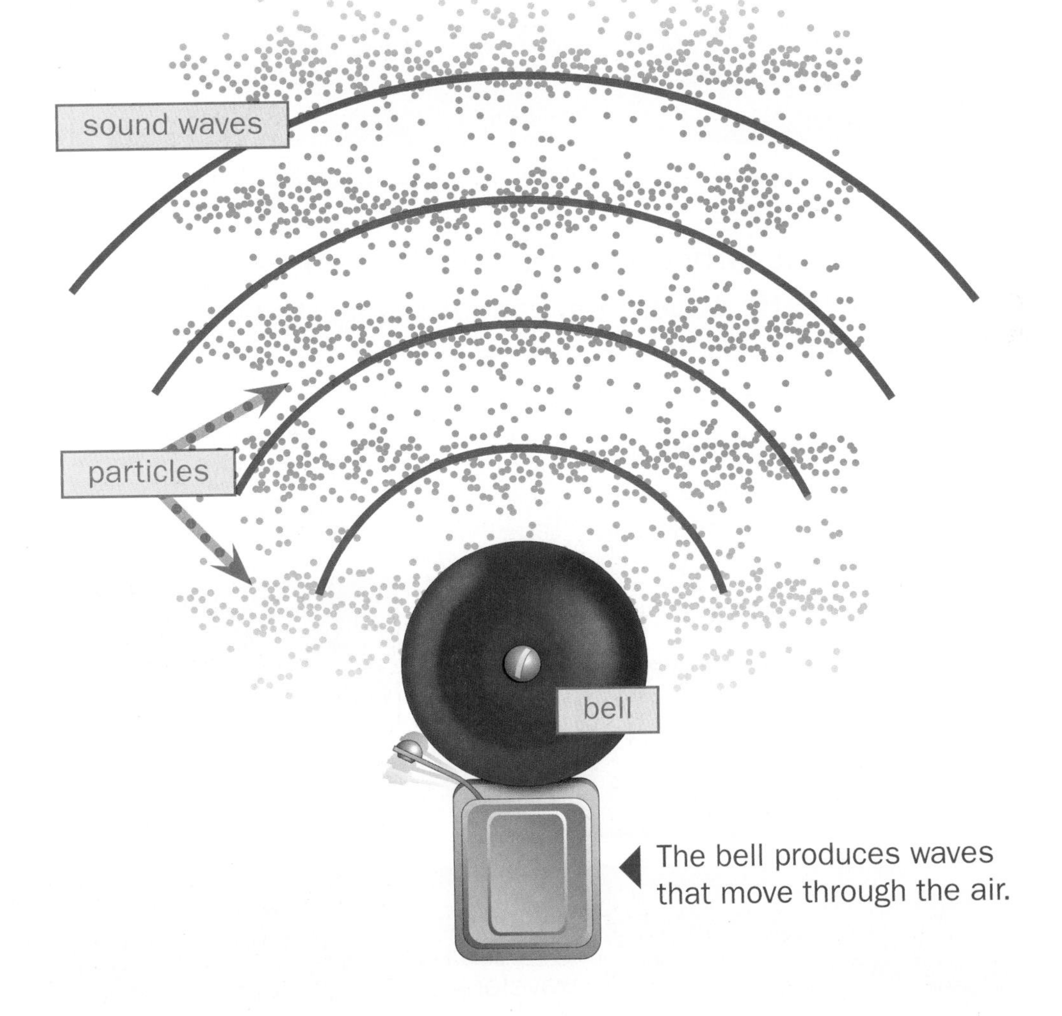

The bell produces waves that move through the air.

WHY IT MATTERS

- Sunlight that you feel traveled to Earth in waves.
- Light that you see and sound that you hear move in waves.

PHYSICAL SCIENCE

Electromagnetic Spectrum

ESSENTIAL IDEA

Scientists classify electromagnetic waves by their wavelengths.

The waves that carry energy from the Sun are called **electromagnetic waves**. You cannot see most of these waves.

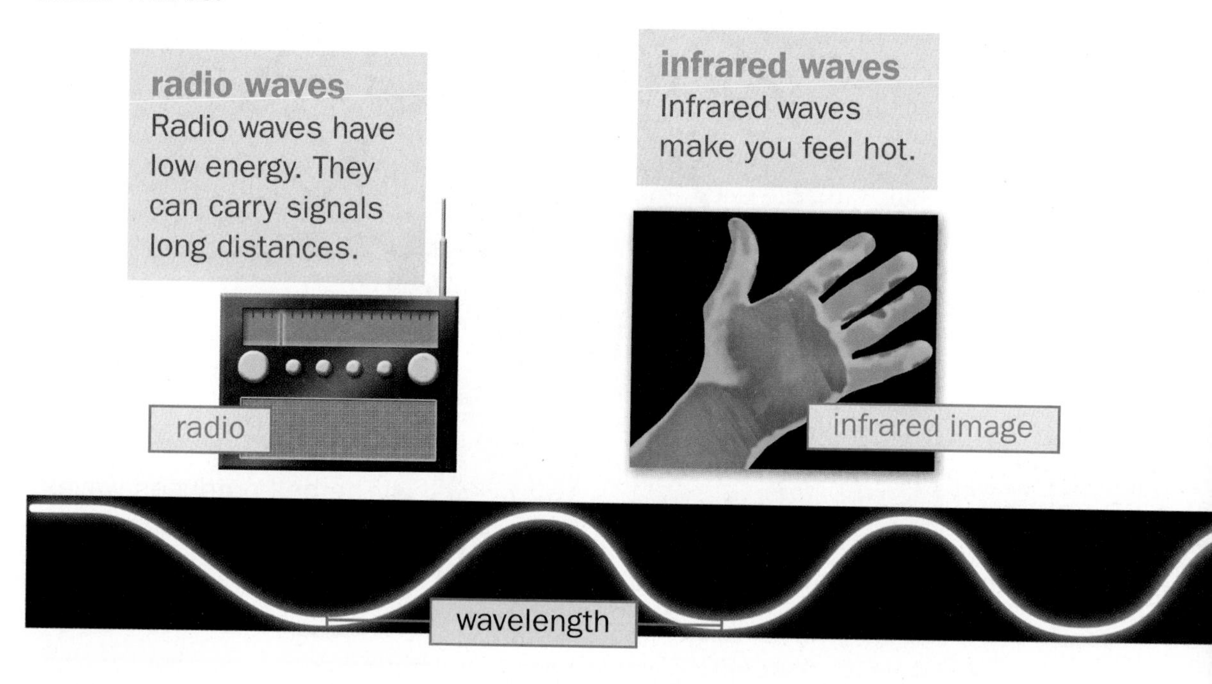

The distance from one wave to the next is the **wavelength**. The number of waves that pass a point in one second is the **frequency**.

Each wave on the electromagnetic spectrum has its own wavelength and frequency. Radio waves have a longer wavelength than X rays. Waves with shorter wavelengths and higher frequencies have a greater amount of energy.

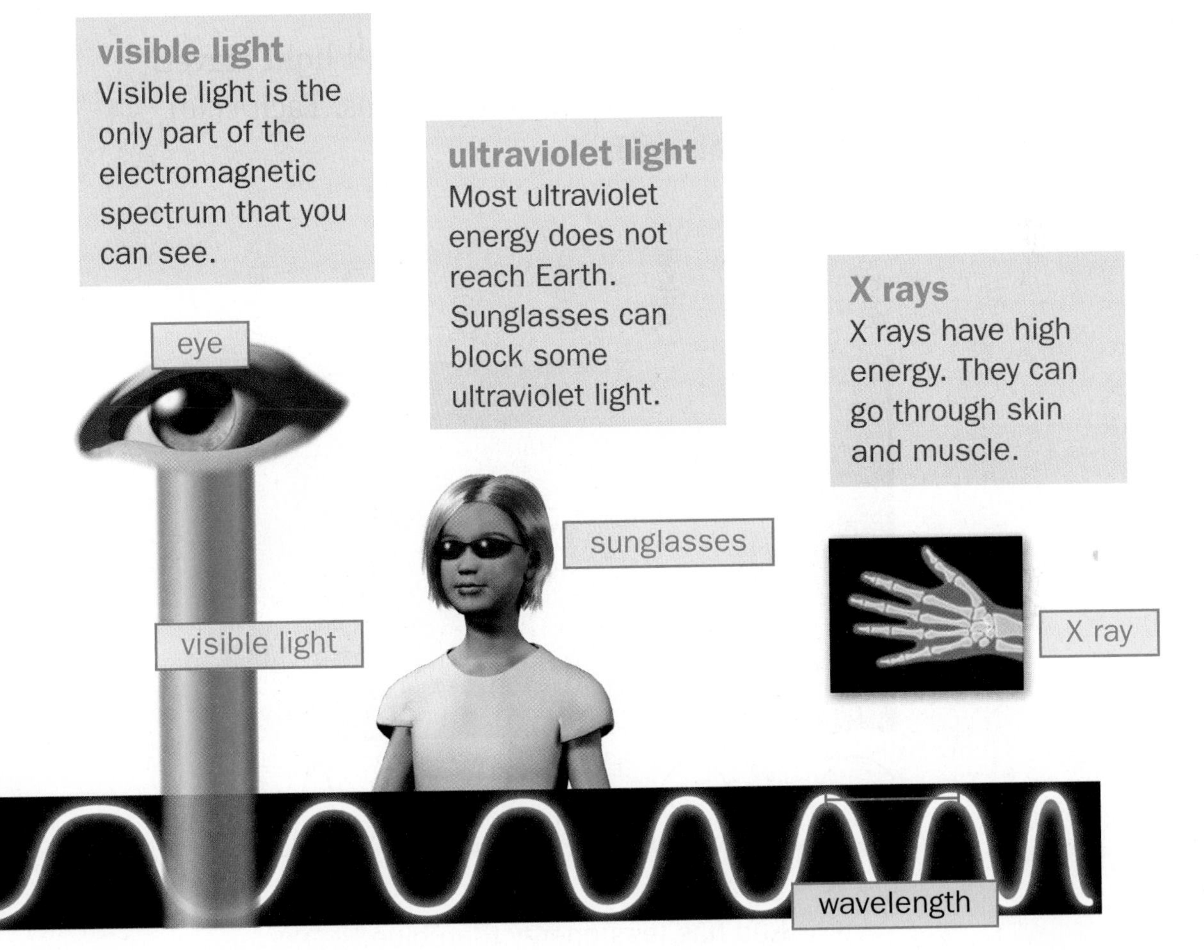

WHY IT MATTERS

Waves from the electromagnetic spectrum are all around you in light, radios, and X rays.

Visible Light

ESSENTIAL IDEA

Light is a form of energy. Each wavelength of visible light carries a different amount of energy.

Visible light is energy that you can see. All light travels in waves. Light waves have different lengths. Each color has a different **wavelength**.

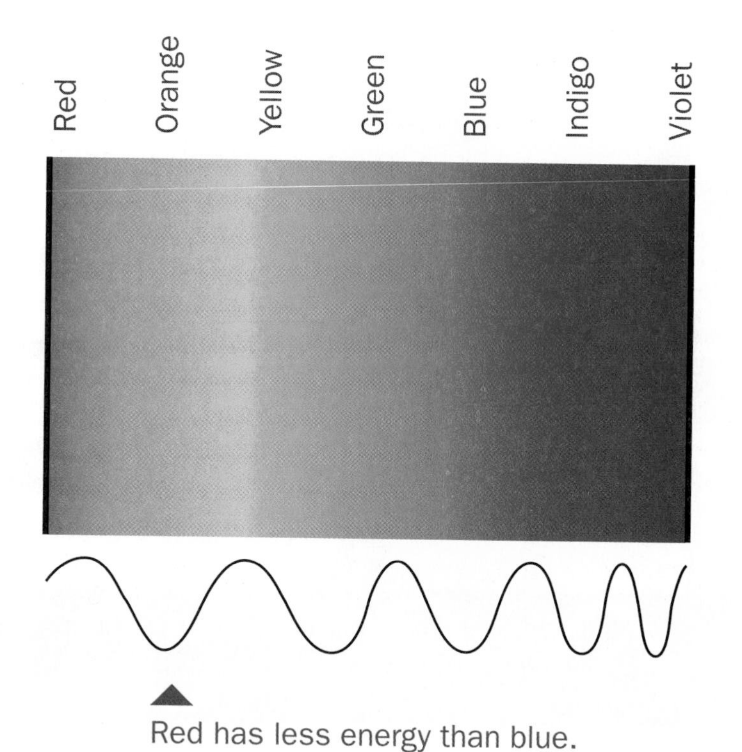

Red has less energy than blue.

Light energy comes in packets called **photons**. Each color of light has photons with a specific amount of energy.

How You See

Photons of light reach the part of your eye called the **retina**. Special cells in your retina send signals to your brain. That is how you see.

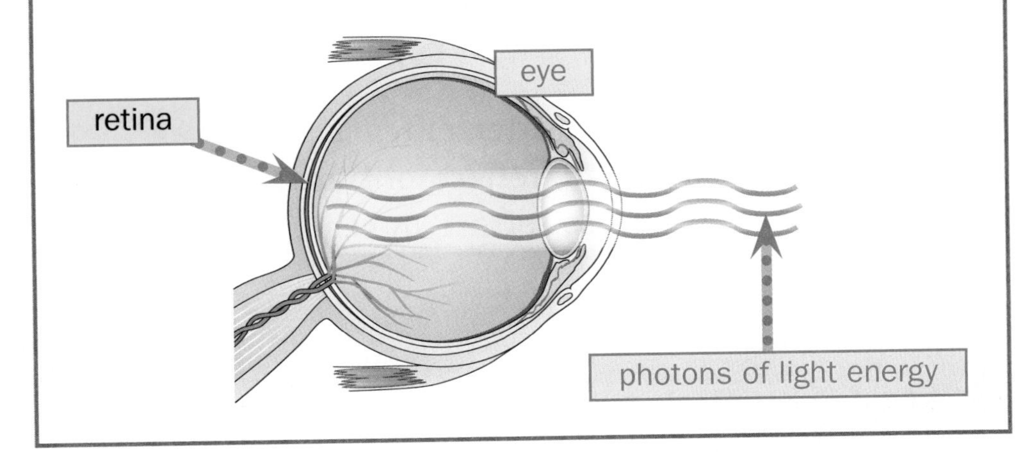

Each **element**, or kind of matter, makes different colors of light. Neon signs are made of glass tubes filled with different elements. When the elements release energy, each element makes a different color.

Each color in a neon sign is a different element.

WHY IT MATTERS

Each color you see has a different amount of energy.

Light and Matter

ESSENTIAL IDEA

Light interacts with matter in three key ways.

When light energy strikes matter, different things can happen. Matter can **absorb**, **reflect**, or **transmit** the light. Sometimes, matter can also **refract**, or bend, the light.

Absorb

Some light energy is always absorbed. It can be just a tiny amount.

When light hits water, some absorbed energy heats the water.

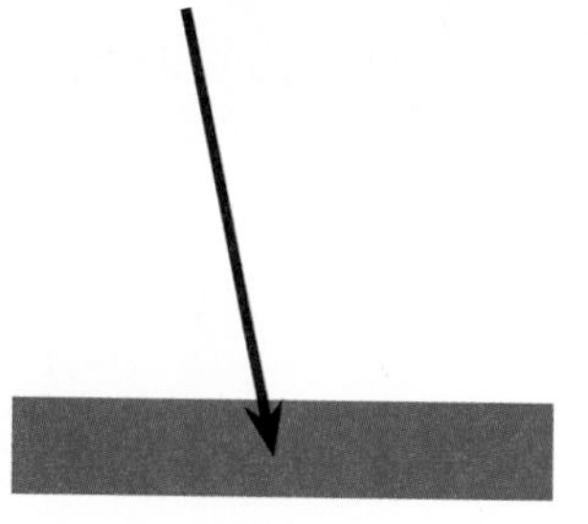

Reflect

Some matter reflects light. The light energy bounces off.

Reflected light causes the water's surface to shine.

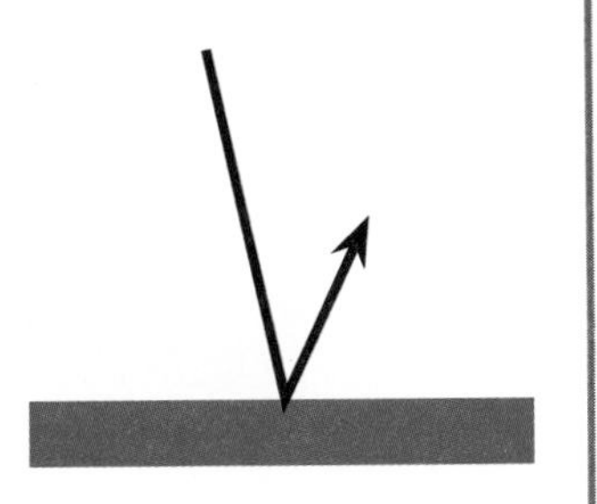

Transmit

Some matter transmits light. The light passes through. Something that transmits light, such as glass or water, is **transparent**.

Some light passes through the surface of water and into the water below.

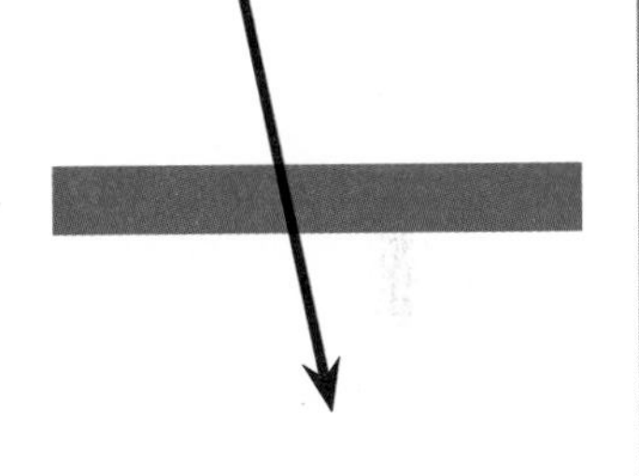

If the light moves at an angle from one clear substance to another, then the direction of the light changes. **Refraction** is the bending of light when it goes from one substance into another substance.

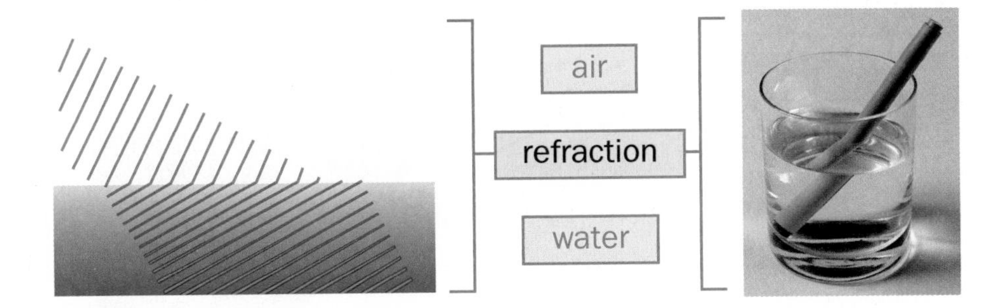

WHY IT MATTERS

The way light interacts with matter affects what you see and where you see it.

PHYSICAL SCIENCE

Color

ESSENTIAL IDEA

You see color when different wavelengths of light reach your eye.

The light you see has many different **wavelengths**. You see each wavelength as a different color. When all of the colors reach your eye at the same time, you see "white" light.

Refraction of Sunlight

A **prism** is a glass object with three sides. If white light passes through a prism, the different wavelengths bend in different ways.

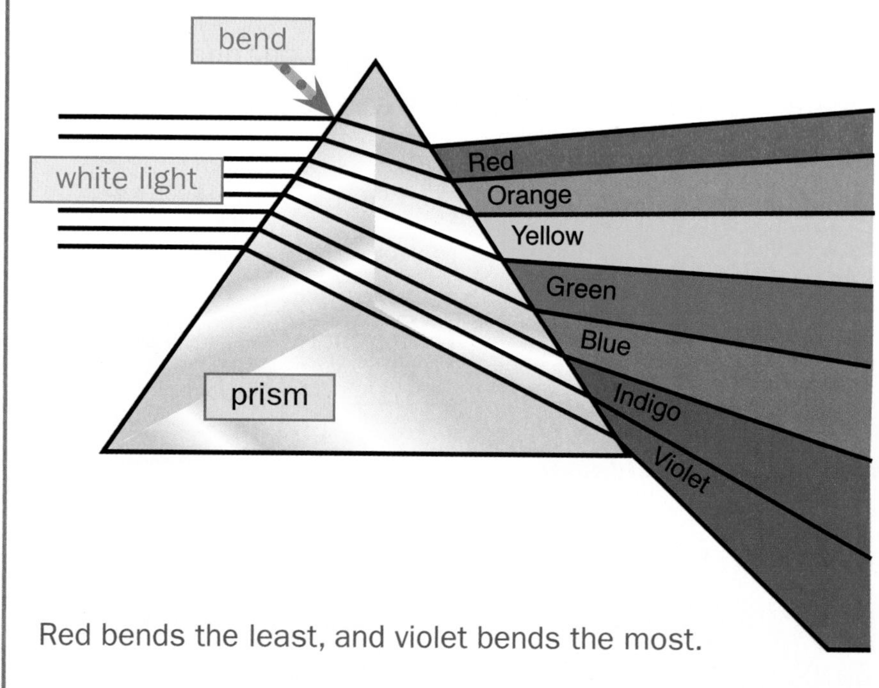

Red bends the least, and violet bends the most.

Light does not pass through an opaque substance. **Opaque** means "not clear." Opaque objects can absorb or reflect light. You see the color that is reflected from the object.

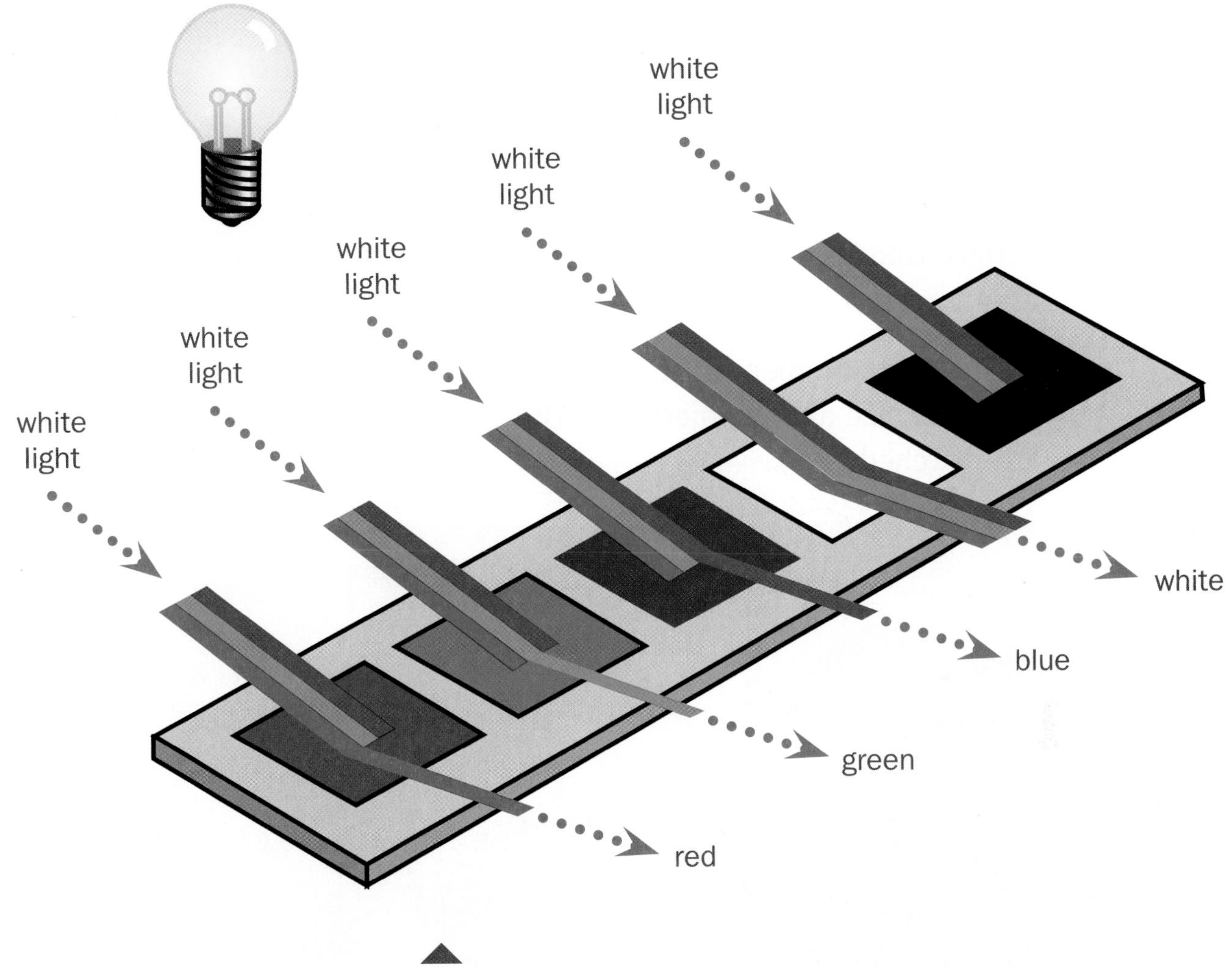

White reflects all colors. Black absorbs all colors.

WHY IT MATTERS

The colors you see depend on the wavelengths that reach your eye.

Mirrors

ESSENTIAL IDEA

A mirror reflects light that strikes it. Mirrors have many important uses.

A **mirror** is a shiny surface that reflects light. Any smooth surface that reflects light and forms **images** can be used as a mirror.

If you hold an object in front of a mirror, the image is the same size as the object, but the left and right sides are switched.

How Mirrors Work

Mirrors work because of light. Light reflects off an object and hits the mirror. Then the light bounces off the mirror.

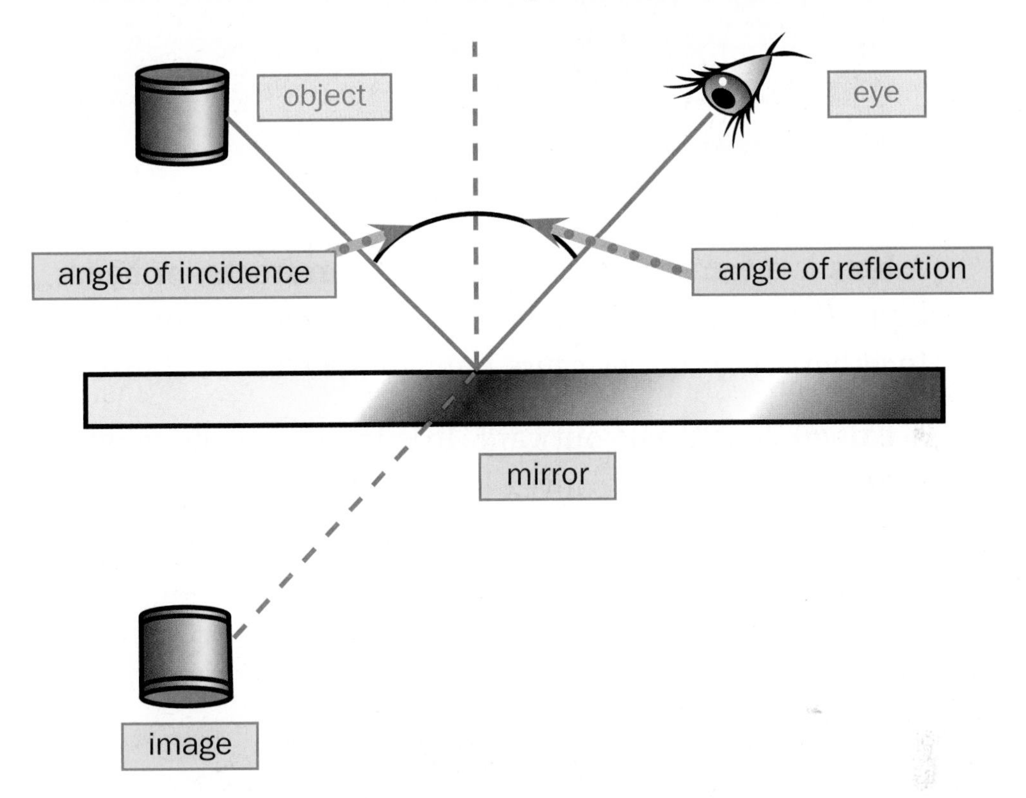

Light from an object hits the mirror at an angle. This is called the **angle of incidence**. The light reflects off the mirror at exactly the same angle on the other side. This angle is the **angle of reflection**. The **Law of Reflection** says that the angle of incidence equals the angle of reflection.

WHY IT MATTERS

You see your reflection in mirrors every day.

Lenses

ESSENTIAL IDEA

A lens bends light waves as they pass through it. A lens is part of your eye. Lenses have other important uses.

A **lens** is a transparent substance that **refracts**, or bends, light. Some lenses cause light rays to **converge**, or come together. Other lenses cause light to **diverge**, or spread out.

A **convex** lens bends outward. It is thicker in the middle than at the edges. A convex lens can bend the light waves so that an object looks larger. Microscopes have convex lenses.

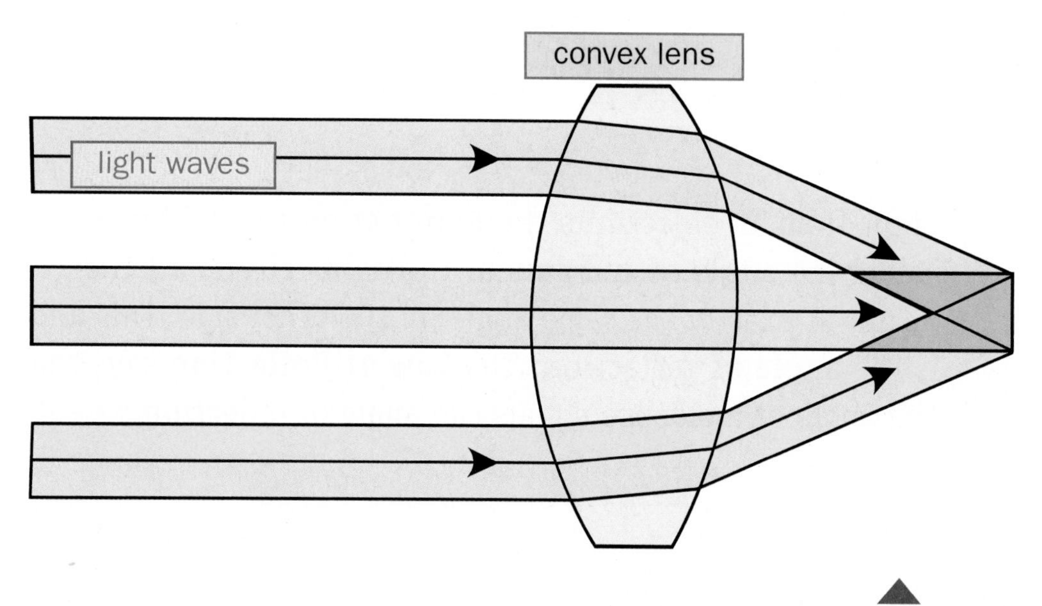

Light waves converge.

A **concave** lens is thicker at the ends than it is in the middle. When light passes through the concave lens, the light spreads out. Concave lenses can make things look smaller.

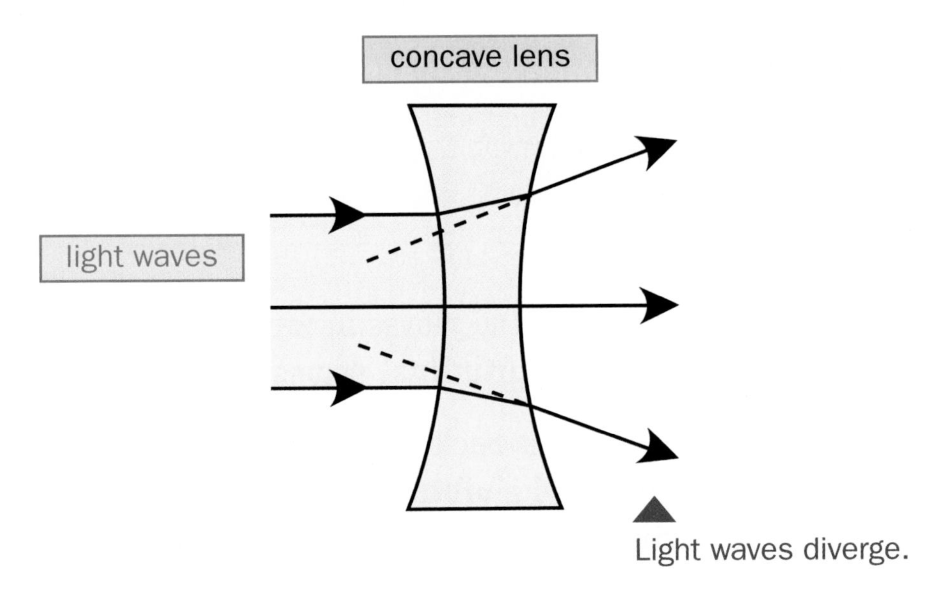

Both convex and concave lenses are used in eyeglasses and contact lenses to help people see better. Telescopes have concave and convex lenses to help people see distant stars clearly.

Kinds of Lenses

type	function
convex	light converges
concave	light diverges

WHY IT MATTERS

- You use a magnifying glass to make things look bigger.
- You might wear lenses to correct your vision.

PHYSICAL SCIENCE

Sound

ESSENTIAL IDEA

Sound is produced when an object vibrates in air or some other material. The vibrations travel through the material.

Sound is a form of energy. Sound moves in waves that go back and forth. These are **longitudinal waves**.

A sound wave pushes particles back and forth. The back-and-forth movement is called a **vibration**. Sound can only travel through a **medium**, or matter. The matter can be a gas, a liquid, or a solid.

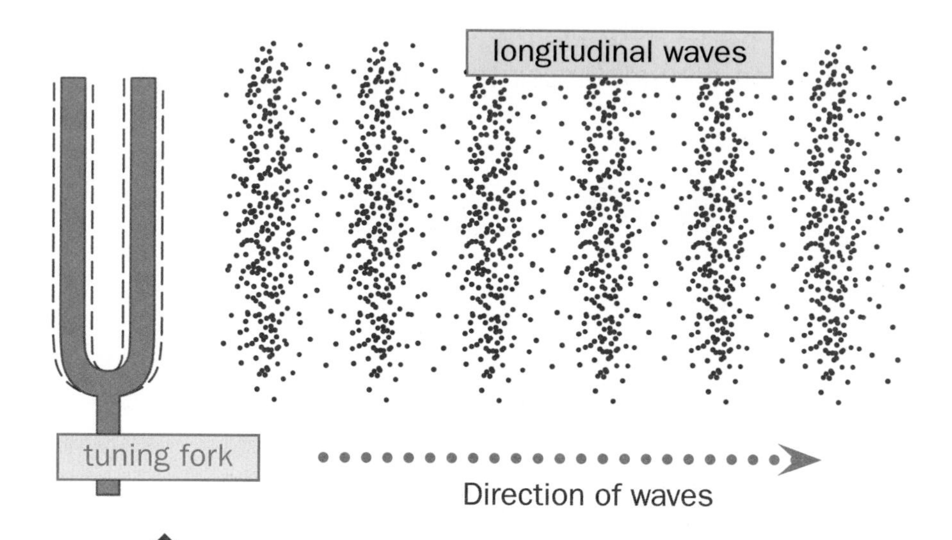

When the tuning fork is struck, it vibrates and pushes particles in the air closer together. The waves move out while the tuning fork vibrates.

How You Hear Sound

When sound waves reach your ear, they cause your eardrum to vibrate. This sends signals to your brain. Your brain recognizes the vibrations as sound.

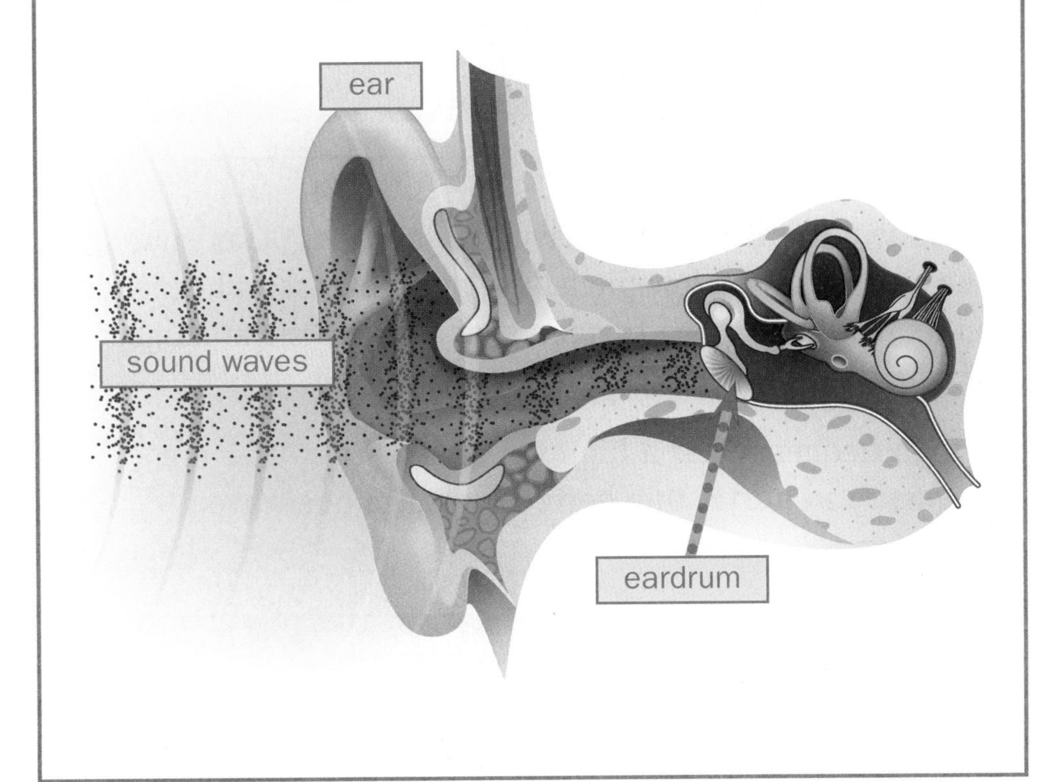

WHY IT MATTERS

You can hear sounds through walls and under water as well as in air.

PHYSICAL SCIENCE

Properties of Sound

ESSENTIAL IDEA

Sound has many properties, such as pitch, intensity, and quality. You can recognize different sounds because of their properties.

Some sounds, like a flute, have a high pitch. Other sounds, like a cello, have a low pitch. The **pitch** of a sound depends on its **frequency**. The frequency of a sound is the number of vibrations that pass a point in one second.

A high frequency has a high pitch. Scientists measure frequency in **hertz**. One hertz is equal to one wave per second.

Pitch and Frequency

The cello has a low pitch and low frequency.

The flute has a high pitch and high frequency.

Amplitude measures how much energy is in a sound wave. The **intensity**, or loudness, of a sound depends on its amplitude.

In a sound with high amplitude, the wave has a lot of energy. The sound wave pushes particles of matter very tightly together.

Low-amplitude sounds have less energy. Those sound waves do not push particles together tightly. Soft sounds are less intense than loud sounds.

Amplitude and Intensity

This boy is blowing loudly. The sound has a high amplitude and high intensity.

This girl is blowing softly. The sound has a low amplitude and low intensity.

Volume tells about the loudness or intensity of sound. Volume is measured in a unit called **decibels**. Listening to sounds over 70 decibels for a long time can cause hearing loss. The more decibels a sound has, the more quickly the sound can hurt your ears.

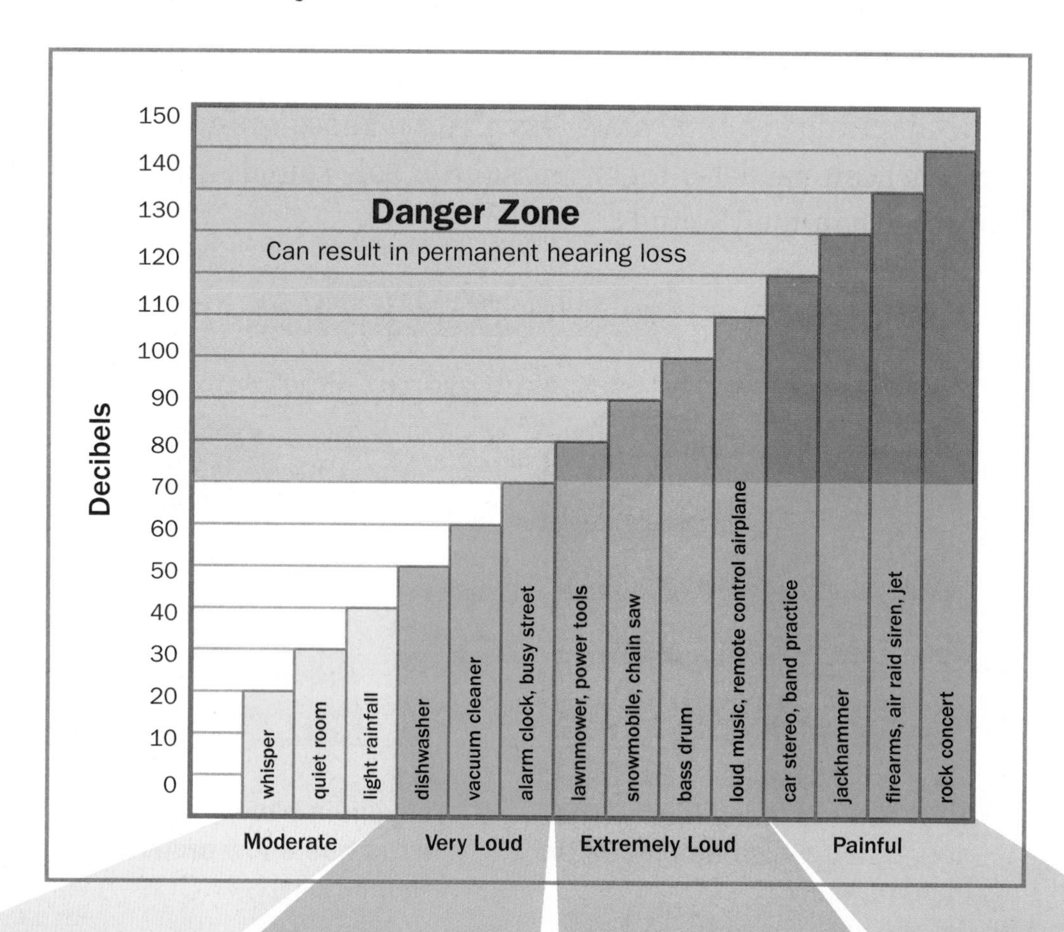

There are many kinds of sounds. For example, a tuba note sounds different from the same note played on a whistle. A human voice sounds different from a violin. A sound's **quality** helps you know what made the sound.

When you listen to music, each instrument might play the same note, or pitch. All the instruments sound different because each instrument vibrates in a different way.

Sound quality helps you determine which instrument a sound comes from.

WHY IT MATTERS

You can hear the difference in sounds because of their pitch, intensity, and quality.

Studying Science

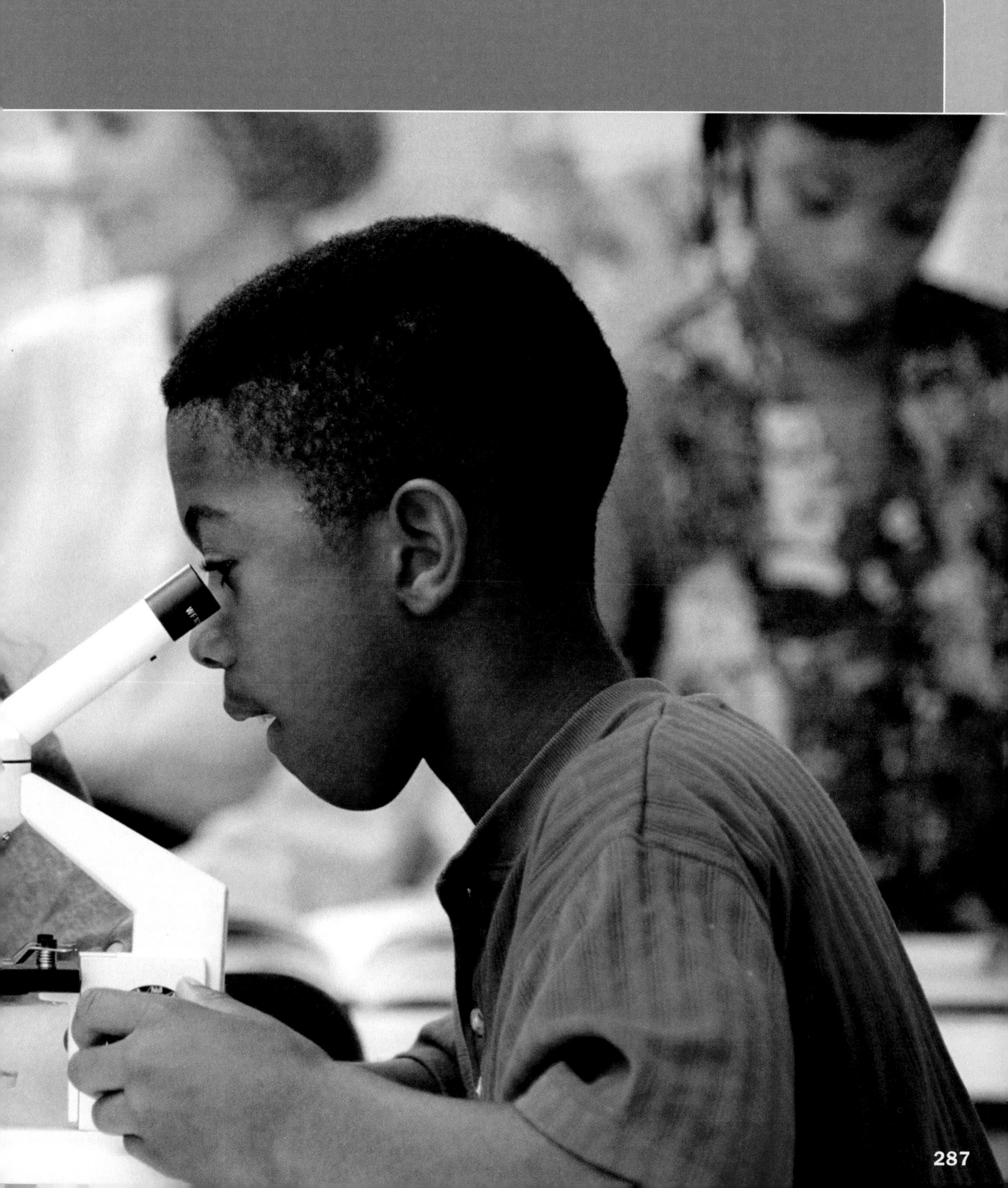

Science Process Skills

ESSENTIAL IDEA

Scientists use a process to answer their questions about the world and how things work.

Science is about asking questions and finding answers to questions. **Scientists** use a series of steps, called a **process**, to look for answers.

Each step in the process is a **skill**, or ability. Scientists use the steps to test their ideas and find out new information.

These scientists are measuring to find information.

Science process skills can help you solve problems and answer questions. You can use the science process skills in any order. Scientists will often **repeat** steps in the science process.

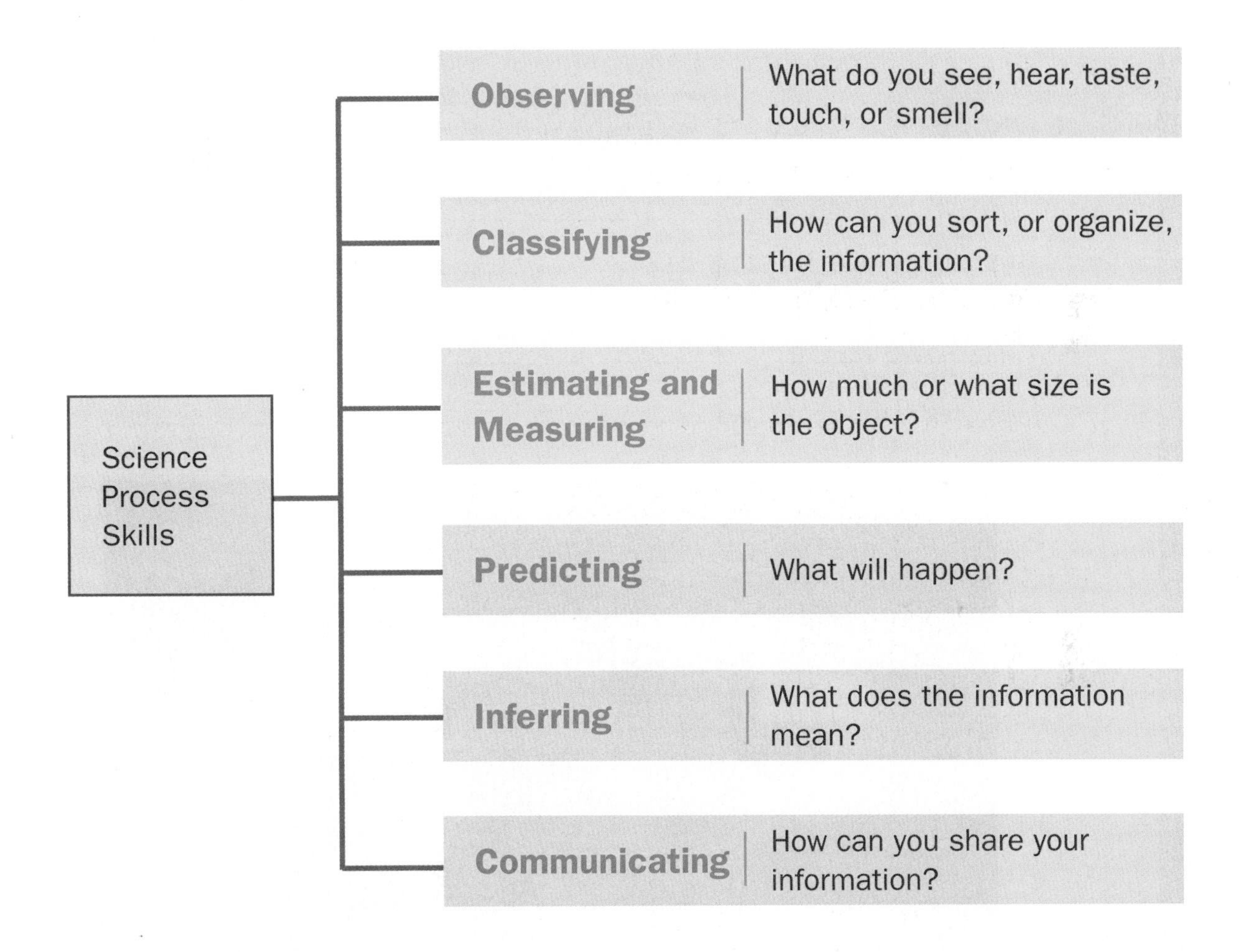

Observing

Observing is one of the most important science process skills. Scientists use their five **senses** to **gather**, or collect, information. Your senses include sight, hearing, taste, touch, and smell. Be careful: it is not always safe to touch, taste, or smell some objects.

	sense	description
	sight	Scientists see many crystals.
	hearing	Scientists hear water dripping.
	taste	It is not safe to taste things in a cave.
	touch	Scientists do not touch crystals. If crystals are touched, then they will stop growing.
	smell	Scientists smell sulfur in caves.

Scientists gather information about the world with their senses.

Your senses give you information about the **properties** of the objects you observe. For example, you could observe an object's color, size, shape, and texture.

Give a description of what you observe.

My Observations

Object: a geode rock

Color: The outside is brown. The inside is full of purple crystals.

Size: 3 inches long

Shape: like a triangle

Texture: The crystals are rough.

Recording your observations is an important part of gathering information.

Classifying

Scientists **classify**, or put into groups, living and nonliving things. Scientists **sort** things by the similarities, or ways things are alike.

When you classify, you separate things into different **categories**, or groups. Things with the same **properties** are grouped together.

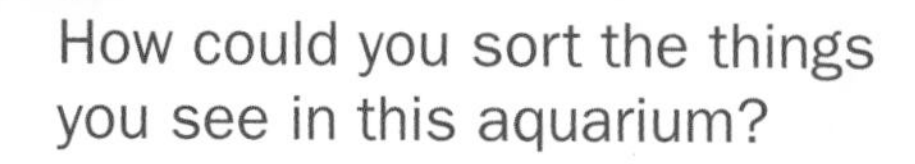
How could you sort the things you see in this aquarium?

Ways to Classify Objects

The way you classify things depends on your purpose. Someone who studies fish might classify fish this way:

big fish (more than 25 lb)	medium fish (1 lb–25 lb)	small fish (less than 1 lb)
sharks	trout	goldfish
halibut	salmon	tetras
swordfish	bass	sunfish

Size is one property of fish. You can also classify fish by where they live. Sharks and swordfish live in salt water. Trout and goldfish live in freshwater.

Estimating and Measuring

Sometimes you do not have to know the **precise**, or exact, size of something. When you do not need an exact answer, you can estimate. **Estimating** means making a **reasonable** guess based on things you know.

Measuring means figuring out the exact amount, or quantity. When you measure, you use a tool marked in **units**. A gram is a unit used to measure mass.

After measuring, you can compare your estimate to your measurement. Comparing helps you check your answer.

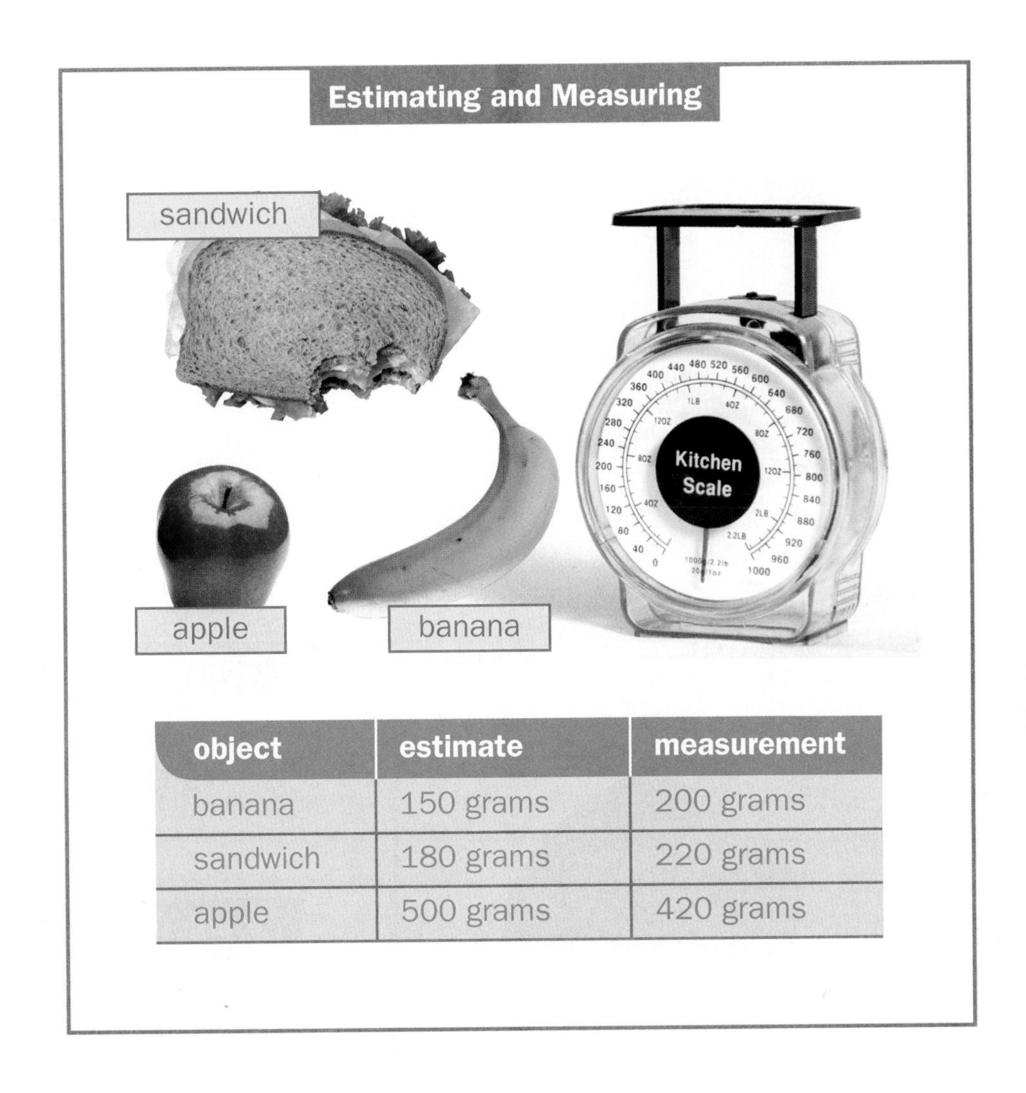

object	estimate	measurement
banana	150 grams	200 grams
sandwich	180 grams	220 grams
apple	500 grams	420 grams

Predicting

When you **predict**, you make a smart guess about **future** events. A prediction tells what you think will happen.

First you observe to figure out what is happening. Then you combine your observations with what you know from past **experiences**.

Predicting

Experience

My dog runs faster than I do.

Prediction

I think the dog will win.

Making a Prediction

When you predict, you think of a possible outcome of an event.

Observation	I see a student running with his dog. The student looks tired. The dog looks excited.

+

Past Experience	It takes a long time for my dog to get tired. My dog can run faster than I can.

=

Prediction	I think the dog will beat the student in a race.

Inferring

Scientists use what they observe to **explain** events. When you **infer**, you start by first making an **observation**. Then you make an **explanation** based on what you observed.

An observation tells what happened. An **inference** tells why something happened.

I observe that the plant looks wilted.

So I infer that the plant needs more sunlight.

Making new observations may cause you to change your **original**, or first, inference. You can make another inference based on the new information.

How to Make an Inference

1. Observe what is happening.
2. Make an inference to explain what you observe.
3. Observe some more.
4. Make a new inference if your original inference was incorrect.

After putting the plant in sunlight, the plant is still wilted. My new inference is that the plant needs more water.

Communicating

Scientists **communicate**, or share what they know or have learned, with others. Communicating helps everyone share and gain **knowledge**.

The students are measuring and recording temperature each hour during the day.

Using Graphs

Your information must be organized so other people can understand it. **Graphs**, tables, and **charts** can help you communicate information. Below are common types of graphs.

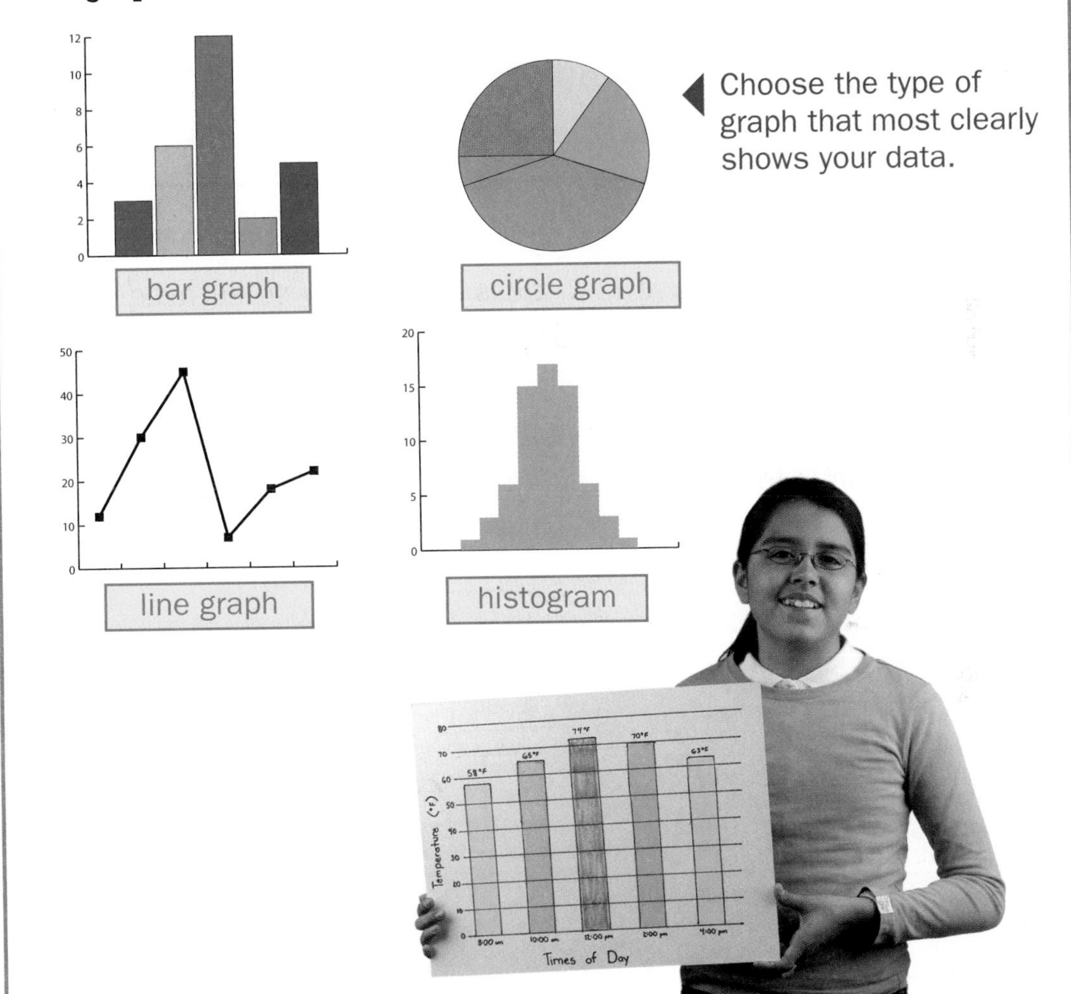

Choose the type of graph that most clearly shows your data.

WHY IT MATTERS

Science process skills can help you answer questions and solve problems.

Using Scientific Methods

ESSENTIAL IDEA

Scientists use scientific methods to help them solve problems and test new ideas.

Scientists often have new ideas about how something in nature works. They use scientific **methods**, or a series of steps, to figure out if their ideas are correct. Scientists also use scientific methods to **solve** problems. The methods do not always follow the same order.

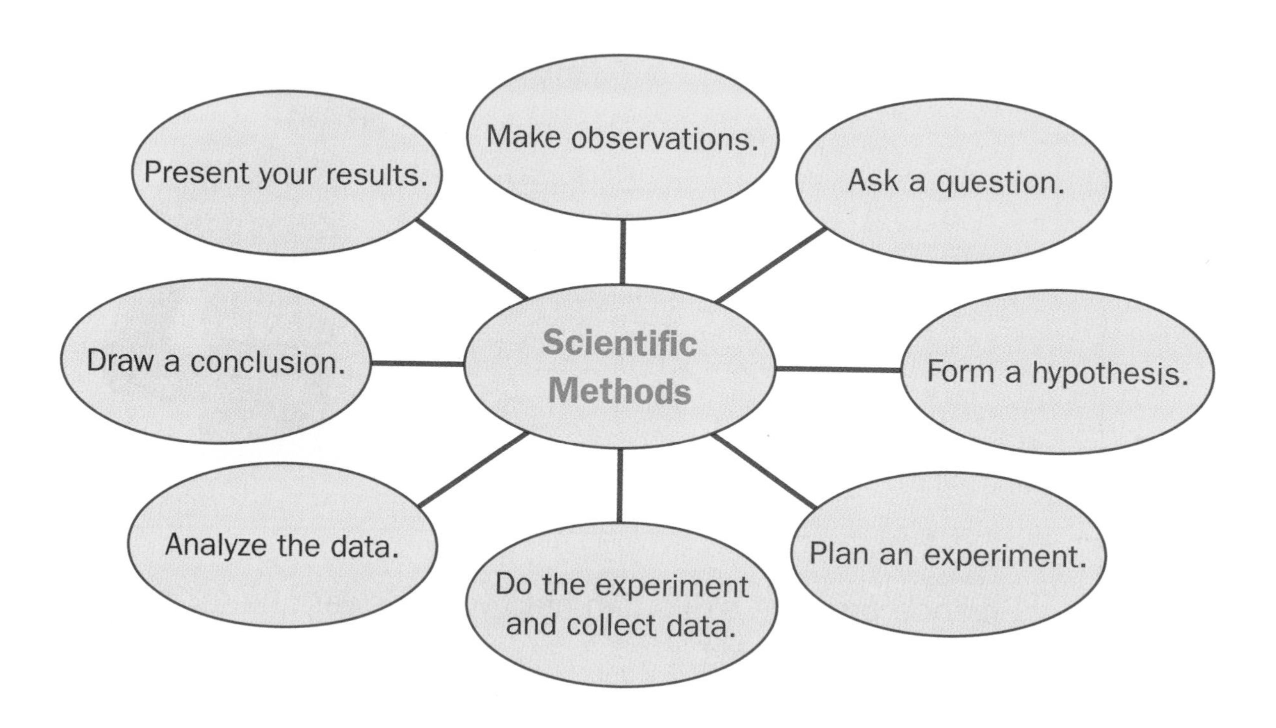

Here are the steps used for one experiment.

1 Make observations.

You use your senses to observe the world around you.

2 Ask a question.

The question should be about your observations.

Question:
Why is it a good idea to wear light clothes in summer and dark clothes in winter?

3 Form a hypothesis. Plan an experiment.

Think about your question and form a **hypothesis**. A hypothesis is an idea about how something works. It is not a fact, because it hasn't been tested.

My Hypothesis:
White clothes absorb less heat than black clothes.

To test a hypothesis, scientists plan and do experiments. An **experiment** is a series of steps that gives information about the hypothesis. A good experiment tests only one **variable**. The variable is the one thing that changes. Things that stay the same are the **controls**.

When you do an experiment, you sometimes use a **model**. A model is a simple version of something. Models **represent**, or show, how things work or look.

Paper can be a model for clothes.

Experiment Plan

1. I will use black and white paper as a model for the clothes.
2. I will use ice as a model for a person.
3. I will put an ice cube on each plate. I will put the white sheet of paper over one plate and the black one over the other plate.
4. I will place both plates under a lamp.
5. I will observe the ice cubes and measure how long the ice cubes take to completely melt.

Variable: white paper or black paper
Controls: lamp, plate, size of ice cube

Do the experiment and collect data.

As you do an experiment, you make observations and record what you observe. **Data** are facts that you collect from your experiment.

Collecting data includes recording the data. You can record by writing or drawing the data in a table. A table is an easy way to show results and measurements.

data

Time (min)	Black paper	White paper
0	Ice cube is the same size.	Ice cube is the same size.
1	Ice cube melts slightly. Small puddle forms.	Ice cube looks wet on sides.
2	Ice cube is about 1/2 melted.	Very small puddle forms.
3	Ice cube is about 3/4 melted.	Puddle is larger, but much of ice cube is still there.
4	Ice cube is completely melted.	Ice cube is almost 1/2 melted.
10		Ice cube is completely melted.

5 Analyze the data.

Analyzing your data is deciding what the information means. You **interpret**, or figure out, the meaning of what you have observed.

Think about your prediction and hypothesis as you analyze the data. Make inferences about what you didn't observe directly.

Analyzing Data

1. The ice cube covered with black paper melted more than twice as fast as the one covered with white paper. (observation)
2. The black paper absorbed more heat from the lamp. (inference)
3. That means that the white paper absorbed less heat than the black paper. (inference)

6 Draw a conclusion.

A **conclusion** is a decision. In your conclusion, you decide if your data **supports** your prediction and hypothesis.

My Conclusion:
The data supports my prediction and hypothesis. The ice cube under the white paper melted slower. So white clothes absorb less heat.

7 Present your results.

The final step in a scientific method is sharing the **results** of your experiment. The results explain what happened. Often you explain the results by writing a report. In a report, you can **present** your data in a **graph**.

Using Scientific Methods

1. Make observations.	I see people wearing light color clothes in summer. I know I wear dark clothes in winter.
2. Ask a question.	Why is it a good idea to wear light clothes in summer and dark clothes in winter?
3. Form a hypothesis. Plan an experiment.	White clothes absorb less heat than black clothes. I will use ice cubes and paper as a model.
4. Do the experiment and collect data.	Under black paper, the ice cube melted in 4 minuntes. Under white paper, the ice cube melted in 10 minutes.
5. Analyze the data.	The white paper absorbed less heat than the black paper.
6. Draw a conclusion.	The data supports my prediction and hypothesis. The ice cube under the white paper melted slower. So, white clothes absorb less heat.
7. Present your results.	I made a graph and wrote a report.

WHY IT MATTERS

You can use a method or plan to solve problems in your daily life.

Part Two

Literacy Essentials

This part of the book will help you read and write about science.

Reading Science

Science Textbooks

ESSENTIAL IDEA

Science textbooks are organized so you can find information easily.

A science textbook includes information about many science **topics**.

Topics in textbooks are arranged into **units**. Units name big topics, like Weather. **Chapters** within the unit tell more about smaller topics, like Seasons and Climate.

You read a science textbook for a specific **purpose**, or reason. Your purpose for reading a science textbook is to find information about science topics.

How to Set a Purpose

Ask yourself three questions before you start a new chapter. Try to answer them while you read.

1. What is the topic?
2. What is the author saying about the topic?
3. How can I connect this new information to facts I already know?

1. The chapter is about Earth in space.
2. The author is telling me that Earth's distance from the Sun affects weather.
3. I know that Earth is the third planet from the Sun.

WHY IT MATTERS

- You use a science textbook to learn about science topics.
- You can use a science textbook as a reference when writing about science topics.

Periodicals

ESSENTIAL IDEA

You can find information about science in periodicals. You can preview the parts of an article before you read it.

You can read science **articles** in **periodicals**, like magazines and newspapers. You can learn about current events and **facts** by reading periodicals.

How to Preview

Before reading an article, **preview** what you are about to read. You can preview the article by looking at the article's **headline**, **photographs**, and **captions**.

headline
An article's headline tells you what the article is about.

photograph
A photograph often shows the subject of an article.

caption
The caption gives information about the photograph.

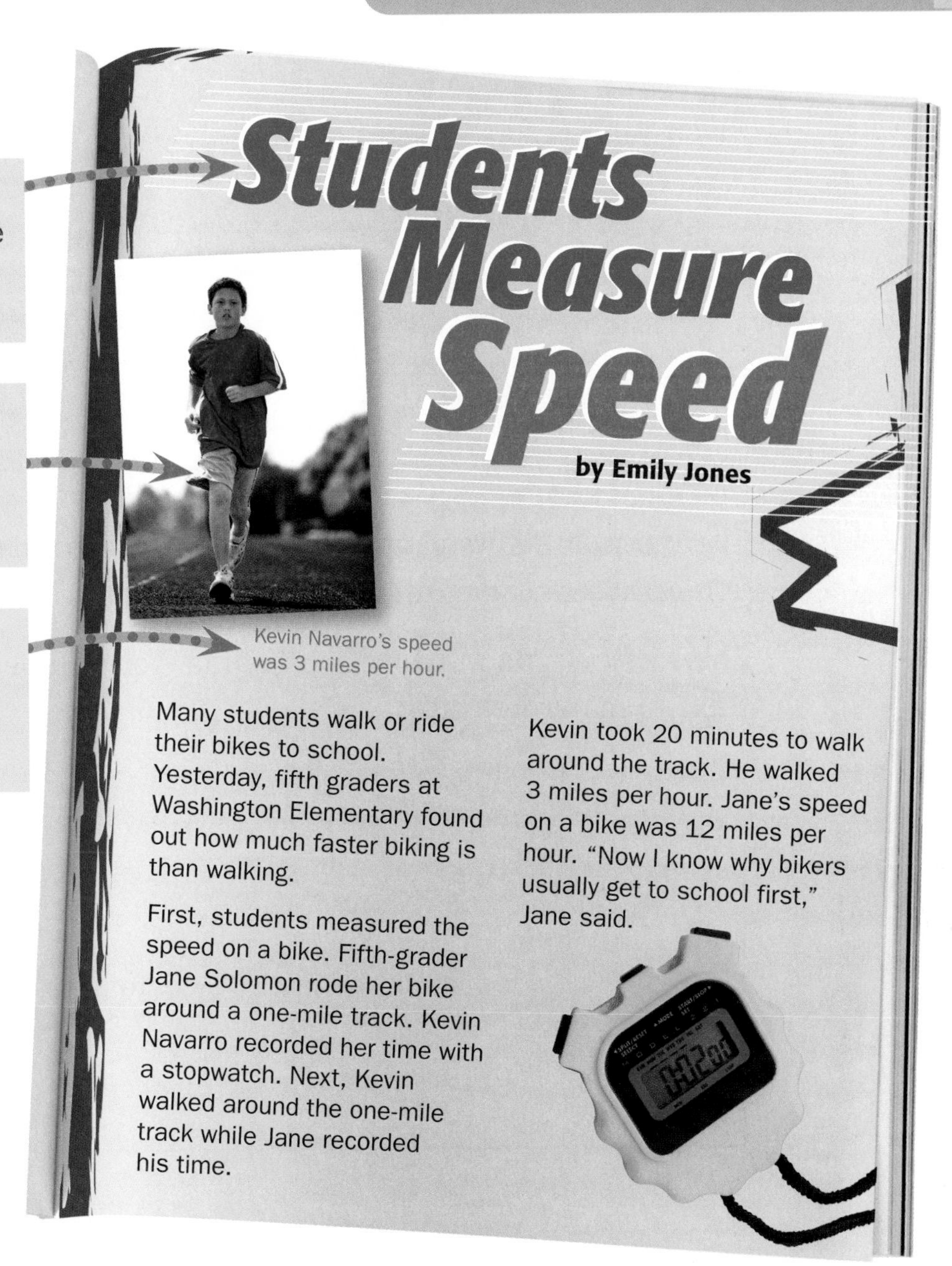

Students Measure Speed

by Emily Jones

Kevin Navarro's speed was 3 miles per hour.

Many students walk or ride their bikes to school. Yesterday, fifth graders at Washington Elementary found out how much faster biking is than walking.

First, students measured the speed on a bike. Fifth-grader Jane Solomon rode her bike around a one-mile track. Kevin Navarro recorded her time with a stopwatch. Next, Kevin walked around the one-mile track while Jane recorded his time.

Kevin took 20 minutes to walk around the track. He walked 3 miles per hour. Jane's speed on a bike was 12 miles per hour. "Now I know why bikers usually get to school first," Jane said.

WHY IT MATTERS

- Science articles tell you information about current events and ideas.
- You can learn about new scientific discoveries by reading periodicals.

Internet

ESSENTIAL IDEA

The Internet is a fast way to find information on a subject. Some sources, or Web sites, are better than others for finding accurate information.

The Internet allows people to find a lot of information fast. You can use a computer to **search** for facts.

Enter **key words** into a search engine. You will get a list of links to many Web sites.

How to Choose Key Words

1. Think of a topic.
2. Find a few key words that connect to the topic.
3. Decide which words to type into a search engine.

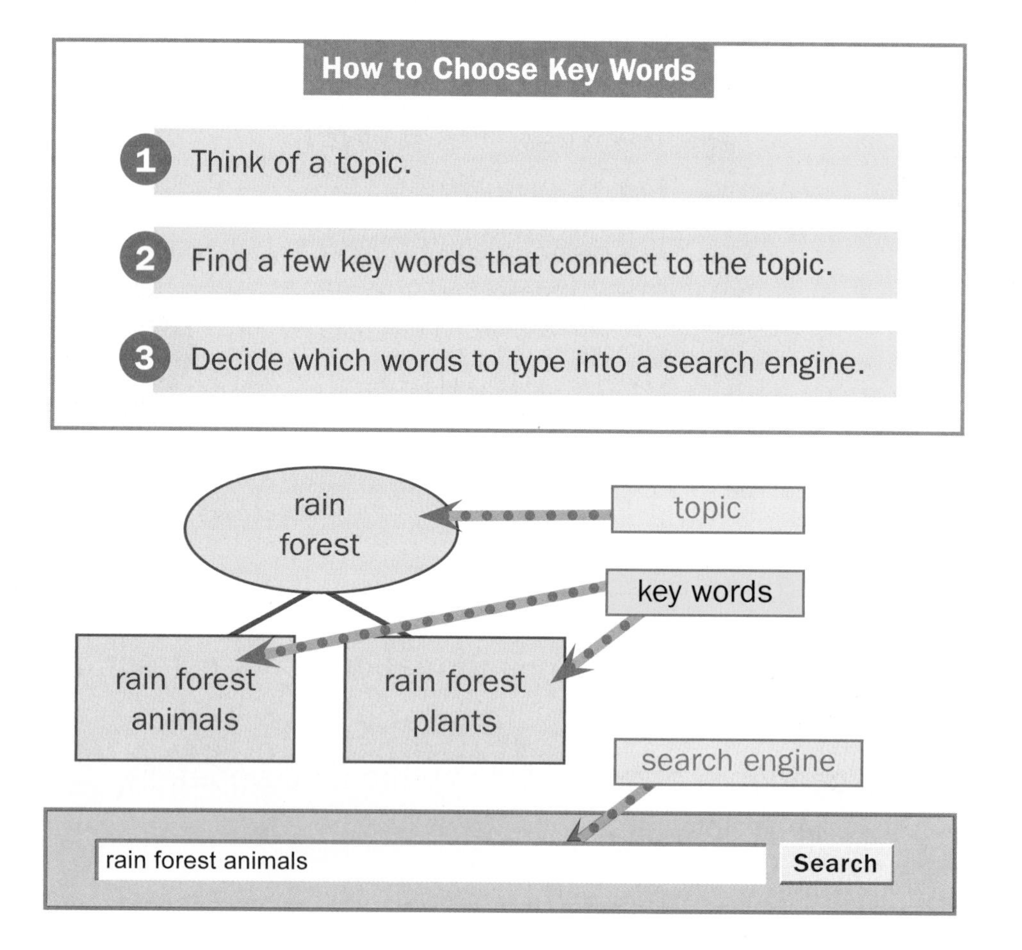

How to Choose Web Sites

Not every Web site is a good **source** of information. You need to **evaluate**, or decide, which sources you can trust.

- ☑ Check who created the Web site. Also check when the Web site was last updated.
- ☑ Look for Web sites ending in .gov or .edu. Government and education Web sites are often better sources of facts.
- ☑ Avoid personal Web sites as sources of information.

WHY IT MATTERS

- The Internet has information that can answer your questions.
- You have to decide if you can trust a source from the Internet.

Parts of a Textbook

ESSENTIAL IDEA

Textbooks have many parts that help you locate information.

The table of contents, glossary, and index are parts of textbooks that can help you find information quickly.

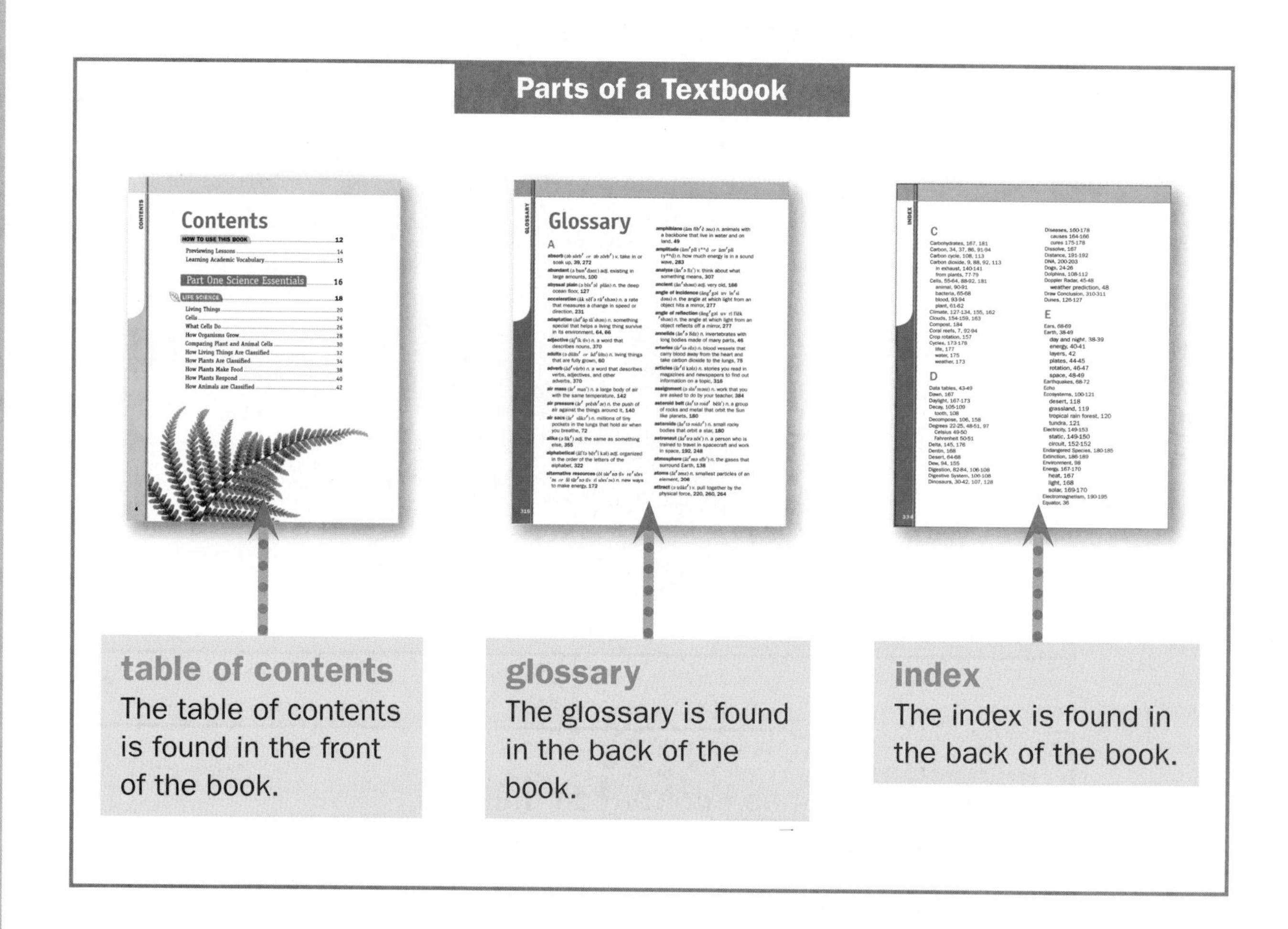

Table of Contents

The **table of contents** lists the **units** and **chapters** in the order they appear. You can use a table of contents to find the starting page number of each unit and chapter.

The table of contents shows only the main topics of a book.

Glossary

A **glossary** lists key words and phrases that appear in a textbook. The words are listed in **alphabetical** order. Use the glossary to find the **definition** so you know what a word means.

A **pronunciation guide** helps you say the word correctly. Sometimes the part of speech is given. This tells you if the word is a noun (n.), verb (v.), adjective (adj.), or adverb (adv.).

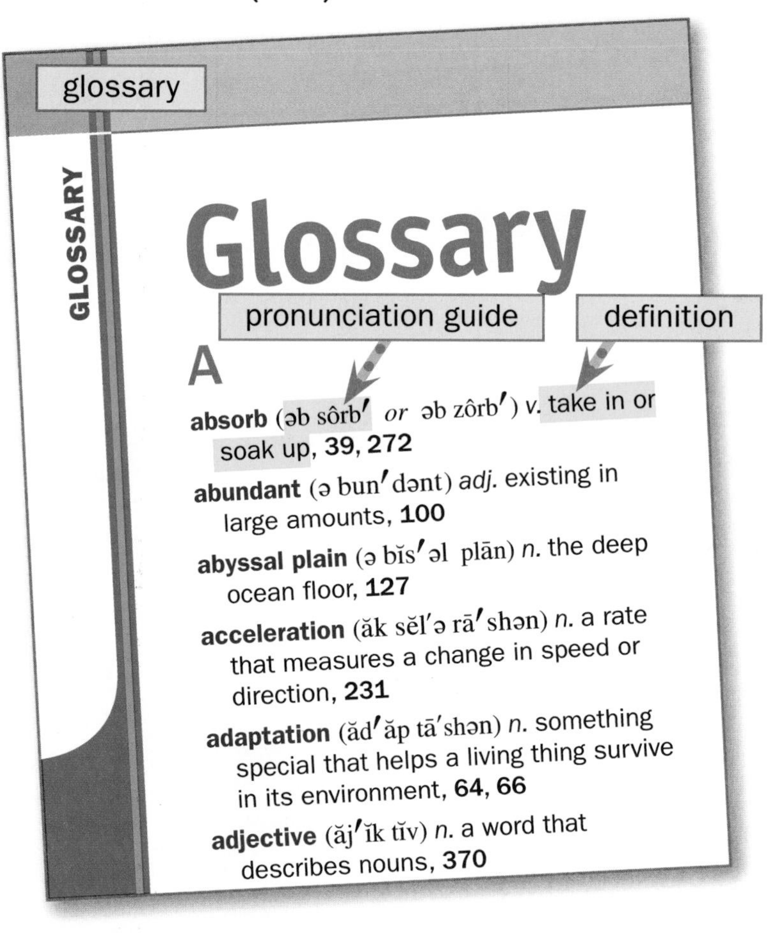

The glossary gives the meaning of the word *adaptation*.

Index

The **index** is a list of topics in a book. The topics are listed alphabetically. Each **entry** gives the topic and the pages where you can read about it.

Subtopics are indented under main topics and are also listed alphabetically.

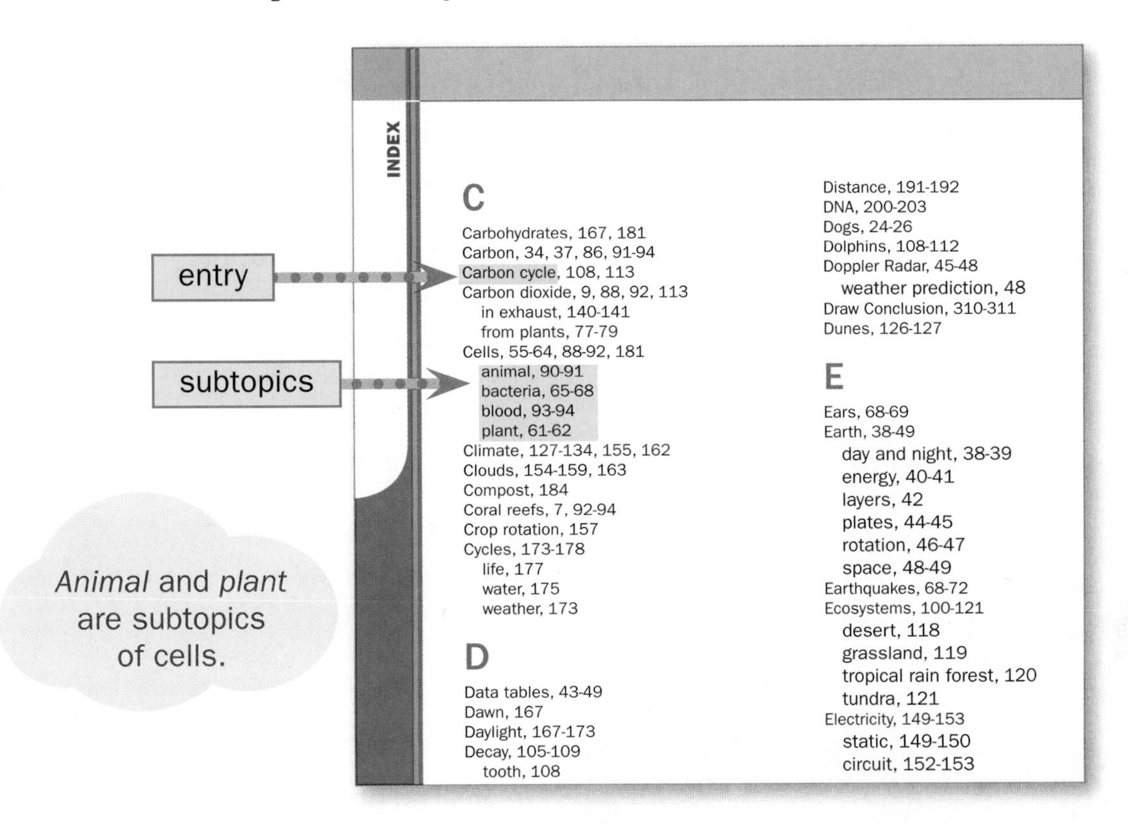

WHY IT MATTERS

- The table of contents shows you the topics you study in a chapter.
- You can use the glossary to study key words.
- The index helps you quickly find the page of a topic.

Textbook Features

ESSENTIAL IDEA

Features in science textbooks show information in different ways.

Science textbooks give you a lot of information. When you read a textbook page, look for features. **Features** are easy to find because they are different from the text.

Some examples of features are headings, terms, photographs, and graphics. You can look at the features for more information on a topic or to help you preview the page.

textbook

Textbook features

titles and headings
terms to know
photographs and illustrations
charts and graphs
diagrams

Titles and Headings

Titles and **headings** tell you the topic of what you are reading. They also give clues to the main ideas. In the example below, you know you will be reading about climate and weather.

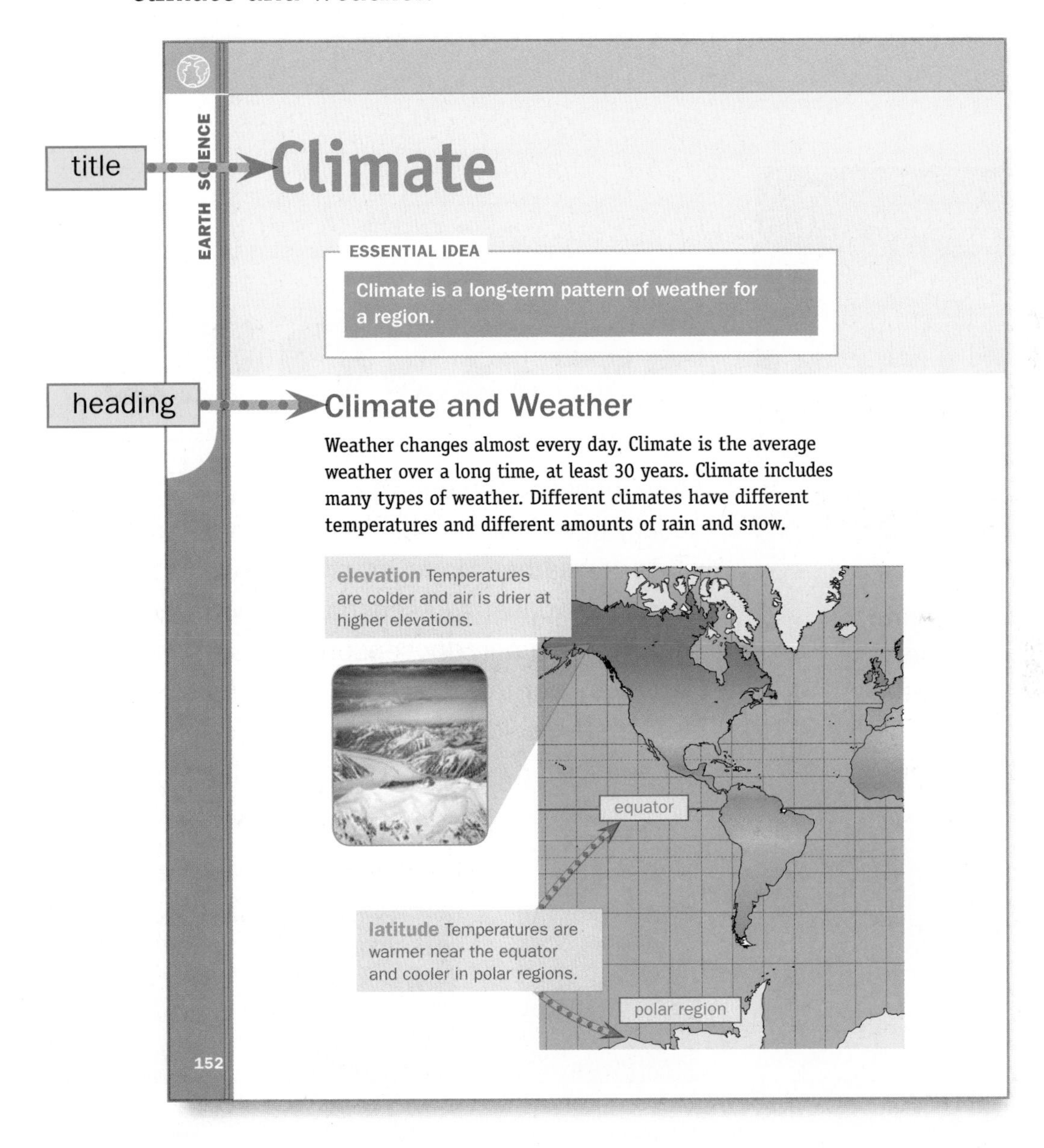

Terms to Know

Science textbooks introduce many new words. As you read, look for clues about what a **term**, or important word, means. Try using context clues, or words near the term, to figure out the **definition** or meaning.

Unit:1 Seasons

terms to know
Words in dark print appear with their meanings in the glossary.

Areas between the **equator** and the poles usually have four seasons, each with different kinds of weather. However, areas close to the equator have just two seasons—a hot, wet season and a hot, dry season. Areas at **latitudes** near the poles also have two seasons—a cold, dry season and a cold, wet season.

4 seasons

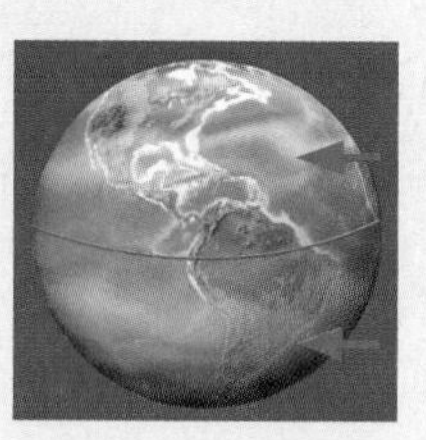

between equator and pole

2 seasons

equator

2 seasons

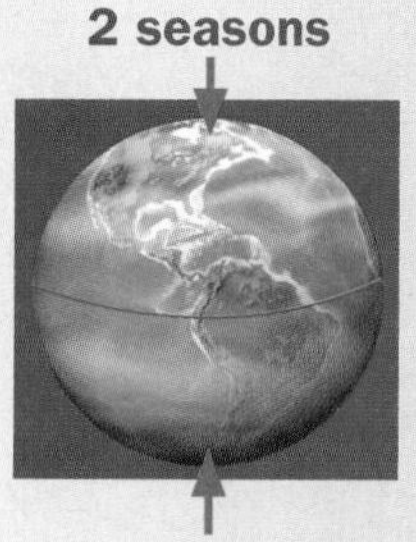

near the poles

Photographs and Illustrations

Photographs are pictures taken with a camera.
Illustrations are drawings used to explain information.

Photographs and illustrations are **graphics**, or features that show information in a visual way. Most graphics have **captions** that explain them.

When it is summer in the United States, it is winter in Australia.

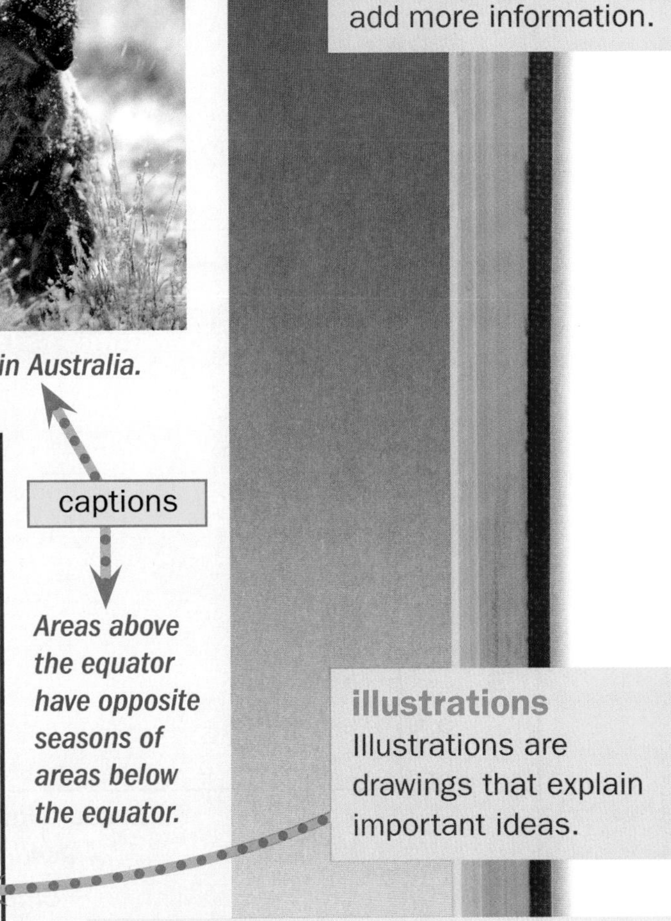

Areas above the equator have opposite seasons of areas below the equator.

Charts and Graphs

Science textbooks often give details in **charts** and **graphs**.

A chart **presents**, or shows, information in rows (↔) and columns (↕). A graph presents information with bars, pictures, shapes, or lines. Charts and graphs make it easy to compare information.

chart

column

row

July Temperatures at Different Latitudes

City	Average July Temperature	Latitude
Bogotá, Colombia	14°C (57°F)	4°N
Comodoro Rivadavia, Argentina	6°C (43°F)	45°S
Toronto, Canada	21°C (70°F)	43°N

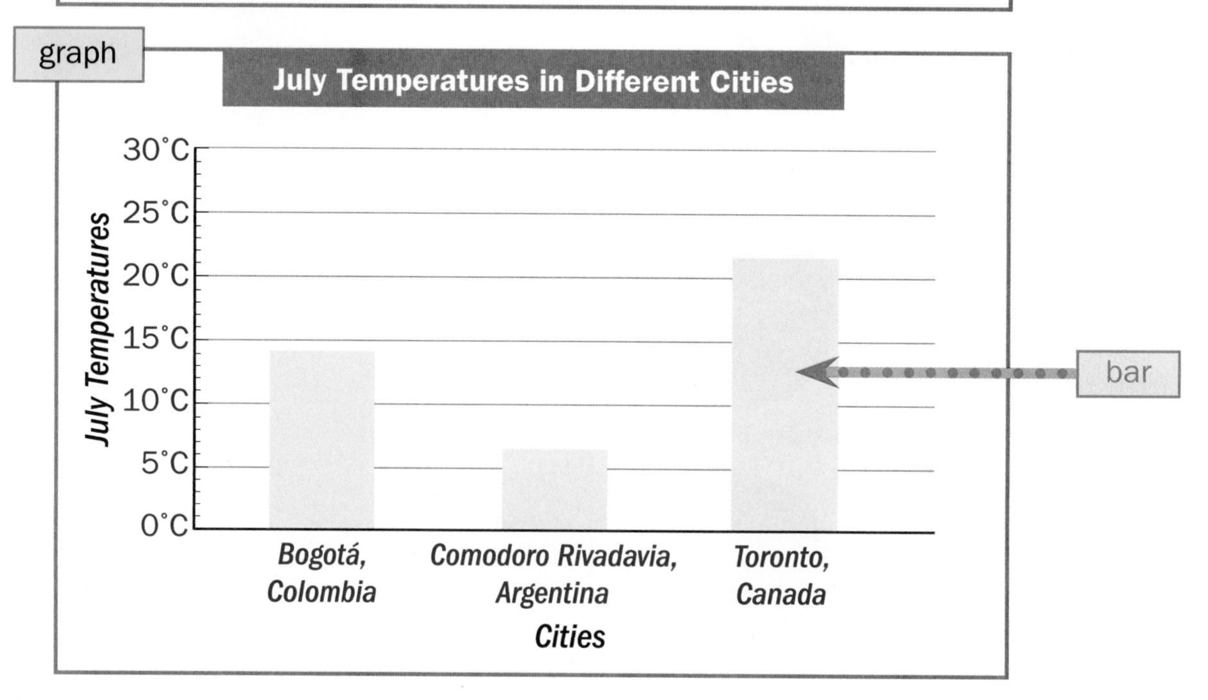

Diagrams

A **diagram** may use arrows, boxes, and words to describe something. Diagrams may **display** how parts go together or how something works.

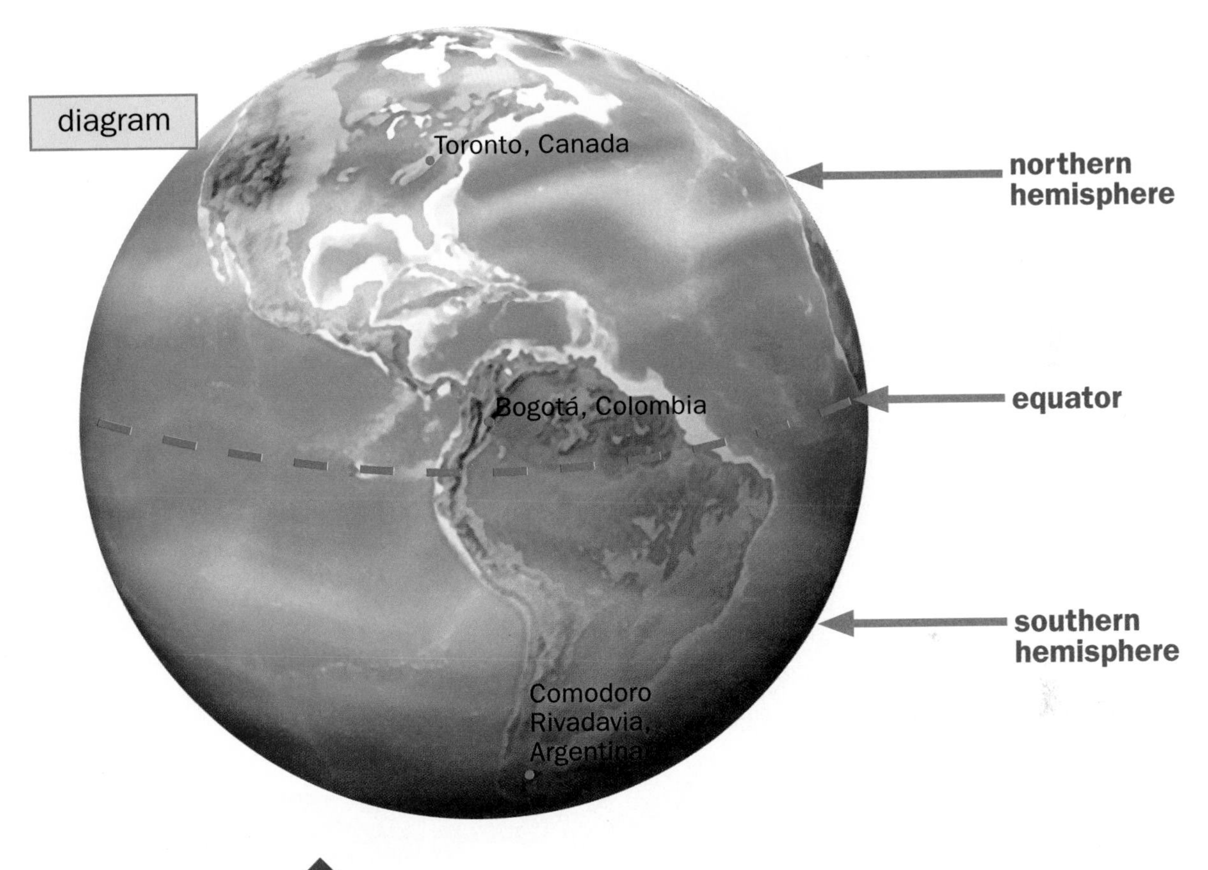

This diagram uses arrows and words to show information.

WHY IT MATTERS

The features in textbooks help you organize information and make it easier to understand.

Comprehension

Comparing and Contrasting

ESSENTIAL IDEA

To understand how things are alike and different, you can compare and contrast them.

Look for **similarities** to **compare** two or more things. Similarities show how things are almost the same.

Differences show how things are not alike. You use differences to **contrast** things.

Inner and Outer Planets

Our solar system can be divided into two parts. Planets closest to the Sun are inner planets. Planets far away from the Sun are outer planets.

Mars

Inner planets, such as Mars, are small, warm, and rocky. These planets have few moons. For example, Mars only has two moons. Mars also has the largest volcano in our solar system.

Outer planets, such as Neptune, are cooler because they are farther away from the Sun. They are also much larger and made mostly of gas and liquid. These planets have many moons. Neptune, for example, has thirteen moons.

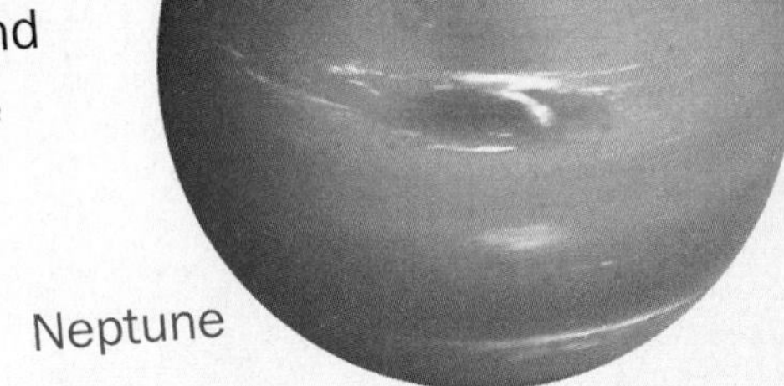
Neptune

Venn Diagrams

A Venn diagram makes it easy to compare and contrast. It helps you see how two or more things are similar or different.

How to Create a Venn Diagram

1. Write similarities in the middle area where the circles overlap.
2. Write differences in the areas where the circles do not overlap.

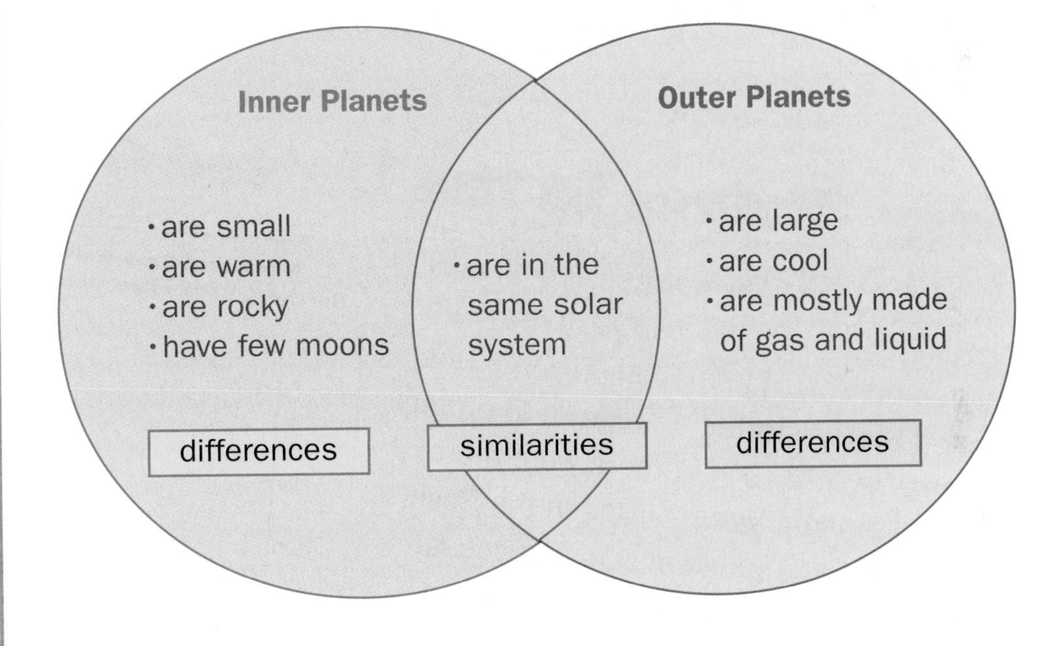

WHY IT MATTERS

- You can find similarities and differences to help you understand the world.
- You can create a Venn diagram to compare and contrast.

Predicting

ESSENTIAL IDEA

You predict when you tell what you think will happen next. When you read, you use facts and details in the text to predict.

Making a **prediction** is thinking about what is most likely to happen in the **future**. Good readers make predictions about what they will read in order to better understand the text.

Gray Wolves in the United States

At one time, gray wolves lived all over North America. By the 1930s, there were almost no wolves left. Then, in 1979, the United States started a program to protect the gray wolf. By 2005, there were more than 1,000 gray wolves living in the Rocky Mountains. The program was a success!

However, not everyone is happy. Sometimes the wolves kill animals that belong to farmers. Now some people want the government to stop protecting the wolves. If the wolves are not protected, they may disappear again. What do you think should happen?

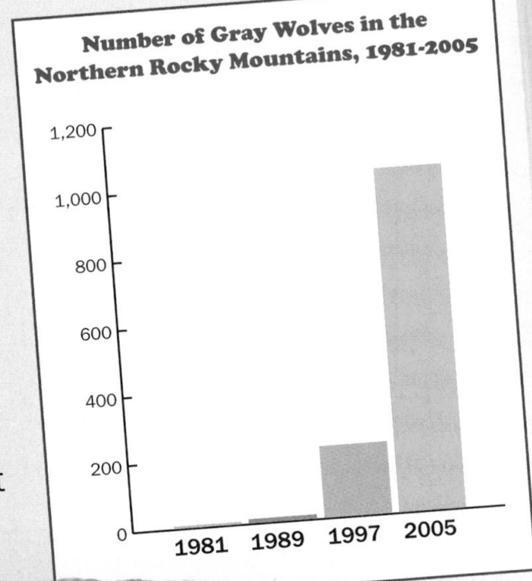

Predicting

To predict, gather **evidence**, or pieces of information, to guide you. Look at titles, pictures, and graphs to help you predict what you will read about.

title Look at the title to find the subject.

Gray Wolves in the United States

picture The pictures often show the subject.

graph You can get more evidence from graphs.

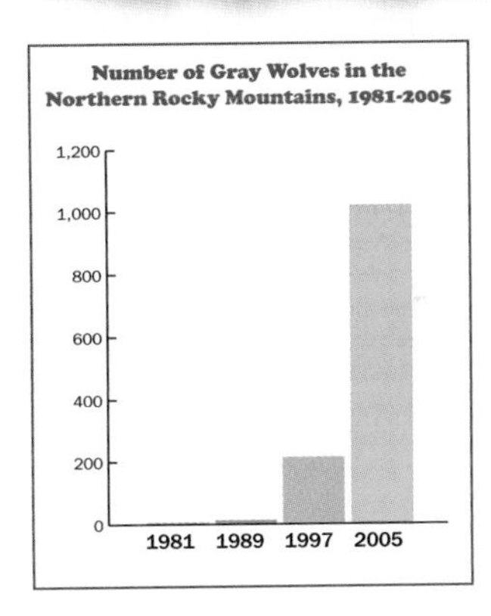

WHY IT MATTERS

Predicting helps you better understand what you read.

You can make a prediction by using pictures, graphs, and titles to give you an idea of what you will read.

Determining Important Information

ESSENTIAL IDEA

Identify the most important information to understand what you read. Look for the main idea and supporting details.

Think about the main idea as you read a paragraph. The **main idea** is the most important point to understand. To **determine**, or find, the main idea, look at the **details** of a passage. The details **support** the main idea.

Sometimes you can find the main idea at the beginning of a paragraph. Other times it is at the end or middle.

WILLIAM GILBERT

William Gilbert was an important scientist. He was born in England in 1544 and was also a doctor. Gilbert was the first person to try to understand how magnets work. He wrote a book about his research so that others could learn too. One of the most important things he discovered is that Earth is magnetic.

Main Idea

William Gilbert was an important scientist.

Detail

He was the first person to try to understand how magnets work.

Detail

He wrote a book about his research.

Detail

He discovered that Earth is magnetic.

The main idea tells the main point in a few words.

The details support, or explain more about, the main idea.

WHY IT MATTERS

- You can determine important information by finding the main idea.
- The details give you more information about the topic.

Summarizing

ESSENTIAL IDEA

You summarize when you put the most important ideas into your own words.

You **summarize** when you give only the most important information. You leave out small details and extra facts. **Determine** the main point as you read. Then **retell**, or describe, the main idea in your words.

Donkeys

Donkeys are like horses, but smaller. They do not need to eat as much as horses because they are smaller. Unlike horses, donkeys have tough hooves that don't need shoes. Therefore, owning a donkey is less expensive than owning a horse.

Donkeys can live a long time. If people take good care of them, donkeys can live over thirty years.

Since donkeys are strong, people use them to carry heavy loads. People also use donkeys for riding on and plowing fields.

First, figure out the main idea and supporting details.

MAIN IDEA	People use donkeys for many different reasons.
Supporting Detail	Donkeys are less expensive than horses.
Supporting Detail	Donkeys can live more than thirty years.
Supporting Detail	Donkeys can carry heavy loads.

The main idea is the most important point.

Supporting details explain the main idea.

Then use the main idea and supporting details to make your summary.

SUMMARY	Donkeys are useful because they are less expensive than horses, can live a long time, and are strong.

WHY IT MATTERS

- You summarize whenever you retell a story or event in your own words.
- When you summarize, it is easier to remember what you read.

Making Inferences

ESSENTIAL IDEA

You make inferences to add meaning to what you read.

Sometimes a text does not provide all the information you need. You need to use **clues** in the text to fill in the missing details. This **strategy** is called making an **inference**.

Making inferences is like filling in the blanks. You combine the information in the text with what you already know. Then you draw a **conclusion**.

Earthquakes

Why do earthquakes happen? Earth is made up of huge chunks called plates. These plates float on top of flowing rock below the surface. The plates are always moving against each other. A fault is where the plates meet. Faults look like giant cracks in the Earth.

Earthquakes often happen when the plates on each side of the fault move in different directions. When the plates move, it causes vibrations that shake the ground.

How to Make Inferences

1. Think about the information you already know.

If I shake a table, the things on the table are likely to fall and break.

2. Look for clues in the text to fill in missing details.

The text says that an earthquake shakes the ground.

3. Combine the information and draw a conclusion. This is your inference.

If an earthquake shakes the Earth, buildings near the fault may be damaged.

WHY IT MATTERS

Making inferences can help you better understand what you read.

COMPREHENSION

Visualizing

ESSENTIAL IDEA

Good readers visualize a process, a place, or an object described in what they read.

You **visualize** something by making a **mental** picture of it. You use the details from the text to help "draw" the **image**, or picture, in your mind.

GROW Your Own Crystals

A crystal is a special kind of rock. Follow these steps to make sugar crystals. Make sure an adult is nearby to help you.

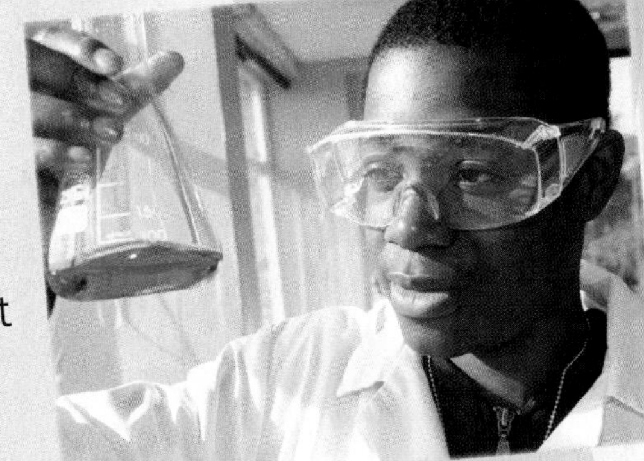

1. Add ¾ cup of sugar and 1¼ cups of hot water to a tall glass. Mix well.
2. Tie a piece of string around a pencil. The string should almost touch the bottom of the glass.
3. Place the pencil over the top of the glass and let the string hang in the water.
4. Set it aside. In a few days you will start to see sugar crystals form on the string.

How to Visualize

You can visualize a **process**, place, or object.
The crystal experiment shows a process, or steps.
Create a mental picture for each step.

WHY IT MATTERS

You visualize by making a mental picture of what you read or hear.

Asking and Answering Questions

ESSENTIAL IDEA

Good readers ask and answer questions about what they read.

Sometimes new material can be **confusing**, or hard to understand. As you read new information, **pause** to ask and answer questions. Stopping and thinking about the material will help you **clarify** a text.

HOME ABOUT CONTACT SEARCH

Asian Lady Beetles–*Outdoor Guest, Indoor Pest*

Multicolored Asian lady beetles are round and small. They can be yellow, light orange, or dark orange. Sometimes they have spots on their back. These beetles eat small insects that damage crops. Many farmers like Asian lady beetles.

Although they are helpful to farmers, Asian lady beetles can be annoying to other people. In the fall, large groups of the beetles look for warm places to spend the winter. They come into homes through cracks in the walls and windows. Once the beetles are in a home, it is hard to get them out. These beetles are nice to have in a garden, but not in a house.

As you read, ask yourself questions and try to answer them. Some common question words are *who, what, when, where, why*, and *how*.

What do multicolored Asian lady beetles look like?

They are small and round. They can have spots. They are yellow or orange.

How long do Asian lady beetles live?

The text doesn't tell me. I need to find another source.

Who likes Asian lady beetles?

Farmers like Asian lady beetles.

Why do some people not like Asian lady beetles?

Asian lady beetles try to come inside people's homes for winter.

WHY IT MATTERS

- You remember more of a text when you ask and answer your own questions.
- If you are confused, you can ask questions to help you understand.

Monitoring Comprehension

ESSENTIAL IDEA

Good readers check that they understand what they read. The most important goal of reading is understanding the subject.

As you read, it is a good idea to check your **comprehension**, or how well you understand what you read.

The Speed of Sound

When sound moves through the air, it usually moves at about 760 miles per hour. This is called the speed of sound. In 1947, Chuck Yeager flew a fighter plane called the X-1 and became the first pilot to travel faster than the speed of sound.

Something that moves at the speed of sound has a speed of Mach 1. Airplanes that travel at twice the speed of sound have a speed of Mach 2. An airplane called the SR-71 Blackbird can fly at Mach 3, or three times the speed of a sound.

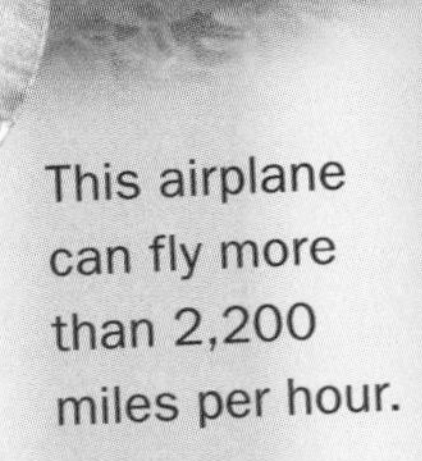

This airplane can fly more than 2,200 miles per hour.

If you do not understand what you read, use a **strategy** to **fix up** anything that is confusing. When you fix up confusing parts, you may need to **adjust**, or change, your thinking.

For example, after you read "The Speed of Sound," you may need to **reread**, or read it again. Rereading is one fix-up strategy for improving comprehension.

How to Monitor Comprehension

As you read, use these strategies to **monitor**, or check, your understanding.

Monitoring comprehension strategies

- ✓ Ask and answer questions as you read.
- ✓ Find the main idea and supporting details.
- ✓ Look for patterns in the text.
- ✓ Think about what you already know.
- ✓ Make a picture of what you read in your mind.
- ✓ Use clues to help you make sense of the text.
- ✓ Reread the text.
- ✓ Summarize the text in your own words.

WHY IT MATTERS

- Use fix-up strategies to improve your comprehension if you don't understand.
- You become a better reader by monitoring your comprehension as you read.

COMPREHENSION

Identifying Cause-Effect

ESSENTIAL IDEA

Identifying cause-effect relationships will help you understand why things happen.

A **cause** is the reason why something happens. The **effect** is what happens. Scientists often research the causes and effects of **events**. When one thing makes another thing happen, they have a cause-effect **relationship**.

Blind Fish in Caves

A cave is a large underground space. **Because** caves are underground, there is no light. Some animals, like the blind fish, live in caves. Why do you think these fish are blind?

Blind fish weren't always blind. Long ago, they had eyes that worked. They lived in caves with no light, **so** they didn't need to use their eyes. Over time their eyes stopped working. **Due to** their blindness, they developed different ways to find food. **Thus**, the blind fish adapted to their environment.

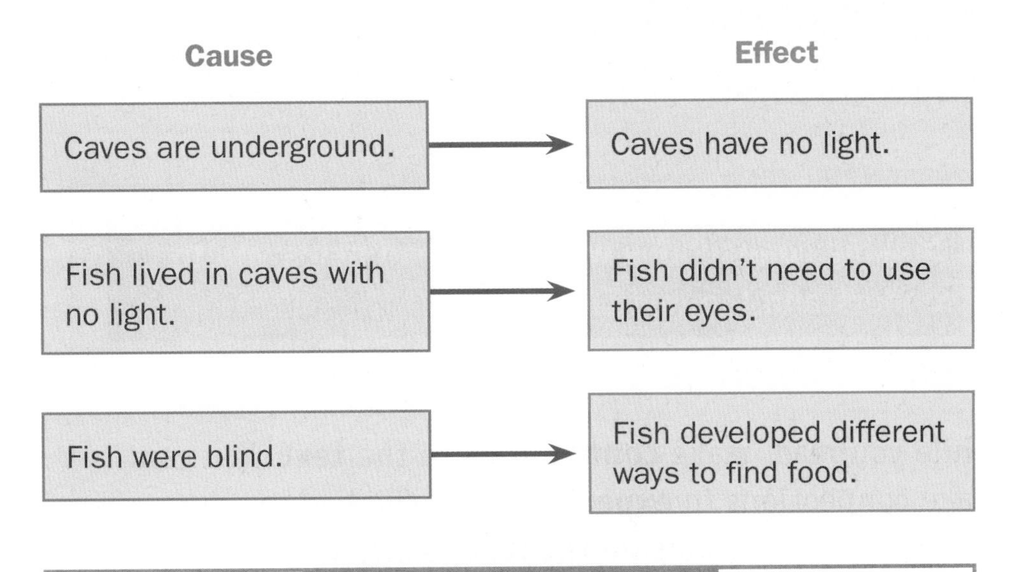

Cause-Effect Signal Words

When you read, look for cause-effect **signal words**. These words can help you identify which part is the cause and which is the effect.

Cause
because
due to
the reason for
created by

Effect
as a result
therefore
so
thus

WHY IT MATTERS

You can identify cause-effect relationships by looking for signal words.

Making Connections

ESSENTIAL IDEA

Making connections while you read helps you to understand the text better.

While you read, make **connections** to the **text**. You can make connections to **experiences** you've had in your life. You can also compare the text to other texts on the same **topic**.

Phases of the Moon

The Moon does not make its own light. We can only see the Moon because it reflects light from the Sun. The Moon's appearance changes as it moves around Earth. Half of the Moon's surface is always lit. The changes in the way the Moon looks are the phases of the Moon.

WHY IT MATTERS

- Making connections helps you understand what you read.
- Connecting a text to what you know adds more meaning.
- Your experiences can help you understand science.

COMPREHENSION

Recognizing Sequence

ESSENTIAL IDEA

Knowing the order of events will help you understand how things happen.

A process or idea makes more sense when you can **recognize** the sequence. **Sequence** is the **order** in which **events** happen.

Elephant Seals in California

Every spring and summer, elephant seals migrate to a beach in Piedras Blancas, California. They go there to molt, or remove a layer of skin.

First, the adult females arrive in May. The female elephant seals weigh between 900 and 1,800 pounds. They look huge, but bigger elephant seals arrive **later**.

The young males arrive **next**, in June. They are about the same weight as the adult females. **Finally**, the adult males arrive in the middle of July. The adult males are the biggest elephant seals. They weigh between 3,000 and 5,000 pounds.

A **flowchart** can help you find the sequence of events in a text. Use a chart like the one below to find the sequence in the text.

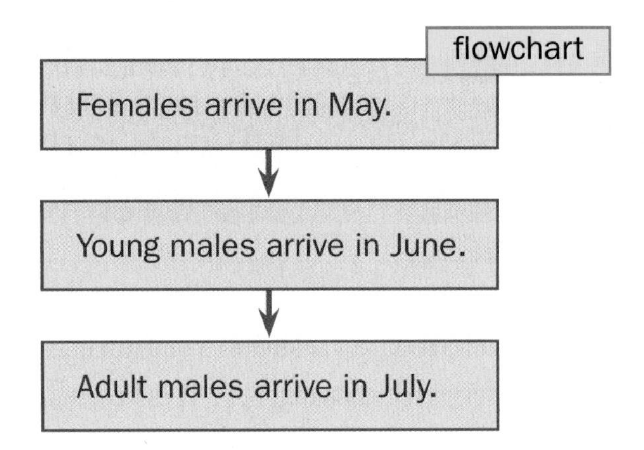

Words that Signal Sequence

When you read, look for words that signal sequence to help you understand the order of events.

beginning	middle	ending
first	next	finally
once	then	eventually
in the first place	later	at last
at the beginning	after	so

WHY IT MATTERS

- You will understand how things happen if you know the sequence, or order, of events.
- Every day you use sequences by deciding what to do in the morning, afternoon, and evening.

Generalizing

ESSENTIAL IDEA

When you read, look for details and examples that are alike. Then make a generalization that shows the similarities.

A **generalization** is a broad statement that joins, or combines, different **examples**. It shows how the examples share a similar idea.

The Dolton Digest

Recycling Works for Dolton

When you recycle, you create a new use for something. You can recycle **many** of the things you use **every** day. For example, an old newspaper can be turned into a brown paper bag. A **few** materials, like lightbulbs, cannot be recycled.

A community can recycle in many ways. **Most** of the time, people sort recyclables by different types, such as paper, plastic, metal, and glass. They then send the recyclables to places that make new products from the old.

You also can recycle by finding other people who want to trade their used item for your used item. Recycling can help save **some** important resources from being wasted.

Making Generalizations

Look for ways that things are **alike** in order to generalize about them.

My generalizations about recycling:

- Communities can recycle many of the things they use.
- Most of the time, communities put recyclables into different bins.
- When every community recycles, it helps protect Earth.

Words used in generalizations		
most	some	none
every	usually	few
many	generally	never
often	much	nothing

WHY IT MATTERS

You generalize to see what different facts, items, or events have in common.

Generalizing also helps you classify, or sort, information about a topic.

Drawing a Conclusion

ESSENTIAL IDEA

Draw a conclusion using information you read and what you already know.

A **conclusion** is an idea you form, or create, yourself. A good conclusion is based on **evidence**. You can get evidence from the facts in the text and your own experiences.

Air in the Mountains

Mountains can have two types of weather at the same time. One side of a mountain might be rainy, and the other side might be dry.

When a mountain is near water, moist air is pushed up one side of the mountain. As the air moves up, it cools. When the moisture in the air cools, it begins to rain.

By the time the air reaches the other side of the mountain, it has lost all its moisture and has become dry. The side that gets the dry air has very little rain.

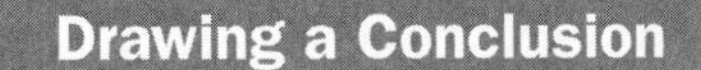

You draw, or form, a conclusion by reviewing all the **facts** and figuring out how they connect.

Experience
I've seen storm clouds on one side of a mountain and sunshine on the other.

Fact
Moist air is pushed up one side of the mountain and forms rain.

Fact
Air on the other side of the mountain is dry.

Conclusion
Mountains block moist air, causing it to rain only on one side.

WHY IT MATTERS

- You use evidence and experience to help you draw conclusions.
- You draw conclusions to solve problems and understand the main ideas of what you read.

Understanding Language

Prefixes

ESSENTIAL IDEA

Learning prefixes helps you read and understand new words.

A **prefix** is a group of letters that is added to the **beginning** of word parts. Two kinds of word parts are base words and roots.

The paragraph below uses many prefixes.

Aquariums

An aquarium holds living and **non**living things. The living and nonliving things **inter**act in the same habitat. An aquarium has important parts. A hood **en**closes the tank. A filter cleans and **re**freshes the water all the time.

A **base word** is a word part that can be separated from the prefix.

Reheat has the base word *heat* and means "to heat again." Adding the prefix *re-*, meaning *again*, changes the meaning of the base word.

A **root** is a word part that is used to form other words. Roots are not words by themselves.

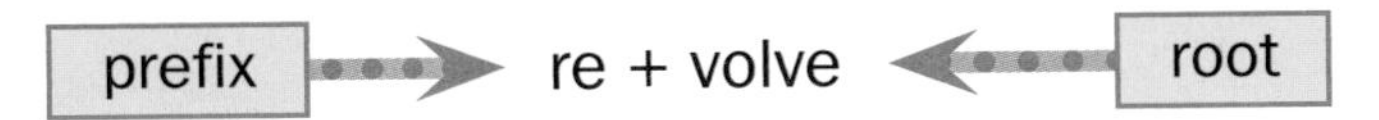

Revolve has the root *volve* and means "to turn again."

Common Prefixes

prefix	meaning	example
non-	not	nonliving, nonfiction
inter-	with, between	interact, interstate
en-	in	enclose, endanger
re-	again	refresh, regrow

WHY IT MATTERS

- Learning common prefixes can help you understand new words.
- Prefixes and roots are common in the science words that you study.

UNDERSTANDING LANGUAGE

Suffixes

ESSENTIAL IDEA

Learn suffixes to help you read and understand new words.

A **suffix** is a group of letters that comes at the **end** of a word. A suffix adds meaning to a **base word** or **root**.

Water Cycle

Have you ever wondered where water comes from? The same water moves through a natur**al** pattern. This movement is called the water cycle.

The Sun heats the water in oceans and lakes. Evapora**tion** turns the liquid water into a gas called vapor. The water vapor rises up into the sky. Then the vapor cools and changes back to its liquid form. This is called condensa**tion**.

The condensation gathers into clouds. Soon the clouds get too heavy. So the water falls back to Earth as precipita**tion**, such as rain or snow. Some water soaks into the soil. Some falls back into the ocean. Water is renew**able**, so the cycle goes on and on.

For example, the word *changeable* has the suffix *-able* after the base word *change*.

base word → change + able ← suffix

Visible has the root *vis* and means "able to be seen."

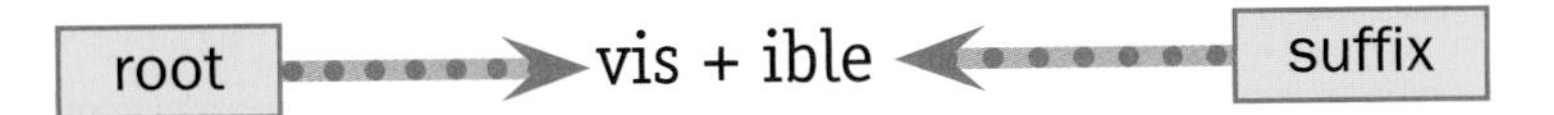

Common Suffixes

Changeable means "able to change." Learning common suffixes can help you understand new words.

suffix	meaning	example
-ion -tion -ness -ous	state or quality of	champion evaporation awareness famous
-able -ible	able to	renewable flexible
-al -ial -ic	relating to	natural partial historic

WHY IT MATTERS

You can understand more words when you know what common suffixes mean.

Cognates

ESSENTIAL IDEA

Cognates are words in different languages that have similar spellings and meanings.

Cognates are words from different languages that come from the same root word. The words have the same **origins**, or came from the same place. Their spellings are the same or **similar**. The words have the same meaning.

The **pronunciation** of cognates might be similar or exactly the same in different languages.

Science Process Skills

Every time scientists do an **experiment**, they use more than one science **process**. Science processes include predicting, observing, and evaluating.

Scientists usually start by asking a question about an **idea**. Then they predict the answer to the question. This **prediction** is called a **hypothesis**.

In an experiment, scientists collect and observe **data**, or

information. Evaluating the data helps scientists draw a conclusion.

A **conclusion** happens when scientists **decide** what the information means and if their hypothesis is **correct**.

English-Spanish Cognates

English	Spanish	meaning
experiment	experimento	controlled test
process	proceso	a number of steps
idea	idea	belief, plan
prediction	predicción	statement about what might happen
hypothesis	hipótesis	prediction
data	datos	factual information
conclusion	conclusión	summary
decide	decidir	make a final choice
correct	correcto	accurate, right

The English word *experiment* is very similar to the Spanish word.

WHY IT MATTERS

- Some words you know are similar to words in other languages.
- Use the languages you know to help you read and understand more English words.

Homophones

ESSENTIAL IDEA

Homophones are words that sound alike but have different spellings and different meanings.

Blue and *blew* are **homophones**. Homophones have the same **sound**, but they have different **spellings** and meanings. To figure out the meaning, look at other words in the sentence.

homophones

Stormy Weather

The blue sky turned dark, and the winds blew hard. This was no ordinary weather. I had to decide whether to find shelter under a tree or in a new building. I knew that going indoors was the right choice.

I went to an inn by the road. I thought I would be safe in there. The whole building shook. The wind tore a hole in the roof. I could see that this was a tornado!

Homophones to Know

Look at the homophones in the article. Use the chart to help you choose the correct meaning.

homophones	meanings
blew blue	what the wind did a color
no know	not *yes* to understand
weather whether	conditions outside if
knew new	was sure of not *old*
right write	correct; not *left* use a pen or pencil to make words
inn in	small hotel not *out*
wood would	material from trees ought to or should
hole whole	empty place everything, all
sea see	ocean or other large body of water visualize, to use your eyes

WHY IT MATTERS

- You can use a dictionary to find the meanings and spellings of homophones.
- Be careful to use the correct homophones when you write.

Homographs

ESSENTIAL IDEA

Homographs are words that are spelled alike but have different meanings.

Words with the same spelling but different meanings are called **homographs**. For example, *wave* can mean "a fold of water in the ocean," or it can mean "a way to greet someone."

Homographs have **multiple meanings**. Look at the **context**, or the words around a homograph, to find out which meaning to use.

MEASURING

Everyone measures things. But people who **live** in the United States use a different measurement system. Americans use inches, **feet**, **yards**, and miles to measure distances. People in other countries measure in centimeters, meters, and kilometers. A person who is five feet tall is **close** to 1.5 meters tall. Height is measured from the bottom of the feet to the **top** of the head.

Americans measure liquid **volume** in units called pints, quarts, and gallons. The **rest** of the world measures liquids in liters.

Some Multiple-Meaning Words

word	meaning
live	occupy a place exist, be alive
foot (plural feet)	the part of the body below the ankle a measurement equal to 12 inches
yard	unit of measure (3 feet) area near a house
close	end near shut
top	highest part a cover or lid a spinning toy
volume	fullness or capacity a book in a series the degrees of loudness
rest	what is left over, the other part to relax

WHY IT MATTERS

- You can read the other words around homographs to find the meaning.
- Look up the word if you don't know the meanings the word can have.

Comparatives and Superlatives

ESSENTIAL IDEA

Comparatives are words used to compare two items. Superlatives are words used to compare three or more items.

You use **adjectives** or **adverbs** to describe something. If you want to compare two or more things, you often add *-er* or *-est* to the describing words.

DINOSAURS

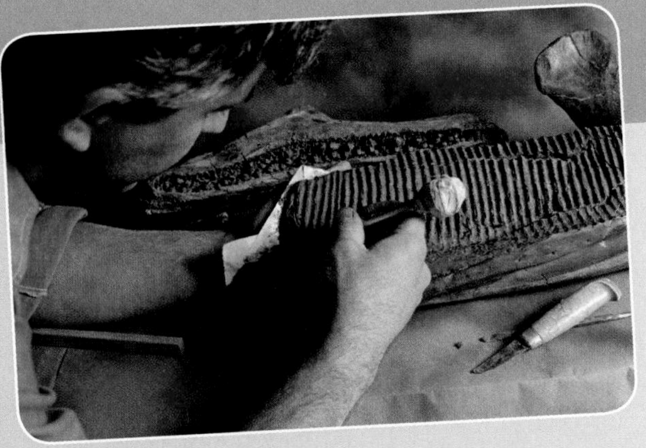

Dinosaurs lived on Earth a long time ago. The **earliest** dinosaurs lived more than 200 million years ago. Archaeologists use clues left in fossils to find the age of dinosaurs.

Archaeologists find fossils in rocks. Rocks are made from compressed layers of soil. **Newer** rocks are in the higher layers. **Older** rocks are in the **deeper** layers. Scientists use this information to compare the ages of fossils.

To find the age of plants and animals that lived the **furthest** back in time, scientists measure an element called Carbon-14. Measuring C-14 and other elements helps scientists find the age of the **most ancient** dinosaurs.

Forming Comparatives and Superlatives

To form a **comparative,** add *–er*. Comparatives show a **comparison** between two things.

To form a **superlative**, add *–est.* Superlatives show a comparison among three or more things.

When a word ends in a consonant and *y*, like *dusty*, change the *y* to *i* before adding *–er* or *–est* (*dustier, dustiest*).

word	comparative	superlative
old	older	oldest
chilly	chillier	chilliest
quick	quicker	quickest
busy	busier	busiest

Many longer words do not use *–er* and *–est* to show comparison. Instead, add *more* or *most* before the word.

word	comparative	superlative
difficult	more difficult	most difficult
important	more important	most important
accurate	more accurate	most accurate
careful	more careful	most careful

WHY IT MATTERS

You use a superlative when you say which of your classes you like best.

Jargon

ESSENTIAL IDEA

Jargon is the language that a special group of people uses.

People in some **professions** or hobbies may use words that outsiders don't know. These words are called **jargon**. Use **context clues** to help you figure out the meaning of jargon.

Space

Imagine being an astronaut. You wear a space suit and sit inside a space shuttle, waiting for **blastoff**. You probably feel excited because you will soon zoom, or quickly fly, into deep space.

You might look down at the control panel and follow the **countdown** on your computer screen. The screen says, "Five, four, three, two, one." You wait to hear "**All systems go**." Finally, **ground control** announces that it's time for **liftoff**! Outside the window, you can see Earth shrinking as you head into the sky.

jargon

Space jargon

blastoff
countdown
all systems go
ground control
liftoff

Medical jargon

prescription
diagnosis
symptoms
blood pressure
heart rate (pulse)

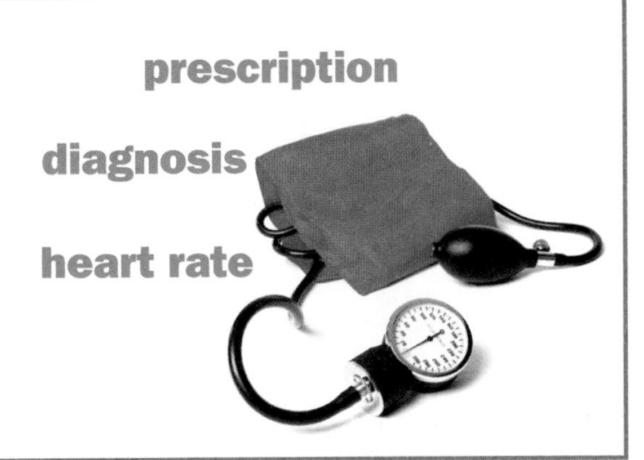

Computer jargon

link
download
bookmark
virtual
start up

WHY IT MATTERS

You can ask someone who knows the subject to help you understand jargon.

Understanding Idioms

ESSENTIAL IDEA

Idioms are phrases that have different meanings from the words alone.

An **idiom** is a group of words that has a different meaning when you **combine** them.

The meaning of an idiom is different from the **literal** meaning of the words. For example, when you "reach for the stars," you do not raise your arms. This idiom means that you "try to do something important."

Understanding Idioms

The English language is full of idioms. When you hear an idiom in a **conversation**, try to figure out what it means or ask someone.

idiom	meaning
look at the big picture	focus on the most important idea and not the details
put two and two together	gather together the facts and reach a conclusion
set in stone	permanent, cannot be changed
a drop in the ocean	a small part of something much bigger

I think I am finally getting the hang of understanding idioms.

WHY IT MATTERS

- You need to know the meaning of idioms just like you do other vocabulary words.
- Learning idioms will help you understand what people are talking about in conversations.

Signal Words

ESSENTIAL IDEA

Signal words give clues to help you understand what you will read next.

Signal words are words in sentences that give **clues** about what you are going to read. Knowing signal words can help you recognize **patterns** in what you read.

SUNDAY NEWS

Deforestation

Forest fires and logging cause more problems than destroying trees. Deforestation, or loss of forests, leads to loss of soil. Tree roots and fallen leaves hold soil in place. The loss of trees and leaves means the soil has no protection.

Erosion is the wearing away of the surface of Earth. It speeds up when there are fewer trees to protect the soil from wind and rain. Then, winds carry topsoil away. Afterward, heavy rains wash away more soil. Eventually, there is not enough soil for trees to grow.

One solution is replanting trees in deforested areas. Another one is protecting trees from forest fires and limiting logging to small areas.

Many science articles present a problem and suggest a solution. They may describe a **process**—the steps that lead to the problem and the steps that are part of the solution.

The article explains the process of erosion. *Then*, *afterwards*, and *eventually* are signal words that show the order of steps.

Common Signal Words in Science

Signal words can show comparisons or contrasts. Other signal words show the **sequence**, or order of events. Some signal words point to cause and effect. Look for summary signal words to find the end result.

comparison/contrast	sequence	cause-effect	summary
like, unlike	first, next	because	as a result
different	then	so	in conclusion
kind, type, category	afterward	due to	overall
fewer	before	leads to	eventually
more	during	therefore	finally

WHY IT MATTERS

- Recognizing signal words helps you know what you are going to read about.
- Signal words help you understand patterns and organization in what you read.

Phrasal Verbs

ESSENTIAL IDEA

Phrasal verbs begin with a verb. One or more words are added after the verb.

A **phrasal verb** is a **phrase**, or a group of words, that work together as a verb in a sentence. The first word is a verb and the other is a short word, often showing direction. Together these words create a different meaning from the **original** verb.

Phrasal verbs are common in the English language. People often use them to state **rules** and give directions.

Science Lab Rules

- Write down each step of your work.
- Always put goggles on before using tools.
- Tie back hair before using burners.
- Immediately clean up spills.
- Speak up if you have any questions.
- Turn the lights off when not in the lab.

Common Phrasal Verbs

An **object** can sometimes **separate** the words in the phrasal verb. For example, with, "I'm going to take the trash out," *the trash* separates the phrasal verbal *take out*.

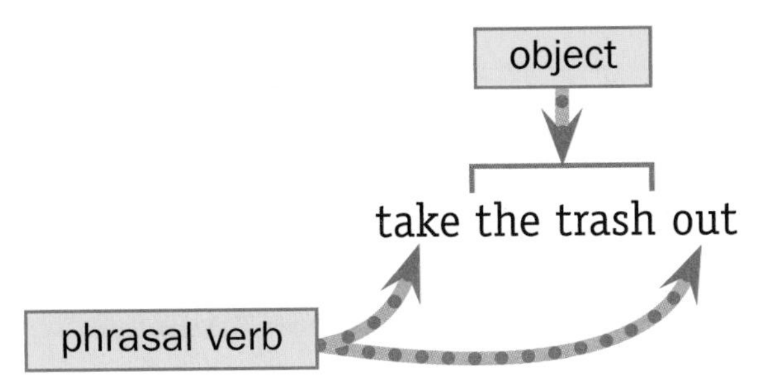

The chart below shows how some phrasal verbs can be separated by objects. Other phrasal verbs are not separated and need to stay together.

phrasal verb	phrasal verb separated by an object
slow down	slow the ball down
get out	get your book out
clean up	clean this mess up
start over	start the process over
watch out	x
hurry up	x
go back	x

WHY IT MATTERS

You hear phrasal verbs every day, especially when listening to rules and directions.

Common Spelling Mistakes

ESSENTIAL IDEA

Some words in science are difficult to spell because they do not follow spelling rules. Other words are not spelled the way they sound.

Some words are easy to **misspell**. Words that do not follow normal spelling patterns can cause **common** spelling mistakes.

Dear Mayor,

We need to improve the quality of the air in our city. In the past, most smog came from ~~firey~~ fiery factories. Smokestacks reached the ~~hite~~ height of a skyscraper. Today, cars cause a lot of pollution. Everyone who has a driver's ~~lisense~~ license adds to the problem. It's not possible to ~~vacume~~ vacuum away the smog. I urge you to reduce the number of cars in the city. I'd ~~prefur~~ prefer to ban them, but my ~~judgement~~ judgment is not shared by many others.

Sincerely,

Eliza Heart

One spelling **rule** says, "Put *i* before *e*, except after *c*, or when sounding like *a* as in *neighbor* and *weigh*." Words that break this rule, such as *height* and *weird*, are often misspelled.

In some other words, letters are silent. One or more letters are not **pronounced**, or said. *Autumn*, *doubt*, *edge*, *island*, *knee*, *listen*, and *write* all have silent letters.

Commonly Misspelled Words

Learning words that are easy to misspell helps you become a better writer.

Commonly misspelled words	
across	environment
argument	island
being	occur
believe	prairie
column	separate
either	theories

WHY IT MATTERS

Spelling words correctly is important because it makes your writing easier for readers to understand.

Writing for Science

Choosing a Topic

ESSENTIAL IDEA

When you write a report for science, the first step is to choose a topic. Brainstorming helps get all your ideas on paper.

After you get a writing **assignment** from your teacher, you might wonder what to write about.

Choosing a **topic** can be difficult. One way to begin is to **brainstorm**. When you brainstorm, you put all your ideas in one place. To make a topic web, you start with a **general** subject and then narrow it down to **specific** topics.

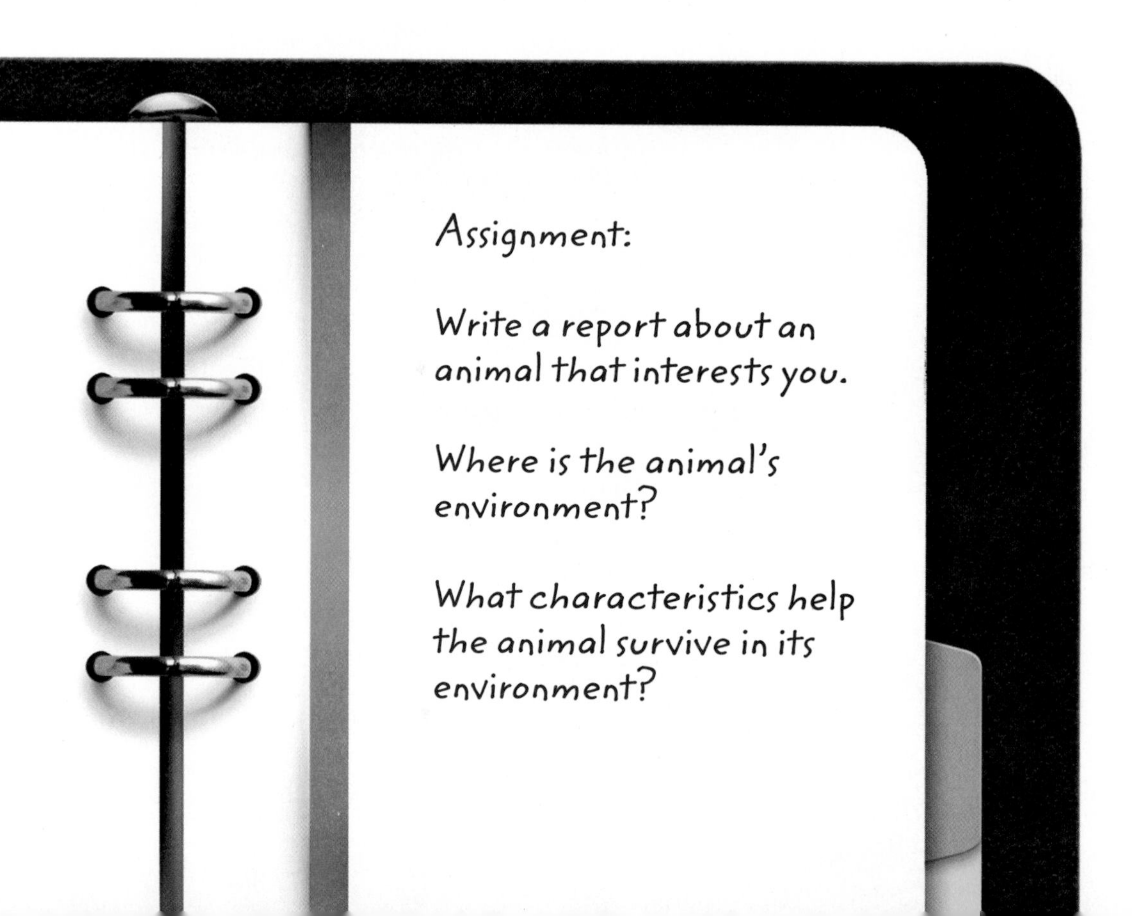

Make a Topic Web

One way to brainstorm is with a topic web.

1. Write a general subject, such as *animals*.
2. Then write down all the specific topics that come to mind, such as *mammals* and *birds*.
3. Narrow the topic even more by thinking of different types of mammals, such as *whales* and *giraffes*.

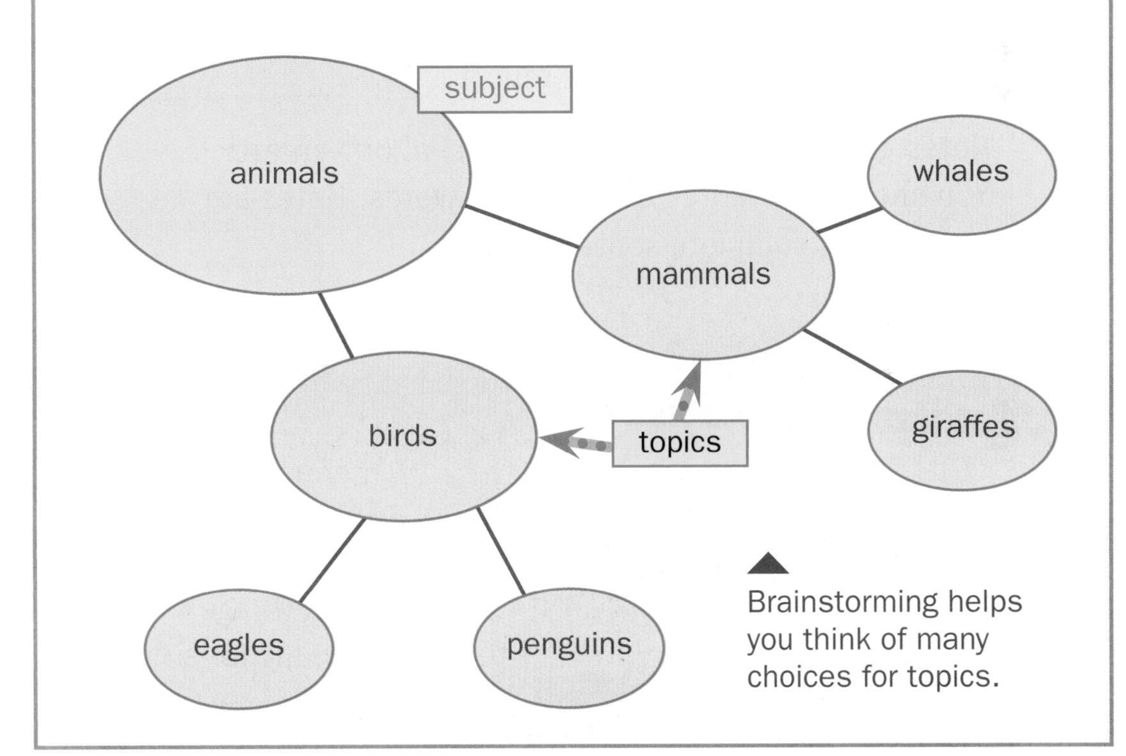

Brainstorming helps you think of many choices for topics.

WHY IT MATTERS

- You can brainstorm to think of topics to write about.
- Making a topic web can help you organize your ideas.

Taking Notes

ESSENTIAL IDEA

When you do research for a report, you take notes about your topic. You can use these notes to help you write.

After you decide on a topic, you can do **research** by reading articles in magazines, newspapers, encyclopedias, and books. As you read, take notes to **gather** information you want to include in your report.

Notes give a summary, or key ideas, about an article. You should put notes in your own words. Notes are usually not complete sentences.

Taiga Biome

The taiga biome covers parts of Asia, Europe, and Canada. Taiga is the largest biome in the world.

Winter and summer are the two main seasons in a taiga. The winters are very cold with lots of snow. The average temperature is below freezing for six months of the year. Summers are warm, rainy, and humid.

Not many species of plants can survive in taigas because of the extreme weather. Taigas are full of evergreen trees, such as spruce, hemlock, and fir. Their needles help them keep warm in the winter.

You can gather your notes on **note cards**.

note card

Taiga Biome
-located in Asia, Europe, and Canada
-world's largest biome
-very cold in the winter
-full of evergreen trees

Science Magazine, p. 15

How to Take Notes

1. Write important words or phrases from the article. You can use abbreviations or symbols, such as ↑ for increasing.
2. Give a short summary of the article's main idea. Remember to use your own words.
3. Write down where the information came from. Ask your teacher which style you should use for a bibliography.

WHY IT MATTERS

Notes help you keep track of important information that you can use when you write a report.

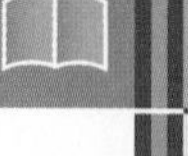

Organizing Ideas

ESSENTIAL IDEA

Organizing ideas before you start writing helps you plan your writing. An outline is a good way to put your ideas in order.

Before you begin writing, **organize** the information about your topic. Making an **outline** helps you put your ideas into a **logical** order.

The Central Nervous System

The central nervous system controls the body's actions and reactions. It is divided into two parts: the brain and the spinal cord.

Brain

The brain is the control center of the body. It sends and receives messages to and from the parts of your body. The average adult human brain weighs 1.3 to 1.4 kilograms (approximately 3 pounds).

Spinal Cord

The spinal cord is a bunch of nerves located in your backbone. A spinal cord is about 43 cm long in adult women and 45 cm long in adult men. It weighs about 35 to 40 grams.

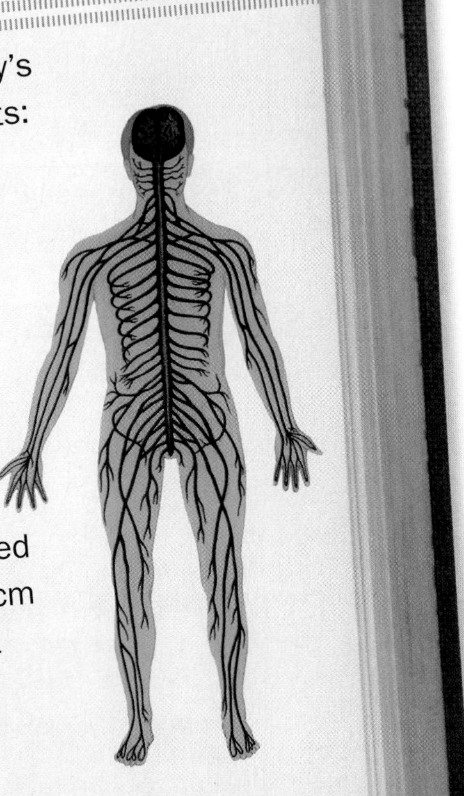

How to Make an Outline

An outline uses **Roman numerals** (I, II, and III) to list each main idea you want to include. Use capital letters for any supporting ideas.

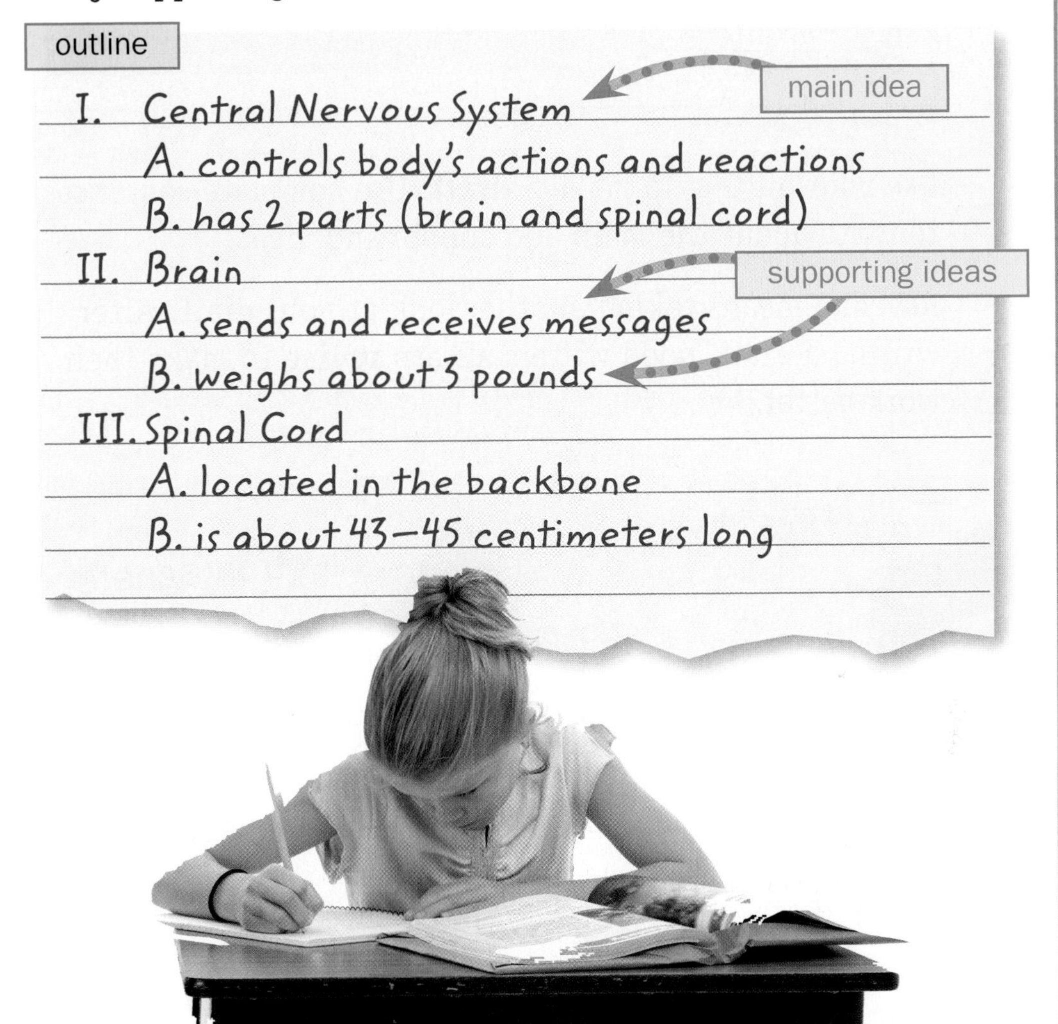

WHY IT MATTERS

You can organize your ideas before you begin to write by making an outline.

Drafting and Revising

ESSENTIAL IDEA

Revising is an important step that improves your draft.

Use your outline to make a **draft**. Use complete sentences to write about the main and supporting ideas.

Revising means taking another look at your draft. After writing a draft, good writers always **revise** to make their work better.

Electromagnets

, which is a force that attracts metals
Electricity can produce magnetism.

, such as iron,
Pieces of metal become magnets when electricity flows through wires wrapped around the metal.

cranes
Electromagnets are used to make ~~machines~~
, such as cars and steel beams
that lift heavy, metal objects.

So, you'll frequently see this type of crane
junkyards
in ~~garbage dumps~~ where metal objects are moved to crushers or burners for recycling.

You can improve your draft by adding **examples** to support your ideas. Replace general words, such as *things*, with more **precise** words. Make sure all your facts are correct in your **revision**.

I added examples to support my main idea.

The word *cranes* is more precise than *machines*.

I read my revision again to make sure the facts are correct.

WHY IT MATTERS

You can revise your work by adding examples and using precise words.

Editing and Proofreading

ESSENTIAL IDEA

Editing and proofreading are the final steps in writing.

Before you finish your writing, you need to reread your revisions. **Edit** your paper to make sure the sentences **flow** together and are **organized** in the right order.

Finally, you need to **proofread** your writing, or check it for mistakes. Make sure that all words are spelled correctly. Then be sure each sentence has correct **punctuation**.

Rovers on Mars

Two space rovers (robots), spirit and Opportunity, were sent to Mars to help scientists on Earth understand Mars. In January 2004, the rovers reached Mars. Mars is about 36 million miles from Earth. Scientists hoped that the rovers would walk for about a mile and collect a few samples.

No one expeckted the rovers to last more than 90 days. However, the rovers have continued to do their jobs for more than three years. The two rovers have sent scientists over 100,000 close-up photos of Mars' surfis. The computers on the rovers have analyzed rocks and minerals and given scientists more information than they've ever had about this planet.

How to Edit and Proofread Your Work

1. Read your revision out loud. Do all the ideas flow from one idea to the next? If the ideas don't flow, decide if you need to delete or reword the ideas.

2. Check your spelling. Are all the words spelled correctly? Use a dictionary for words you're not sure how to spell.

3. Next, check all the punctuation. Does each sentence end with a question mark, period, or exclamation point? Are commas used correctly?

Proofreading Marks

Mark	Meaning
≡	capitalize letter
⊙	add period
^,	add comma
(sp)	fix spelling
	take out

WHY IT MATTERS

Editing and proofreading improve your writing and help the reader understand your report.

Science References

Science Tools

ESSENTIAL IDEA

Science tools help you make investigations.

Scientists make **investigations** by asking and answering questions about things. Scientists use tools to help answer their questions.

A **thermometer** helps you measure temperature. People in the United States measure temperature in degrees Fahrenheit (°F). Scientists measure temperature in degrees Celsius (°C).

	boiling point	freezing point
Celsius	100°C	0°C
Fahrenheit	212°F	32°F

A **graduated cylinder** is a tool used to measure the volume of liquids.

graduated cylinder

A **stopwatch** measures time. To find the speed or power of something, you need to measure time.

stopwatch

A **microscope** lets you see tiny things that you cannot see with only your eyes.

microscope

WHY IT MATTERS

You use science tools in your everyday life.

Standard and Metric Units

ESSENTIAL IDEA

Scientists and people in other countries use a different measuring system than people in the United States.

People in the United States use standard units. Scientists and people in most other countries use metric units. The **metric system** is based on multiples of 10. For example, 1 millimeter multiplied by 10 equals 1 centimeter.

Length and Distance Conversions

metric units		
1 centimeter (cm)	=	10 millimeters (mm)
1 decimeter (dm)	=	10 centimeters (cm)
1 meter (m)	=	100 centimeters (cm)
1 kilometer (km)	=	1,000 meters (m)

standard units		
1 foot (ft)	=	12 inches (in.)
1 yard (yd)	=	3 feet (ft)
1 mile (mi)	=	5,280 feet (ft)

To measure length, you can use a tape measure.

Mass and Weight Conversions

metric units	
1 gram (g)	= 1,000 milligrams (mg)
1 kilogram (kg)	= 1,000 grams (g)

standard units	
1 pound (lb)	= 16 ounces (oz)
1 ton (t)	= 2,000 pounds (lb)

This balance uses grams to measure the mass of the object.

Volume Conversions

metric units	
1 liter (L)	= 1,000 milliliters (mL)

standard units	
1 pint (pt)	= 2 cups (c)
1 quart (qt)	= 2 pints (pt)
1 gallon (gal)	= 4 quarts (qt)

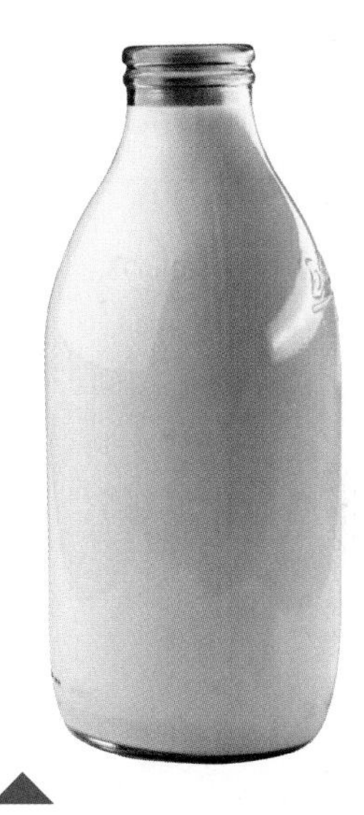

Liquids, like milk, can be measured in volume.

WHY IT MATTERS

- Measurements from your daily life, like your height, are usually in standard units.
- Measurements in science class are usually in metric units.

The Periodic Table

ESSENTIAL IDEA

The periodic table groups elements by their properties.

The **periodic table** is a chart that helps scientists understand **elements**.

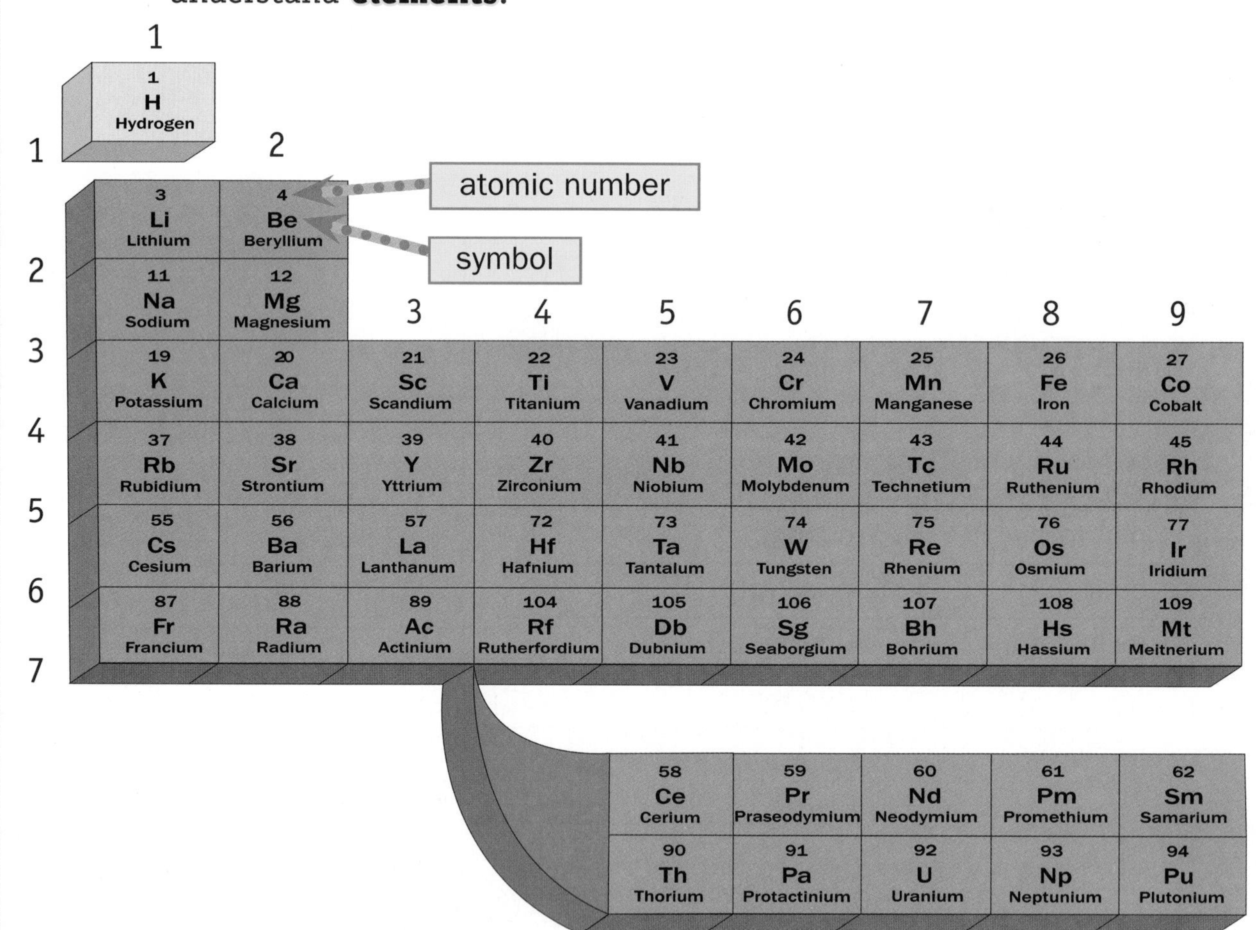

Each element has a **symbol** in the chart. The number above the symbol is the **atomic number**. The atomic number tells how many protons are in the nucleus of the atom.

WHY IT MATTERS

You can use the periodic table to find the symbol or atomic number of an element.

The green boxes show elements that are metalloids. They have properties of both metals and nonmetals.

The yellow boxes show elements that are not metals. Many of these elements are gases.

The orange boxes show elements that are metals.

10	11	12	13	14	15	16	17	18
								2 He Helium
			5 B Boron	6 C Carbon	7 N Nitrogen	8 O Oxygen	9 F Fluorine	10 Ne Neon
			13 Al Aluminum	14 Si Silicon	15 P Phosphorus	16 S Sulfur	17 Cl Chlorine	18 Ar Argon
28 Ni Nickel	29 Cu Copper	30 Zn Zinc	31 Ga Gallium	32 Ge Germanium	33 As Arsenic	34 Se Selenium	35 Br Bromine	36 Kr Krypton
46 Pd Palladium	47 Ag Silver	48 Cd Cadmium	49 In Indium	50 Sn Tin	51 Sb Antimony	52 Te Tellurium	53 I Iodine	54 Xe Xenon
78 Pt Platinum	79 Au Gold	80 Hg Mercury	81 Tl Thallium	82 Pb Lead	83 Bi Bismuth	84 Po Polonium	85 At Astatine	86 Rn Radon
110 Ds Darmstadium	111 Rg Roentgenium	112 Uub Ununbium	113 Uut Ununtrium	114 Uuq Ununquadium	115 Uup Ununpentium	116 Uuh Ununhexium	117 Uus Ununseptium	118 Uuo Ununoctium

63 Eu Europium	64 Gd Gadolinium	65 Tb Terbium	66 Dy Dysprosium	67 Ho Holmium	68 Er Erbium	69 Tm Thulium	70 Yb Ytterbium	71 Lu Lutetium
95 Am Americium	96 Cm Curium	97 Bk Berkelium	98 Cf Californium	99 Es Einsteinium	100 Fm Fermium	101 Md Mendelevium	102 No Nobelium	103 Lr Lawrencium

Science Safety

ESSENTIAL IDEA

Follow safety rules to stay safe during science experiments.

You need to follow safety rules to protect yourself and avoid injuries in a science **laboratory**.

Follow Directions

Always read through all **directions** before starting any experiment. Make sure you follow the steps of the **experiment** in the order they are given. If you don't understand a direction, ask your teacher to explain it again.

Dress for Science Safety

Always protect your eyes by wearing **goggles**. Gloves protect your hands when you handle chemicals. Wear a lab **apron** or coat to protect your clothing.

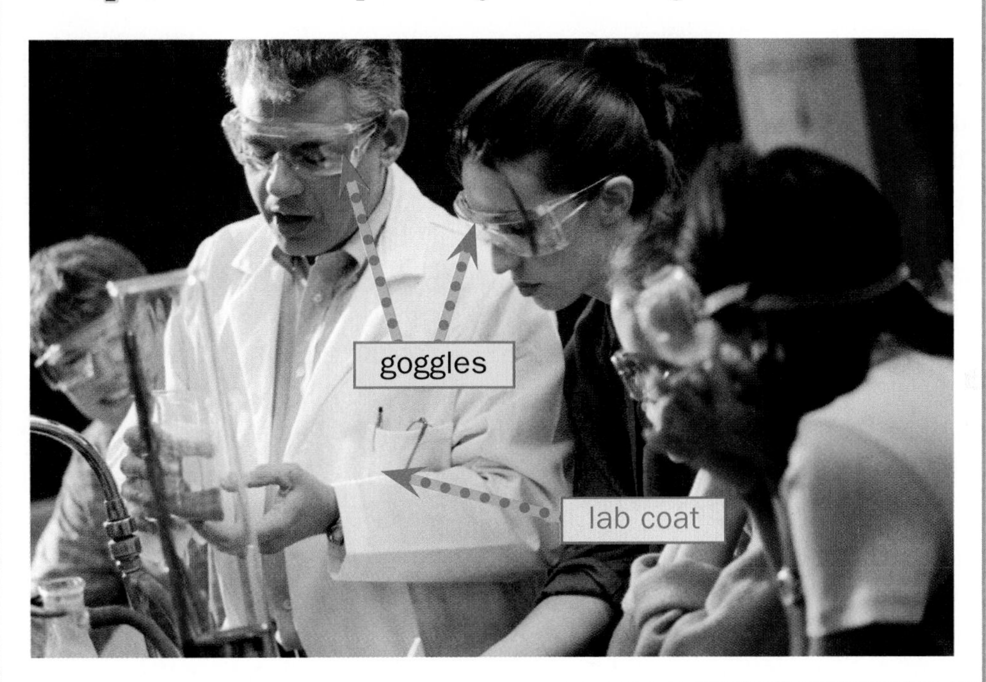

Keep a Safe Work Area

Organize the tools and materials in your work area. Clean up **spills** right away. After you finish the experiment, return materials safely. Always wash your hands after an experiment.

WHY IT MATTERS

Following safety rules will prevent you and others from injury during a science experiment.

Glossary

A

absorb (əb sôrb′ *or* əb zôrb′) *v.* take in or soak up, **272**

abundant (ə bun′dənt) *adj.* existing in large amounts, **100**

abyssal plain (ə bĭs′əl plān) *n.* the deep ocean floor, **127**

acceleration (ăk sĕl′ə rā′shən) *n.* a rate that measures a change in speed or direction, **231**

adaptation (ăd′ăp tā′shən) *n.* something special that helps a living thing survive in its environment, **64, 66**

adjectives (ăj′ĭk tĭvz) *n.* words that describe nouns, **370**

adjust (ə jŭst′) *v.* change, **347**

adults (ə dŭlts′ *or* ăd′ŭlts) *n.* living things that are fully grown, **60**

adverbs (ăd′vûrbz) *n.* words that describe verbs, adjectives, and other adverbs, **370**

air mass (âr′ mas′) *n.* a large body of air with the same temperature, **142**

air pressure (âr′ prĕsh′ər) *n.* the weight of air pushing against the things around it, **140**

air sacs (âr′ săkz′) *n.* millions of tiny pockets in the lungs that hold air when you breathe, **72**

alike (ə līk′) *adj.* the same as something else, **355**

alphabetical (ăl′fə bĕt′ĭ kəl) *adj.* organized in the order of the letters of the alphabet, **322**

alternative resources (ôl tûr′nə tĭv rē′sôrs′əs *or* ăl tûr′nə tĭv rĭ′sôrs′əs) *n.* new ways to make energy, **172**

amphibians (ăm fĭb′ē ənz) *n.* animals with a backbone that live in water and on land, **49**

amplitude (ăm′plĭ to͞od *or* ăm′plĭ tyo͞od) *n.* how much energy is in a sound wave, **283**

analyze (ăn′ə līz′) *v.* think about what something means, **307**

ancient (ān′shənt) *adj.* very old, **166**

angle of incidence (ăng′gəl ŭv ĭn′sĭ dəns) *n.* the angle at which light from an object hits a mirror, **277**

angle of reflection (ăng′gəl ŭv rĭ flĕk′shən) *n.* the angle at which light from an object reflects off a mirror, **277**

annelids (ăn′ə lĭdz) *n.* invertebrates with long bodies made of many parts, **46**

antennae (ăn tĕn′ē) *n.* a pair of organs on the heads of insects, **46**

applied force (ə plīd′ fôrs′ *or* ə plīd′ fōrs′) *n.* a force given to an object, **233**

apron (ā′prən) *n.* something you wear during an experiment to protect your clothing, **403**

arteries (är′tə rēz) *n.* blood vessels that carry blood away from the heart, **75**

articles (är′tĭ kəlz) *n.* stories you read in magazines and newspapers to find out information on a topic, **316**

assignment (ə sīn′mənt) *n.* work that you are asked to do by your teacher, **384**

asteroid belt (ăs′tə roid′ bĕlt′) *n.* a group of rocks and metal that orbits the Sun like planets, **180**

asteroids (ăs′tə roidz′) *n.* small rocky bodies that orbit a star, **180**

astronaut (ăs′trə nôt′) *n.* a person who is trained to travel in spacecraft and work in space, **192, 248**

Pronunciation Key

ă	bat	oi	toy
ā	ape	ou	shout
âr	air	ŏŏ	book
ä	father	ōō	moon
ĕ	let	s	sun
ē	easy	sh	pressure
ĭ	if	th	the, thing
ī	lie	ŭ	nut
îr	dear	ûr	circle
k	cause	ə	ago
ŏ	lot	ər	mother
ō	go	′	primary stress
ô	all	′	secondary stress

atmosphere (ăt′mə sfîr′) *n.* the gases that surround Earth, **138**

atomic number (ə tŏm′ĭk nŭm′bər) *n.* the number above the symbol on the periodic table that tells how many protons are in the nucleus of the atom, **401**

atoms (ăt′əmz) *n.* smallest particles of an element, **206**

attract (ə trăkt′) *v.* pull together by physical force, **220, 260, 264**

autumn (ô′təm) *n.* fall or the season in which leaves fall off trees, **154**

axis (ăk′sĭs) *n.* an imaginary line running through the center of Earth, **154**

B

backbones (băk′bōnz′) *n.* the large bones in the backs of some animals, **42**

bacteria (băk tîr′ē ə) *n.* a group of single-celled organisms, **93**

balanced (băl′ənst) *adj.* equal, **219**

balanced diet (băl′ənst dī′ĭt) *n.* a healthy way of eating that gives a body the right amount of nutrients, **82**

base word (bās′ wûrd′) *n.* the word part that is a word by itself, **361, 362**

beginning (bĭ gĭn′ĭng) *n.* the start, **360**

benefit (bĕn′ə fĭt) *v.* help, **94**

biome (bī′ōm′) *n.* a place with a certain climate and environment that meets the needs of organisms that live there, **104**

birds (bûrdz) *n.* warm-blooded animals that have wings and are covered in feathers, **48**

bladder (blăd′ər) *n.* the part of the excretory system that stores liquid waste, **80**

blizzard (blĭz′ərd) *n.* a winter storm with high winds and heavy, blowing snow, **148**

blood (blŭd) *n.* a tissue made of blood cells floating in liquid that carries things throughout the body, **74**

blood vessels (blŭd′ vĕs′əlz) *n.* tubes that carry blood throughout the body, **74**

bogs (bôgz *or* bŏgz) *n.* wetlands with spongy grounds that have lots of decaying plants, **136**

bonds (bŏndz) *n.* things that hold other things together, **212**

born (bôrn) *v.* become alive or begin life, **60**

boundary (boun′də rē *or* boun′drē) *n.* where Earth's plates meet, **116**

brain (brān) *n.* part of a body that controls all living functions, **76**

brainstorm (brān′stôrm′) *v.* think about as many ideas as possible, **384**

C

calculate (kăl′kyə lāt′) *v.* find an answer by using math, **203**

canyon (kăn′yən) *n.* a deep, narrow valley with steep sides, **124**

capillaries (kăp′ə lĕr′ēz) *n.* small blood vessels that connect arteries and veins, **75**

captions (kăp′shənz) *n.* words that describe photographs or illustrations on a page, **316, 327**

carbohydrates (kär′bō hī′drāts′) *n.* nutrients that are found in bread, **82**

carbon dioxide (kär′bən dī ŏk′sīd′) *n.* a gas in the air that lungs exhale during breathing, that things create when burning, and that plants use to make food, **72**

carnivores (kär′nə vôrz′) *n.* animals that get all their energy by eating other animals, **96**

cartilage (kär′tl ĭj) *n.* tough, bendable tissue, like the tip of the nose or ears, **55**

cast fossil (kăst fŏs′əl) *n.* a fossil that is a copy of a three-dimensional shape made from a mold, **167**

categories (kat′ĭ gôr′ēz *or* kăt′ĭ gōr′ēz) *n.* groups, **292**

cause (kôz) *n.* the reason something happens, **348**

cell membrane (sĕl mĕm′brān) *n.* the part of a cell that acts like a wall and holds it together, **25, 30**

cell wall (sĕl wôl) *n.* the part of a plant cell that supports and protects the cell, **31**

cells (sĕlz) *n.* the smallest living parts that make up all living things, **24**

cement (sĭ mĕnt′) *v.* bring things together tightly, **163**

chapters (chăp′tərz) *n.* parts of a unit in a textbook, **314, 321**

characteristics (kăr′ək tər ĭs′tĭks) *n.* traits, **66**

charge (chärj) *n.* the property that explains why electrons and protons repel or attract each other, **260**

charts (chärts) *n.* ways to organize information in rows and columns, **301, 328**

chemical energy (kĕm′ ĭ kəl ĕn′ər jē) *n.* the energy that holds atoms together in matter, **251**

chemical property (kĕm′ĭ kəl prŏp′ər tē) *n.* a quality of a substance that is observed when one substance is changed into a new substance, **197**

chemical reaction (kĕm′ĭ kəl rē ăk′shən) *n.* something that takes place when bonds are made or broken, **216**

chlorophyll (klôr′ə fĭl) *n.* the green substance found in plants that absorbs light, **39**

chloroplasts (klôr′ə plăsts′ *or* klōr′ə plăsts′) *n.* the parts of a cell that capture the Sun's energy, **31**

chromosomes (krō′mə sōmz′) *n.* the parts of the nucleus that contain information on the cell's traits, **28, 30, 84**

chromosphere (krō′mə sfîr′) *n.* the middle part of the Sun's atmosphere, **175**

circuit (sûr′kĭt) *n.* a closed path that allows electricity to move through it, **262**

circulatory system (sûr′kyə lə tôr′ē sĭs′təm) *n.* a system that moves blood around the body, **74**

clarify (klăr′ə fī′) *v.* make something easier to understand, **344**

Pronunciation Key

ă	bat	oi	**toy**
ā	ape	ou	sh**ou**t
âr	**air**	ŏŏ	b**oo**k
ä	f**a**ther	ōō	m**oo**n
ĕ	**le**t	s	**s**un
ē	**ea**sy	sh	pre**ss**ure
ĭ	**i**f	th	**th**e, **th**ing
ī	**lie**	ŭ	n**u**t
îr	**dear**	ûr	**cir**cle
k	**c**ause	ə	**a**go
ŏ	**lo**t	ər	moth**er**
ō	**go**	**ʹ**	primary stress
ô	**all**	ʹ	secondary stress

class (klăs) *n.* a group of things that are alike in some way, **48**

classify (klăsʹ ə fīʹ) *v.* sort; put things into groups, **32, 292**

claws (klôz) *n.* sharp, curved nails found on mammals, reptiles, and birds, **52**

climate (klīʹ mĭt) *n.* the usual weather of a place, **104, 152**

climax community (klīʹ măksʹ kə myōōʹ nĭ tē) *n.* a community of plants and animals that has been living in an area for a long time and is well adapted to its surroundings, **102**

clues (klōōz) *n.* information that helps you solve a problem, **340, 376**

coal (kōl) *n.* a solid fossil fuel formed from plants that were buried under swamps, **168**

cognates (kŏgʹ nātsʹ) *n.* words from different languages that have the same meaning and similar spellings, **364**

cold-blooded (kōldʹ blŭdʹ ĭd) *adj.* having a body temperature that changes when the outside temperature changes, **49**

collect data (kŏ lĕktʹ dāʹ tə *or* kŏ lĕktʹ dătʹ ə) *v.* make observations and measurements, **306**

collide (kə līdʹ) *v.* hit; crash together, **115**

combine (kəm bīnʹ) *v.* put together, **374**

comets (kŏmʹ ĭts) *n.* chunks of ice and dust that orbit the Sun, **181**

common (kŏmʹ ən) *adj.* happening often, **380**

communicate (kə myōōʹ nĭ kātʹ) *v.* share information with other people, **300**

community (kə myōōʹ nĭ tē) *n.* populations of different organisms in an area, **86, 90**

comparative (kəm părʹ ə tĭv) *n.* a word that shows a comparison between two things, **371**

compare (kəm pârʹ) *v.* look for ways that things are the same, **332**

comparison (kəm pârʹ ĭ sən) *n.* the way that two or more things are alike, **371**

compete (kəm pētʹ) *v.* fight against one another, **95**

composition (kŏmʹ pə zĭshʹ ən) *n.* the number and kind of atoms, **213**

compound (kŏmʹ poundʹ) *n.* a substance made of two or more elements, **212**

comprehension (kŏmʹ prĭ hĕnʹ shən) *n.* understanding of a topic, **346**

compress (kəm prĕsʹ) *v.* push together, **163**

concave (kən kāvʹ) *adj.* being thicker at the ends than in the middle, **279**

conclusion (kən klōōʹ shən) *n.* a decision based on what you know or have read, **308, 340, 356**

condensation (kŏnʹ dĕn sāʹ shən *or* kŏnʹ dən sāʹ shən) *n.* what happens when a gas changes into a liquid, **201**

condense (kən dĕns′) *v.* cause a gas to change into a liquid, **135**

conditions (kən dĭsh′ənz) *n.* the settings or surroundings, **40**

conduction (kən dŭk′shən) *n.* what happens when heat energy moves from one substance to another, **258**

conductors (kən dŭk′tərz) *n.* substances that allow electricity and heat to move through easily, **210**

confusing (kən fyo͞o′zĭng) *adj.* difficult to understand, **344**

conifers (kŏn′ə fərz *or* kō′nə fərz) *n.* plants that grow their seeds inside cones, **36**

connection (kə nĕk′shən) *n.* the way things relate to each other, **350**

conserve (kən sûrv′) *v.* do not waste, **172**

constellations (kŏn′stə lā′shənz) *n.* groups of stars that make up pictures in the sky, **190**

consumers (kən so͞o′mərz) *n.* living things that must eat other living things to get their energy, **88**

context (kŏn′tĕkst′) *n.* the text around a word that helps you figure out the meaning of the word, **368**

context clues (kŏn′tĕkst′ klo͞oz) *n.* information that you use to understand a word or words you don't know, **372**

continental margin (kŏn′tə nĕn′tl mär′jĭn) *n.* the underwater part of the continental crust, **126**

continental plates (kŏn′tə nĕn′tl plāts′) *n.* plates that Earth's land is on, **116**

contrast (kən trăst′ *or* kŏn′trăst′) *v.* look for ways that things are different, **332**

control (kən trōl′) *n.* something that stays the same in an experiment, **304**

convection (kən vĕk′shən) *n.* what happens when liquids and gases carry heat energy with them when they move, **258**

converge (kən vûrj′) *v.* come together, **278**

conversation (kŏn′vər sā′shən) *n.* talk between two or more people, **375**

convert (kən vûrt′) *v.* change, **92**

convex (kŏn′vĕks′ *or* kən vĕks′) *adj.* bending outward, **278**

cool (ko͞ol) *v.* make particles move slower, **200**

core (kôr) *n.* the center, **175**

corona (kə rō′nə) *n.* the outer layer of the Sun's atmosphere, **175**

crater (krā′tər) *n.* a large, shallow hole that forms when meteorites hit the surface of a moon or planet, **181, 184**

crescent moon (krĕs′ənt mo͞on) *n.* a moon that has curved sides and pointed edges, **183**

crest (krĕst) *n.* the top of a wave, **266**

crust (krŭst) *n.* the outside layer that covers Earth, **113**

crustaceans (krŭ stā′shənz) *n.* invertebrates with exoskeletons that live in the water, **45**

crystal structure (krĭs′təl strŭk′chər) *n.* a three-dimensional shape that the particles in most minerals form, **158**

current electricity (kûr′ənt ĭ lĕk trĭs′ĭ tē *or* kûr′ənt ē′lĕk trĭs′ĭ tē) *n.* electricity that flows along a wire, **262**

Pronunciation Key

ă	bat	oi	**toy**
ā	**ape**	ou	sh**out**
âr	**air**	o͝o	b**oo**k
ä	father	o͞o	**moon**
ĕ	let	s	**sun**
ē	**easy**	sh	pre**ss**ure
ĭ	**if**	th	**th**e, **th**ing
ī	**lie**	ŭ	**nut**
îr	**dear**	ûr	**circle**
k	**c**ause	ə	**a**go
ŏ	**lot**	ər	moth**er**
ō	**go**	′	primary stress
ô	**all**	′	secondary stress

cycle (sī′kəl) *n.* a set of events where the last event leads back to the first event, **134**

cyclones (sī′klōnz′) *n.* large storms that form over warm, tropical oceans, **146**

cylinder (sĭl′ən dər) *n.* a solid tube, **242**

cytoplasm (sī′tə plăz′əm) *n.* a jellylike substance that supports all the structures in a cell, **25**

D

data (dā′tə *or* dăt′ə) *n.* information about the variable you test, **306**

daughter cells (dô′tər sĕlz) *n.* the two cells that come from a divided parent cell, **29**

decay (dĭ kā′) *v.* break apart; rot, **164**

decibels (dĕs′ə bəlz *or* dĕs′ə bĕlz′) *n.* a unit used to measure volume of a sound, **284**

decline (dĭ klīn′) *v.* become less, **108**

decomposers (dē′kəm pō′zərz) *n.* living things that feed on dead plants and animals, **89**

decrease visibility (dĭ krēs′ vĭz′ə bĭl′ ĭ tē) *v.* make it hard to see, **149**

definition (dĕf′ə nĭsh′ən) *n.* the meaning of a word, **322, 326**

delta (dĕl′tə) *n.* a fan-shaped area of land at the mouth of a river, **125**

density (dĕn′sĭ tē) *n.* the mass of a certain volume of matter, **204**

depend (dĭ pĕnd′) *v.* need for survival, **100**

depletion (dĭ plē′shən) *n.* when something is used faster than it can be replaced, **165**

deposition (dĕp′ə zĭsh′ən) *n.* what happens when wind and water put down loose rocks and sediment, **123**

deposits (dĭ pŏz′ĭts) *n.* places where you find fossil fuels or minerals, **168, 187**

desert (dĕz′ərt) *n.* a dry biome that gets little rain and has few plants, **106**

destruction (dĭ strŭk′shən) *n.* damage or the act of being broken apart, **108**

details (dĭ tālz′ *or* dē′tālz′) *n.* small facts or pieces of information that support the main idea, **336**

determine (dĭ tûr′mĭn) *v.* decide or find, **336, 338**

develop (dĭ vĕl′əp) *v.* change and grow, **60**

diagram (dī′ə grăm′) *n.* a picture that may use arrows, boxes, and words to describe something, **329**

differences (dĭf′ər əns əs *or* dĭf′rəns əs) *n.* ways that things are not the same, **332**

digest (dī jĕst′ *or* dĭ jĕst′) *v.* break down food, **78**

direction (dĭ rĕk′shən *or* dī rĕk′shən) *n.* the way something moves, **228**; an instruction to follow, **402**

discharge (dĭs chärj′) *v.* release, **143, 261**

discoveries (dĭ skŭv′ə rēz) *n.* things you find out or learn, **131**

display (dĭ splā′) *v.* show, **329**

dissolve (dĭ zŏlv′) *v.* become part of a liquid, **215**

distance (dĭs′təns) *n.* the space between two objects or places, **227, 234**

diverge (dĭ vûrj′ *or* dī vûrj′) *v.* spread out, **278**

divide (dĭ vīd′) *v.* split into parts, **29**

dominant (dŏm′ə nənt) *adj.* having a strong influence, **85**

draft (drăft) *n.* written ideas in an unfinished form for a report, **390**

dunes (do͞onz *or* dyo͞onz) *n.* hills of loose sand grains, **125**

dwarf planet (dwôrf plăn′ĭt) *n.* a small planet, like Pluto, **177**

E

earthquake (ûrth′kwāk′) *n.* a sudden movement in Earth's crust, **118**

echo sounding (ĕk′ō soun′dĭng) *n.* process when sound waves are used to measure how far away something is, **130**

ecological succession (ĕk′ə lŏj′ĭ kəl sək sĕsh′ən *or* ē′kə lŏj′ĭ kəl sək sĕsh′ən) *n.* a process in which communities of plants and animals slowly replace one another, **102**

ecosystem (ĕk′ō sĭs′təm) *n.* all the nonliving and living things in a given area, **86**

ectothermic (ĕk′tə thûr′mĭk) *adj.* cold-blooded, **57**

edit (ĕd′ĭt) *v.* read something to make sure the sentences are clear and have no errors, **392**

effect (ĭ fĕkt′) *n.* the result or outcome of events, **348**

efficiently (ĭ fĭsh′ənt lē) *adv.* working without wasting materials or energy, **172**

effort force (ĕf′ərt fôrs *or* ĕf′ərt fōrs) *n.* the force you apply, **237**

eggs (ĕgz) *n.* the earliest stage of animal development, **58**

electric charge (ĭ lĕk′trĭk chärj′) *n.* the property that explains why electrons and protons repel or attract each other, **260**

electromagnetic energy (ĭ lĕk′trō măg nĕt′ ĭk ĕn′ər jē) *n.* energy that comes in forms such as light, radio waves, and electricity, **251**

electromagnetic waves (ĭ lĕk′trō măg nĕt′ ĭk wāvz) *n.* waves that carry energy, **268**

electrons (ĭ lĕk′trŏnz′) *n.* parts of an atom with a negative charge, **206**

element (ĕl′ə mənt) *n.* a substance made up of only one kind of atom, **208, 271, 400**

elevation (ĕl′ə vā′shən) *n.* the height above the surface of Earth or water, **152**

El Niño (ĕl′ nēn′yō) *n.* a warming of ocean currents in the Pacific Ocean every three to seven years, **156**

end (ĕnd) *n.* the last part, **362**

endangered (ĕn dān′jərd) *adj.* describing a population of a species in danger of not surviving, **109**

energy (ĕn′ər jē) *n.* what is needed to do work, **88, 218, 250, 252**

energy pyramid (ĕn′ər jē pĭr′ə mĭd) *n.* a diagram that shows the many steps in a food chain, **99**

entry (ĕn′trē) *n.* something on a list, **323**

Pronunciation Key

ă	bat	oi	toy
ā	ape	ou	shout
âr	air	o͝o	book
ä	father	o͞o	moon
ĕ	let	s	sun
ē	easy	sh	pressure
ĭ	if	th	the, thing
ī	lie	ŭ	nut
îr	dear	ûr	circle
k	cause	ə	ago
ŏ	lot	ər	mother
ō	go	′	primary stress
ô	all	′	secondary stress

environment (ĕn vī′rən mənt *or* ĕn vī′ərn mənt) *n.* place animals live and includes nonliving things, **86, 90**

epicenter (ĕp′ĭ sĕn′tər) *n.* a point on Earth's surface above the focus of an earthquake, **119**

erosion (ĭ rō′zhən) *n.* what happens when wind and water carry loose rocks and sediment away, **123, 165**

erupt (ĭ rŭpt′) *v.* burst open very quickly, **120**

esophagus (ĭ sŏf′ə gəs) *n.* a long tube that forces food into the stomach, **78**

estimate (ĕs′tə māt′) *v.* form a reasonable answer based on what you know, **294**

evaluate (ĭ văl′yo͞o āt′) *v.* decide the value of something, **319**

evaporate (ĭ văp′ə rāt′) *v.* cause a liquid to change into a gas, **135**

evaporation (ĭ văp′ə rā′shən) *n.* what happens when a liquid changes to a gas, **201**

events (ĭ vĕnts′) *n.* things that happen, **348, 352**

evidence (ev′ĭ dəns) *n.* information used to make a decision, **335, 356**

examples (ĭk zăm′pəlz) *n.* things that can help you understand ideas, **354, 391**

excess (ĭk sĕs′ *or* ĕk′sĕs′) *adj.* extra; not needed, **137**

excrete (ĭk skrēt′) *v.* remove waste from the body, **80**

excretory system (ĕk′skrĭ tôr′ē sĭs′təm *or* ĕk′skrĭ tōr′ē sĭs′təm) *n.* the body system that removes waste, extra water, and extra nutrients from the body, **80**

exercise (ĕk′sər sīz′) *n.* activity that moves muscles to keep you healthy, **82**

exert (ĭg zûrt′) *v.* use or apply, **218**

exhale (ĕks hāl′ *or* ĕk sāl′) *v.* breathe air out of lungs, **72**

exoskeleton (ĕk′sō skĕl′ĭ tn) *n.* a hard shell on the outside of crustaceans and insects, **45**

experiences (ĭk spîr′ē əns əs) *n.* events that happened, **296, 350**

experiment (ĭk spĕr′ə mənt) *n.* a scientific test, **304, 402**

explain (ĕk′splān′) *v.* tell why something happens, **298**

explanation (ĕk′splə nā′shən) *n.* reason why or how something happens, **298**

extinction (ĭk stĭngk′shən) *n.* what happens when all the members of a species disappear from Earth, **108**

extreme (ĭk strēm′) *adj.* being on two ends of a range, **248**

eye (ī) *n.* the calm center of a storm, **147**

F

facts (făkts) *n.* information about something that is true, **316, 357**

fats (făts) *n.* one of the six main nutrients that provides energy, **82**

fault (fôlt) *n.* the place where two plates move past each other, **118**

feathers (fĕth′ərz) *n.* the soft things that cover the bodies of birds, **52**

features (fē′chərz) *n.* special qualities or characteristics about something, **324**

filter (fĭl′tər) *v.* clean; separate materials, **137**

fins (fĭnz) *n.* the parts of a fish that help it swim, **54**

first-class lever (fûrst′klăs′ lĕv′ər *or* fûrst′ klăs′ lē′vər) *n.* a lever that is pressed downwards with the load on one end and the fulcrum in the middle, **245**

fish (fĭsh) *n.* cold-blooded animals that have gills, a backbone, and live in water, **49**

fix up (fĭks′ ŭp′) *v.* make better, **347**

fixation (fĭk sā′shən) *n.* a process that changes something that cannot be used into something useful, **92**

fixed (fĭkst) *adj.* not moving, **247**

flippers (flĭp′ərz) *n.* limbs that animals have to help them move through water, **57**

flood (flŭd) *n.* what happens when water fills land that is normally dry, **137**

flow (flō) *v.* move along smoothly, **392**

flowchart (flō′chärt) *n.* a graphic organizer that shows a sequence of events, **353**

flowering plants (flou′ər ĭng plănts′) *n.* plants that grow their seeds inside flowers, **36**

focus (fō′kəs) *n.* the place underground where rock first breaks apart in an earthquake, **119**

food chain (fo͞od′ chān) *n.* a diagram that shows what organisms eat in a habitat, **98**

food web (fo͞od′ wĕb) *n.* a group of many food chains for one habitat, **100**

force (fôrs *or* fōrs) *n.* the capacity to do work or cause physical change, **218, 230, 234**

formula (fôr′myə lə) *n.* a combination of symbols that represents the elements in a compound, **213**

fossil fuels (fŏs′əl fyo͞o′əlz) *n.* natural, nonrenewable resources that come from the remains of dead plants and animals, **168, 255**

fossils (fŏs′əlz) *n.* evidence of the remains of organisms that lived and died long ago, **166**

frame of reference (frām′ ŭv rĕf′ər əns *or* frām′ ŭv rĕf′rəns) *n.* the point of view of a person, **224**

frequency (frē′kwən sē) *n.* the number of waves or vibrations that pass a point in one second, **268, 282**

freshwater (frĕsh′ wô′ tər *or* frĕsh′ wŏt′ ər) *n.* water that you can drink; about 3 percent of Earth's water, **132**

friction (frĭk′shən) *n.* a force that happens when two things rub against each other, **222**

front (frŭnt) *n.* the area where two air masses meet, **142**

fulcrum (fo͝ol′krəm *or* fŭl′krəm) *n.* a fixed point, **244**

function (fŭngk′shən) *n.* a job, **24, 26**

fungi (fŭn′jī *or* fŭng′gī) *n.* decomposers that feed on dead plants and animals, **33**

future (fyo͞o′chər) *n.* things that will happen, **296, 334**

G

galaxies (găl′ək sēz) *n.* huge collections of stars, gas, and dust, **188**

gas (găs) *n.* the state of matter that will fill whatever space it is put in; the particles in a gas are more spread out than the particles in both solids and liquids, **198**

gather (găth′ər) *v.* collect, **290, 386**

gems (jĕmz) *n.* products of minerals that are used in jewelry, **158**

gene (jēn) *n.* a part of a chromosome that contains information about a living thing's traits, **84**

general (jĕn′ər əl) *adj.* applies to many things or situations, **384**

generalization (jĕn′ər ə lĭ zā′shən) *n.* a broad idea based on many examples or patterns, **354**

geotropism (jē′ō trō′pĭz′əm) *n.* when the roots of a plant grow down into the soil in response to Earth's gravity, **41**

gibbous moon (gĭb′əs mo͞on) *n.* a moon that seems to bulge on one side, **183**

gills (gĭlz) *n.* things that help fish get oxygen from water, **54**

glaciers (glā′shərz) *n.* slow moving masses of ice and snow that contain freshwater, **133**

global warming (glō′bəl wôrm′ĭng) *n.* an increase in greenhouse gases that leads to a warmer climate, **157**

glossary (glô′sə rē *or* glos′ə rē) *n.* the part of a book that lists and defines key words, **322**

Pronunciation Key

ă	**b**a**t**	oi	**toy**
ā	**ape**	ou	**sh**ou**t**
âr	**air**	o͝o	**b**oo**k**
ä	**f**a**ther**	o͞o	**m**oo**n**
ĕ	**l**e**t**	s	**s**un
ē	**eas**y	sh	pre**ss**ure
ĭ	**if**	th	**th**e, **th**ing
ī	**lie**	ŭ	**n**u**t**
îr	**d**ear	ûr	cir**cle**
k	**c**ause	ə	**a**go
ŏ	**l**o**t**	ər	moth**er**
ō	**go**	′	primary stress
ô	**all**	′	secondary stress

goggles (gŏg′əlz) *n.* things you wear to protect your eyes during an experiment, **403**

gradually (grăj′o͞o əl lē) *adv.* slowly, **102**

graduated cylinder (grăj′o͞o āt′ĕd sĭl′ən dər) *n.* a tool used to measure the volume of liquids, **397**

gram (grăm) *n.* a unit of mass equal to 1,000 milligrams, **202**

graph (grăf) *n.* a way to organize information with bars, pictures, shapes, or lines, **301, 308, 328**

graphics (grăf′ĭks) *n.* images that support text, **327**

grassland (grăs′lănd′) *n.* a biome covered by grasses and wildflowers, **105**

gravitational force (grăv′ĭ tā′shən əl fôrs *or* grăv′ĭ tā′shən əl fōrs) *n.* the attraction of objects due to mass and distance, **220**

gravity (grăv′ĭ tē) *n.* a force that pulls objects toward one another, **176, 220, 248**

great ocean conveyor belt (grāt ō′shən kən vā′ər bĕlt) *n.* the subsurface water current that carries water around the entire Earth, **129**

greenhouse gases (grēn′hous′ găs′əs) *n.* gases in the air that trap heat and make the climate warmer, **157**

groundwater (ground′wôt′ər *or* ground′wŏ′tər) *n.* water that is collected in the soil, **133, 135**

grow (grō) *v.* become bigger, **60**

H

habitat (hăb′ĭ tăt) *n.* a place where an organism lives, **94**

hail (hāl) *n.* balls of ice, **143**

headings (hĕd′ĭngz) *n.* words before text that tell what the text is about, **325**

headline (hĕd′līn′) *n.* the title of an article, **316**

heart (härt) *n.* the organ that pumps blood around the body, **74**

heat (hēt) *v.* make particles move faster, **200**; *n.* the movement of energy from one place to another, **257**

herbivores (hûr′bə vôrz′ *or* ûr′bə vôrz′) *n.* animals that get all their energy by eating plants, **96**

heredity (hə rĕd′ĭ tē) *n.* the passing of traits from parents to children, **85**

hertz (hûrts) *n.* a unit used to measure frequency, **282**

highlands (hī′ləndz) *n.* areas of the surface of the Moon that have rocks that reflect a lot of sunlight, **184**

homograph (hŏm′ə grăf′ *or* hō′mə grăf′) *n.* a word with one spelling but many meanings, **368**

homophones (hŏm′ə fōnz′ *or* hō′mə fōnz′) *n.* words that have the same sound but different spellings and meanings, **366**

humidity (hyo͞o mĭd′ĭ tē) *n.* the amount of water vapor in the air, **142**

humus (ho͝om′əs *or* hŭm′əs) *n.* a layer of soil made up of the remains of dead plants, **164**

hurricane (hûr′ĭ kān′ *or* hŭr′ĭ kān′) *n.* a large storm that forms over the Atlantic Ocean, **146**

hydrosphere (hī′drə sfîr′) *n.* a system that contains all Earth's water in the oceans, rivers, lakes, air, and ground, **134**

hypothesis (hī pŏth′ĭ sĭs) *n.* a possible answer or explanation, **304**

I

ice caps (īs′ kăps) *n.* sheets of frozen freshwater, **133**

idiom (ĭd′ē əm) *n.* a group of words that means something different from the words themselves, **374**

igneous rocks (ĭg′nē əs rŏks′) *n.* rocks that form when magma hardens, **160**

illustrations (ĭl′ə strā′shənz) *n.* drawings used to explain information, **327**

image (ĭm′ĭj) *n.* a picture, **276, 342**

impact (ĭm′păkt′) *v.* hit, **181**

import (ĭm pôrt′ *or* ĭm′pôrt′ *or* ĭm′pōrt) *v.* bring in, **169**

inclined (ĭn klīnd′) *adj.* slanted or angled, **238**

index (ĭn′dĕks′) *n.* a list of topics in a book, **323**

individual (ĭn′də vĭj′o͞o əl) *adj.* relating to one organism, **90**

Pronunciation Key

ă	bat	oi	toy
ā	ape	ou	shout
âr	air	o͝o	book
ä	father	o͞o	moon
ĕ	let	s	sun
ē	easy	sh	pressure
ĭ	if	th	the, thing
ī	lie	ŭ	nut
îr	dear	ûr	circle
k	cause	ə	ago
ŏ	lot	ər	mother
ō	go	′	primary stress
ô	all	′	secondary stress

inertia (ĭ nûr′ shə) *n.* the reason why an object at rest will stay at rest and a moving object will continue to move, **230**

infer (ĭn fûr′) *v.* make a conclusion by using information you observe or know, **298**

inference (ĭn′ fər əns) *n.* a conclusion made by putting together what you know, **298, 340**

inhale (ĭn hāl′) *v.* breathe air into lungs, **72**

inherit (ĭn hĕr′ ĭt) *v.* pass traits to children from parents, **64, 85**

inner core (ĭn′ ər kōr′ *or* ĭn′ ər kôr′) *n.* the layer in the center of Earth made of solid metal, **113**

inorganic (ĭn′ôr găn′ ĭk) *adj.* never having been alive, **158**

insects (ĭn′ sĕkts′) *n.* invertebrates with an exoskeleton and six legs, **46**

insulation (ĭn′sə lā′ shən *or* ĭns′yə lā′ shən) *n.* something that keeps something warm, like hair on the body of a mammal, **50**

intensity (ĭn tĕn′ sĭ tē) *n.* the level of strength or weakness of something, **150, 283**

interact (ĭn′tər ăkt′) *v.* have an effect on or change one another, **87, 90**

interactions (ĭn′tər ăk′ shənz) *n.* things organisms do that have an effect on or change one another, **91**

interpret (ĭn tûr′ prĭt) *v.* figure out the meaning, **307**

inventor (ĭn vĕn′ tŏr) *n.* a person who creates new technology, **243**

invertebrates (ĭn vûr′ tə brāts) *n.* animals that have no backbone, **43**

investigations (ĭn vĕs′tĭ gā′ shənz) *n.* ways to find out answers to questions, **396**

J

jargon (jär′ gən) *n.* special words that are used by people with a certain hobby or job, **372**

K

key words (kē′ wûrdz′) *n.* words that you type into a search engine to find information about a topic, **318**

kidneys (kĭd′ nēz) *n.* the parts of the excretory system that remove waste from the blood, **80**

kilogram (kĭl′ ə grăm′) *n.* a unit of mass equal to 1,000 grams, **202**

kinetic energy (kĭ nĕt′ ĭk ĕn′ ər jē *or* kī nĕt′ ĭk ĕn′ ər jē) *n.* the energy of moving objects, **252, 256**

kingdoms (kĭng′ dəmz) *n.* groups of different types of organisms, **32**

knowledge (nŏl′ ĭj) *n.* information that you learn, **300**

L

laboratory (lăb′rə tôr′ē *or* lăb′rə tōr′ē) *n.* a place where you do experiments, **402**

landform (lănd′fôrm′) *n.* a physical feature on Earth's surface, **124**

large intestine (lärj′ ĭn tĕs′tĭn) *n.* the part of the digestive system where water from digested food returns to the body and solid waste leaves the body, **78**

latitude (lăt′ĭ to͞od′ *or* lăt′ĭ tyo͞od′) *n.* the distance north or south of the equator; measured in degrees, **152**

Law of Reflection (lô′ ŭv rĭ flĕk′shən) *n.* the angle of incidence equals the angle of reflection, **277**

layers (lā′ərz) *n.* things stacked on top of each other to create a whole, **112**

lens (lĕnz) *n.* a curved piece of glass that refracts light, **278**

lever (lĕv′ər *or* lē′vər) *n.* a bar that moves on a fixed point, **244**

life processes (līf′ prŏs′əs′əs) *n.* the things animals do to stay alive, **20**

light-year (līt′yîr′) *n.* the distance that light travels in one year, **188, 190**

lightning (līt′nĭng) *n.* a spark in the sky during a thunderstorm, **143**

limbs (lĭmz) *n.* parts of an animal used for moving, **52**

limited (lĭm′ĭ tĭd) *adj.* not having an endless supply, **171**

liquid (lĭk′wĭd) *n.* the state of matter that takes the shape of whatever space it is put in, **198**

literal (lĭt′ər əl) *adj.* having the exact meaning of the words, **374**

lithosphere (lĭth′ə sfîr′) *n.* Earth's crust and upper mantle together, **114**

living (lĭv′ĭng) *adj.* uses energy and can reproduce, **20**

load (lōd) *n.* something that is lifted, **244**

logical (lŏj′ĭ kəl) *adj.* making sense, **388**

longitudinal waves (lŏn′jĭ to͞od′n əl wāvz *or* lŏn′jĭ tyo͞od′n əl wāvz) *n.* waves that go back and forth, **280**

lungs (lŭngz) *n.* the parts in an animal's chest that help it breathe, **72**

luster (lŭs′tər) *n.* shininess, **211**

M

machines (mə shēnz′) *n.* tools that make work easier, **236**

magma (măg′mə) *n.* the hot, liquid substance that becomes igneous rock when it hardens, **120**

magnet (măg′nĭt) *n.* an object or material that attracts certain metals, such as iron, **264**

magnetic field (măg nĕt′ĭk fēld′) *n.* the area around a magnet where the push and pull of the magnet is felt, **265**

magnify (măg′nə fī) *v.* become greater, **246**

main idea (mān ī dē′ə) *n.* the most important point to understand, **336**

maintain (mān tān′) *v.* keep, **109**

mammals (măm′əlz) *n.* warm-blooded animals that have a backbone and fur or hair, **48**

mantle (măn′tl) *n.* the layer of Earth between the crust and the core, **113**

maria (mä′rē ə) *n.* flat plains on the Moon that formed when lava flowed over the surface, **184**

Pronunciation Key

ă	bat	oi	toy
ā	ape	ou	sh**ou**t
âr	**air**	o͝o	b**oo**k
ä	father	o͞o	m**oo**n
ĕ	let	s	**s**un
ē	**ea**sy	sh	pre**ss**ure
ĭ	**i**f	th	**th**e, **th**ing
ī	l**ie**	ŭ	n**u**t
îr	d**ear**	ûr	c**ir**cle
k	**c**ause	ə	**a**go
ŏ	l**o**t	ər	moth**er**
ō	g**o**	′	primary stress
ô	**a**ll	′	secondary stress

marine (mə rēn′) *adj.* relating to the sea, **51**

marshes (märsh′əs) *n.* low-lying wetlands with lots of grasses, **136**

mass (măs) *n.* the amount of matter in an object, **196, 202**

matter (măt′ər) *n.* anything that has mass and takes up space, **196**

measure (mĕzh′ər) *v.* find out the amount of something, **295**

mechanical energy (mĭ kăn′ĭ kəl ĕn′ər jē) *n.* energy that comes from the motion or position of matter, **250, 252**

mechanical weathering (mĭ kăn′ĭ kəl wĕth′ər ĭng) *n.* what happens when rocks split or break into smaller pieces, **122**

medium (mē′dē əm) *n.* matter that a wave travels through, **280**

mental (mĕn′tl) *adj.* relating to the mind, **342**

metals (mĕt′lz) *n.* shiny, hard substances that conduct heat and electricity, **210**

metamorphic rock (met′ə môr′fĭk rŏk′) *n.* a type of rock that forms from heat and pressure, **160**

meteorite (mē′tē ə rīt) *n.* a piece of rock from space that lands on Earth, **181**

meteorologists (mē′ tē ə rŏl′ə jĭsts) *n.* people who study and predict the weather, **150**

meteors (mē′tē ərz′ *or* mē′tē ôrz′) *n.* pieces of rock from space that burn up as they enter Earth's atmosphere, **181**

methods (mĕth′ədz) *n.* plans of action, **302**

metric system (mĕt′rĭk sĭs′təm) *n.* a system of measurement used all over the world, **398**

microscope (mī′krə skōp′) *n.* a tool that lets you see tiny things that you cannot see with only your eyes, **397**

minerals (mĭn′ər əlz) *n.* solid, nonliving substances that form in the earth, **82, 158**

mirror (mĭr′ər) *n.* a shiny surface that reflects light, **276**

misspell (mĭs spĕl′) *v.* spell wrong, **380**

mitochondria (mī′tə kŏn′drē ə) *n.* the parts of a cell that turn nutrients into energy, **30**

mitosis (mī tō′sĭs) *n.* what happens when cells divide and make exact copies of themselves, **29**

mixture (mĭks′chər) *n.* something that contains two or more substances, **214**

model (mŏd′l) *n.* a simple version of something, **304**

moist (moist) *adj.* wet, **58**

mold (mōld) *n.* an imprint of a solid shape, **167**

molecule (mŏl′ĭ kyo͞ol′) *n.* the smallest unit of a compound, **212**

mollusks (mə lŭsks′) *n.* invertebrates with soft bodies that often have a hard outer shell, **45**

molten (mōl′tən) *adj.* melted, **120**

moneran (mə nîr′ən) *adj.* relating to all bacteria, **33**

monitor (mŏn′ĭ tər) *v.* check, **347**

moons (mo͞onz) *n.* things in space that revolve around a planet, **177**

motion (mō′shən) *n.* movement, **224, 252**

movable (mo͞o′və bəl) *adj.* changing position, **247**

movement (mo͞ov′mənt) *n.* a change in position, **233**

multiple meanings (mŭl′tə pəl mē′nĭngz) *n.* something that can be understood in different ways, **368**

multiply (mŭl′tə plī′) *v.* make more, **240**

muscle tissue (mŭs′əl tĭsh′o͞o) *n.* a group of cells that works together to form muscles, **26**

muscular system (mŭs′kyə lər sĭs′ təm) *n.* the group of muscles that helps a body move, **71**

mutations (myo͞o tā′shənz) *n.* changes, **68**

N

natural cycle (năch′ə rəl sī′kəl *or* năch′rəl sī′kəl) *n.* a process that repeats in nature over a long time, **156**

natural gas (năch′ə rəl găs′ *or* năch′rəl găs′) *n.* a gas formed from plants and animals that lived long ago; a fossil fuel, **168**

natural resource (năch′ə rəl rē′sôrs′ *or* năch′ə rəl rĭ sôrs′) *n.* any useful thing that is found in nature, **170**

natural selection (năch′ə rəl sĭ lĕk′shən *or* năch′rəl sĭ lĕk′shən) *n.* survival and reproduction of organisms that are best adapted to live in an environment, **69**

negative charge (nĕg′ə tĭv chärj′) *n.* a charge that has more electrons than protons, **207**

nerves (nûrvz) *n.* the things that carry messages between the brain and the other parts of a body, **76**

nervous system (nûr′vəs sĭs′təm) *n.* the group of parts that controls how a body moves, **76**

neutral (no͞o′trəl *or* nyo͞o′trəl) *adj.* not electrically charged, **260**

neutron (no͞o′trŏn′ *or* nyo͞o′trŏn′) *n.* part of an atom with neither a positive charge nor a negative charge, **206**

newton (no͞ot′n *or* nyo͞ot′n) *n.* a unit that measures the strength of a force, **219**

niche (nĭch *or* nēsh) *n.* the role an organism plays in its habitat, **94**

nitrogen (nī′trə jən) *n.* a gas that plants and animals need to grow, **92**

nonliving (nŏn′lĭv′ĭng) *adj.* describes things that do not do all of the life processes, **20**

nonrenewable (nŏn′rĭ no͞o′ə bəl *or* non′rĭ nyo͞o′ə bəl) *adj.* not able to be replaced, **255**

nonrenewable resource (nŏn′rĭ no͞o′ə bəl rē′sôrs′ *or* nŏn′rĭ no͞o′ə bəl rĭ sôrs′) *n.* a natural resource that cannot be replaced, **255**

nonvascular plants (nŏn văs′kyə lər plănts) *n.* plants that do not have tubes, **34**

northern hemisphere (nôr′thərn hĕm′ĭ sfîr′) *n.* one-half of Earth's surface above the equator, **154**

note cards (nōt′ kärdz′) *n.* small pieces of paper that you write notes on, **387**

nourish (nûr′ĭsh *or* nŭr′ĭsh) *v.* feed, **50**

Pronunciation Key

ă	**bat**	oi	**toy**
ā	**ape**	ou	sh**ou**t
âr	**air**	ŏŏ	b**oo**k
ä	f**a**ther	ōō	m**oo**n
ĕ	**le**t	s	**s**un
ē	**ea**sy	sh	pre**ss**ure
ĭ	**i**f	th	**th**e, **th**ing
ī	**lie**	ŭ	**n**u**t**
îr	**dear**	ûr	**c**ir**c**le
k	**c**ause	ə	**a**go
ŏ	**l**o**t**	ər	moth**er**
ō	**g**o	′	primary stress
ô	**a**ll	′	secondary stress

nuclear energy (nōō′klē ər ĕn′ər jē *or* nyōō′klə ər ĕn′ər jē) *n.* energy that is stored in the nucleus of an atom, **251**

nucleus (nōō′klē əs *or* nyōō′klē əs) *n.* the center of a cell that controls how the cell grows, **25, 30, 206**

nutrients (nōō′trē ənts *or* nyōō′trē ənts) *n.* something that organisms must have to live and grow, **21**

O

object (ŏb′jĕkt′) *n.* a thing, **379**

observation (ŏb′zər vā′shən) *n.* something you notice, **298**

observe (əb zûrv′) *v.* look closely at, **290**

occupy (ŏk′yə pī′) *v.* take up space, **203**

oceanic ridge (ō′shē ăn′ĭk rĭj) *n.* an underwater mountain range, **127**

ocean (ō′shən) *n.* a marine biome or water environment, **107**

offspring (ôf′sprĭng′ *or* ôf′sprĭng′) *n.* babies, **50**

oil (oil) *n.* a fossil fuel, usually a liquid, formed from plants and animals that lived long ago, **168**

omnivores (ŏm′nə vôrz′ *or* ŏm′nə vōrz′) *n.* animals that get their energy from eating both plants and animals, **96**

opaque (ō pāk′) *adj.* not clear, **275**

orbit (ôr′bĭt) *v.* move around something in a path, **151, 176**

order (ôr′dər) *n.* an arrangement of things, **352**

organelles (ôr′gə nĕlz′) *n.* the parts inside a cell that have special jobs, **30**

organisms (ôr′gə nĭz′əmz) *n.* living things, **20**

organize (ôr′gə nīz′) *v.* put things in a way that is easy to find and understand, **388, 392**

organs (ôr′gənz) *n.* groups of tissues in a body that work together to do a job, **70**

organ system (ôr′gən sĭs′təm) *n.* a group of organs that work together, **70**

original (ə rĭj′ə nəl) *adj.* first; relating to the thing you started with, **299, 378**

origins (ôr′ə jĭnz *or* ŏr′ə jĭnz) *n.* the places where things come from, **364**

outer core (ou′tər kôr′ *or* ou′tər kōr′) *n.* the layer near the center of Earth made of liquid metal, **113**

outline (out′līn′) *n.* a short, written plan of what you are going to write or say later, **388**

overuse (ō′vər yōōz′) *v.* use something too much, **165**

oxygen (ŏk′sī jən) *n.* a gas in air or water that animals must breathe to live, **72**

ozone layer (ō′zōn′ lā′ər′) *n.* a band of a special form of oxygen in the stratosphere that absorbs many of the Sun's ultraviolet rays, **139**

P

parallel circuit (păr′ə lĕl′ sîr′kĭts) *n.* an electric circuit that has several paths; if one light burns out, the other lights still work, **263**

parent cell (pâr′ənt sĕl *or* păr′ənt sĕl) *n.* the one cell that divides to form two daughter cells, **29**

particles (pär′tĭ kəlz) *n.* tiny pieces that make up all matter, **199**

patterns (păt′ərnz) *n.* models that show a relationship between things, **376**

pause (pôz) *v.* stop briefly, **344**

perform (pər fôrm′) *v.* do, **26**

periodicals (pîr′ē ŏd′ĭ kəlz) *n.* magazines, newspapers, or journals that come out every day, week, month, or year, **316**

periodic table (pîr′ē ŏd′ĭk tā′bəl) *n.* a chart that helps scientists understand elements, **400**

phases (fāz′əz) *n.* the different forms in a cycle, **182**

photographs (fō′tə grăfs′) *n.* pictures taken with a camera, **316, 327**

photons (fō′tŏnz) *n.* packets of light energy, **270**

photosphere (fō′tə sfîr′) *n.* the part of the Sun you see, **175**

photosynthesis (fō′tō sĭn′thĭ sĭs) *n.* a process where plants use the energy in sunlight to change carbon dioxide and water into food, **38**

phototropism (fō tŏt′rə pĭz′əm *or* fō′tō trō′pĭz′əm) *n.* process when plants grow in response to light, **40**

phrasal verb (frāz′ŭl vûrb) *n.* a verb plus one or more other words that makes a new verb, **378**

phrase (frāz) *n.* a group of words that works together, **378**

physical (fĭz′ĭ kəl) *adj.* relating to the body, **67**

physical features (fĭz′ĭ kəl fē′chərz) *n.* characteristics of something that are visible, **124**

physical property (fĭz′ĭ kəl prŏp′ər tē) *n.* something you observe with your senses, such as shape, color, and texture, **196**

pioneer plants (pī′ə nîr′ plănts) *n.* grasses and small shrubs that grow first in a forest after a fire, **103**

pitch (pĭch) *n.* the high or low frequency of a sound, **282**

plane (plān) *n.* a wide area of flat surface, **238**

planets (plăn′ĭts) *n.* large objects that move around a sun, **176**

plates (plāts) *n.* the parts that make up Earth's crust and solid upper mantle, **114**

polar (pō′lər) *adj.* cold, **148**

population (pŏp′yə lā′shən) *n.* all the organisms of the same species that live in the same place, **68, 108**

pores (pôrz *or* pōrz) *n.* small openings, **44**

position (pə zĭsh′ən) *n.* the place where something is, **224, 252**

positive charge (pŏz′ĭ tĭv chärj′) *n.* a charge that has more protons than electrons, **207**

potential energy (pə tĕn′shəl ĕn′ər jē) *n.* energy that is stored, **252**

power (pou′ər) *n.* how much work is done in a certain time, **235**

precipitate (prĭ sĭp′ĭ tāt′) *v.* fall to Earth as rain or snow, **135**

Pronunciation Key

ă	bat	oi	toy
ā	ape	ou	shout
âr	air	o͝o	book
ä	father	o͞o	moon
ĕ	let	s	sun
ē	easy	sh	pressure
ĭ	if	th	the, thing
ī	lie	ŭ	nut
îr	dear	ûr	circle
k	cause	ə	ago
ŏ	lot	ər	mother
ō	go	′	primary stress
ô	all	′	secondary stress

precipitation (prĭ sĭp′ĭ ta′shən) *n.* a form of water that falls back to Earth, **148**

precise (prĭ sīs′) *adj.* exact or detailed, **294, 391**

predators (prĕd′ə tərz) *n.* consumers that must eat other animals to get energy, **67, 95, 101**

predict (prĭ dĭkt′) *v.* use what you know or observe to say what will happen, **296**

prediction (prĭ dĭk′shən) *n.* a statement about what will happen in the future based on what you know, **334**

prefix (prē′fĭks′) *n.* a group of letters found at the beginning of a base word or root, **360**

present (prĭ zĕnt′) *v.* show, **308, 328**

prevailing winds (prĭ vā′lĭng wĭndz) *n.* the directions that winds usually blow from, **141**

preview (prē′vyo͞o′) *v.* look ahead, **316**

prey (prā) *n.* an animal a predator kills and eats, **67, 95, 101**

primary (prī′mĕr′ ē *or* prī′mə rē) *adj.* first, **98**; most important, **174**

prism (prĭz′əm) *n.* a glass object with three sides, **274**

process (prŏs′əs′) *n.* a number of steps; the way that something happens, **288, 343, 377**

producers (prə do͞o′sərz *or* pre dyo͞o′sərz) *n.* living things that make their own food, **38, 88**

products (prŏd′əkts) *n.* things that are made, **216**

professions (prə fĕsh′enz) *n.* the jobs people have, **372**

pronounce (prə nouns′) *v.* say words, **381**

pronunciation (prə nŭn′sē ā′shən) *n.* the way a word is said out loud, **364**

pronunciation guide (prə nŭn′sē ā′shən gīd) *n.* the part of a glossary that helps you say a word correctly, **322**

proofread (pro͞of′rēd) *v.* read something in writing to find and fix mistakes, **392**

propel (prə pĕl′) *v.* move forward, **57**

properties (prŏp′ər tēz) *n.* special qualities or characteristics that describe things and events, **196, 291, 292**

proteins (prō′tēnz′) *n.* nutrients that are found in meat, beans, and nuts, **82**

protist (prō′tĭst) *adj.* relating to one-celled organisms that are not bacteria, **33**

protons (prō′tŏnz′) *n.* parts of an atom with a positive charge, **206**

pulley (po͝ol′ē) *n.* a simple machine made of a wheel and axle and a rope, **247**

punctuation (pŭngk′cho͞o ā′shən) *n.* marks, like periods and commas, that separate sentences or clarify meaning, **392**

pure substances (pyŏŏr′ sŭb′stəns əs) *n.* substances that contain only one kind of matter, **208**

purpose (pûr′pəs) *n.* a goal or reason to do something, **315**

Q

quality (kwŏl′ĭ tē) *n.* a property that makes something special, **285**

R

radar (rā′där) *n.* a tool that helps people predict the weather, **150**

radiation (rā′dē ā′shən) *n.* the movement of energy through space without using particles, **258**

ramp (rămp) *n.* an inclined plane that people use to move to a higher or lower place, **238**

rate (rāt) *n.* a measurement of how much something changes over time, **226**

rays (rāz) *n.* thin lines of light that radiate from the center, **184**

react (rē ăkt′) *v.* respond to something, **22**; change chemically, **216**

reactants (rē ăk′tənts) *n.* the elements or compounds you start with in a chemical reaction, **216**

reasonable (rē′zə nə bəl) *adj.* making sense; thoughtful, **294**

recessive (rĭ sĕs′ĭv) *adj.* having an influence that is weaker than other influences, **85**

recognize (rĕk′əg nīz′) *v.* understand; remember something from past experience, **352**

rectangular solid (rĕk tăng′gyə lər sŏl′ĭd) *n.* a three-dimensional figure with six sides that are rectangular, **203**

recycle (rē sī′kəl) *v.* break down to use again, **173**

reflect (rĭ flĕkt′) *v.* bounce back, **272**

reflexes (rē′flĕks′əs) *n.* automatic responses, **77**

refract (rĭ frăkt′) *v.* change direction; bend, **272, 278**

refraction (rĭ frăk′shən) *n.* the bending of light when it goes from one substance into another substance, **273**

region (rē′jən) *n.* an area, **104**

regulate (rĕg′yə lāt′) *v.* control, **50**

relationship (rĭ lā′shən shĭp) *n.* a connection between two or more things, **348**

rely (rĭ lī′) *v.* depend, **53**

remains (rĭ mānz′) *n.* things that are left over, **166**

renewable (rĭ nōō′ə bəl *or* rĭ nyōō′ə bəl′) *adj.* being easily replaced, **254**

renewable resource (rĭ nōō′ə bəl rē′sôrs′ *or* rĭ nyōō′ə bəl rē′sôrs′) *n.* a natural resource that is used and then replaced, **170**

repeat (rĭ pēt′ *or* rē′pēt′) *v.* do again, **289**

repel (rĭ pĕl′) *v.* push apart by physical force, **260, 264**

represent (rĕp′rĭ zĕnt′) *v.* show, **304**

reproduce (rē′prə dōōs′ *or* rē′prə dyōōs′) *v.* make more of the same type of thing, **22, 36, 60**

reptiles (rĕp′tīlz′ *or* rĕp′tīlz) *n.* cold-blooded animals that have scales and a backbone, **49**

reread (rē′rēd) *v.* read something again, **347**

research (rĭ sûrch′ *or* rē′sûrch) *n.* focused study of a topic, **386**

Pronunciation Key

ă	bat	oi	toy
ā	ape	ou	sh**ou**t
âr	**air**	ŏŏ	b**oo**k
ä	f**a**ther	ōō	m**oo**n
ĕ	let	s	sun
ē	**easy**	sh	pressure
ĭ	**if**	th	**the**, **th**ing
ī	lie	ŭ	nut
îr	**dear**	ûr	c**ir**cle
k	**c**ause	ə	**a**go
ŏ	lot	ər	moth**er**
ō	g**o**	′	primary stress
ô	**a**ll	′	secondary stress

resist (rĭ zĭst′) *v.* work against, **222**

resistance force (rĭ zĭs′təns fôrs *or* rĭ zĭs′təns fōrs) *n.* the force working against effort force, **237**

resources (rē′sôrs′əs *or* rĭ sôrs′əs) *n.* things that can be used to help living things, **254**

respiratory system (rĕs′pər ə tôr′ē sĭs′təm *or* rĭ spīr′ə tôr′ē sĭs′təm) *n.* the group of parts that help a body breathe, **72**

respire (rĭ spīr′) *v.* breathe, **23**

respond (rĭ spŏnd′) *v.* react, **40**

results (rĭ zŭlts′) *n.* things that happen in the end, **308**

retell (rē tĕl′) *v.* tell again, **338**

retina (rĕt′ĭn ə) *n.* the part of the eye that is sensitive to light and carries images to the brain, **271**

revise (rĭ vīz′) *v.* look at something to find ways to make it better, **390**

revision (rĭ vĭzh′ən) *n.* an edited version of a piece of writing, **391**

revolution (rĕv ə lōō′shən) *n.* the completion of going around once, **178**

revolve (rĭ vŏlv′) *v.* move around something, **178**

rift valleys (rĭft′ văl′ēz) *n.* long and narrow valleys that form where Earth's plates pull apart, **117**

rilles (rĭlz) *n.* trenches or ditches on the surface of the Moon, **184**

robots (rō′bəts *or* rō′bŏts′) *n.* machines that help people do work, **249**

rock cycle (rŏk′ sī′kəl) *n.* the cycle in which rocks change from one kind to another, **162**

rockets (rŏk′ĭts) *n.* things that send astronauts, spacecrafts, and satellites into space, **192**

Roman numerals (rō′mən nōō′mər əlz *or* rō′mən nyōō′mər əlz) *n.* a system of writing numbers that is used in outlines, **389**

root (rōōt) *n.* the word part that is used to form other words, **361, 362**

rotate (rō′tāt) *v.* spin, **179**

rough (rŭf) *adj.* uneven; having a lot of friction, **222**

rule (rōōl) *n.* a direction that must be followed, **378, 381**

rust (rŭst) *n.* a chemical change that happens to metal, **197, 211**

S

salinity (sə lĭn′ĭ tē) *n.* amount of salt, **132**

salt water (sôlt′ wô′tər *or* sôlt′ wŏt′ər) *n.* water that humans cannot drink; 97 percent of Earth's water, **132**

satellite (săt′l īt′) *n.* a tool in space that moves around the Earth and measures many properties of land and water, **130, 151, 192**

scales (skālz) *n.* the things that cover the bodies of reptiles and some fish, **54**

scavengers (skăv′ən jərz) *n.* animals that eat dead animals that they did not kill, **96**

scientists (sī′ən tĭsts) *n.* people who study the natural world, **288**

screw (skro͞o) *n.* an inclined plane wrapped around a tube, **242**

screwdriver (skro͞o drī′vər) *n.* a tool that turns the top of a screw to put it in a material, **243**

search (sûrch) *v.* look for, **318**

season (sē′zən) *n.* a major division, or part, of the year, **154**

second-class lever (sĕk′ənd klăs′ lĕv′ər *or* sĕk′ənd klăs′ lē′vər) *n.* a lever that is lifted upward with the load in the middle and the fulcrum on the end, **245**

secondary (sĕk′ən dĕr′ē) *adj.* second, **98**

sediment (sĕd′ə mənt) *n.* small pieces of rocks, **123, 161**

sedimentary rock (sĕd′ə mĕn′tə rē rŏk′ *or* sĕd′ə mĕn trē rŏk′) *n.* a type of rock that forms from layers of sediment that push down on other layers, **160**

seed (sēd) *n.* the first stage of a plant life cycle, **62**

seedlings (sēd′lĭngz) *n.* young plants that grow from seeds, **62**

senses (sĕns′əz) *n.* the five ways you take in information about the things around you, **76, 290**

separate (sĕp′ ə rāt′) *v.* divide or split apart, **214, 379**

sequence (sē′kwəns) *n.* the order in which events happen, **352, 377**

series circuit (sîr′ēz sûr′kĭt) *n.* an electric circuit that has one path; if one light burns out, the other ones stop working, **262**

shelf (shĕlf) *n.* the flat part of land that is covered by water, **126**

shell (shĕl) *n.* a layer that protects animals from things in the natural world, **56**

signal words (sĭg′nəl wûrdz′) *n.* words in sentences that give clues about what you are going to read, **349, 376**

similar (sĭm′ə lər′) *adj.* the same as something else, **364**

similarities (sĭm′ə lăr′ĭ tēz) *n.* ways that things are the same, **332**

skeletal system (skĕl′ĭ tl sĭs′təm) *n.* the group of bones that gives shape to a body, **71**

skeleton (skĕl′ĭ tn) *n.* a system of bones in a body, **54**

skill (skĭl) *n.* something you can do, **288**

sleet (slēt) *n.* partially frozen rain, **148**

slope (slōp) *n.* the slanted part of land that is covered by water, **126**

small intestine (smôl′ ĭn tĕs′tĭn) *n.* the part of the digestive system where most nutrients are absorbed into the blood, **78**

smooth (smo͞oth) *adj.* even; having little friction, **222**

snow drifts (snō′ drĭfts) *n.* large piles of snow that have been moved by the wind, **149**

solar energy (sō′lər ĕn′ər jē) *n.* energy that comes from the Sun, **254**

Pronunciation Key

ă	bat	oi	toy
ā	ape	ou	shout
âr	air	o͝o	book
ä	father	o͞o	moon
ĕ	let	s	sun
ē	easy	sh	pressure
ĭ	if	th	the, thing
ī	lie	ŭ	nut
îr	dear	ûr	circle
k	cause	ə	ago
ŏ	lot	ər	mother
ō	go	′	primary stress
ô	all	′	secondary stress

solar system (sō′lər sĭs′təm) *n.* the Sun and all the objects that orbit it, **176, 190**

solid (sŏl′ĭd) *n.* the state of matter that has a defined shape; the particles in a solid are less spread out than the particles in both liquids and gases, **198**

solution (sə lo͞o′shən) *n.* a mixture that looks like one substance, **215**

solve (sŏlv *or* sôlv) *v.* find an answer to a question or problem, **302**

sonar (sō′när′) *n.* a tool that measures distance using sound waves, **130**

sort (sôrt) *v.* classify; put things into groups, **292**

sound (sound) *n.* something that can be heard, **366**

source (sôrs) *n.* the place where something comes from, **319**

southern hemisphere (sou′thərn hĕm′ĭ sfîr′) *n.* one-half of Earth's surface below the equator, **154**

spacecrafts (spās′krăfts′) *n.* vehicles that travel into space, **186, 192**

specialized (spĕsh′ ə līzd′) *adj.* focused on one thing, **27**

species (spē′shēz *or* spē′sēz) *n.* a group of living things that are alike in many ways, **68**

specific (spĭ sĭf′ĭk) *adj.* special in some way, **70, 384**

speed (spēd) *n.* the measure of how quickly an object changes position, **226, 228**

spellings (spĕl′ ĭngz) *n.* the order of letters in words, **366**

spills (spĭlz) *n.* liquid that has fallen on the ground, **403**

spinal cord (spī′nəl kôrd′) *n.* a bunch of nerves that runs from the brain through the middle of the back, **76**

spines (spīnz) *n.* sharp, pointy growths that come out of plants like cacti, **64**

spiral galaxy (spī′rəl găl′ək sē) *n.* a galaxy with a spiral shape that is bright in the center, **189**

sponges (spŭn′jəs) *n.* the simplest animals that have no muscle or nerve cells and live in the ocean, **44**

spores (spôrz) *n.* small cells that can become new plants, **37**

stages (stāj′əs) *n.* steps in a cycle or process, **60**

standard system (stăn′dərd sĭs′təm) *n.* the system of measurement used in the United States, **398**

starch (stärch) *n.* food stored in plants, **39**

state (stāt) *n.* form, **198**

static electricity (stăt′ĭk ĭ lĕk trĭs′ĭ tē *or* stăt′ĭk ē′lĕk trĭs′ĭ tē) *n.* electric charges that build up, **261**

stationary (stā′shə nĕr′ē) *adj.* not moving, **219**

stomach (stŭm′ək) *n.* an organ that uses its muscles to mix food with digestive juices, **78**

stopwatch (stŏp′wŏch′) *n.* a tool used to measure time, **397**

storm surge (stôrm′ sûrj′) *n.* ocean water that moves to the shore during a hurricane, **147**

strategy (străt′ə jē) *n.* method or plan of action, **340, 347**

stratosphere (străt′ə sfîr′) *n.* the layer of the atmosphere that is above the troposphere and contains the ozone layer, **139**

streamlined (strēm′līnd′) *adj.* designed to move smoothly in water, **54**

structures (strŭk′chərz) *n.* parts, **24**

submersibles (səb mûr′sə bəlz) *n.* small submarines, **131**

subsurface (sŭb′sûr′fəs) *adj.* below the surface or top level, **129**

subtopics (sŭb tŏp′ĭks) *n.* small or narrow topics, **323**

suffix (sŭf′ĭks) *n.* a group of letters found at the end of a base word or root, **362**

summarize (sŭm′ə rīz′) *v.* give only the most important ideas, **338**

superlative (so͞o pûr′lə tĭv) *n.* a word that shows a comparison among three or more things, **371**

support (sə pôrt′) *v.* give reasons to make something more believable, **308, 336**

surface (sûr′fəs) *n.* the top layer, **116**

surface current (sûr′fəs kûr′ənt *or* sûr′fəs kŭr′ənt) *n.* the movement of the top level of ocean water, **128**

swamps (swŏmps *or* swômps) *n.* wetlands that have many large bushes and trees, **136**

symbiosis (sĭm′bē ō′sĭs *or* sĭm′bī ō′sĭs) *n.* a close relationship between two different species, **94**

symbol (sĭm′bəl) *n.* a thing that represents other things, **209, 401**

T

table of contents (tā′bəl ŭv kŏn′tĕnts′) *n.* the part of a book that names the units and chapters in order, **321**

tadpoles (tăd′pōlz′) *n.* baby frogs that have tails, **58**

taiga (tī′gə) *n.* a cold and moist forest biome, **105**

tail (tāl) *n.* a part of some animals that grows out of the back end of the body, **58**

tarnish (tär′nĭsh) *v.* form a dark coating, **211**

technology (tĕk nŏl′ə jē) *n.* the useful tools that were made by inventors applying science ideas, **130, 192, 249**

telescopes (tĕl′ĭ skōps′) *n.* tools that help scientists see things that are very far away, **193**

temperate forest (tĕm′pər ĭt fôr′ĭst *or* tĕm′pər ĭt fŏr′ĭst) *n.* dry and moist biomes with four seasons, **105**

temperature (tĕm′pər ə cho͝or′ *or* tĕm′prə cho͝or′) *n.* a measure of how fast the particles move in a substance, **256**

term (tûrm) *n.* an important word, **326**

tertiary (tûr′shē ĕr′ē) *adj.* third, **98**

Pronunciation Key

ă	bat	oi	toy
ā	ape	ou	shout
âr	air	o͝o	book
ä	father	o͞o	moon
ĕ	let	s	sun
ē	easy	sh	pressure
ĭ	if	th	the, thing
ī	lie	ŭ	nut
îr	dear	ûr	circle
k	cause	ə	ago
ŏ	lot	ər	mother
ō	go	′	primary stress
ô	all	′	secondary stress

text (tĕkst) *n.* words on a page, **350**

thermal energy (thûr′məl ĕn′ər jē) *n.* the motion of particles in matter, **250, 256**

thermometer (thər mŏm′ĭ tər) *n.* a tool used to measure temperature, **396**

third-class lever (thûrd′klăs′ lĕv′ər *or* thûrd′klăs′ lē′vər) *n.* a lever that is lifted upward with the load on one end and the fulcrum on the other end, **245**

threads (thrĕdz) *n.* the ridges on a screw, **242**

threatened (thrĕt′nd) *adj.* having a population of a species that decreases, **109**

thunderstorm (thŭn′dər stôrm′) *n.* a strong storm with lightning and thunder, **142**

tissue (tĭsh′o͞o) *n.* a group of cells that work together to do the same kind of job, **26, 70**

titles (tīt′lz) *n.* words at the top of a page that tell you what is on the rest of the page, **325**

topic (tŏp′ĭk) *n.* what something is about, **314, 350, 384**

tornado (tôr nā′dō) *n.* a fast-moving storm that forms over land, **144**

trace fossil (trās′ fŏs′əl) *n.* a mark of something that used to be in a place, **167**

trade winds (trād′ wĭndz′) *n.* winds that blow west toward the equator, **156**

traits (trāts) *n.* characteristics or special things about an organism, **28, 64, 84**

transfer (trăns fûr′ *or* trăns′fər) *v.* move from one place to another, **78, 258**

transmit (trăns mĭt′ *or* trănz mĭt′) *v.* send, **272**

transparent (trăns pâr′ənt *or* trăns păr′ənt) *adj.* allowing light to pass through, **273**

transport (trăns pôrt′ *or* trăns pōrt′) *v.* carry, **123**

trench (trĕnch) *n.* a deep crack in Earth's crust, **127**

tropical (trŏp′ĭ kəl) *adj.* relating to the warm areas of Earth that are close to the equator, **146, 148**

tropical rain forest (trŏp′ĭ kəl rān fôr′ĭst *or* trŏp′ĭ kəl rān fŏr′ĭst) *n.* a hot and moist forest biome where many different kinds of organisms live, **106**

tropism (trō′pĭz′əm) *n.* growth that happens based on something in the environment, **40**

troposphere (trō′pə sfîr′ *or* trŏp′ə sfîr′) *n.* the layer of the atmosphere that is closest to Earth, **138**

trough (trôf *or* trŏf) *n.* the bottom of a wave, **266**

tubes (to͞obz *or* tyo͞obz) *n.* the round passages that move water through plants, **35**

tundra (tŭn′ drə) *n.* a cold and dry biome with a lot of snow and very few plants, **105**

typhoons (tī fo͞onz′) *n.* large storms that form over the western Pacific Ocean, **146**

U

ultraviolet rays (ŭl′trə vī′ə lĭt rāz) *n.* the kind of electromagnetic rays that can cause sunburn, **139**

units (yōō′nĭts) *n.* parts used to measure things, **295**; parts of a textbook that organize topics together, **314, 321**

universe (yōō′nə vûrs′) *n.* a huge collection of galaxies, **188**

unmanned missions (ŭn mănd′ mĭsh′ənz) *n.* spacecrafts with no people, **186**

updraft (ŭp′drăft′) *n.* air moving upward, **145**

ureters (yŏŏ rē′tərz *or* yŏŏr′ĭt ərz) *n.* the pathways through which waste travels from the kidneys to the bladder, **80**

urethra (yŏŏ rē′thrə) *n.* the pathway through which the liquid of the bladder leaves the body, **80**

V

vacuoles (văk′yōō ōlz′) *n.* the parts of a cell that store water and nutrients, **25**

valley (văl′ē) *n.* a low, flat area of land between hills or mountains, **124**

variable (vâr′ē ə bəl *or* văr′ē ə bəl) *n.* something that can change, **304**

vascular plants (văs′kyə lər plănts) *n.* plants that have tubes that carry liquid, **35**

vegetation (vĕj′ĭ tā′shən) *n.* the plant growth of a place, **153**

veins (vānz) *n.* thin tubes in the body that carry blood to the heart, **75**

velocity (və lŏs′ĭ tē) *n.* speed in a specific direction, **228**

vertebrae (vûr′tə brā′ *or* vûr′tə brē′) *n.* bones that form a backbone, **42**

vertebrates (vûr′tə brāts′ *or* vûr′tə brĭts′) *n.* animals that have a backbone, **42**

vibrate (vī′brāt) *v.* move back and forth, **256**

vibration (vī bra′shən) *n.* what happens when things shake, or move back and forth, **280**

visible light (vĭz′ə bəl līt′) *n.* electromagnetic waves you can see, **270**

visualize (vĭzh′ōō ə līz′) *v.* make a picture of something in your mind, **342**

vitamins (vī′tə mĭnz) *n.* nutrients that are found in many fruits and vegetables, **82**

volcano (vŏl kă′nō) *n.* a crack in Earth's crust that sometimes erupts and forms a hard landform, **120**

volume (vŏl′yōōm *or* vŏl′yəm) *n.* the amount of space an object takes up, **203**; loudness of a sound, **284**

W

wane (wān) *v.* have less and less visibility, **183**

warm-blooded (wôrm′ blŭd′ ĭd) *adj.* adapted to help keep a constant body temperature, **48**

waste (wāst) *n.* something that you don't need anymore; something that is not useful anymore, **23**

wave (wāv) *n.* a moving vibration, **266**

wavelength (wāv′lĕngkth′ *or* wāv′lĕngth′ *or* wāv′lĕnth′) *n.* the distance from one wave to the next, **268, 270, 274**

wax (wăks) *v.* have more and more visibility, **183**

Pronunciation Key

ă	**b**a**t**	oi	**t**oy
ā	ape	ou	**sh**ou**t**
âr	air	o͝o	**b**oo**k**
ä	**f**a**th**e**r**	o͞o	**m**oo**n**
ĕ	**l**e**t**	s	**s**u**n**
ē	**e**a**s**y	sh	pre**ss**ure
ĭ	**i**f	th	**th**e, **th**ing
ī	**l**ie	ŭ	**n**u**t**
îr	**d**ea**r**	ûr	**c**ir**c**le
k	**c**ause	ə	**a**go
ŏ	**l**o**t**	ər	mo**th**er
ō	**g**o	**ʹ**	primary stress
ô	**a**ll	ʹ	secondary stress

weather forecasting (wĕthʹər fôrʹkăstʹĭng *or* wĕthʹər fōrʹkăstʹĭng) *n.* when people use science and technology to predict future weather, **150**

weathering (wĕthʹər ĭng) *n.* the breaking down of landforms by the Sun, water, and wind, **122, 164**

wedge (wĕj) *n.* an inclined plane turned on edge, **240**

weight (wāt) *n.* a measure of the force of gravity on an object, **221**

wetlands (wĕtʹlăndzʹ) *n.* environments where water is near the surface, **136**

wheel and axle (hwēl ănd ăkʹsəl *or* wēl ănd ăkʹsəl) *n.* a simple machine that is made of a rod that goes through the middle of a wheel, **246**

wind (wĭnd) *n.* moving air caused by differences in pressure, **140**

windpipe (wĭndʹpīpʹ) *n.* a tube that air travels down to your lungs to help you breathe, **72**

wings (wĭngz) *n.* the parts of a bird that help it fly or swim, **52**

work (wûrk) *n.* when force is applied to an object and the object moves, **232, 234**

Art Credits

Kenneth Batelman, pp. **101, 239, 266, 267**; Linda Bittner, p. **32-33**; Annamarie Boley, pp. **35, 39, 164**; Dan Bridy, pp. **104, 114, 156**; Barbara Cousins, pp. **29, 30, 213**; Dusty Deyo, pp. **73, 79, 145, 183** *right,* **182, 188**; Thomas Gagliano, pp. **116, 117** *top,* **168, 176–177, 178, 206, 271** *top,* **280, 281**; L.R. Galante, pp. **242, 243** *bottom;* Jeff Grunewald, pp. **126–127, 128, 141, 142, 154** *bottom,* **155, 229, 265, 268, 269**; George Hamblin, pp. **119** *top,* **134–135, 138–139, 140, 262, 263, 356**; Reggie Holladay, pp. **66-67, 90**; Michael Hortens, pp. **84, 175, 199, 200, 204, 256** *bottom,* **258** *top,* **259** *right;* Judith A. Hunt, pp. **92, 98, 99**; Victor Kennedy, p. **374**; John Lambert, pp. **75, 77, 80, 121, 160, 274, 275, 277, 278, 279, 401**; Jonathan Massie, pp. **133, 191** *bottom,* **148, 190, 246, 247**; Mike Nicastre, p. **184–185**; Nadine Sokol, p. **24**; Rich Stergultz, pp. **86–87, 236, 237**; Kate Sweeny, pp. **71** *bottom,* **76.**

Photo Credits

Cover: ©Walter Geiersperger/Corbis, *bottom left;* ©Creatas/Punchstock, *bottom middle;* ©Royalty-Free/Corbis, *right;* ©Gary Hincks/Photo Researchers Inc.: **cover front and back.**

©Age Fotostock, pp. **21** *bottom,* **37** *middle, bottom right,* **85** *right,* **145** *left,* **169** *top right,* **181** *bottom*, **198, 222, 233** *right,* **245** *middle,* **282** *right,* **322, 341, 354, 365, 368, 391**; ©Age Fotostock/SuperStock, p. **167** *bottom;* ©Alamy, pp. **46** *middle,* **61** *bottom,* **149** *top,* © B. & C. Alexander/Photo Researchers Inc., p. **105** *top right;* ©Steve Allen/Getty Images, p. **251** *bottom;* ©ARCO/F. Pölking/Age Fotostock, p. **50**; ©ARCO/H. Reinhard/Age Fotostock, p. **97** *bottom;* ©Authors Image/PunchStock, p. **27** *left;* ©BananaStock/PunchStock, p. **85** *bottom;* ©Anthony Bannister/Gallo Images/Corbis, p. **60**; ©Barros & Barros/Getty Images, p. **285**; ©Scott Barrow/Veer, p. **362**; ©Scott Bauer, p. **344**; ©Niel Beer/Getty Images, p. **338**; ©Robert J. Bennett/Age Fotostock, p. **366**; ©George Bernard/Photo Researchers Inc., p. **108**; ©Walter Bibikow/Age Fotostock, p. **380**; ©Biodisc/Visuals Unlimited, p. **27** *bottom;* ©Melanie Blanding/Stringer/Getty Images, p. **144**; ©Steve Bly/Getty Images, pp. **110–111**; ©Werner Bollmann/Age Fotostock, p. **22** *bottom;* ©Mark Boulton/Photo Researchers Inc., p. **137**; ©Brand X Pictures/PunchStock, pp. **51** *bottom,* **55** *top,* **64, 102** *top,* **217** *bottom,* **220, 230, 257, 340, 373** *bottom;* ©Dr. Jeremy Burgess/Photo Researchers Inc., p. **25** *bottom;* C Squared Studios/Getty Images, p. **208**; ©John Cancalosi/Age Fotostock, p. **327** *right;* ©Myrleen Cate/Photo Edit Inc., pp. **250** *bottom,* **291** *left;* ©M. Celebi/U.S. Geological Survey, p. **119** *bottom;* ©David C. Clegg/Science Photo Library, p. **376**; ©Steve Cole/Getty Images, p. **209** *bottom;* ©Martial Colomb/Getty Images, p. **171** *middle;* ©Comstock Images/Alamy, p. **201** *middle;* ©Comstock Images/PictureQuest, pp. **55** *bottom,* **107**; ©Comstock Images/PunchStock, pp. **106** *top,* **170** *top left;* ©Corbis, pp. **26** *bottom,* **44** *middle*, **62–63, 81, 97** *middle right,* **169** *middle left,* **172** *right,* **223** *bottom,* **228** *left,* **241** *bottom right,* **243** *bottom,* **250** *top,* **329, 364**; ©Corbis/PunchStock, p. **378**; ©Creatas/PictureQuest, pp. **47, 226**; ©Creatas/PunchStock, pp. **23, 46** *bottom right,* **46** *bottom left,* **286, 315**; ©Creatas/SuperStock, p. **169** *bottom left;* ©Design Pics/PunchStock, p. **201** *left;* ©Alejandro Díaz Díez/Age Fotostock, p. **56**; ©Digital Archive Japan/Alamy, pp. **34, 170** *bottom left;* ©Digital Vision, pp. **95** *right,* **123**; ©Digital Vision/Getty Images, pp. **42** *middle,* **57** *bottom;* ©Digital Vision/PunchStock, pp. **48** *top,* **49** *bottom,* **53** *top,* **102** *bottom,* **133** *top,* **181** *top;* ©Joe Drivas/Getty Images, p. **372**; ©Gerry Ellis/Getty Images, p. **94**; ©Enigma/Alamy Images, p. **295** *middle;* ©Douglas Faulkner/Photo Researchers,

p. **51** *top;* ©Mauro Fermariello/Photo Researchers Inc., p. **203** *bottom;* ©Berndt Fischer/Age Fotostock, p. **136** *bottom;* ©Michael & Patricia Fogden/Corbis, p. **61** *middle right;* ©Jules Frazier/Getty Images, p. **295** *top;* ©Maryann Frazier/Photo Researchers Inc., p. **40**; ©Tony Freeman/ PhotoEdit Inc., p. **276**; ©Mark Garlick/Photo Researchers Inc., p. **180** *right;* ©Geostock/ Getty Images, p. **59**; ©Getty Images, pp. **18–19, 28, 42, 42** *middle,* **52** *top,* **72, 82** *middle,* **82** *bottom right,* **151** *left,* **153** *right,* **171** *left,* **201** *right,* **224** *bottom,* **224** *top,* **252** *bottom,* **283** *left,* **283** *right,* **284** *left,* **303, 343, 360**; ©Max Gibbs/Getty Images, p. **54** *top,* ©Robert Glusic/Getty Images, p. **132**; ©Spencer Grant/Photo Researchers Inc., pp. **271, 272**; ©Jeff Greenberg/Photo Edit Inc., p. **214** *right;* ©Jeffrey Greenberg/Photo Researchers, p. **402**; ©Steve Gschmeissner/ Photo Researchers Inc., p. **71**; ©Jaume Gual/ Age Fotostock, p. **381**; ©Hagg and Kropp/Age Fotostock, p. **143** *bottom;* ©Gary Hincks/Photo Researchers Inc., pp. **112, 113**; ©Willocx Hugo/Age Fotostock, p. **58** *right;* ©Arnulf Husmo/Getty Images, p. **288**; ©Russell Illig/ Photodisc/Getty Images, pp. **172** *left;* ©Image100/Corbis, pp. **312–313**; ©Imagebroker/Alamy, p. **197** *right;* ©Image Ideas/PictureQuest, pp. **120** *left,* **161** *middle;* ©Image Source Ltd., pp. **337, 345**; ©IMS Communications Ltd./Capstone Design, p. **169** *bottom right;* ©Index Stock Imagery Inc., pp. **13, 136** *middle,* **310, 390**; Ingram Publishing/ Alamy, pp. **45** *middle right,* **56** *top,* **82** *top middle;* ©InsideOut Pix/SuperStock, p. **159** *bottom right;* ©iStock International Inc., pp. **6–7, 36** *top right,* **37** *bottom left,* **38** *middle,* **57** *top,* **70, 74, 82** *bottom,* **97** *middle top,* **100, 105** *bottom right,* **106** *bottom,* **154** *left,* **154** *right,* **158** *bottom right,* **163** *top,* **163** *middle,* **167** *top,* **169** *middle right,* **170** *bottom right,* **174, 196, 203** *top,* **212, 214** *left,* **216, 225, 227, 231, 241** *top left,* **242, 243** *top,* **253** *left,* **254, 255, 284** *right center,* **293** *left,* **327** *bottom*, **342, 376, 396** *right,* **398**; IT Stock Free/Alamy, p. **45** *top;* ©Jacana/Photo Researchers Inc., p. **158** *top left;* ©Mark Jones/Age Fotostock, p. **95** *left;* ©Joubert/ Photo Researchers, Inc., p. **388**; ©Jupiter Images Corporation, pp. **83** *top,* **125** *top,* **143** *top,* **197** *left,* **228** *right,* **238** *bottom,* **317** *bottom,* **319, 357, 373** *top,* **375**; ©Koichi Kamoshida/Getty Images, p. **118**; ©Breck P. Kent/Animals Animals-Earth Science, p. **348**; ©Dorling Kindersley Limited, pp. **115, 162** *left,* **215, 240, 245** *top,* **261, 273** *right,* **396** *left,* **399** *bottom;* ©David King/Getty, p. **52** *bottom,* **399** *top;* ©Pat LaCroix, p. **351**; ©Lawrence Lawry/Science Photo Library, pp. **194–195**; ©Roine Magnusson/Age Fotostock, p. **386**; ©Marevision/Age Fotostock, p. **43** *top;* ©Matt Matthews/iStock, p. **256**; ©Mauritius Images/ Age Fotostock, p. **292**; ©Buddy Mays/Corbis, p. **61** *middle left;* © The McGraw-Hill Companies Inc., pp. **26** *left,* **46** *top right,* **71, 103** *top,* **159** *middle left,* **159** *bottom left,* **161** *top,* **173** *right,* **241** *top right;* ©C. McIntyre/PhotoLink/Getty Images, pp. **36** *bottom right,* **37** *bottom middle;* ©Ryan McVay/Getty Images, pp. **171** *right,* **245** *bottom;* ©Medioimages/PunchStock, p. **49** *top,* ©Astrid & Hanns-Frieder Michler/Photo Researchers Inc., p. **169** *top left;* ©Lawrence Migdale/Photo Researchers, p. **397** *bottom;* ©Larry L. Miller/Photo Researchers Inc., p. **89**; ©Dr. Brad Mogen/Getty Images, p. **27** *top,* ©Cordelia Molloy/Photo Researchers Inc., p. **117** *bottom;* ©Morales/Age Fotostock, pp. **5, 53** *bottom;* ©Juriah Mosin/Getty Images, p. **321**; ©Juan Carlos Muñoz/Age Fotostock, p. **124** *bottom;* ©NASA, pp. **157** *left,* **157** *right,* **179, 186** *left,* **187** *bottom,* **187** *top,* **189** *top,* **248** *left,* **346**; ©NASA/Calvin J. Hamilton/ Jupiter Images, p. **180** *left;* ©NASA/EPA/ Corbis, p. **393**; ©NASA Goddard Space Flight Center/NOAA, pp. **147** *top,* **151** *right;* ©NASA/ JPL/Photo Researchers., p. **186** *right;* ©NASA/ Photo Researchers Inc., p. **248** *right;* ©NASA/ Roger Ressmeyer/Corbis, p. **221**; ©NASA/ Science Source, p. **249**; ©Michael Newman/ PhotoEdit Inc., pp. **78, 202, 233** *left;* ©NOAA, pp. **129** *middle,* **130** *left;* ©Shigemi Numazawa/ Atlas Photo Bank/Photo Researchers Inc., pp. **181** *middle,* **189** *bottom;* ©David Nunuk/ Science Photo Library, p. **193** *top,* ©Nuridsany & Perennou/Photo Researchers Inc., p. **58** *left;* ©Perennou Nuridsany/Photo Researchers Inc., p. **10**; ©Ainsley Perry, p. **211** *bottom;* ©Pixtal/

Age Fotostock, p. **105** *bottom left;* ©Photodisc/Getty Images, pp. **173, 358–359, 387, 403;** ©Photodisc/PunchStock, p. **49** *middle;* ©Siede Preis/Getty Images, **158** *bottom left,* **291** *right;* ©Louie Psihoyos/Getty Images, p. **166;** ©PunchStock, p. **41;** ©Purestock/PunchStock, p. **48** *bottom;* ©Radomir Rezny/Age Fotostock, p. **284** *right;* ©Jim Reed/Getty Images, p. **147** *bottom;* ©G.R. Roberts/Photo Researchers Inc., p. **125** *bottom;* ©Helene Rogers/Almay, p. **218;** ©Benjamin Rondel/Zefa/Corbis, p. **36** *bottom left;* ©Alexis Rosenfeld/Photo Researchers Inc., p. **131;** ©RubberBall, p. **296;** ©Martin Ruegner/Getty Images, p. **16;** ©Eileen Ryan, pp. **298** *left,* **298** *right,* **299, 300, 301, 303** *left,* **304** *right,* **305, 307, 308;** ©Joel Sartore/Contributor/Getty Images, p. **97;** ©Steve Satushek/Getty Images, p. **327** *left;* ©Kevin Schafer/Corbis, p. **61** *top;* ©Elliot J. Schechter/Stringer/Getty Images, p. **192** *right;* ©Science Museum/Science and Society Picture Library, p. **336;** ©Science Source, p. **68;** ©Dr. Parvinder Sethi, p. **161** *bottom;* ©Martin Shields/Photo Researchers Inc., p. **22** *top,* ©Shutterstock Inc., pp. **36** *top left,* **37** *top,* **45** *middle left,* **45** *bottom,* **46** *top left,* **65** *top,* **65** *bottom*, **82** *top,* **88** *middle,* **88** *bottom*, **91** *left,* **96, 103** *bottom,* **105** *top left,* **149** *bottom,* **158** *top right,* **159** *top right,* **163** *bottom,* **170** *top right,* **209** *top,* **223** *top,* **232** *left,* **232** *right,* **238** *top,* **241** *bottom left,* **251** *top,* **252** *top,* **253** *top,* **253** *right,* **258, 259** *bottom,* **282** *left,* **293** *middle,* **293** *right,* **294, 295** *bottom left,* **295** *right,* **304** *right,* **320, 352, 369** *left,* **369** *right,* **373** *middle,* **384, 389, 397** *top,* **397** *middle;* ©Victoria Snowber/Getty Images, p. **21** *middle;* ©Tyler Stableford/Getty Images, p. **290;** ©Sinclair Stammers/Photo Researchers Inc., p. **167** *middle;* ©Kim Steele/Photodisc/Getty Images, p. **370;** ©Torrione Stefano/Age Fotostock, p. **211** *top,* ©James Steinberg/Photo Researchers Inc., p. **122;** ©Stockbyte, pp. **43** *bottom,* **159** *middle right;* ©Stock Trek/Getty Images, pp. **193** *bottom,* **314, 332** *top,* **332** *bottom;* ©Stringer/Time Life Pictures/Getty Images, p. **192** *left;* ©Bob Torrez/PhotoEdit Inc., p. **251** *middle;* ©Michael Willmer Forbes Tweedie/Photo Researchers Inc., pp. **69** *right,* **69** *left;* ©USDA Natural Resources Conservation Service, pp. **8, 165** *top;* ©U.S. Department of Agriculture, pp. **152** *right,* **153** *left;* ©U.S. Department of Agriculture, Soil Conservation Service/Getty Images, p. **165** *bottom,* **325** *right;* ©U.S. Fish and Wildlife Service/James C. Leupold, p. **21** *top;* ©USGS, p. **120** *right;* ©USGS/Photo Researchers Inc., p. **130** *right;* ©Jeff Vanuga/Corbis, p. **350;** ©Veer Inc., pp. **91** *right,* **124** *top,* **259** *top,* **316, 317** *top*, **330–331, 382–383, 394–395;** ©John W. Warden/Age Fotostock, pp. **334, 335;** ©Weinhäupl/Age Fotostock, p. **219;** ©George Whitely/Photo Researchers Inc., p. **159** *top left;* ©Roger Wilmshurst/Photo Researchers Inc., p. **54** *bottom;* ©Charles D. Winters/Photo Researchers, p. **217** *top,* ©David Young Wolf/PhotoEdit Inc., pp. **85** *left,* **150, 210, 234, 235** *left,* **235** *right,* **284** *left center,* **297;** ©David Zurick/Getty Images, p. **152** *left,* **325** *left.*